FAMILY

FAMILY

Pa Chin

Introduction by Olga Lang

ANCHOR BOOKS
Doubleday & Company, Inc.
Garden City, New York
1972

EDITOR'S NOTE

Family was first published in China in 1931, and has for some time been available in English from Peking's Foreign Languages Press. This new Anchor Books edition uses as its basic text the 1958 Foreign Languages Press edition, translated by Sidney Shapiro. However, the three Prefaces by Pa Chin, as well as certain parts of the text, were deleted from the 1958 edition, and have been newly translated for Anchor Books by Lu Kuang-huan. The following "Editor's Note" which appeared in Peking's 1958 edition will indicate why some of these deletions were made.

Family is the first part of a long trilogy called *Turbulent Currents* which Pa Chin completed in 1931. The translation is based upon the first printing of the edition put out in June 1953 by the People's Literature Publishing House, Peking. According to the "Afterword" appended, in anticipation of this edition going to press, the author made some corrections in phrasing and eliminated certain redundancies. During the course of the English translation, the author made further changes, but on the whole the content has remained the same.

Pa Chin is a prolific author. He began writing in 1927. His works, especially the novel *Family*, were widely read by Chinese young people and exercised a considerable influence on them during the democratic revolution against imperialism and feudalism.

The novel exposes the hypocrisy and evils of the feudal social code, and reveals the seamy side of feudal family relations. Because it aroused young intellectuals to fight against the rotten social system, it served a positive function.

Family has its shortcomings. Its main failing is that the author sings the praises of spontaneous, individual resistance and prettifies the essential weakness of petty-bourgeois intellectuals, instead of pointing out the absolute necessity of joining with the workers and peasants. He thus does not really show his readers the road from darkness to light.

The events in Pa Chin's *Family* occurred in 1931. By then the Chinese Communist Party had been in existence for ten years. Socialist thought was spreading and many bitter battles were being waged under Party leadership. But in *Family* the author does not offer his young readers a solution based on these most significant elements. Chueh-hui, the hero of the novel, although extremely dissatisfied with existing conditions, never has any clear idea of what he is fighting for, only a vague belief that society some day will change. He resists, but it is the emotional resistance of an individual. Although he breaks out of the Kao family "prison," he is not at all sure what he will do next. From start to finish, his struggle is divorced from social realities, is divorced from the struggles of the masses.

Generally speaking, Pa Chin's works, in spite of their shortcomings, portray the darkness of a semi-feudal, semi-colonial society, the dissatisfaction of petty-bourgeois intellectuals, their confusion, their distress, their wavering and vacillation after the defeat of the 1927 revolution. Pa Chin can write very movingly and colourfully, particularly on matters in which he has had personal experience.

To sum up, we feel that Pa Chin, inspired by anti-imperialist, anti-feudal democratic thought, has written a number of novels, based on his own life and experience, which exercised a progressive influence on the anti-imperialist, anti-feudal democratic revolution of his day, and that of these novels *Family* is his representative work.

INTRODUCTION

Pa Chin (Li Fei-kan) is one of the outstanding figures of modern Chinese literature. He was very popular in China during the 1930s and 1940s, especially among the youth who were increasingly influential in Chinese political life in the twentieth century. Pa Chin wrote fiction, literary essays, and political articles, but his best works, and those which made him famous, were his novels describing the life of educated Chinese youth. The most successful of these has been *Family*, which forms the first part of his autobiographical trilogy, *Turbulent Stream*.

Pa Chin owed his popularity to the fact that his young readers readily identified with his characters. In his novels they saw the reflection of their own lives, their own sufferings and struggles. They were attracted not only by his ability to grapple with the crucial problems of the times, but also by his warm humanitarianism and his belief in the ultimate victory of his ideals. Though primarily realistic, Pa Chin's fiction contains a great deal of romanticism which struck a responsive chord in his young readers.

Pa Chin did not belong to the most influential political movements of the period. At the age of fifteen he became an anarchist, and he continued to identify with anarchism until the Communist revolution of 1949. Few of his readers, however, followed in his political footsteps: the majority of those who became politically active joined either the Kuomintang or the Communist Party. Pa Chin, nevertheless, did influence them. True to his anarchist ideas, he taught them to rebel against despotism and oppression in every form. A particular target of his attacks was the old Chinese family system, which deprived the young of their freedom of action and their right to love and marry according to their own choice. Young men and women growing up during a period in which they felt they had "to shoulder the responsibility for their country," as Pa Chin put it, often asked the question: "What is to be done?" Pa Chin gave them an answer. He called for action and tried to convince his readers that the only effective way to act was the revolutionary way. In his fiction and essays he presented models for emulation in the Russian revolutionary idealists of the nineteenth and early twentieth centuries as well as in the Chinese revolutionaries of his time.

Like so many other intellectuals of his generation, Pa Chin keenly felt the impact of Western political and moral ideas and literary trends. His disposition, his innate craving for freedom and justice, led him to embrace the Western humanist tradition. Three Western ideologies were of primary importance in the formation of his political ideas: international anarchism, Russian populism, and the French Revolution.

The greatest literary influences on Pa Chin's works were the Russian classical writers, above all Turgenev, as well as the memoirs of Russian revolutionaries. But he was also influenced by French writers, especially Zola, Maupassant, and Romain Rolland. All these influences were superimposed on the style and methods inherited by the young writer from the magnificent old Chinese realist novels and short stories and from Chinese poetry. It must be stressed, however, that when Pa Chin used foreign ideas and literary devices he did so because they helped him to perceive and represent the new realities of Chinese life, which often bore a closer resemblance to Western life than to that of Old China. In many cases the resemblance between the situations and motivations described by Pa Chin and those apparent in Western literature are due less to influences and borrowings than to the similarity of circumstances described. This also explains the preponderance of Russian influence. As he himself once put it, "I liked them [the Russian writers] tremendously because the conditions of life in Russia resembled those of the Chinese people of that period. The character, the aspirations, and tastes of the Russians were somewhat similar to ours."

The reader of *Family* will see, however, that foreign influences did not change the essentially Chinese nature of Pa Chin's novels. At the same time the poetic quality of his descriptions and the vividness of his characters lend them a universal appeal.

In many respects Pa Chin was a typical Chinese intellectual of the twentieth century. Even his fascination with anarchism could be found in the biographies of many men and women who played an important role in shaping the life of China in our time, including some prominent members of the Kuomintang and the Communist Party.

Pa Chin was born in 1904 of the wealthy and educated Li family in Chengtu, the capital of the province of Szechuan in southwest China. From the age of twenty-three, when he signed his first novel *Destruction,* the journalist, known until then as Li Fei-kan, used the pen name Pa Chin under which he became famous. He chose this name to express his adherence to anarchism; "Pa" in Chinese transcription stands for the first syllable of the name Bakunin and "Chin" for the last syllable of the name Kropotkin. Those who gave him the name Fei-kan drew their inspiration from an entirely different source: these words, meaning "sweet shelter," were taken from the *Book of Odes,* one of the ancient sacred books of China.

The change from Fei-kan to Pa Chin is symbolic of the great change that took place in China during the writer's life time. When Pa Chin was born the structure of the old Empire was still standing, though already deeply shaken by foreign aggression and internal strife. In 1911–12, when he was seven years old, the monarchy was overthrown and the Republic proclaimed. His adolescence and early youth spanned civil wars, the victory of the Kuomintang (Sun Yat-sen's

Nationalist Party) over the warlords, and the appearance on the Chinese scene of the Communist Party, soon to develop into a formidable force. The time when he became an influential writer coincided with the twenty-first year of Kuomintang rule and the war with Japan. He was a mature man of forty-five when, in 1949, the Communist Party seized power, and he lived through the tumultuous years of the establishment of socialism in his ancient country.

The first nineteen years of Pa Chin's life were spent, with a short interruption, in the large family mansion in Chengtu, a household consisting of fifty Li family members and their forty-five servants, ruled autocratically by his grandfather. After his parents' death, the twelve-year-old boy was very unhappy and lonely in this family, which he called "a despotic kingdom." He felt the pressure of his grandfather's iron hand especially painfully when the old man forbade him to enter a modern school. But after the grandfather's death in 1917 the family had to yield to the wishes of the younger generation. Without the authority of the strongwilled patriarch, the family could not resist the fresh wind of change created by the New Culture Movement of 1915–22 (also known as the May 4th Movement). The initiators of this movement were convinced that in order to survive as a free and independent state, China had to reject completely the traditional outlook on life, particularly Confucianism, and to create a new culture. Most significant was the demand for a leading role of youth in the new China. And the New Culture Movement itself provided the first example: it was initiated and led exclusively by the younger generation of professors and students.

In working out the principles of the new culture the participants of the movement accepted from the West not only its technology, as did some enlightened members of the older generation, but also many of its political, social, and moral values. The publications of that time were full of material intended to familiarize readers with various Western political, social and philosophical theories, including Marxism and anarchism. Anarchism was already rather influential among the radically inclined intelligentsia at that time, and Marxism gained momentum after the Russian Revolution of 1917. The importance of science and democracy, the respect for the individual and his duty toward society, and a critical attitude toward life and ideas were especially emphasized. An important feature of the New Culture Movement was the impetus it provided for the tendency to establish the spoken language as the literary medium in place of the dead classical language. Simultaneously new themes, new style and new content reflecting modern life and ideas were introduced into literature. All these and also some Western influence had a beneficial effect on Chinese literature and the subsequent three decades belong to one of the most productive periods in its history.

In 1919 the youth actively and successfully intervened in Chinese political life. In a demonstration on May 4th the students of Peking University initiated a protest movement against the decisions of the Versailles Peace Conference which were detrimental to China's interests. The initiative of the young intellectuals found wide support among the people of China, and under the pressure of public opinion, the Chinese delegation at Versailles refused to sign the peace treaty. This political action provided a great stimulus for the New Culture Movement. Periodicals and books spreading its ideas filled bookstores all over the country, and the anarchist groups numerous at that time greatly contributed to this flow.

In due course the wave of the movement reached the city of Chengtu, and the new literature came into the hands of the fifteen-year-old Pa Chin. From early childhood the sensitive, frail boy was sympathetic to the poor and oppressed. He realized that his grandfather's mansion harbored two worlds: the upper world where the family lived, and the lower world—the cold dingy rooms relegated to the servants. "I don't want to be a young master," he decided, "I want to be on their [the servants] side, I want to help them." Lonely and not understood by his family, the boy found his friends in books. He was greatly impressed by the new literature which helped him articulate his desire "to sacrifice himself for the happiness of humanity." Of decisive importance in his life were the popular anarchist publications in Chinese translation: Kropotkin's "An Appeal to the Young," Emma Goldman's articles on anarchism, and a drama called *On the Eve*, depicting the life of Russian revolutionary terrorists before the 1905 revolution. These books decided Pa Chin's fate; he became a "Kropotkinite"—an anarchist-communist—and found in Emma Goldman his "spiritual mother."

The next step was the desire to carry his ideas into practice, and the young man joined the local anarchist group. He became the group's most active member, taking part in the students' demonstrations against the local war lords, distributing revolutionary leaflets, and organizing a reading room on the premises of the local anarchist journal, to which he began to contribute articles. Thus at the early age of fifteen Pa Chin became an anarchist and a writer.

Relations between the young members of the Li family improved at that time, when many of them became interested in the new trends. Pa Chin was especially fond of his eldest brother. Yet his greatest emotional satisfaction was derived from his friendship with the members of his group. From then on friendship played a great role in his life and in the role of the characters in his fiction.

This period of Pa Chin's life gave him the material for his trilogy, *Turbulent Stream*.

In 1923, after an energetic struggle, he won the consent of his family to continue his studies in a big city, and moved first to Shanghai and then to Nanking. In 1925 he graduated from a high school in Nanking but he did not enter the University of Peking as he had planned. He was carried away by a new upsurge of the revolutionary movement in China, the May 30th Movement, which derived its name from the date of the great demonstration in support of the striking workers of a Japanese-owned factory in Shanghai. The demonstration was brutally suppressed by the British police of the International Settlement and many of the participants were killed.

After May 30th Pa Chin lived in Shanghai and was very active in the anarchist movement. He translated from English, French and Esperanto, wrote on social and political problems, and did some work in the trade unions. The most important of his works at that time was a pamphlet called *Chicago*

Tragedy, telling the story of the Haymarket affair of 1886 in which five Chicago anarchists were sentenced to death on trumped-up charges.

In the 1920s the anarchist movement in China, as everywhere in the world, was on the decline. Many of its adherents were forsaking it for the Kuomintang and the Communist Party, which promised more practical ways to achieve their aims. The cause of communism was greatly helped by the victory of Bolshevism in Russia and by the Soviet government's abrogation of unequal treaties. But Pa Chin remained faithful to anarchism. He was a young man imbued with a feeling of compassion for the people and a desire to help them, with a craving for justice and freedom. Anarchism, striving for a happy, just and free society, through the teaching of Kropotkin, which has been aptly described as "applied ethics," was his choice. It was also the choice of other idealists who abhorred "the practical ways" of the Communists who accepted the cruelties, human sufferings and lack of freedom in the Soviet Union on the ground that the end justifies the means, an explanation Pa Chin considered thoroughly immoral.

Pa Chin and a few other genuine anarchists were modern counterparts of those idealists, poets, and dreamers of Old China who adhered to the teachings of Buddha and Lao Tzu instead of following the practical ways and becoming Confucian scholars and administrators.

His disappointment not in the anarchist ideal but in the results of his work in Shanghai were responsible for Pa Chin's decision to study in France. Studies abroad were not unusual for Chinese intellectuals of that time. But Pa Chin left China during one of the most critical moments of the Chinese revolution, January 1927, when the revolutionary nationalist army was moving toward Nanking and Shanghai. He knew that it was not the right thing to do for "a sincere anarchist." But evidently, for all his devotion to the cause, Pa Chin was not a political fighter. He was an artist. During the next few years this became evident.

Pa Chin spent the next twenty-two months in Paris and in the small town of Château-Thierry on the Marne, with occasional trips to London. These two years greatly widened his cultural and political horizons and provided the intellectual stimulation and experience necessary for a writer. Contrary to his family's expectations, he did not pursue much formal education, except for his study of the French language, but he read widely in philosophy, economics, and social problems as well as in Western fiction, mainly Russian and French. At that time he became thoroughly familiar with the history of the Russian populist movement, in which he found a rich source of inspiration for his writings.

No less important was Pa Chin's involvement in political life. He immediately joined the Chinese anarchist group in Paris and became associated with anarchists and other exiles of various nationalities, including such prominent figures as Alexander Berkman and T. H. Keell (London). He continued his correspondence with Emma Goldman, begun in 1924 when he was still in China, and began to exchange letters with the Austrian anarchist Max Nettlau. He also associated with middle class and working class Frenchmen. His greatest emotional experience at that time was the execution of Sacco and Vanzetti in August 1927. While still in China he had participated in the campaign for new trials for these Italian-American anarchists. In Paris he read Vanzetti's autobiography, and, fascinated by this unusual man, wrote him a letter, received an answer and from then on referred to him as his "beloved teacher."

But as submerged as Pa Chin was in Western culture and the Western revolutionary movement, he never became an expatriate and constantly kept in touch with China and its problems. He was a frequent contributor to anarchist periodicals in Shanghai and to the journal *Equity* published by the Chinese anarchist group in San Francisco. His translation of Kropotkin's *Ethics: Origin and Development,* "immortal masterpiece," as he called it, was done for a Shanghai anarchist publishing house.

The break between the Kuomintang and the Chinese Communist Party and the massacre of Communists in Shanghai on April 12, 1927, was of course heatedly discussed in the meetings of the Chinese anarchist group in Paris, and Pa Chin and his friends were definitely against the Kuomintang in this conflict.

Not only the contemporary events in China but also those of the recent past were constantly on Pa Chin's mind. In Paris he wrote his first novel, *Destruction,* in which he described the life of Shanghai revolutionists, and whose protagonist is recognizable as an autobiographical figure. The novel deals with problems of the greatest concern for revolutionists: the main motive of revolutionary activities, i.e. love for the oppressed or hatred of their enemies; the right to personal happiness; terror as a method of revolutionary struggle. Pa Chin also dealt with the last problem in an article entitled "Anarchism and Terrorism." He was against political assassinations. "There is no other way to bring about anarchism but an organized mass movement," he said. But he was sympathetic toward the terrorists and held the present immoral society responsible for their desperate acts. After finishing his novel Pa Chin sent it to a friend in Shanghai. When he returned to Shanghai in December 1928 he discovered that it had been accepted by a leading literary journal, *The Short Story Monthly.*

Although he had already written his first novel, upon his return to Shanghai Pa Chin considered himself primarily a political writer. Even when it became clear that *Destruction* was a great success, he still did not recognize himself as a creative writer par excellence. He continued to translate, finishing Kropotkin's *Ethics,* the work he considered his revolutionary duty and which "gave him courage [and] strengthened his faith" at the time of the consolidation of the reactionary Kuomintang government and the growing menace of Japanese aggression. Another important work of that time was the book *From Capitalism to Anarchism* based on Alexander Berkman's *Now and After: The ABC of Communist Anarchism.*

But "in his free time" Pa Chin continued to write fiction. His first volume of short stories, describing the Westerners he had met in France, aroused considerable interest, since Westerners were rare figures in Chinese fiction. The readers also liked the new Western literary devices in Pa Chin's stories. *The Setting Sun,* a novel set against the background of the May 30th Movement and which dealt with foreign aggression and the role of bourgeois intellectuals in the revolutionary labor movement, was also favorably received by the critics.

In 1931 Pa Chin wrote the novel *Family,* his masterpiece. The topic was a timely one. The struggle for the liberation of youth and women from the fetters of the old patriarchal family system had been going on for many years. The New Culture Movement gave it an impetus and many outstanding writers and scholars supported it. But the battle was not yet won. In the eldest brother Kao and the other young victims of a family dominated by old men and old traditions, many young men and women recognized themselves, their friends and brothers. Many of them found courage reading about the rebellion and victory of the younger brothers Kao. The poetic and tragic figure of the slave girl Ming-feng, the vivid dialogues and descriptions of the family and youth group life fascinated the readers. The novel was a tremendous success and it definitely brought Pa Chin into the ranks of first-class writers. For many years *Family* was the favorite book of Chinese students.

Two more novels followed: *New Life,* a sequel to *Destruction,* dealing with an intellectual who overcomes his despondency and loss of faith in the revolutionary movement, rejoins the fight and dies a heroic death; and *Fog,* the first part of the trilogy *Love.* Then appeared new collections of short stories. Pa Chin's artistic skill was developing. In 1931 he began to consider himself a "regular writer of fiction." He was full of energy and apart from fiction wrote political articles, literary essays, and book reviews, and devoted much time to editorial work.

The year 1931 marked the beginning of difficult times for China. In September the Japanese army occupied Manchuria and in January–February 1932 the Japanese attacked Shanghai. Pa Chin's house was occupied and looted by the Japanese soldiers and the manuscript of his novel *New Life* was burned in a fire in the printing office. The acute feeling of indignation and national danger prompted Pa Chin to write a novel, *Dream on the Sea*, the story of a country occupied by foreign invaders, easily recognizable as China and the Japanese. The story is a passionate indictment of the invaders, of the foreigners who sympathized with them and of the upper class collaborators, with praise for the resistance offered by the common people and revolutionary intellectuals.

Almost all of Pa Chin's novels dealt with the intellectuals. But after his extensive travels in North and South China, described in detail in two travelogues, peasants and workers began to appear in his stories; one of the best of these stories is "Dog." In 1933 Pa Chin wrote the rather successful novel *Snow*, based on his own observations of a coal miners' strike in North China.

In 1934 Pa Chin finished the trilogy *Love*, which consisted of three novels, *Fog, Rain*, and *Lightning*, and a novelette *Thunder*. The trilogy describes the life of revolutionary intellectuals and (in *Thunder* and *Lightning*) their work in mass organizations. In a series of dramatic episodes, tense dialogues and interior monologues, it tackles many vital problems: the purpose of human life, political convictions, revolutionary tactics, friendship, loyalty, family, love. In spite of the trilogy's title, love does not play the main role in the life of its characters. "More important for them is their faith," said the author. Like almost all of Pa Chin's fiction, *Love* has a didactic purpose: to show the readers how to live and to give them a model for emulation. Pa Chin considered *Love* his favorite work. The critics and the public did not agree with this judgement and found some of his other works, in particular, *Turbulent Stream*, to be greater achievements.

Pa Chin wrote with enthusiasm, regarding his literary work as a mission. He felt "an inner urge to describe the life, feelings and ideas of Chinese youth and to influence life with my writings." This attitude toward literature naturally brought him close to those writers who advocated "art for life's sake" rather than to those of the "art for art's sake" school. But sharing anarchist distrust of organizations, he did not join any of the literary groups of his time. As an anarchist he was an avowed enemy of the Kuomintang regime. Some of his books and the books of other anarchists were banned, and in 1934, afraid of being arrested, he escaped to Japan for a while. This situation naturally brought him close to the other enemies of the regime, the Communists, with whom he shared some views on the aim of literature. But his cooperation with the Communists did not proceed smoothly. Some of the left wing critics praised Pa Chin but more often he was reproached for being a "petty bourgeois writer" who "does not understand history, does not understand revolution" and attacked for his "vague humanitarianism" and adherence to anarchism. His defense of the Spanish anarchists during the Spanish Civil War (1936–38) also made him a target of attack by the adherents of the Communist Party line. His refusal to join the Chinese Writers' Organization in 1936 was denounced as an attempt to wreck the writers' united front for resistance against Japan. This reproach was utterly unjust and the great writer Lu Hsün, who valued Pa Chin highly, came out in his defense. Pa Chin warded off these attacks but they did hurt him, especially when the critics spoke of his "petty bourgeois origin." Like many other left wingers (not only in China) he was ashamed of not hailing from a worker or peasant family which would have been a guarantee of a correct attitude toward life.

In general, in spite of his great success and his readers' devotion, Pa Chin was not happy and was not at all convinced of the usefulness of his literary work. It is also evident from his writings that he felt guilty about drifting farther and farther away from his work in the anarchist movement after he became a popular fiction writer. In almost all his writings Pa Chin called on his readers to rebel against the establishment and to recognize that progress can be achieved only at a price of great sacrifice. But he felt it hard to demand these sacrifices from the young people whom he loved so much. Moreover he often asked himself, "What right have I to do that? What did I sacrifice for the sake of the people?" All these scruples and torments show what an honest and sensitive person Pa Chin was. And it should be remembered that until 1947 he never expressed his doubts and despair in his works of fiction, all of which are basically optimistic. Even the sad "cries of the soul," as he calls them in his autobiographical works, always end in a proud positive assertion that he "never lost his faith," the faith in a better future for humanity.

After the war with Japan finally broke out (July 7, 1937) Pa Chin eagerly participated in the struggle against the enemy. In his attitude toward war Pa Chin did not follow the orthodox anarchist view that "a man ought never to fight except in the social revolution." He could not consider the Japanese invasion merely a conflict between the Chinese and Japanese ruling classes, the outcome of which was irrelevant for the working people. Yet during the war Pa Chin repeatedly stressed his continued faith in anarchism. Maybe he felt that to fight against foreign aggression was compatible with anarchist ideals, remembering that two famous anarchists whose names he adopted as his own also did not "stand above the battle": Bakunin during the Franco-Prussian War of 1870 and Kropotkin during the First World War.

Pa Chin spent the war years (1937–45) moving from one city to another in the part of China not occupied by the Japanese. At that time he was one of the leaders of the "All China Association of Artists and Writers for Resistance to the Enemy." He edited periodicals dedicated to the cause of resistance and worked in the publishing house "Culture and Life," whose editorial director he had been since 1935. He also participated in the translation and publication of Kropotkin's most important works. And of course he continued to write fiction.

In the two first parts of the novel *Fire*, the bard of Chinese youth described their lives and deeds during the first years of the war. He depicted in volume one their participation in the battle for Shanghai in the fall of 1937 and, after the retreat of the Chinese army, in the underground resistance against the Japanese. In volume two we see the youth group spreading propaganda for the war of resistance among the peasants near the front. At about the same time (in 1939–40) Pa Chin wrote the second and third parts of *Turbulent Stream*, the novels *Spring* and *Autumn* in which he portrayed the development of three young members of the Kao family into rebels and revolutionists and the destruction of those who submit to the cruel family authority. The two first volumes of *Fire*, the novel *Spring* and to a lesser extent the novel *Autumn* are imbued with an optimistic spirit. Undaunted by the series of defeats, Pa Chin believed in final victory because he believed in the fighting spirit of the Chinese people.

During the last two years of the war, however, a mood of apathy and exhaustion permeated those parts of China occupied by the Japanese and ruled by the Kuomintang government, and this reflected also on Pa Chin. He was restless, unhappy and often sick. His restlessness expressed itself in his renewed philosophical quests and his interest in Christianity, although he remained an atheist. In the third volume of *Fire* he described the cooperation of young revolutionary atheists with Chinese Christians in the war. In contrast with Pa Chin's other novels, the protagonist of the third volume of *Fire*, a Christian minister, is not a young man. It is significant that he is presented as a very attractive figure. In this part of the novel Pa Chin again asserts his belief in victory and the possibility of all men of good will to work together. But streaks of sadness appear here more often than usual in Pa Chin's works and it has a sad ending. The good minister dies. The revolutionist who worked underground in Shanghai is betrayed and killed. His girl, who returns to Shanghai to avenge his death, fails in an attempt to assassinate a collaborator responsible for his death and also perishes. Moreover the novel shows a gallery of repulsive characters among the modern Chinese youth. Sad too is the charming novelette *The Garden of Rest* (1944), a psychological family story unrelated to the war.

After the Japanese defeat in 1945 Pa Chin returned to Shanghai. He translated Kropotkin and other writers, wrote short stories, published a book of obituaries of his deceased friends, and finished two novels started during the last year of the war. One of them, *Ward Number Four* (1946) describes the terrible conditions in a wartime hospital and the vain attempts of an idealistic woman doctor to change them. This ward looks very much like a symbolic picture of Kuomintang China of that time.

Another novel, *The Cold Nights*, along with *Family* is one of

Pa Chin's masterpieces and ironically became the last novel he was destined to publish. The action takes place during the last years of the war. The protagonists, Wang Wen-hsuan and his wife, now in their thirties, had been idealists in their youth. Now they are completely absorbed in their personal affairs and the struggle for existence. Like so many other intellectuals in war time, they live in an atmosphere of privation and disease. Their family life is very unhappy, and Wen-hsuan's devoted and possessive mother further aggravates the situation. Finally the wife, a healthy and vivacious woman, leaves her sick husband. He dies soon after the Japanese surrender. Gloom penetrates the life of poor people at the end of the war. One of the last sentences of the novel is pronounced by a woman on the street who says, "Victory is for them, not for us. We have not made profit out of our country's misfortune. Victory does not bring us luck."

This novel, more than any other written after 1943, reveals the unhappiness that took hold of Pa Chin at that time. After the war the situation in Kuomintang-ruled China went from bad to worse. The trend to the right in the government, the shameless corruption in the administration, the continued misery among the people, the constant terrorism against the dissenters—all these further alienated from the government even those intellectuals who did not share Pa Chin's condemnation of the capitalist regime. On the other hand the record of the Chinese Communists during the war was one of considerable achievement and presented a picture of integrity and dedication to the ideal of socialism which Pa Chin so cherished. The difference between these two images must have been of great importance when, after the Communist victory, he decided not to leave his country. Here again Pa Chin acted as a typical Chinese intellectual. The majority, including the major Chinese writers and many anarchists, did not emigrate. Pa Chin shared their fate also in the next twenty-odd years.

During the first seventeen years after the establishment of the Chinese People's Republic, Pa Chin was accepted by its rulers. They knew that in spite of his past criticism of the Russian and Chinese Communists Pa Chin helped to create among the intellectuals an emotional climate which induced them to accept the Communist revolution. The revolutionists in his novels and short stories attacked not only Old China but also modern capitalism as "the systems obstructing the development of society and of human personality," as "the forces destroying love." Many of the moral values which Pa Chin inculcated into his readers were in keeping with Communist ideas: to sacrifice oneself for the cause, to live for others, to enjoy group living, to practice self-criticism. During the time of the Russian-Chinese honeymoon in the 1950s, Pa Chin also benefitted by the friendly attitude toward him in the Soviet Union. His anti-Soviet articles and remarks published in the obscure anarchist journals were forgotten or forgiven. The Soviet critics evidently realized that Pa Chin's high respect for the nineteenth-century Russian revolutionists greatly increased the popularity of the Bolsheviks who were—rightly or wrongly —considered as their heirs.

Pa Chin had to pay heavily for this acceptance, however. He was often criticised and many concessions were demanded of him. The new editions of his works were published only after thorough revision. He began by removing from his stories everything that revealed his characters' anarchist identities and even sympathies: the titles of the books they read, pictures on their walls, quotations from anarchist authors, mention of their names. Then he removed all traces of his own adherence to anarchism from his purely autobiographical works. Finally in 1958 he had to make an open break with his past, attributing his adherence to anarchism and admiration of Kropotkin to his "petty bourgeois feelings" and "lack of power of judgement."

These changes have destroyed the historical value of his purely autobiographical works. The new expurgated editions no longer present a true portrait of a young Chinese intellectual of the 1920s and 1930s. The removal of anarchist traits from his works of fiction did not affect them that much: Pa Chin always preferred not to present his characters as anarchists. Only politically experienced readers could see their true identity. For average readers they were just revolutionaries, enemies of the establishment. But some of the concessions he had to make in the 1950s did hurt the artistic value of his stories, especially when he had to give them happy endings.

Why did he make all these concessions? Why did he repudiate his "beloved anarchism," his teacher Kropotkin, his "spiritual mother" Emma Goldman? What had he to undergo when doing that?

We have no way of knowing. But perhaps the following speculation can provide some clues. To begin with, there was a social revolution in China, an event he had advocated his whole life. What emerged as a result of it did not conform to his image of a free and happy society, but some features of the new life in China must certainly have met with his approval. He shared fully the condemnation of the Kuomintang regime so often used in Communist propaganda and was completely sincere when he related the stories of the hard life of the peasants and workers in the past. And he certainly was happy to see that the material life of the common people was constantly improving and that there was a new dignity in it after the revolution. There can be no doubt that he expressed his own ideas when joining in the attacks on the survival of the old family system. The criticism of "petty bourgeois intellectuals" and their selfishness also was not new to him. Maybe his desire to become an organic part of the new society was strengthened also by the fact that in postrevolutionary China the Communists set more value on ethics than they had before. And as to freedom, maybe he still hoped that it would not be restricted forever and that "future generations will see it," as he had said in 1930.

He tried hard to become a disciplined member of the new society. Did he succeed?

During the first seventeen years of the Chinese People's Republic Pa Chin was a respected "writer of the last generation." His old books in new expurgated editions sold well. A play based on *Family* was often performed. Two films were made of this novel, two more were based on *Autumn* and *Cold Nights*. He lived in Shanghai in comfortable circumstances with his wife, whom he married in 1944, and their two children. His readers continued to write to him. He occupied leading positions in the writers' and artists' organizations, often represented China at various international conferences, and was even a deputy in the National People's Congress. But was he happy?

To be happy the writer has to write. Yes, he did write: short stories, essays, accounts of his travels, appeals for peace, commentaries on his works and he did editing and translations. "But I am not satisfied either by the quantity or by the quality of my works," he wrote in 1961. He could not but feel that nothing of significance had come from his pen since 1949. His stories were flat and he did not publish a single new novel—a literary genre in which he formerly excelled. "It is difficult to describe one's heroes in the imposed style," he said to the French writer Simone de Beauvoir in 1956. It was also obvious that he could not approve of all that he saw around him. He had misgivings and as soon as an opportunity arose he would voice them.

In 1956–57, during the "Hundred Flowers Period" when Mao Tse-tung proclaimed a new era under the slogan "Let the hundred flowers bloom, let the hundred schools of thought contend," Pa Chin, like scores of other intellectuals, trustfully followed Mao's invitation to express his criticism. It was a loyal and constructive criticism inspired by a desire to improve the life in his country. But the flowers of criticism did not bloom long. They were not as red as Mao wanted, and the era of permissiveness came to an abrupt end. Pa Chin was severely scolded in the press for his temerity and, following the rules of the game, he admitted his mistakes, blaming them on his "feudal-bourgeois origin." But as soon as the new relaxation came in 1962, when the party seemed to tolerate and even promote a more creative and spontaneous style in literature, Pa Chin came out with a speech under the title "Courage and Sense of Responsibility of Writers." It was a strong protest against the literary bureaucrats and an admonition to writers to be fighters, to uphold the truth and their own vision of reality.

During the Cultural Revolution (1966–68) Pa Chin was severely punished for these and previous expressions of his true opinions. The Cultural Revolution was perhaps really meant by Mao as an onslaught against the bureaucratism, inequality, and ossification which began to dominate life in

China at that time, but in fact it hit the intellectuals hardest and Pa Chin was one of the victims. His books, together with the books of other writers of his generation and the works of Chinese classical literature, were removed from bookstores and libraries and in some cases even burned. Pa Chin was again criticised and compelled to criticise himself in an open meeting. A most vicious attack on him was launched by the Shanghai newspaper *Wen-hui* on February 26, 1968. Pa Chin was denounced as "the big literary tyrant" and "the oldest, most notorious anarchist in China." "In 1930," the newspaper said, "he had vigourously attacked the Soviet Union and the Bolshevik Party led by Stalin but his real target was the Chinese Communist Party . . . he actually dared to point the spearhead of his attack on our most revered and beloved leader Chairman Mao. He really deserves to die ten thousand deaths for his crime . . ." Pa Chin's attempts at criticism were recalled and used as proofs of his "counterrevolutionary anti-Maoist attitude." The attack on Pa Chin gave the authors of this article another opportunity to strike at those party leaders who were now declared enemies of Mao, and to accuse them of the desire to restore capitalism in China. They allowed Pa Chin to function as a "progressive old writer."

A few months later the Red Guards carried into practice the threats contained in this article. These members of the new generation of Chinese youth whom Pa Chin loved so much ransacked the writer's house and destroyed his Chinese art objects as well as his library, which was said to contain one of the best collections of anarchist literature in the world. Similar outrages were perpetrated against hundreds and perhaps thousands of writers, professors and other intellectuals. Finally, on June 20, 1968, Pa Chin was dragged to the People's Stadium of Shanghai. Those present and those who watched the scene on television saw him kneeling on broken glass and heard the shouts accusing him of being a traitor and enemy of Mao. They also heard him break his silence at the end and shout at the top of his voice, "You have your thoughts and I have mine. This is the fact and you can't change it even if you kill me." This desperate cry speaks not only for Pa Chin. For a while Pa Chin was kept under virtual house arrest.

Then, as rumor has it, this sick old man was "sent to labor for reeducation."

But now the Cultural Revolution has abated. Pa Chin and some other intellectuals who survived the ordeal returned to their homes. It seems that now in China they have a desire to forget the hardships of the recent past. If Pa Chin's books again become accessible to Chinese readers, there is no doubt that they will be read.

Olga Lang
New York, 1972

FAMILY

PREFACE TO *CHILIU*
(Turbulent Stream)

Several years ago I read Tolstoy's *Resurrection* with tears in my eyes, and on the title page I wrote the line "Life is in itself a tragedy."

This is not true. Life is not a tragedy. It is only a "jeu." What do we live for? Or in other words why do we have life? The answer given by Romain Rolland is "for making a conquest of life." I think it is well said.

Since I have had this life of mine, although I have only passed through twenty some years in this world, these years were not spent like a blank, with no impressions made. I have witnessed a lot of happenings, and was made aware of a lot of things. I found that I was surrounded with unbounded darkness, but I was never alone, never destitute of hope. I see everywhere the movement made by the current of life, breaking through to create its own path and direction, to wind its way through the darkness of rugged hills and craggy stones.

The life current moves on all the time, without a moment's rest, because it is unstoppable; nothing can check it. Along its course, it shoots forth a variety of sprays, which contain a variety of elements such as love, hate, joy and pain. All these congregate into the main stream of the life current, moving on with a tremendous force that can wipe out mountains, heading towards a definite sea or ocean. What this sea is, and how long it would take for the life current to reach it, are questions to which nobody has a definite answer.

Like everybody else, I live in this world for the conquest of life. I have had my part in this "jeu." I have had my love, my hate, my joy, and my pain. But I never did lose my faith, my faith in life. My life is not yet ended, I do not know what is lying in wait for me, but I have some vague notion of the future, for the past is not totally mute, it is capable of giving us information on many things.

What I wish to display before my readers here is a picture presenting a description of the past events of more than ten years. It is of course only a small section of life, but from it one can readily see how the main current of life, a congregation of love and hate, joy and pain, performs its movement. Not being a preacher, I am not able to point out a definite course to take, but the reader can search for it himself from the picture.

It was said that there is no definite course or way, but when lots of people march forward, a course or way is formed. It was also said that there is a way, and because of that lots of people march on. I would not like to pass judgment on which idea is right. I am still young, I still want to live, I still want to conquer life. Aware that the life current will never stop, I would like to see where it is going to take me.

Pa Chin
April, 1931

DEDICATION
IN PLACE OF A PREFACE

Three years ago winter, I wrote to tell you that I was thinking of writing a novel dedicated to you, but that there were certain discretional considerations. You wrote back with enthusiasm and encouragement, saying that you couldn't wait to see it written, that you were impatient to read it. You mentioned further how Dickens wrote *David Copperfield*, the novel you loved the most.

Your letter was in my drawer for more than a year before my novel ever got started. I was fully aware of how anxiously you must have been waiting. It was not until April last year, when I made an agreement with the *shih pao* (Shanghai *Times*), that I seriously decided to start writing. I was then thinking that at last I won't let you wait any longer. Furthermore I was planning to keep the issues of the paper that were to carry my installments, so that accumulated clippings could be sent you. What a shock it was then to me, that as my writing first appeared one Saturday, that very Sunday the radiogram came reporting your death. You were not given the chance to set your eyes on my novel!

That you should have such an exit was not beyond my anticipation, but I certainly never expected that it would come so soon, nor did I ever imagine that you were indeed going to bring an end to your life by your own hands, in spite of the

3

mention you made eight or nine years ago of contemplating suicide.

You have lived only over thirty, and have died a young man. But did you ever have youth? What a tragic history is your more than thirty years of life. You have died of being made a victim of totally unnecessary sacrifices. This you had never been able to understand, not even at the end of your life.

You once had a lofty, beautiful dream, you yourself destroyed it; you had for a time a bright, promising future, you yourself ruined it. For a short while you had created for yourself a new ideal, but then you let your own head be numbed by the "philosophy of bows" and "principle of non-resistance." You had loved a young girl, but you submissively let father have your fate decided by lot and accepted marriage to a different girl. You loved your wife, but then you let others' senseless words influence you to send your expecting wife to that desolate place out of town. You had, with tears in your eyes, tolerated all the injustice done to you, without ever uttering a single word of protest. You lived your life totally for the sake of giving satisfaction to others, letting them do whatever they like to you. You knew that you were stepping close to the abyss, yet instead of turning to some other path, you walked straight ahead towards that abyss, and when the day of falling into it came, you could do nothing but resort to taking poison as your only relief. Maybe you have died for the sake of saving face; or maybe you have died for being unable to take any more of the tortures that were in store for you. Although I have read your last words over and over, I failed to divine an answer to this question. But all the same, the eventuality was that you had lost face, and had bequeathed a life of more bitter sufferings to your wife and children, or even to another woman. (Whose existence I feel certain of, as you used to talk to me vaguely of your spiritual love for her. Yet even such a love your lot failed to save, making it clear what a minor position love has in life.)

If only you could come back to life, and read my novel, or see how those whom you loved suffer after your death, you might wake up, you might come up with the courage and res-

4

olution to walk a new path in a new direction. But now it is too late. Even your flesh and bones have already decomposed.

Yet would it be that on account of your having done all these, on account of your being weak and vulnerable, I would have detested and abhorred you? No, definitely not. After all, you are a brother whom I loved and who had loved me, although for the past seven to eight years we have been driven further and further apart by ideological differences and other things. Even as of this period I still loved you. But you would not know what this love is now doing to me! It is going to leave many painful recollections in my head to remain and recur forever and ever.

I remember three years ago you came to Shanghai to visit me. On the day you left for home I saw you to your boat. The dingy cabin and hot weather forced me and three others who came to say goodbye to get off the boat, and we were about to part without any further exchanges, for tears streaming down your face must have choked your words. I shook your hand and managed to say "take care" and was about to leave, when you stopped me. I asked you what it was, and without a word you went back into the cabin and opened your suitcase. I was thinking that you might have forgotten something that you meant to give someone, and would like me to deliver it. I was blaming you for being so forgetful. But what you took out was a phonograph record which you handed to me, saying in sobs, "have this and enjoy it." I took it and found it to be Gracie Fields's "Sonny Boy." You knew that it was my favorite, and thus wanted me to have it, but I knew quite well that it was your favorite too. At other times I would have accepted it gladly, but by then I was quite unwilling to take it away from you. Yet it then occurred to me that I have many times failed to comply with your wishes, and that at this time of parting it would be hurting you too much to deny your wish again, for I understood very well that you meant to leave me something for a souvenir. I took the record unable to say a word, for my feeling at the time was inexpressible in words. I moved on into a sampan; while rocking on the Whampoo following the river gale and billows, I gazed at the vista of lights along the river front, and it brought to my mind how I parted with a certain

5

person and my heart began to ache, and my eyes, not used to crying, were wet with tears.

How would I know that that parting was to be the last between us brothers! Now, after lying solitarily for three years in my study, the record was done for, a victim of the War, and the hands that had once caressed it had decomposed into a part of the earth that lay atop them.

From your last words I gathered how reluctantly you had come to face death, how you were wavering, having written your bequeathed words three times, and three times you destroyed them. How much you must have lingered for the love of life, for the love of those whom you loved! Yet eventually you wrote it the fourth time. It is clear that your last moment must have been one that was filled with the terrible and horrible struggle between life and death. But finally death won out.

You were not willing to die, you had held out for the love of life, so much so that even in the fourth version, the voice of life was everywhere discernible from between the lines, and you were still mutely crying out that you don't want to die! But now you are dead. You have died a victim of totally unnecessary sacrifices. You have now become a man of the past.

But I am not going to die. I want to live on. I want to write, to write with this pen all and everything that I want to write. This pen, this fountain pen you bought me when you were in Shanghai three years ago, I have used in writing all the fiction and stories I published except *wo ti mieh wang* (*My Destruction*). It will make me remember you all the time, it will make you come back to life, to live again to witness how I am going to step over all the flesh and bones to go forward, to march on.

Pa Chin
April, 1932

PREFACE TO THE FIFTH EDITION

Family has been published for five and a half years, but it was not until now on starting to write its sequential story that I have had a chance to reread it. On its publication I did the proof reading twice myself, but unexpectedly I now come across quite a few typographical errors, which I must say were due to my own carelessness. Now I take the opportunity of its fifth edition to correct as many of these errors as possible, and in addition I have also revised and reset five pages, in which I found places disagreeable to myself. These were all inadvertently committed during the first writing, for which I can only tender my sincere apologies to my readers.

As I reread my own work, I was quite moved. I felt that I really liked it. I myself am not in the novel, but I see in it my childhood and adolescence. I am over thirty now, and have grown to be more rebellious and impetuous than I was in my youth. A friend of mine was worried lest I go insane. I am grateful to him, but I have more confidence in myself. As I finish reading *Family* I can't help loving Chueh-hui. He is not a hero, he is quite childish. But when I see him, I have in my mind Danton's words, "have courage, have courage, always have courage!" I should use this line to encourage myself.

Pa Chin
May, 1936

I

The wind was blowing hard; snowflakes, floating like cotton fluff from a ripped quilt, drifted down aimlessly. Layers of white were building up at the foot of the walls on both sides of the streets, providing broad borders for their dark muddy centres.

Pedestrians and sedan-chair porters struggled against the wind and snow, but to no avail. They looked weary, and the snowfall was becoming heavier. Snow filled the sky, falling everywhere—on umbrellas, on the sedan-chairs, on the reed capes of the chair carriers, on the faces of the pedestrians.

The wind buffeted the umbrellas in all directions; it blew one or two out of their owners' hands. Howling mournfully, the wind joined with the sound of footsteps in the snow to form a strange, irritating music. This snowstorm will rule the world a long, long time; it seemed to warn the people on the streets, the bright warm sun of spring will never return again. . . .

It was nearly evening, but the street lamps had not yet been lit. Everything was gradually disappearing into a pall of grey. Water and mud filled the streets. The air was icy cold. Only one thought sustained the walkers struggling through these dismal surroundings—they would soon be back in the warmth and brightness of their homes.

"Walk faster, Chueh-hui, or we'll be late for dinner," said a youth of eighteen. He carried an umbrella in one hand and held up the skirt of his cotton-padded gown with the other. His

8

round face was red with cold as he turned around to speak to his brother; a pair of gold-rimmed spectacles rested on the bridge of his nose.

Chueh-hui, the boy walking behind him, although the same size and wearing the same kind of clothes, was a bit younger. His face was thinner, his eyes were very bright.

"No, it's alright, we're almost there. . . . Brother, you were the best in today's rehearsal, your English comes naturally, fluently. You play the part of the doctor just right, you've got the lines and everything quite well now," Chueh-hui said with enthusiasm, quickening his pace at the same time. Mud was sent splashing, more clots were collected on the legs of his trousers.

"There is nothing to it, it's only that I am bolder," the elder brother, Kao Chueh-min, said with pride and satisfaction, while halting to wait for his brother to come abreast. "You are too timid, your Black Dog is not right at all. Didn't you learn your lines so well yesterday? Why can't you deliver them at the rehearsal? If it were not for Teacher Chu's prompting, you couldn't have finished the scene!" Thus the elder brother spoke with great tenderness, without a hint of reproach.

Chueh-hui was embarrassed, and blood rushed to his face as he spoke with perplexity as well as for self-retrieval, "I don't know why, once I was on that stage I got frightened; I felt like I was in front of a great many people with all their eyes on me. I tried to do my very best, I wanted to render my lines without a single slip. . . ." A gust of wind turned his umbrella awhirl, cutting short his speech while he held on to the handle without much avail. But the gust was over sooner than it came. The road was covered with unmelted snow, a patch of white all the way, spattered with footsteps one on top of the other, the newly made covering up the old.

"I wanted to deliver the whole thing without a single slip," Chueh-hui went on with his interrupted words, "but once I opened my lips everything was gone, even the best learned lines were lost by that time. Only after Teacher Chu had prompted a word or two did they come back so that I could go on. If it's like this at the rehearsals now, I wonder what it would be like at the opening. If it is going to be the same, what a disgrace it will be!" On his childlike and naive face there were expressions of gravity and gloom, and in his words a tone of slight self-reproach. His footsteps were making rhythmic squeaky sounds on the soft snow surface, each step a sound, marking his pace.

"Chueh-hui, don't be scared," Chueh-min said to comfort him. "Two or three more rehearsals and you will be alright, just brace up your courage. . . . To tell you the truth, Teacher Chu's rendering of *Treasure Island* into a play is not really successful, the staging probably won't be much of a success anyway."

Chueh-hui did not say anything, and was only grateful for his brother's loving care for him. His mind turned intensely on how he could do that scene to its perfection, to win the applause of the audience, the praise of his schoolmates, and the appreciation of his brother. As he so thought, over quite a long while, he began to feel that he was in a dream land; all of a sudden everything in front of his eyes underwent a transformation. There was the inn where his old pal Bill lived. He, the Black Dog, a figure of the seamen's world, after losing two fingers and undergoing a number of other incidents, finally was able to locate the whereabouts of Bill. The joy of revenge and the threatening imminence of the showdown crisscrossed his heart. He began to figure how he was going to approach Bill, how to upbraid him, condemning him for breaking his vow and hiding the treasure chart, selling out the good name of the fraternity of the high seas. As these visions passed, the English lines he had learned so well popped up one by one from his head, without the slightest effort. He shouted with joy as if suddenly aroused, "Brother, I have got it!"

Chueh-min looked at him with surprise and asked, "What was it? What made you so pleased?"

"Brother, I just found out the secret of play acting," Chueh-hui said with smiles of boyish pride. "If I could bring myself to feel as if I myself were Black Dog, the lines would come out spontaneously, without any effort of searching or recollecting."

"That's right, that is the way to perform," Chueh-min smiled. "Now that you have mastered this, you will surely suc-

10

ceed. . . . . It looks like the snow is over, let's shut our umbrellas. The gust makes open umbrellas hard to hold on to." So saying he jerked his umbrella to get rid of the snow collected on it, and shut it. Chueh-hui did the same thing, and they walked side by side, with their umbrellas on their shoulders, very close to each other.

The snow was indeed over, and the ferocious wind was gradually abating. Over the walls and house tops much snow was collected, reflecting gleams of brightness in the darkening dusk. Shop fronts, brightly lit, interspersed between residential houses with huge gates of black lacquer, decorated the quiet street, giving it a spattering of warmth and light in this cold winter evening.

"Chueh-hui, are you cold?" Chueh-min asked suddenly with fond care.

"No, I feel quite warm; as we walk along while talking, I don't feel cold at all."

"Then why are you trembling?"

"It's because I am excited. I am like this whenever I'm excited, always trembling, with my heart beating very fast. As I have been thinking of our play, I have the urge to do it right away. To tell you the truth I very much want success, I am after the admiration and praise of everybody. Brother, won't you be laughing at me for being too vain, too childish?" So said Chueh-hui as he turned his head to cast a glance at his brother, showing embarrassment, as if anticipating with dismay his brother's disapproving ridicule.

"Chueh-hui," said Chueh-min tenderly and full of sympathy, "no, not at all. I am just like that. I also want success, want the applause of everybody, just like you do. We are all the same. Didn't you notice, in class, any approval from the teacher, no matter how simple it is, is always taken with great pleasure by the one it is intended for."

"Yes, you have said it," said Chueh-hui, edging closer to his brother. The two of them walked on side by side, forgetting the cold, forgetting the wind and snow, forgetting night and darkness.

"Brother, you are indeed my beloved, good elder brother." Chueh-hui looked at his brother's face and said this with a childlike smile. Chueh-min also turned to look at his brother's shining eyes, smiled, and said very slowly, "You are too . . . my beloved, good younger brother." He then glanced around, and was aware of their approaching home. Thus in a happy mood he said to his brother, "Chueh-hui, hurry up, our home is just around the corner."

Chueh-hui nodded his consent. The two of them quickened their steps, and in a wink they turned into a still quieter street.

Here the oil lamps had been lit, and their dull gleam, casting pale shadows of the lamp posts on the snow, looked particularly lonely in the frigid windy atmosphere. Few persons were abroad, and these walked quickly, leaving their footprints in the snow and silently vanishing. The deep imprints rested exhausted, without even a thought of moving, until new feet pressed down upon them. Then they uttered low sighs and were transformed into queer shapes; on the interminably long, white-mantled street the regular patterns of footprints became only large and small dark shapeless holes.

A row of residential compounds, with large solid wood gates painted black, stood motionless in the icy gale. Pairs of eternally mute stone lions crouched outside their entrances—one on each side. Opened gates gave the appearance of the mouths of fantastic beasts. Within were dark caverns; what was inside them, no one could see.

Each of these residences had a long history; some had changed owners several times. Each had its secrets. When the black veneer peeled off the big gates, they were painted again. But no matter what changes took place, the secrets were kept. No outsider was ever permitted to know them.

In the middle of this street, before the gates of an especially large compound, the two brothers halted. They scuffed their leather shoes on the stone flagging, shook the snow from their clothing, and let their robes fall straight. Holding their umbrellas, they strode in, the sound of their footsteps being quickly swallowed up in the dark cavern of the long entranceway. Silence again descended on the street.

The outside of this compound resembled the others in that a pair of crouching stone lions flanked its entrance and two big red paper lanterns also hung from the eaves of its gate. What made it distinctive was the pair of large rectangular stone vats placed before the gate.

On the walls on either side of the entrance, hung vertically, were red veneered plaques inscribed with black ideographs. Reading from top to bottom, first the right board then the left, the wishful motto was set forth: *Benevolent rulers, happy family; long life, good harvests.*

II

Although the wind now died down completely, the air was still as cold as before. Night came, but did not bring darkness. The sky remained grey, the ground was paved with snow. In the large snow-covered courtyard, pots of golden plum blossoms were ranged on either side of a raised stoneflagged path. Coated with frosty white, the branches were like lovely jade.

Advancing along this path, Chueh-min, the elder of the two brothers, had just reached the steps of the one-storey wing on the left side of the courtyard, and was about to cross the threshold, when a girl's voice called:

"Second Young Master, Third Young Master, you've come back just in time. Dinner has just started. Hurry. We have guests."

The speaker was the bondmaid Ming-feng, a girl of sixteen. She wore her hair in a long single braid down her back. Her trim young frame was encased in a padded jacket of blue cloth. When she smiled, dimples appeared in the firm healthy flesh of her oval-shaped face. She regarded the brothers innocently with bright sparkling eyes, quite free of any timidity or hesitation.

Standing behind Chueh-min, Chueh-hui smiled at her.

"Right. We'll get rid of these umbrellas and be there directly," Chueh-min retorted. Without giving her another glance, he entered the door.

"Ming-feng, who are the guests?" Chueh-hui called from the steps.

"Mrs. Chang and Miss Chin. Hurry up." Ming-feng turned and went into the main building.

Chueh-hui smiled after her retreating figure until the door closed behind her. Then he entered his own room, bumping into his brother, who was coming out.

"What were you and Ming-feng talking about that kept you so long?" Chueh-min demanded. "Get a move on! The food will be all gone if you delay much longer."

"I'll go with you now. I don't have to change my clothes. They're not very wet." Chueh-hui tossed his umbrella on the floor.

"Sloppy! Why can't you do things right? The old saying is certainly true—It's easier to move a mountain than change a man's character!" Though he spoke critically, Chueh-min still wore a pleasant expression. He picked up the dripping umbrella, opened it and carefully placed it on the floor again.

"What can I do?" said Chueh-hui, watching with a grin. "That's the way I am. But I thought you were in a hurry. You're the one who's holding us up."

"You've got a sharp tongue. Nobody can out-talk you!" Chueh-min walked out as if in a great huff.

Chueh-hui knew his brother as well as Chueh-min knew him, so he wasn't alarmed. Smiling, he followed behind Chueh-min, his mind filled with the pretty bondmaid. But his thoughts of her vanished at the scene which met his eye as he entered the main building.

Seated around a square table were six people. On the side farthest from the door—the seats of honour—sat his stepmother Madam Chou and his aunt—his father's sister—Mrs. Chang. On the left sat his cousin Chin—Mrs. Chang's daughter—and Jui-chueh, wife of his eldest brother Chueh-hsin. On the near side sat Chueh-hsin and their young sister Shu-hua. The two seats on the right side were vacant.

Chueh-hui and his brother bowed to Mrs. Chang and greeted Chin, then slipped into the two empty seats. A maid quickly served them bowls of rice.

"Why are you so late today?" Madam Chou, holding her rice

14

bowl, asked them kindly. "If your aunt hadn't come for a visit we would have finished eating long ago."

"We had no classes this afternoon, but Mr. Chu wanted us to rehearse our play," Cheuh-min replied. "That's what took us so long."

"It must be cold outside after that heavy snowfall," said Mrs. Chang, half concerned, half for the sake of politeness. "Did you take sedan-chairs home?"

"No, we walked. We never take sedan-chairs!" said Chueh-hui quickly.

"Chueh-hui would never let it be said that he rode in a sedan-chair. He's a humanitarian," Chueh-hsin explained with a mocking grin.

Everyone laughed. Angry and embarrassed, Chueh-hui kept his head down, concentrating on his food.

"It's not actually very cold outside, and the wind has stopped," Chueh-min replied courteously to his aunt. "We chatted as we walked, in fact we felt quite comfortable."

"When is your school going to put on that play you mentioned?" Chin asked him. She was a few months younger than Chueh-min. Chin was considered the most beautiful of all the girl relatives of the Kao family, and the most vivacious. She had entered a girls' school at an early age, and was now a third-year student in the provincial Normal School for Girls.

"Probably when the next spring term begins. There's only a little more than a week of this term left. When does your winter vacation start?"

"We started last week. They say the school is short of money, that's why we were let off early this year." Chin had already finished eating and put down her bowl.

"All the provincial educational funds are being used for military purposes. Every school is in the same fix. The only difference with us is that our principal is bound by contracts with our foreign teachers. They get their salaries whether we hold classes or not. We cut our losses by holding class, so to speak. . . . I hear our principal has some connection with the governor, so our money is not so tight."

Chueh-min also put his bowl down. Ming-feng handed him a damp face-cloth.

"As long as you can go to school, what's the difference?" Chueh-hsin said.

"What's the name of their school? I've forgotten," Mrs. Chang asked Chin.

"Mama has a terrible memory," Chin said pleasantly. "They're in the Foreign Languages School. You've already asked several times."

"You're quite right, Chin. I'm getting old; my memory's failing me," Mrs. Chang smiled. "I won a trick at mahjong today and forgot to take it."

By now everyone had finished eating and had wiped their faces with the damp napkins. "Let's go into the next room," Madam Chou proposed, pushing back her chair and rising. The others also stood up, and all walked out together.

In the rear of the group, Chueh-min said to Chin in a low voice, "After next summer vacation our school is going to accept girl students."

Chin glowed with pleasure. She fixed her large limpid eyes on him as if he had given her the best possible news.

"Really?" she asked, a trifle doubtfully. She was afraid Chueh-min might be teasing her.

"Really. Have I ever lied to you?" Chueh-min looked at his younger brother, standing beside him. "If you don't believe me, you can ask Chueh-hui."

"It's not that I don't believe you, it's just that this good news came too suddenly," Chin replied with an excited laugh.

"It's true all right. But whether the plan can be put through or not is another question," said Chueh-hui. "Szechuan has entirely too many feudal moralists, and their influence is very strong. They're sure to oppose this thing. Boys and girls in the same school? That's something they never thought of in their wildest dreams!" Chueh-hui grew heated.

"It doesn't matter about them. As long as our principal sticks to his guns, we can do it," Chueh-min retorted, thinking to comfort Chin. "Our principal says if no girls have the courage to register, he'll get his wife to put her name down!"

"I'm going to be the first to apply!" Chin said firmly.

"Chin, why don't you come in here?" Mrs. Chang called

16

from the next room. "Why are you still standing there by the door?"

"Ask your mother if you can come to our room," Chueh-min urged Chin quietly. "I'll tell you the whole story in detail."

Chin nodded, then walked over to her mother and said a few words in her ear. Mrs. Chang laughed. "Very well, but don't be too long."

As the girl and the two brothers were leaving the main building, Chin could hear the clicking of the ivory pieces on the wooden table. She knew that her mother was good for at least four games of mahjong.

III

"This term we finished reading *Treasure Island*. Next term we're going to do Tolstoy's *Resurrection*," Chueh-min said to Chin with a pleased smile as they walked down the steps. "Our Chinese literature teacher is going to be the man who wrote that article, 'Cannibal Confucian Morality'[1] in the *New Youth* magazine![2] Isn't that wonderful?"

"You're really lucky," cried Chin, her face flushing with admiration. "We always get old-fashioned scholars for our 'lit' teachers, the kind whose favourite texts are books like *Selected Ancient Chinese Essays*.[3] As for English, we've been on *Chamber's English Reader* for the past few years and now I hear we'll be switching to *Tales from Shakespeare*—always the

[1] Article by Wu Yü (1872–1949) published in the November 1919 issue of *New Youth*.

[2] Originally entitled *Youth*, this most influential magazine of the New Culture Movement (see Introduction) was published first in Shanghai, then in Peking, and finally in Canton during the period 1915–26.

[3] A collection of essays from ancient times until the seventeenth century, written in classical prose. Compiled by Lin Hsi-chung in 1696.

17

same dull old antiques! . . . I'd give anything if your school would lift its ban on girl students right now and let me transfer."

"What's wrong with *Chamber's English Reader?*" Chueh-hui queried sarcastically. "It's already been translated into Chinese under the title of *Smiles from the Poets!*"[4]

Chin gave him a severe glance. "You're always joking. We're talking seriously."

"All right, I'll shut up," said Chueh-hui with a grin. "You two go ahead and talk." He slowed down to let Chueh-min and Chin enter the wing first, while he paused in the doorway and gazed around the courtyard.

Lights were burning brightly in both the left and right sections of the main building as well as in the wing opposite the one in which the two brothers lived. Mahjong tiles clicked in the left section of the main building. All sides of the courtyard were alive with voices. How beautiful the snow-covered garden was, how pure! Chueh-hui wanted to shout for joy, to laugh loud and clear. He flung his arms wide, greeting the broad vistas before him. He felt free, unrestrained.

He remembered how Black Dog, the role he played in *Treasure Island,* pounded the table at the inn and roared for rum. The gusto of it all surged up within him. Throwing back his head he shouted:

"Ming-feng, bring three cups of tea!"

There was a call of acknowledgement, and a few minutes later the girl emerged from the left section of the main building with the tea.

"Why only two cups? I distinctly asked for three!" Chueh-hui was still shouting and Ming-feng, as she came up to him, was startled. Her hands trembled, spilling some of the tea.

"I've only got two hands," she said, smiling.

"Clever, aren't you? You could have brought a tray." Chueh-hui laughed. "All right, take these in to Miss Chin and Second Young Master." He pressed back against the left side of the doorway to let her go by.

[4] Translated by the famous writer and translator Lin Shu (1852–1924).

After a moment, hearing her returning footsteps, Chueh-hui planted his legs wide in the doorway and stood facing the courtyard. She came up quietly behind him and, after a pause, said:

"Third Young Master, let me pass." Her voice was not very loud.

Either Chueh-hui didn't hear, or he pretended not to; in any event he continued to stand where he was.

"Ming-feng . . . Ming-feng!" It was the voice of Madam Chou, Chueh-hui's stepmother, calling from the main building.

"Let me go; Madam Chou wants me," Ming-feng pleaded. "She'll scold me if I'm late."

"What if she does?" Chueh-hui turned and smiled. "Just tell her I asked you to do something for me."

"She won't believe me. If I make her angry, she'll give me the devil after the guests leave." The girl's voice was low, audible only to Chueh-hui.

The voice of another girl, Chueh-hui's sister Shu-hua, came ringing across the courtyard. "Ming-feng, Madam wants you to put tobacco in the water-pipes!"

Chueh-hui stepped aside and Ming-feng hurried past.

Shu-hua came out of the main building. "Where have you been?" she demanded of Ming-feng. "Why don't you answer when you're called?"

"I brought some tea for Third Young Master," Ming-feng answered, hanging her head. Her voice was emotionless.

"Bringing tea shouldn't take all that time! You're not a mute. Why didn't you answer when I called you?" Shu-hua was only fourteen, but she had already learned how to scold the bondmaids, just like her elders, and she did it very naturally. "Now get in there. If Madam Chou knew you deliberately refused to answer, she'd tell you a thing or two."

Shu-hua turned and went back into the house. Ming-feng quietly followed her.

Chueh-hui had heard every syllable of this exchange, and the words cut him like the blows of a whip. His face burned with shame. It was he who had brought this on Ming-feng. His sister's attitude sickened him. He had wanted to come forward and defend Ming-feng, but something had held him back. He had stood silently in the dark, watching, as though it had nothing to do with him.

Alone in the courtyard, he could still see Ming-feng's lovely face. It was subservient, uncomplaining. Like the sea, it accepted everything, swallowed everything, without a sound.

From his room, another feminine voice reached his ear, and he pictured another girl. Her face was also beautiful, but it reflected very different kinds of emotion. Resistance, ardour, determination, refusal to submit to the least injustice. The expressions on the two faces were manifestations of two different ways of life, of two different fates. Somehow, even though the latter girl enjoyed a much greater abundance of happiness and gaiety, more of his sympathy and affection lay with the former.

The face of the first girl again loomed large in his mind, drawing him with its docile, beseeching expression. He wanted to comfort her, to offer her some kind of consolation. But what could he give her? Her fate was predetermined before she came into the world. Many other girls in her circumstances had suffered the same fate. Of course, she couldn't be any exception. Chueh-hui wanted to cry out against the unfairness of this fate, to fight it, to change it. Suddenly, a strange thought came to him. After a moment, a faint laugh escaped him.

"It could never be. That sort of thing just can't be done," he said half-aloud.

Ah, if it only could, he mused. But when he thought of the consequences that might ensue, his courage left him. It's only a dream, he said to himself with a wry smile, only a dream.

Dream or no, the idea fascinated him and he was reluctant to abandon it. Suppose she had Chin's social status? he wondered.

There'd be no question about it! he told himself positively. For the moment it seemed to him that she really was a girl like Chin and that his relationship with her was quite ordinary.

Then he laughed, laughed at himself. Preposterous! . . . Anyhow, who says I love her? She's just fun to be with.

Gradually Ming-feng's submissive face was replaced in

Chueh-hui's mind by the stubborn, ardent visage of the other girl. But soon this too faded.

"Can a man remain at home while the Huns are still undefeated?"[5] Although he didn't usually care for that hoary aphorism, it now seemed to contain a miraculous solution to all his problems. He boldly shouted it aloud. His "Huns" were not foreign invaders, nor was he intending to take up sword and spear to slay them on a battlefield. What the cry meant to him was that a real man ought to cast off family ties; he should go out into the world and perform great deeds. As to what kind of deeds these should be, he had only the vaguest notion. Chueh-hui strode into the room with the heroic quotation still on his lips.

"He's gone crazy again!" Chueh-min, standing beside his desk, had looked round at the sound of Chueh-hui's voice, then laughed and addressed this remark to Chin, who was seated in a cane armchair.

Chin glanced at Chueh-hui. "Don't you know he's a great hero?" she asked with an amused smile.

"More likely than not, he's the Black Dog. Black Dog was also a great hero!" Chueh-min said, laughing. Chin laughed too.

"Anyhow, the Black Dog was a lot better than Dr. Livesey," Chueh-hui retorted warmly, somewhat angered by their laughter. "Dr. Livesey was only one of the gentry."

"Now what in the world do you mean by that?" Chueh-min queried, half surprised, half in jest. "Aren't you also going to be one of the gentry?"

"No, I'm not!" Chueh-hui cried hotly. "Just because our grandfather and father are members of the gentry, does that mean we, also, have to become gentry?" He clamped his lips and waited for his brother to reply.

Chueh-min had only been joking at first, but now, seeing

[5] These words are attributed to Ho Ch'ü-ping, the famous general of the Han Dynasty (second century B.C.) who won several brilliant victories over the Huns. When asked to look at the mansion built for him by the emperor, he answered that he could not think about houses when the Huns were still undefeated.

that Chueh-hui was really angry, he tried to find words to calm him. For the moment, however, he could think of nothing appropriate, and could only stare at Chueh-hui in stupefaction. Chin, seated off to one side, was observing the two brothers, but she did not speak.

"I've had enough of this kind of life!" Chueh-hui could contain himself no longer. "Why does Chueh-hsin sigh all day long? Isn't it because he can't stand being one of the gentry, because he can't stand the oppressive atmosphere of this gentry household? You know it is. . . . We've got four generations under one roof, only one generation less than the 'ideal' family, but never a day goes by without open quarrels and secret wrangles. They're all trying to grab a bit more of the family property. . . ."

Chueh-hui was almost choking with rage. He had a lot more to say but he couldn't get the words out. What was infuriating him, in fact, was not his eldest brother's fate, but that of the girl whose expression was so docile. He felt he was being cut off from her by an invisible high wall, and this wall was his gentry family. It prevented him from attaining the object of his desire; therefore he hated it.

Chueh-min looked at his brother's red face and flashing eyes. He came up and grasped Chueh-hui's hand, then patted him on the shoulder.

"I shouldn't have teased you," he said in an agitated voice. "You're right. Your unhappiness is my unhappiness. . . . We two will always stand side by side. . . ." He still didn't know about the girl in Chueh-hui's heart.

Chueh-hui, quickly mollified, mutely nodded his head.

Chin stood up and walked over to them. She addressed Chueh-hui in a voice that trembled. "I shouldn't have laughed at you either. I want to stick together with both of you, always. I have to fight too. My condition is even worse than yours."

They looked at her. There was a melancholy light in her lovely eyes; her usual vivaciousness was gone. A troubled expression bespoke her inner struggle. The boys had never seen her like this before, but they knew at once what was disturbing her. She had spoken correctly—her condition was much worse than theirs. They were touched by this melancholy, so

22

rare in her. They were ready to sacrifice themselves completely, if only it would bring this girl's wishes to an earlier fulfilment. This was just an idle hope, for there was nothing specific they could do, but they felt it was their duty to help her.

The boys immediately forgot their own problems and thought only of Chin.

"Don't worry," Chueh-min assured her, "we'll figure something out for you. I'm a firm believer in 'where there's a will, there's a way.' Remember when we first wanted to go to a public school? Yeh-yeh[6] was dead set against it. But in the end we won out."

Chin steadied herself with one hand on the desk. She gazed at them as if out of a dream.

"Chueh-min is right. Don't worry about a thing," Chueh-hui earnestly beseeched Chin. "Just concentrate on reviewing your lessons. Put a lot of time in on English. As long as you can pass the Foreign Languages School entrance exams, solving the other problems won't be so hard."

With deft fingers, Chin adjusted her hair. She smiled, but there was a note of concern in her voice. "I hope so. There's no question about Mama; she's sure to let me transfer. But I'm afraid my grandmother won't agree, and there's bound to be a lot of talk among our relatives. Take your family—except for you two, everyone else will probably be opposed."

"What have they got to do with you? Going to school is your own affair. Besides, you're not a member of our family!" Chueh-hui was a little surprised that Chin should have mentioned his family. Although Chin's mother was a daughter of the Venerable Master Kao, when she married she came under the jurisdiction of her husband's family, according to custom, and she no longer had any say in the affairs of her original home.

"You don't know what Mama had to put up with when I entered the provincial Normal School for Girls. Our relatives said—A big girl like her, out on the street every day; what will people think! What well-brought-up young lady would ever act like that? . . . Mama is very old-fashioned. She's more

[6] Grandfather.

enlightened than most of them, but she has her limits. She's willing to take the brunt on her shoulders, no matter how our relatives sneer, because she loves me. Not that she thinks it right for me to go to school—it wasn't easy for her to let me do even that. Now I'm going to ask to enter a boys' school, to sit in the same classroom with male students! Can you think of one of our relatives who would dare approve of such a thing!"

The more she talked the more excited Chin became. She was standing very straight, her shining eyes fixed on Chueh-min's face, as if seeking the answer from him.

"Our Big Brother wouldn't oppose it," Chueh-min remarked.

"If Chueh-hsin were the only one, what use would it be?" said Chin. "Aunt Chou will be against it, and it will only be material for more gossip for Aunt Wang and Aunt Shen."

"Let them talk!" Chueh-hui interjected. "They've nothing to do but stuff themselves all day. Naturally, they're full of gossip. Even if you never did anything wrong, they'd invent something to criticize. Since they're going to sneer anyhow, let them."

"Chin, there's something in what he says. Make up your mind," Chueh-min encouraged.

"I'm deciding right now." Chin's face suddenly grew radiant, and her usual vivacity and firmness flooded back. "I know that a high price must be paid for any reform to be put through, that many sacrifices must be made. I'm ready to be the victim."

"If you're determined as all that, you're sure to succeed," said Chueh-min soothingly.

Smiling, Chin said with her old stubbornness, "Whether I succeed or not doesn't matter very much. But I'm going to make the try." The brothers gazed at her admiringly.

In the next room, the clock struck nine.

Chin adjusted her hair. "I must be going. Those four games of mahjong are probably over by now." She walked towards the door, then turned to say, smiling, "Come and see us when you have time. I'm home all day with nothing to do."

"We will," the brothers replied in unison. They walked with her to the door and watched until she disappeared into the main building. It was cold outside in the courtyard, but there was considerable warmth in the hearts of both brothers as they returned to their room.

"Chin is certainly a brave girl," said Chueh-min. He lapsed into a reverie, then again burst out: "Even a vivacious girl like Chin has problems. That's something I would never have believed."

"Everyone has his troubles. I've got mine too," said Chueh-hui. He abruptly broke off, as if he had revealed something he had not intended to.

"You have troubles?" Chueh-min asked, surprised. "What's wrong?"

Chueh-hui blushed. "Nothing. I was only kidding."

Chueh-min looked at him suspiciously.

"Mrs. Chang's sedan-chair!" the clear, crisp voice of Ming-feng was calling outside.

"Mrs. Chang's sedan-chair!" echoed the hoarse tones of Yuan Cheng, a middle-aged male servant. A few minutes later, the inner compound gates swung open and two men came into the courtyard carrying a sedan-chair. They set it down beside the steps of the main building.

On the street, the watchman's gong resounded deep and mournful—once, twice. It was ten o'clock.

IV

The night died, and with it the glow of the electric lights died too. Darkness ruled the big compound. The dismal cry the electric lamps uttered as they expired still quivered in the air. Although the sound was low, it penetrated everywhere; even the corners of the rooms seemed to echo with soft weeping. The time for happiness had passed. Now was the hour of tragic tears.

Lying in their beds, stripped of the masks they had worn all day, people took stock of themselves. They opened their hearts

25

and examined their innermost secrets, peering into the recesses of their souls. Stricken with remorse and anger, they wept over the waste, the losses, the bitterness of the day gone by. Of course there were a few pleased individuals among them, but these were already wrapped in satisfied slumber. The rest were disappointed, miserable creatures in unwarm beds, tearfully bemoaning their fate.

Whether in the brightness of day or the darkness of night the world always has these two different aspects for these two different kinds of people.

In the female servants' room a wick floating in an earthen cup of oil sputtered feebly and grew dim, deepening the darkness of the humble quarters. Two women were snoring lustily on wooden beds on the right side of the room. On the left were two other beds, one occupied by Mama Huang, an elderly servant whose hair was streaked with grey, the other by the sixteen-year-old bondmaid, Ming-feng. The girl was sitting up, gazing dully at the lamp wick.

After working hard all day, now that the madams and misses of the household had retired and she had temporarily recovered her freedom, Ming-feng might, quite reasonably, have gone to sleep early. But lately, these hours of freedom had become especially dear to her; she treasured every minute of them. Thinking, remembering, she felt very much at peace. No one disturbed her. The noisy commands, the scoldings that were dinned in her ears from morning till night, were finally stilled.

During the day, wearing her mask like everyone else, she rushed around busily, a pleasant smile on her face. Now, in these precious hours of freedom, she could take the mask off; she could unlock her mind and spread out its secrets for her heart to see.

I've been here for seven years. That was the first thought. It had been constantly tormenting her of late. Seven years was a long time! She often marvelled that they should have gone by so uneventfully. She had wept many tears in that period, received many a curse and many a blow. But these had become commonplace, mere frills to her dull existence. Unavoidable things which, while she didn't relish them, had to be endured. All that happened in the world was decreed by an omnipotent being; it was her fate to be where she was and what she was. This was her own simple belief, and it coincided with what others told her.

But something else was now stirring in her heart. Though she was not yet aware of it, it was beginning to waken, bringing her hope.

More than seven years I've been here. It's soon going to be eight! She was swept with a wave of revulsion for the emptiness of her life. Like other girls in her position, she began to bemoan her fate. When the Eldest Young Miss was still alive she often talked to me about a home of one's own. Who knows where my final home will be.

Ahead Ming-feng could see only a dreary wilderness, without a trace of light anywhere. The familiar face of the Eldest Young Miss again floated before her. . . . If only she were still alive, there would be someone who cared for me. She helped me understand many things, she taught me to read and write. Now she's dead. The good don't live very long! . . . Tears filled Ming-feng's eyes.

How much longer must I go on like this? she asked herself tragically. She remembered a snowy day seven years ago. A fierce-looking woman had led her from the side of her father, bereft over the loss of his wife, and brought her to this wealthy household. From then on orders, exhausting toil, tears, curses and blows became the principal elements of her existence. A life of dullness, of drab, unvarying monotony.

Like other girls her age, she had dreamed beautiful dreams, but they all passed quickly, blotted out by reality. She had dreamed of lovely baubles, of beautiful clothes, of delicious food, of warm bedding, of all the things the young ladies she waited on possessed. She even prayed that these wonderful objects might soon be hers. But the days continued to flit by, bearing her pain with them. Nothing new ever came her way, not even a new hope.

Fate, everything is decided by fate. When she was beaten and cursed she used these words to console herself. Suppose

I had been fated to be a young lady too? Ming-feng luxuriated in fanciful imagination: She wore pretty clothing; she had parents who loved and cherished her; she was admired by handsome young gentlemen. One of them came and took her away to his home, and there they lived together happily ever after.

How silly. Of course it could never happen! She scolded herself with a smile. I'll never have a home like that! Her smile faded and her face fell. She knew very well what would happen to her. When she reached the proper age, Madam would say to her, "You've worked here long enough." And she would be placed in a sedan-chair and carried to the home of a man Madam had chosen, a man Ming-feng had never seen. He might be thirty or forty years old. Thereafter she'd toil in his house, work for him, bear him children. Or perhaps after a few weeks she'd come back to serve the same wealthy family, the only difference being that now she would not be scolded and beaten so frequently, and would receive a small wage which she would have to turn over to her husband. Isn't that what happened to Madam Shen's maid, Hsi-erh?

How terrible! That kind of a home is no home at all! . . . Ming-feng shivered. She remembered when Hsi-erh returned after her marriage, her long single braid done up in a bun in the back of her head. Ming-feng often saw her alone in the garden, furtively weeping. Sometimes Hsi-erh told of the brutality of her husband. All this gave Ming-feng a frightening premonition of what her own destiny would be.

Darkness, only darkness! I'd be better off dead, like the Eldest Young Miss! Ming-feng thought bitterly. The gloom of the room closed in on her as the wick again dwindled. She could hear the snores of her companions. Listlessly she rose and adjusted the wick. The room brightened and her heart felt a bit lighter. She looked at the stout Sister Chang, sleeping buried in bed clothes; only a tangled mop of hair and half a fat face were visible. The woman emitted queer regular little snores that sounded like yelps. Emerging half muffled from beneath the thick comforters they were particularly frighten-

28

ing. Her massive body a great lump on the bed, the stout maid slept very deeply; she never stirred.

Like a pig, thought Ming-feng with a wry smile. But her heart was heavy. She was still surrounded by darkness, darkness filled with evil grinning faces. The faces came closer. Some of them grew angry, opened their mouths, shouted at her. Frightened, she covered her eyes with her hands and sank down on the bed again in a sitting position.

Outside, the wind began to howl. It shook the window frames, causing the paper pasted over the wooden latticework to cry out dismally. Icy air seeped in through the paper and the room became cold. The lamp flame flickered. A chill crept up Ming-feng's sleeves to her body. With a shiver, she removed her hands from her eyes and gazed around.

I'd better go to sleep, she thought dully, opening the buttons of her padded jacket. She slipped it off. Two mounds of firm young flesh pressed out against her undershirt.

I'm growing up, Ming-feng sighed. But who knows what kind of a home I'll have. . . . Then the face of a smiling young man appeared before her. She recognized him and her heart burst into flower. Warmed by a thread of hope, she prayed that he would stretch forth his hand. Perhaps he could rescue her from her present life. But then the face gradually floated away into the sky, higher and higher until it vanished. And her dream-filled eyes found themselves looking only at the dirty ceiling.

A cold gust swept across her exposed breast, wrenching her back to reality. She rubbed her eyes and sighed. Only a dream! After a final lingering glance around the room, she gathered her courage and removed her warm cotton-padded trousers. Piling them and the padded jacket on top of the bedding, with a quick motion she plunged beneath the covers.

She had nothing. The phrase the Eldest Young Miss had always used in talking of woman's lot revolved in her brain— "wretched fate."

It cut her heart like a whip, and she began to weep beneath the bedding, softly, so as not to disturb the others. The lamp flame dimmed. Outside, the high wind howled mournfully.

V

On the snow-covered street, the clash of the watchman's gong sounded with deep solemnity through the quiet night. Reverberating in the icy air, it rolled past the sedan carriers' footfalls in the snow.

The men carrying the sedan-chairs walked very slowly, as if fearful that if they overtook the gong sound they would lose this solemn friend. But after travelling two more blocks, the gong turned off, leaving only its fading regretful sound to linger in the ears of the sedan porters and their passengers.

Middle-aged servant Chang Sheng led the way with a lantern, his head hunched between his shoulders against the cold. From time to time his sharp cough broke the rather frightening stillness.

The chair porters shouldered their heavy loads silently, walking freely with large strides. It was bitterly cold and the icy snow stung the bare flesh of their straw-sandaled feet. But they were accustomed to this and they knew the road ahead was not long. They would soon reach their destination. Then they could while away their time beside the opium lamp or at the card table. Walking quietly, with even footfalls, they occasionally shifted the carrying pole of the sedan-chair from one shoulder to the other, or blew hot breath on one of their hands. Exertion sent warm blood coursing through their bodies. They began to perspire, the sweat on their backs soaking through their tattered old padded jackets.

Chin's mother, Mrs. Chang, sat in the leading sedan-chair. Although she had only just turned forty, she already showed signs of age. A few games of mahjong had exhausted her. Her mind was numb. At times the wind swept open the curtain of her sedan-chair, but she was unaware of it.

Chin, on the other hand, was very alert and excited. She was thinking of what was soon to happen, the first important event of her life. She could almost see it before her, adorable, dazzling. She wanted to grasp it, but she knew the moment she stretched out her hand, people would hinder her. Although not sure she could succeed, she was determined to try. Yet, in spite of having made up her mind, she still was a little worried that she would fail, and she was rather afraid. These complicated thoughts made her alternately happy and gloomy. Wrapped in her problems, Chin was oblivious to her surroundings. She came back to herself only when the sedan-chairs passed through the gates of her family compound and were set down in front of the main hall.

As usual, Chin first accompanied Mrs. Chang to her room and watched the maid change her mother's clothes. Chin herself hung the clothing in the closet.

"I don't know why I'm so tired today," Mrs. Chang sighed. She had put on a fur-lined silk jacket and sat wearily in a cane chair beside the bed.

"You played too long today, Ma," Chin said with a smile. She sat down on a chair diagonally opposite. "Mahjong takes too much out of people, and you played twelve games."

"You always scold me for playing mahjong, but what else is there for a woman of my age to do?" Mrs. Chang laughed. "Sit around all day reciting Buddhist scriptures, like your grandmother? I just couldn't do it."

"I'm not saying you shouldn't play, I only mean you shouldn't play too long."

"I know," said Mrs. Chang pleasantly. She observed the maid, standing half asleep on her feet beside the clothes closet. "Go to bed, Sister Li. I don't need you any more," she instructed.

After the maid had gone, Mrs. Chang turned again to her daughter. "What were you saying? Oh, yes, that I shouldn't play too much mahjong. I know that. But somehow I seem to get tired even when I don't do anything tiring. A life with nothing to do is boring if it lasts too long. People who live too long are a nuisance, anyhow." Mrs. Chang closed her eyes and folded her arms across her chest. She seemed to doze.

Except for the ticking of the clock, the room was very still. Evidently Chin would have no opportunity to discuss that important matter with her mother tonight. She stood up, thinking she had better waken her mother and put her to bed so that she wouldn't catch a chill.

But as Chin rose, her mother opened her eyes and said, "Chin, dear, give me some tea."

The girl took a teapot from a low-burning charcoal brazier, poured out a cup and placed it on a stool beside her mother.

"Here's your tea, Ma," she said. She stood awkwardly. She felt her chance to speak had come, but she couldn't get the words out.

"You're tired too, Chin. Go to sleep."

Chin hesitated. Finally she screwed up her courage. "Ma," she began. Her voice trembled a bit with excitement.

"What is it?"

"Ma," Chin said again. Head down, she toyed with the edge of her jacket. She spoke slowly. "Chueh-min says next year their school will be accepting girl students. I'd like to take the entrance exam."

"What are you saying? Girl students in a boys' school? You want to go there?" Mrs. Chang couldn't believe her ears.

"Yes," Chin replied timidly. She explained, "There's nothing wrong with it. Peking University[7] already has three girl students. Co-ed schools have been started in Nanking and Shanghai."

"What is the world coming to? It isn't enough to have schools for girls, now they want to have co-ed schools too!" Mrs. Chang sighed. "When I was a girl, I never dreamed there'd be such things!"

These words struck Chin like a gourd ladleful of cold water. Chilled and dazed, she stood in silence. But she refused to give up hope. Slowly, her courage returned. She said:

"Ma, times have changed. After all, it's more than twenty years since you were my age; something new comes into the world every day. Girls are human beings the same as boys. Why shouldn't they study in the same classroom?"

[7] Founded in 1898, Peking University (or National University of Peking) is one of the greatest modern Chinese institutions of higher learning. It played a great part in the New Culture Movement and in the revolutionary and nationalist movements of the later period.

Mrs. Chang interrupted with a laugh: "I won't try to argue the merits of the case; I'd never be able to outtalk you. I'm sure you can find lots of reasons in those new books of yours to use against me. You probably think I'm a reactionary old mossback."

Chin laughed too, then she pleaded, "Let me go, Ma. You usually trust me. You've never refused me anything!"

Mrs. Chang weakened a little. "And I've taken a good deal of abuse for that very reason," she sighed. "But I'm not afraid of gossip, and I do trust you. No matter what it's been, I've always done what you wanted. . . . But this thing is too special. Your grandmother will be the first to oppose. Surely you don't want me to fall out with her because of this? And of course all our relatives will be sure to talk."

"Didn't you just say you're not afraid of gossip?" Chin retorted. "Grandma is in a nunnery. At most she visits us once a month, and then only stays two or three days. The last few months she hasn't come home at all. Besides, who cares what she says? Since she usually doesn't concern herself with family affairs, you can decide—like the time you let me enter the girls' normal school. Our relatives won't have any reason to oppose. If they want to gossip, we'll just ignore them."

After a silence, Mrs. Chang said in a deflated voice, "I used to be brave, but I'm old now. I don't want to be the butt of any more idle chatter by our relatives. I want to live in peace another few years, without any trouble. You know I've been a devoted mother to you. Your father died when you were very young, leaving me with the full burden of bringing you up. I never bound your feet like other young girls. I let you study with your cousins' private tutor at your grandfather Kao's house. Later, in spite of everything, I sent you to a girls' school. Your cousin Shu-chen has tiny bound feet, and she can barely read. Even your cousin Shu-hua had very little schooling! On the whole, you must admit I've treated you pretty well."

Mrs. Chang was to weary to go on. But when she saw that Chin was on the point of tears, her heart went out to the girl and she said kindly:

"Go to sleep, Chin dear. It's late. We can talk again about

what will happen next autumn some other time. I'll do my best for you."

With a murmur of assent, the disappointed Chin walked out, crossed a small hall and went to her own room. Although downcast, she did not blame her mother, in fact she was grateful for her mother's affection.

Chin's room was dreary, as if devoid of all hope. Even her dead father's picture, hanging on the wall, seemed to be weeping. Chin felt her eyes grow damp. She took off her skirt and laid it on the bed, then walked over to the desk, turned up the wick of the pewter lamp and sat down. Picking up a *New Youth* magazine, she idly thumbed through a few pages. The following words caught her eye:

". . . I believe that before all else I am a human being, just as much as you are—or at least that I should try to become one. . . . I can't be satisfied with what most people say. . . . I must think things out for myself, and try to get clear about them. . . ."

Lines from Ibsen's play *A Doll's House*. . . .[8]

To her they were a revelation, and her eyes grew bright. She saw clearly that her desire was not hopeless, that it all depended on her own efforts. In other words, there was still hope, and the fulfilment of that hope rested with her, not with others.

With this realization, her despair melted away, and she cheerfully picked up her pen and wrote this letter to Chien-ju, one of the girls in her class:

Today, my cousins told me that the Foreign Languages School has decided to accept girl students commencing next autumn. I am determined to take the entrance exam. What about you? Would you like to go with me? I hope you're willing to take the plunge. We have to fight, no matter what the cost, to open a road for sisters who come after us.

Please come and see me if you have time. I have a lot to tell you. My mother will be glad to see you, too.

Chin

[8] Ibsen was introduced to China by Hu Shih and was very popular among the Chinese students at the time of the New Culture Movement.

Chin read through the finished letter, wrote in the date, then painstakingly added punctuation marks, which had only recently come into vogue. Her mother despised letters written in colloquial. She said they were " . . . much longer than the classical style, and unbearably vulgar!" But Chin liked them, and she studied the colloquial letters in the "To the Editor" column of *New Youth* as a means of improving her own style.[9]

VI

To Chueh-min and Chueh-hui, Chueh-hsin was "Big Brother." Though born of the same mother and living in the same house, his position was entirely different from theirs. In the large Kao family, he was the eldest son of an eldest son, and for that reason his destiny was fixed from the moment he came into the world.

Handsome and intelligent, he was his father's favourite. His private tutor also spoke highly of him. People predicted that he would do big things, and his parents considered themselves fortunate to be blessed with such a son.

Brought up with loving care, after studying with a private tutor for a number of years, Chueh-hsin entered middle school. One of the school's best students, he graduated four years later at the top of his class. He was very interested in physics and chemistry and hoped to go on to a university in Shanghai or Peking, or perhaps study abroad, in Germany. His mind was full of beautiful dreams. At that time he was the envy of his classmates.

[9] In Old China only the dead classical language (*wen-yen*) was used in literature considered respectable by the Chinese educated class, i.e., poetry, short stories, literary essays, treatises, and history, as well as official documents. The colloquial (*pai hua*) was used by popular novelists and, beginning with the nineteenth century, by translators of the Bible and some revolutionary publications. Only the New Culture Movement firmly established the colloquial as the literary medium.

In his fourth year at middle school, he lost his mother. His father later married again, this time to a younger woman who had been his mother's cousin. Chueh-hsin was aware of his loss, for he knew full well that nothing could replace the love of a mother. But her death left no irreparable wound in his heart; he was able to console himself with rosy dreams of his future. Moreover, he had someone who understood him and could comfort him—his pretty cousin Mei, "mei" for "plum blossom."

But then, one day, his dreams were shattered, cruelly and bitterly shattered. The evening he returned home carrying his diploma, the plaudits of his teachers and friends still ringing in his ears, his father called him into his room and said:

"Now that you've graduated, I want to arrange your marriage. Your grandfather is looking forward to having a great-grandson, and I, too, would like to be able to hold a grandson in my arms. You're old enough to be married; I won't feel easy until I fulfil my obligation to find you a wife. Although I didn't accumulate much money in my years away from home as an official, still I've put by enough for us to get along on. My health isn't what it used to be; I'm thinking of spending my time at home and having you help me run the household affairs. All the more reason you'll be needing a wife. I've already arranged a match with the Li family. The thirteenth of next month is a good day. We'll announce the engagement then. You can be married within the year. . . ."

The blow was too sudden. Although he understood everything his father said, somehow the meaning didn't fully register. Chueh-hsin only nodded his head. He didn't dare look his father in the eye, although the old man was gazing at him kindly.

Chueh-hsin did not utter a word of protest, nor did such a thought ever occur to him. He merely nodded to indicate his compliance with his father's wishes. But after he returned to his own room, and shut the door, he threw himself down on his bed, covered his head with the quilt and wept. He wept for his broken dreams.

He had heard something about a match with a daughter of the Li family. But he had never been permitted to learn the whole story, and so he didn't place much credence in it. A number of gentlemen with unmarried daughters, impressed by his good looks and his success in his studies, had become interested in him; there was a steady stream of matchmakers to his family's door. His father weeded out the applicants until only two remained under consideration. It was difficult for Mr. Kao to make a choice; both of the persons serving as matchmakers were of equal prestige and importance. Finally, he decided to resort to divination. He wrote each of the girls' names on a slip of red paper, rolled the slips up into balls, then, after praying for guidance before the family ancestral tablets, picked one.

Thus the match with the Li family was decided. But it was only now that Chueh-hsin was informed of the result.

Yes, he had dreamed of romance. The one in his heart was the girl who understood him and who could comfort him—his cousin Mei. At one time he was sure she would be his future mate, and he had congratulated himself that this would be so, since in his family marriage between cousins was quite common.

He was deeply in love with Mei, but now his father had chosen another, a girl he had never seen, and said that he must marry within the year. What's more, his hopes of continuing his studies had burst like a bubble. It was a terrible shock to Chueh-hsin. His future was finished, his beautiful dreams shattered.

He cried his disappointment and bitterness. But the door was closed and Chueh-hsin's head was beneath the bedding. No one knew. He did not fight back, he never thought of resisting. He only bemoaned his fate. But he accepted it. He complied with his father's will without a trace of resentment. But in his heart he wept for himself, wept for the girl he adored—Mei, his "plum blossom."

The day of his engagement he was teased and pulled about like a puppet, while at the same time being shown off as treasure of rare worth. He was neither happy nor sad. Whatever people told him to do, he did, as if these acts were duties which he was obliged to perform. In the evening, when the comedy had ended and the guests had departed, Chueh-hsin was exhausted. He went to bed and slept soundly.

After the engagement, he drifted aimlessly from day to day. He stacked his books neatly in the bookcase and didn't look at them again. He played mahjong, went to the opera, drank, and went about making the necessary preparations for his marriage, in accordance with his father's instructions. Chueh-hsin thought very little. He calmly awaited the advent of his bride.

In less than six months, she arrived. To celebrate the marriage, Chueh-hsin's father and grandfather had a stage specially built for the performance of theatricals in the compound.

The marriage ceremony turned out to be not as simple as Chueh-hsin had anticipated. He too, in effect, became an actor, and he had to perform for three days before he was able to obtain his bride. Again he was manipulated like a puppet, again he was displayed as a treasure of rare worth. He was neither happy nor sad—he was only tired, though roused a bit by the general excitement.

This time, however, after his performance was over and the guests departed, he was not able to forget everything and sleep. Because lying in bed beside him was a strange girl. He still had to continue playing a role.

Chueh-hsin was married. His grandfather had obtained a grand-daughter-in-law, his father had obtained a daughter-in-law, and others had enjoyed a brief period of merry-making. The marriage was by no means a total loss for Chueh-hsin either. He had joined in wedlock a tender, sympathetic girl, just as pretty as the one he adored. He was satisfied. For a time he revelled in pleasures he had not believed possible, for a time he forgot his beautiful dreams, forgot the other girl, forgot his lost future. He was sated, he was intoxicated, intoxicated with the tenderness and love of the girl who was his bride. Constantly smiling, he hung about her room all day. People envied him his happiness, and he considered himself very lucky.

Thus one month passed.

One evening his father called him into his room and said:

"Now that you're married you should be earning your own living, or people will talk. I've raised you to manhood and found you a wife. I think we can say that I've fulfilled my duties as a father. From now on you must take care of yourself. We have enough money to send you to a university, down-river, to study, but in the first place you already have a wife; secondly the family property has not yet been shared out among me and my brothers, and I am in charge of the accounts. It would look like favouritism if I advanced money from the family funds for your university education. Besides, your grandfather might not agree. So I've found you a position in the West Szechuan Mercantile Corporation. The salary's not very large, but it will give you and your wife a little spending money. Moreover, if you do your work diligently, you're sure to advance. You start tomorrow. I'll take you down myself. Our family owns some shares in the company and several of the directors are my friends. They'll look after you."

Chueh-hsin's father spoke in an even voice, as if discussing something quite commonplace. Chueh-hsin listened, and assented. He didn't say whether he was willing or unwilling. There was only one thought in his mind—"Everything is finished." Though he had many words in his heart, he spoke not a one.

The following day after the midday meal his father told him something of how a man going out in the world should behave, and Chueh-hsin made careful mental notes. Sedan-chairs brought him and his father to the door of the West Szechuan Mercantile Corporation. Entering, he first met Manager Huang, a man of about forty with a moustache and a stooped back; Chen, the accountant, who had a face like an old woman; Wang, the tall, emaciated bill-collector; and two or three other ordinary-looking members of the office staff. The manager asked him a few questions; he answered simply, as if by rote. Although they all addressed him very politely, he could tell from their actions and the way they spoke that they were not the same as he. It occurred to him with some surprise that he had seldom met people of this sort before.

His father departed, leaving Chueh-hsin behind. He felt

frightened and lonely, a castaway on a desert island. He was not given any work. He just sat in the manager's office and listened to the manager discuss things with various people. After two full hours of this, the manager suddenly noticed him again and said courteously, "There's nothing for you to do today, Brother. Please come back tomorrow."

Like a pardoned prisoner, Chueh-hsin happily called a sedan-chair and gave his address. He kept urging the carriers to walk faster. It seemed to him that in all the world there was no place more wonderful than the Kao family compound.

On arriving home, he first reported to his grandfather, who gave him some instructions. Then he went to see his father, who gave him some more instructions. Finally, he returned to his own apartment. Only here, with his wife questioning him solicitously and at great length, did he find peace and relaxation.

The next day after breakfast he again went to the corporation and did not return home until five in the afternoon. That day he was given his own office. Under the guidance of the manager and his colleagues, he commenced to work.

Thus, this nineteen-year-old youth took his first big step into the world of business. Gradually, he grew accustomed to his environment and learned a new way of life. Gradually, he forgot all the knowledge he had acquired in his four years of middle school. He began to feel at home in his work. The first time he received his salary of twenty-four *yüan*,[10] he was torn between joy and sorrow. It was the first time he had ever earned any money, yet the pay was also the first fruits of the sale of his career. But as the months went by, the regular installments of twenty-four *yüan* no longer aroused in him any special emotions.

Life was bearable, without happiness, without grief. Although he saw the same faces every day, heard the same uninteresting talk, did the same dull work, all was peaceful and secure. None of the family came to bother him at home; he and his wife were permitted to live quietly.

10 *Yüan* is the basic Chinese monetary unit. Its exchange rate varies. Twenty-four *yüan* was not considered a high salary in 1917–18.

Less than six months later, another big change occurred in his life. An epidemic struck his father down; all the tears of Chueh-hsin and his brothers and sisters were unable to save him. After his father died, the family burdens were placed on Chueh-hsin's shoulders. In addition to looking after his stepmother, he also became responsible for his two younger sisters and his two young student brothers. Chueh-hsin was then only twenty years of age.

Sorrowfully, he wept for his departed father. He had not thought that fate could be so tragic. But gradually his grief dissipated. After his father was buried, Chueh-hsin virtually forgot him. Not only did he forget his father, he forgot everything that had passed, he forgot his own springtime. Calmly he placed the family burdens on his own young shoulders.

For the first few months they didn't seem very heavy; he was not conscious of any strain. But in a very short time, many arrows, tangible and intangible, began flying in his direction. Some he was able to dodge, but several struck home. He discovered something new, he began to see another side of life in a gentry household. Beneath the surface of peace and affection, hatred and strife were lurking; he also had become a target of attack. Although his surroundings made him forget his springtime, the fires of youth still burned in his heart. He grew angry, he struggled, because he considered himself to be in the right. But his struggles only brought him more troubles and more enemies.

The Kao family was divided into four households. Originally Chueh-hsin's grandfather had five sons, but the second son had died many years ago. Uncle Ke-ming and his Third Household were on fairly good terms with the First Household, which Chueh-hsin now headed. But the Fourth and Fifth Households were very unfriendly to Chueh-hsin; the wives of both secretly waged a relentless battle against him and his First Household, and spread countless rumours about him.

Struggling didn't do the least bit of good, and he was exhausted. What's the use of this endless strife? he wondered. Those women would never change and he couldn't make them give in. Why waste energy looking for trouble? Chueh-hsin evolved a new way of managing affairs—or perhaps it would be better to say of managing the family. He ended his battle with the women. He pretended to go along with their wishes whenever he could. Treating them with deference, he joined them in mahjong, he helped them with their shopping. . . . In brief, he sacrificed a portion of his time to win his way into their good graces. All he wanted was peace and quiet.

Not long after, the elder of his two young sisters died of tuberculosis. Although he mourned for her, his heart felt somewhat eased, for her death lightened his burden considerably.

Some time later, his first child was born—a boy. Chueh-hsin felt an immense gratitude towards his wife. The coming of this son into the world brought him great happiness. He himself was a man without hope; he would never have the chance to fulfil his beautiful dreams. His only function in life was to bear a load on his shoulders, to maintain the family his father had left behind. But now he had a son, his own flesh and blood. He would raise the child lovingly, and see in him the realization of the career he had lost. The boy was part of him and the boy's happiness would be his own. Chueh-hsin found consolation in this thought. He felt that his sacrifices were not in vain.

Two years later, in 1919, the May Fourth Movement began. Fiery, bitter newspaper articles awakened in Chueh-hsin memories of his youth. Like his two younger brothers, he avidly read the Peking dispatches carried in the local press, and news of the big strike in Shanghai on June third which followed. When the local paper reprinted articles from the *New Youth* and *Weekly Review* magazines, he hurried to the only bookstore in town that was selling these journals, and bought the latest issue of the first, and two or three issues of the second. Their words were like sparks, setting off a conflagration in the brothers' hearts. Aroused by the fresh approach and the ardent phrases, the brothers found themselves in complete agreement with the writers' sentiments.

Therefore they bought up all the progressive periodicals they could lay their hands on, including back numbers. These

42

included the *New Youth, New Tide,*[11] *Weekly Critic,*[12] *Weekly Review;*[13] even old issues of the *Youth Magazine,* the predecessor of *New Youth,* were searched out from under his old piles by the dealer and handed to them. Every night he and his two brothers would take turns reading every one of these, without skipping even the letters to the editor. Sometimes they had lively discussions on subjects raised in the periodicals. Chueh-hsin's brothers were more radical than he was, for he was only a follower of Hu Shih,[14] whose "On Ibsenism" even seemed a little too extreme to him. He was an admirer of Liu Pan-nung's "philosophy of compliant bows,"[15] and he liked Tolstoy's "principle of non-resistance," although he had read none of Tolstoy's own writings on the subject beside the story of *Ivan the Fool.*

Indeed, Chueh-hsin found the "compliant bow" philosophy and the "policy of non-resistance" most useful. It was thanks to them that he was able to reconcile, with no difficulty at all, the theories expressed in *New Youth* with the realities of his big family. They were a solace to him, permitting him to believe in the new theories while still conforming to the old feudal concepts. He saw no inconsistency.

[11] Also entitled *Renaissance,* this was published by the students of Peking University (1919–22), and was the most influential student magazine of the period.

[12] Published in Peking (1918–19). Very influential magazine, similar in attitude to *New Youth,* but especially concerned with current political problems.

[13] Organ of the Kuomintang (1919–20). Very widely read.

[14] A well-known philosopher, literary critic, poet, playwright, political writer, professor and diplomat. A student of John Dewey, Hu Shih received his Ph.D. from Columbia University and was connected with Peking University from 1917 until 1949, first as professor and later as chancellor. During World War II Hu Shih was Chinese Ambassador to the United States. He played a great role in the "literary revolution" initiated by the New Culture Movement.

[15] Formulated by Liu Pan-nung (1889–1934) in his article by that title published in *New Youth* (September 1918). Its basis was that one should not waste time and effort on discussion, but rather outwardly agree with one's adversary and greet his statements with a bow. This would not entail losing one's own convictions.

Chueh-hsin became a man with a split personality. In the old society, in the midst of his old-fashioned family, he was a spineless, supine Young Master; in the company of his brothers, he was a youth of the new order.

Naturally, this way of life was something the younger boys could not understand. They berated Chueh-hsin for it frequently, and he placidly accepted their criticism. But he continued to read new books and periodicals, and continued to live in the same old-fashioned manner.

He watched his first son learning to crawl, then to walk, then to speak a few simple words. The child was adorable, intelligent, and Chueh-hsin lavished nearly all his affection on him. "He's going to do all the things I couldn't," thought Chueh-hsin. He refused to hire a wet-nurse, insisting that his wife suckle the child herself. Fortunately, she had enough milk. Such goings-on were virtually unprecedented in a wealthy family, and they led to a great deal of gossip. But Chueh-hsin bore it all, convinced that he was acting in the child's best interests.

Every night, after his wife and child had retired, he would sit beside them, feasting his eyes on the baby sleeping in its mother's arms. Looking at the child's face, he was able to forget about himself completely. Chueh-hsin couldn't resist planting a kiss on the baby's satiny cheek. He softly breathed words of thanks and hope and love, rather vague words, but they gushed naturally from his lips like water from a fountain.

Chueh-hsin didn't know that his parents had loved him with the same fervour when he was an infant. They too had breathed words of thanks and hope and love.

VII

On Sunday, Chueh-hsin went as usual to the West Szechuan Mercantile Corporation. In that office there were no Sundays off.

He had no sooner sat down and taken a few sips of tea, than Chueh-min and Chueh-hui also arrived. They visited him at the office almost every Sunday. As had become their custom, they brought with them several new periodicals.

The company Chueh-hsin worked for, besides renting out shops in the arcade which it owned, ran a small power plant which supplied electricity—for a price—to its tenants and other neighbouring shopkeepers. The arcade was very large, and housed all kinds of enterprises, including the manager's office of the West Szechuan Mercantile Corporation. Near the rear door of the arcade, in the left corner, was a bookstore specializing in new publications. Because of its proximity, the bookstore became very well known to the three brothers.

"Only a few issues of *New Tide* came this time. This was the only one thay had left, and I grabbed it. A few minutes later and it would have been gone. We might have had to wait ages before getting to see a copy!" Chueh-hui lay back in a reclining cane chair beside the window of Chueh-hsin's office, reverently holding a magazine with a white cover lettered in red. His face was wreathed in smiles.

"I left word with the bookseller—come what may, he must keep a copy for us of everything new that comes in," said Chueh-hsin, looking up from his account book.

"Leaving word isn't enough," Chueh-hui explained excitedly. "There are too many people wanting them, mostly subscribers, too. The bookstore only gets three bundles at a time. In less than two days they're all gone." He turned to an editorial and began reading it with interest.

"More will be coming in. Didn't the bookseller say they're on the way? These three packages came special delivery." Chueh-min, who had just sat down, now got up again, walked over to the desk and picked up a copy of *Young China*.[16] He seated himself beside the wall to the right. His chair was one of a row of three, interspersed with two tea tables. Chueh-min chose the chair nearest the window; between him and the window stood Chueh-hsin's swivel chair.

None of the brothers spoke. Except for the sharp clicking of Chueh-hsin's abacus counters, all was still. The warm rays of the winter sun, filtered by the pale blue curtains, slanted

[16] Organ of the *Young China Association*. Published in Peking, later in Shanghai (1919–24). Very popular among young readers.

into the room as only blurry shadows. Leather shoes, ringing smartly on the cement walk outside, rose above the other noise in the arcade. They were coming closer. Mounting the stone steps, they went through the company's door. A moment later the door curtain of Chueh-hsin's office moved and a tall thin young man entered. The three brothers looked up, and Chueh-hsin hailed him with a smile:

"Ah, Chien-yun."

After greeting each of the brothers, Chen Chien-yun picked up a copy of the local paper and sat down beside Chueh-min. He glanced through the provincial news, then placed the paper on the tea table and asked:

"When does your school start its winter vacation?"

"Classes are over already. Exams begin next week," Chueh-min replied briefly, in a rather cool voice. He resumed his reading of *Young China*.

"I hear that the Students' Federation is putting on some plays in the Wanchun Theatre today to raise money for a free school for poor people," Chien-yun persisted.

Chueh-min raised his head slightly. "That may be. I haven't paid much attention," he retorted in the same cold way. "It's not necessarily the Students' Federation. More likely it's two or three schools doing the show together."

Indeed, Chueh-min seldom took part in student activities. He attended class each day, and when class was over he returned home. The only reason he was going to play Dr. Livesey in the school dramatization of *Treasure Island* during the coming Spring Festival was because his English teacher had chosen him for the role.

"Aren't you fellows going? They say they're doing Hu Shih's *When a Girl Marries* and *The Strange Orchid*.[17] They ought to be pretty good."

"It's too far. Anyhow we're getting ready for exams. Got no time to think about plays," replied Chueh-min. This time he didn't even raise his head.

[17] A play created by the theatrical group "Spring Willow," organized by Chinese students in Japan on the eve of the 1911 Chinese revolution. The group was propagandizing the realist drama.

46

"I'd like to go. Those are two good plays," Chueh-hsin interjected, still manipulating his abacus. "Unfortunately, I haven't the time."

"It's too late even if you did. They've already started," laughed Chueh-hui. He closed the magazine he had been reading and placed it on his knees.

Chien-yun silently buried his head in a newspaper he took from one of the tea tables and leafed through it listlessly.

"Are you still tutoring the Wang family children? Why is it we haven't seen you for so long?" Chueh-hsin asked in a friendly voice. He had finished his accounts and had noticed Chien-yun's awkward manner. "Is your health any better?"

"I had a bad cold for several days. That's why I haven't come around. I'm all right now. Yes, I'm still tutoring at the Wang's, and I still often run into Miss Chin."

Whether addressing her directly or talking about her with others, Chien-yun always referred to Chin as "Miss" Chin. Distantly related to the Kao family, he was Chueh-hsin's junior by a few months, and called him "Big Brother" just as the younger boys did. His parents had both died when he was a child and he was brought up by his father's brother. After graduating from middle school, he was unable to afford going on to a university. The only work he could find was a small tutoring job, teaching English and mathematics to the Wang children. The Wangs were relatives of Chin's mother, Mrs. Chang, and both families lived in the same compound. Chien-yun therefore met Chin frequently.

"You're pale, and much thinner. You've always been delicate. You ought to take better care of yourself," said Chueh-hsin sympathetically.

"You're quite right, Big Brother," Chien-yun replied, moved by his solicitude. "I know that very well."

"Then why do you always look so downcast?"

Chien-yun smiled, in an obviously forced manner. "Many people have asked me that. I don't know why myself. Maybe it's because I'm so frail, or because I lost my parents at an early age." Chien-yun's voice trembled as if he were about to weep, but there were no tears in his eyes.

"If you're frail you ought to exercise. Just moping won't do

47

any good," Chueh-min raised his head and said harshly. Before the words had all left his mouth, footsteps were heard outside and a feminine voice called:

"Cousin Chueh-hsin!"

"It's Miss Chin." A touch of brightness stole across Chien-yun's face. His low voice sounded happy.

"Please come in," Chueh-hsin called with pleasure, rising to his feet.

The door curtain was swept aside and Chin entered, followed by her mother and their male servant Chang Sheng. Having seen them to their destination, Chang Sheng immediately went out.

Chin was dressed in a pale blue silk padded jacket and a dark blue skirt. There was a faint dusting of powder on her cheeks; a strand of hair curving down beside each ear flattered the oval configuration of her face. Beneath the neat bangs on her forehead long eyebrows arched over large eyes set on either side of a well-formed nose. Those eyes were exceptionally bright and penetrating; they shone with a warmth that not only added a glow to her enthusiastic vivacious face, but seemed to light up a room the moment she came into it. She magnetized the attention of everyone in Chueh-hsin's office as she and her mother smilingly greeted them all.

Chueh-min and Chien-yun quickly offered their chairs to the two ladies, they themselves taking other seats further away from the window. Chueh-hsin ordered tea.

"We hear that the Hsinfahsiang Department Store has some new dress material. I wonder whether they have anything nice we can buy," said Mrs. Chang after a few minutes of general conversation.

"They have quite a variety now, mostly silks. I've seen them," Chueh-hsin replied promptly.

"Would you mind going with me some time?"

"Not at all. I'll be glad to. How about now?" asked Chueh-hsin cheerfully.

Mrs. Chang was very pleased. "If you're not too busy, that would be fine." She rose and looked at Chin inquiringly.

"I'll wait for you here, Ma," Chin said with a smile. She

also stood up and walked over to the desk. Chueh-hsin had already risen.

Chueh-hsin held aside the door curtain for her. "I'll be back soon," Mrs. Chang said as she crossed the threshold. Chueh-hsin followed her.

"What are you reading?" asked Chin, observing the magazine in Chueh-hui's hand.

Chueh-hui looked at her. "*New Tide*—a new publication," he answered in a satisfied tone. He was clutching the magazine lovingly with both hands.

Chin laughed. "Don't hold it like that. I'm not going to take it from you."

Chueh-min laughed too. "I have a new issue of *Young China* here, Sister Chin. Would you like to see it?"

Chueh-hui hastily sat up and offered his magazine to the girl. "Take it, take it. I don't want you saying I hoard new magazines!"

Chin shook her head. "After you've all finished reading it, I'll take it home and go through it at my leisure."

Lying back in his reclining cane chair, Chueh-hui resumed his reading. A moment later he asked gaily, "Have you succeeded, Sister Chin? You're so happy today. Did your mother consent?"

"Not yet. I don't know what I'm so happy about. But it doesn't matter whether Ma agrees or not. I can make my own decisions. I'm a person, the same as the rest of you." She seated herself in Chueh-hsin's swivel chair, and idly leafed through the account book on his desk.

"Well said. Bravo," cried Chueh-min. "Spoken like a true New Woman!"

"Don't mock me," smiled Chin. Then her face fell and she said in a different tone of voice, "I have some special news for you. Your aunt Mrs. Chien has come back."

That was special news indeed. Everyone's mood changed instantly.

"What about Cousin Mei? Has she come back too?" Chueh-hui sat up and asked anxiously.

"Yes. Mei's husband died a year after their marriage. She's

49

a widow now. Her mother-in-law didn't treat her well, so she went back to her mother. Now they've come together to Chengtu."

"How do you know all these details?" asked Chueh-min, gazing round-eyed at Chin through his gold-rimmed spectacles.

"She came to the house to see me yesterday," replied Chin slowly.

"She came to your house? Is she still the same?" asked Chueh-min.

"She looks a little haggard, but not too thin. Maybe a little thinner than before. It's only in those limpid eyes of hers that you see she's been through a lot. But I didn't dare ask her too much. I was afraid to stir up old memories. The only things she talked about were the county town she had been living in—the people there, what it was like—and a little about herself. But she never mentioned Chueh-hsin or the Kao family."

Chin's voice had become very sad. Then in a different tone, she suddenly asked Chueh-min, "How does Big Brother feel about her?"

"He seems to have long since forgotten her. I've never heard him mention her name. He's very satisfied with Sister-in-law," Chueh-min retorted frankly.

Chin shook her head slightly. She said in a rather pained voice. "But Mei probably hasn't forgotten him so easily. I can tell from her eyes that she still thinks of him. . . . Ma says I shouldn't tell Big Brother that Mei is here."

"It wouldn't matter. Anyhow Mei and her mother won't come to our house, so she and Chueh-hsin aren't likely to meet. Big Brother's forgotten the whole affair. Everything changes after a few years. What's there to worry about?" said Chueh-hui.

"I agree it's better not to tell him," said Chueh-min. "If he's forgotten there's no sense in reminding him again. And who can guarantee that he's really forgotten her?"

"That's right," Chin nodded. "It's better not to let him know."

Seated in a corner, Chien-yun shrunk back, struggle and unhappiness reflected on his face. His lips moved several times as if he wanted to speak, but no sound emerged. His eyes were riveted on Chin as he listened to her talk. The girl didn't look in his direction. At times he gazed at Chueh-min and Chueh-hui admiringly, but they paid no attention to him. Deeply moved by what Chin had said—as well as for another reason —he sighed:

"If only Big Brother had been able to marry Miss Mei, it would have been a perfect match."

Chin glanced at him warmly, then turned her eyes away. Chien-yun treasured the brief look like a blessing. He delicately savoured her reply:

"That's how we all felt."

"I don't know who stirred up the trouble between our mother and Mrs. Chien, but they certainly ruined Mei's and Big Brother's happiness once and for all!" Chueh-hui said angrily.

"You don't know? Well, I do. Ma told me the whole story. Even Big Brother himself doesn't know it," Chin said in a mournful voice. "Your father had already sent a matchmaker and Mrs. Chien had consented. But then she took their horoscopes to a fortune-teller who said that they were ill-mated and couldn't marry; that if they did, Mei would die young. So Mrs. Chien refused the match. But there was also another reason. She and your stepmother had a tiff over a mahjong game. Mrs. Chien felt very much abused and used breaking the match as a form of retaliation. Your stepmother had been quite fond of Mei—so was your whole family, for that matter—and she was put out when it was called off. Later, when Big Brother's engagement to a girl of the Li family was announced, Mrs. Chien was displeased too. The relations between the two mothers grew worse. Finally they stopped seeing each other altogether."

"So that's the way it was! We didn't know," said Chueh-min, surprised. "We didn't know that their marriage had been proposed. In fact we blamed our father and stepmother for not knowing what was in Big Brother's heart and not caring about his happiness. It wasn't their fault after all."

"That's right. We all wanted Big Brother to marry Cousin Mei. When we heard of the engagement with the Li family, we felt that a cruel wrong had been done to Mei. We thought Big Brother should have resisted. Instead, he gave in, like a fool," cried Chueh-hui hotly. "After that, Cousin Mei stopped coming to our house. Then, not long afterwards, she left Chengtu. When Big Brother married Sister-in-law, we were sorry for Cousin Mei and secretly blamed him. It's funny when you come to think of it. We seemed to be more upset about the thing than Big Brother. . . . At the time we thought he and Mei were fated for each other." Chueh-hui smiled in spite of himself.

"I'm afraid we can't say they were really in love. It's just that they were about the same age and well suited to each other temperamentally," mused Chueh-min. "That's why Big Brother wasn't too hurt after they parted."

"You are the limit!" said Chueh-hui. "'About the same age and well suited to each other temperamentally!' What else do you want?"

Everyone sighed, including Chien-yun.

"What's wrong with *you*, Chien-yun?" asked Chueh-min, startled.

There was no reply from Chien-yun. It was as if he had not heard.

"He's always like that," said Chueh-hui with a laugh.

Chien-yun suddenly became aware of the three pairs of eyes fixed upon him, and he dropped his head. But he immediately raised it again and looked timidly at Chin with a mournful gaze. When Chin made no attempt to avoid his scrutiny, he lowered his eyes at once. Shaking his head, he said softly:

"None of you understand Big Brother, you simply don't understand him. Big Brother hasn't forgotten Cousin Mei. I've seen it for a long time. He's always thinking about her."

"Then why haven't we seen any sign of it? He hardly ever even mentions her name. According to you, the more one loves in his heart, the colder an appearance he should present to the world!" Chueh-min thought he was making a crushing retort.

"Yes. Only it's not a question of should or shouldn't. In

52

cases like that, sometimes the person doesn't know what he feels," Chien-yun explained.

"I don't believe it!" said Chueh-hui firmly.

"Nor I," said Chin earnestly. "I don't think there could be a situation like that. Love is shining and righteous; there's nothing hidden about it. If a man's heart is really ardent, how can he give the appearance of being cold and disinterested?"

Chien-yun blanched as if stricken by a severe blow. His lips trembled and his eyes, the light gone out of them, gazed vacantly at the wall. He lowered his head and remained silent.

Looking through a new book on the desk, Chin hadn't observed his changed expression. The brothers, whose eyes were all on Chin, were not aware of it either. But at last Chin noticed him.

"Mr. Chen, what's wrong?" she cried, rising to her feet in astonishment.

Chien-yun's body twitched, and he turned and looked at Chin with a doubtful expression. Then he smiled and his eyes shone again, but with their usual melancholy light. Soon the smile faded and gloom quickly overcast his features, as if he had never smiled at all.

The gaze of the two brothers had gone with Chin's stare at Chien-yun's face. They observed the play of emotions there but couldn't imagine what was the cause of them.

"Nothing, nothing," replied Chien-yun in a somewhat pained tone. A smile returned to his face momentarily. "I was only thinking of something. Something I can't figure out."

"Can you tell us what it is—this thing you can't figure out?" Chin asked him pleasantly.

Chien-yun looked very ill at ease. His eyes on Chin's pretty face, he couldn't bring out a single word. Blushing, he finally stammered, "I hardly know, myself. My brain is too weak. Sometimes I don't know what I'm thinking." He smiled a dismal smile.

"Why be so modest, Mr. Chen?" smiled Chin. "We're not strangers."

"It's not modesty. I really am useless. Compared with you people, why, I'm miles behind. I don't even deserve to be in your company." Chien-yun's face was red, not with embarrassment, but with the earnestness of his speech. He spoke with a special effort for fear that his words might not be believed.

"Don't talk like that. We don't like to hear it. Let's talk about something else," Chin ordered. Her tone was still friendly, for she knew Chien-yun was a little queer and no amount of explanation would do any good.

Chueh-min said nothing. His eyes were watching Chin, at times shifting for a glance at Chien-yun. Listening carefully to their conversation, he smiled occasionally with satisfaction.

Chueh-hui paid no attention to what the others were saying, but buried himself in his *New Tide*.

Chien-yun's expression kept changing constantly. It was difficult to guess what was going on in his mind. Chin's "We" had hurt him. He repeated it to himself several times, but in a voice so low that even Chin couldn't hear him.

"All right, I won't say any more. I must be going. I have something to do." Chien-yun stood up abruptly and walked towards the door.

Chin watched him in surprise, but didn't say anything. It was Chueh-min who urged:

"Why not stay a while? It's nice, chatting together like this. Big Brother will be back soon."

"Thanks very much, but I have to go," Chien-yun said resolutely, after a moment's hesitation. He nodded to them and went out.

"What does he have to do?" queried Chin dubiously.

Chueh-min's reply was brief. "Heaven only knows!"

"Something definitely is troubling him. Otherwise, why has he become so strange? He used to be a little better before."

"Yes. He's getting queerer all the time. I don't know what's bothering him," Chueh-min answered. "Probably because he's poor, he's always being irritated; that's what makes him so peculiar."

"I want to be nicer to him, but every time I meet him, he shuts up like a clam—as if he's hiding some secret he's afraid people will discover." Chin spoke warmly, almost argumentatively. When the brothers did not reply, she continued: "How can you get close to a person like that? Sometimes, when we

54

meet, he seems to limit our talk deliberately to idle chatter. The moment I try to discuss anything serious with him, he does his best to change the subject, as if he were afraid of something."

"Maybe he's harbouring some secret heart-break. Unfortunately for him, he's living in the wrong age," Chueh-min said mockingly. "Yet sometimes he reads new books!" he added in wonderment.

"Oh, forget him!" Chueh-hui closed his magazine and banged it down on his knee. "The world is full of people like that. Can you worry about them all?"

The room was silent for a while. A face peered in through the door, looked around, then withdrew, muttering, "Oh, Young Master Kao has gone out."

"I've already decided to take the exam for your school," Chin suddenly announced to Chueh-min. "I'm working hard on my lessons now. Would you be willing to help me review my English?"

"Of course. What a question!" Chueh-min cried happily. "But what about the time?"

"That's up to you. In the evening, naturally. We both have class during the day . . . I don't think we have to wait till school starts next year. We can begin right now."

"Fine. I'll call at your house later and we can talk it over. They've come back." Chueh-min had heard the voices of Chueh-hsin and Mrs. Chang outside.

And indeed it was Chueh-hsin who held aside the door curtain and let Mrs. Chang enter first, he himself then coming in, followed by Chang Sheng, carrying the packages.

"Let's go, Chin. It's getting late." Mrs. Chang had just sat down and taken a few sips of tea, when she addressed these words to her daughter. To Chang Sheng, who was still in the room, she said, "Call a couple of sedan-chairs for us and get everything ready."

With a word of assent, Chang Sheng departed. A few minutes later Chin and her mother left. Chueh-hsin escorted them to the office door. Then the two younger brothers walked with them to the entrance of the arcade and saw both ladies safely seated in their sedan-chairs.

55

VIII

After leaving the West Szechuan Mercantile Corporation, Chueh-hui and Chueh-min separated. Chueh-min went to visit Chin; Chueh-hui intended to call on a friend.

Chueh-hui had walked a few blocks when he ran into his classmate Chang Hui-ju at an intersection. Breathing heavily, Hui-ju was hurrying along with his head down. Chueh-hui grabbed him by the arm.

"What's up, Hui-ju? You're in such a rush you don't even recognize your friends!"

The triangular-faced youth stared at Chueh-hui, perspiration beading his forehead. He was panting so hard, for the moment he couldn't speak. At last he gasped, "Awful . . . things . . . happened!"

"What is it?" Chueh-hui asked in alarm.

Hui-ju's breathing was a bit more even now, but his voice still quavered with anger and excitement. "We had a fight with the comrades today . . . in the Wanchun Theatre."

"What? Tell me about it—quick!" Chueh-hui's blood froze in his veins. He shook Hui-ju's arm with a hand that trembled. "You mean the soldiers attacked the students? Give me the details!"

"I'm going back to school to tell the rest of the boys. Come along. I'll tell you as we go. . . ." Hui-ju's eyes were blazing with anger.

Automatically, Chueh-hui turned and walked with Hui-ju. His heart was beating wildly; his body was beginning to burn. He silently gnawed his lips.

"Today we were putting on our plays in the Wanchun Theatre," Hui-ju said in an agitated voice, as the two boys walked quickly together. "I was just one of the audience. When the first play started, three soldiers tried to get in without buying tickets. The man at the door told them this wasn't

56

one of the usual Wanchun Theatre performances; that they couldn't go in unless they paid. There was no reasoning with them, and when they still insisted, our people drove them away. Not long afterwards, they came back with a dozen more comrades, all demanding free admission. Our people were afraid they'd disturb the audience with the racket they were making, so they let them in, just to keep them quiet. After they took their seats, they began cheering and yelling and behaving even worse than they usually do in theatres.

"Finally our people couldn't stand it any longer and asked them to be quiet. But they still kept on. We warned them they'd either have to behave or get out. That made them mad; they began to fight. Some of them climbed on the stage and wrecked the props. The riot lasted until a company of soldiers came from the garrison command. But the theatre was already a shambles. Several of the students had been hurt. The rioters all got away; they didn't catch a single one. A whole company of armed troops can't nab a couple of weaponless comrades! What fool would believe that? Obviously, the whole thing was planned in advance. . . ."

"Of course. They planned it all together!" Chueh-hui pressed his hands against his chest. It felt ready to burst, the anger was seething within him so! "There've been plenty of rumours lately that the authorities were cooking up something against the students. We've been too much of a headache to them the last few years—demanding checks on stores to see whether they were selling enemy goods, holding parades and demonstrations, our movement growing bigger and stronger all the time. . . . They just had to put us in our place. That's why they sicked their comrades on us. And this is only the first step. Wait and see. There'll be more to follow!"

"We immediately held a meeting of everyone who was there, in Shaocheng Park. We've decided to call on all students of the schools still in session to go in mass with a petition to the governor. The demands have already been agreed upon. Are you with us?" Hui-ju quickened his pace.

"Naturally!" replied Chueh-hui. They had arrived at the school, and they strode into the grounds in a highly excited state.

57

Many students were already gathered on the athletic field, conversing noisily in groups. The whole school seemed to be up in arms. Evidently they had already heard about the fight with the comrades. Hui-ju observed Huang Tsun-jen, who played the role of the father in *When a Girl Marries,* the first of the two plays to be performed that day. *When a Girl Marries* was already over when the rioting started, and Tsun-jen must have gone back to school directly with the news.

Chueh-hui and Hui-ju joined one of the groups and listened to what the students were saying. Hui-ju told them everything he knew of the situation, and was still heatedly speaking when the time came for the students to set forth.

Shaocheng Park was the rallying place. When the students from Chueh-hui's school arrived they found boys from other schools already there. But because it was a Sunday, it had not been possible to notify everybody; what's more, several schools were in the middle of their winter vacations. Many less than the entire student body were present, and these were only from the more important schools. The turn-out was much smaller than for previous demonstrations. In all, there was a total of only about two hundred students.

Dusk had fallen. Lamps were being lit in the gathering gloom. The students began their march to the office of the governor.

Chueh-hui looked around him tensely as he walked. Knots of people lined the streets, gazing at the students curiously. A few made guarded remarks; some timidly hurried away.

"They must be out for another blasted check on enemy goods. Which store is going to catch it this time?" Chueh-hui caught the sound of an out-of-town accent. He turned to look at the speaker and found himself confronted with a pair of small shifty eyes in a small pasty face. Scowling, Chueh-hui bit his lips. He couldn't be sure he had heard correctly, so he continued to march.

It was night by the time they reached the governor's headquarters. The pressing darkness increased the tension in every student's heart, assailing them with a nameless fear. They had the peculiar feeling that this was not merely the darkness of night, but the darkness of society and the political situation.

Against all these, alone among an indifferent populace, they pitted their youthful hearts.

On the field in front of the governor's compound a platoon of soldiers stood awaiting them with levelled bayonets, gleaming, chest high. The soldiers watched in grim silence as the students excitedly demanded to be let in. Neither side was willing to fall back. The students held a conference and decided to send a deputation of eight, but these too were stopped by the soldiers. Finally a junior officer emerged and addressed them curtly:

"Please leave, gentlemen. The governor has gone home."

The deputies replied courteously but firmly that if the governor was not in, his secretary would do just as well. But this was not of the slightest avail. The junior officer shook his head in a cold, pompous manner, as if to say—The power is in my hands now; I can handle you students myself!

When the deputies reported the results of this conference to their mates, the students were furious.

"Nothing doing," they shouted. "The governor must come out!"

"We're going in! We're going in!"

"If the governor's not here, let his secretary come out!"

"Charge! Let's go in first and talk afterwards!"

Heads were bobbing all over the field. A few students began to push forward but were held back by their mates.

"Quiet down a bit, fellows. Order. We must keep order!" one of the deputies shouted.

"Order!" "Order!" Others took up the cry.

"Never mind about order," someone yelled. "The first thing to do is get inside!"

"It can't be done. They've got guns!"

"Order! Order! Listen to our deputies!" was the cry of the majority.

Gradually the hubbub subsided. In the dark night, a fine drizzle began to fall.

"Fellows, they won't let us in, and the governor refuses to send anyone out to see us. What shall we do? Shall we go back? Or shall we wait here?" So that everyone might hear

59

him, a deputy shouted at the top of his lungs, his voice going hoarse with the effort.

"We won't go back!" roared the students.

"We insist on seeing someone in authority. Our demands must be met. We're not falling for any tricks!" several of the students cried.

The junior officer approached the deputies. "It's raining," he said in a more conciliatory tone. "I urge you to go home. I promise to deliver your requests to the governor. There's no use your waiting out here all night." The deputies relayed his words to the students.

"No, we're not going!" was the noisy response. The whole field seethed with agitation. Finally, quiet was slowly restored.

"All right then. We're all staying right here," a deputy shouted through cupped hands. "We deputies will make another try at reasoning with them. We're not leaving till they meet our demands!"

A few students clapped their hands, and in an instant the whole assembly burst into applause. The deputies set out. This time, eight of them were permitted to enter the governor's compound.

Chueh-hui clapped with all his might as rain drenched his hatless head. Though at times he shaded his eyes with his hand or held his wrist over his forehead, his eyes continued to be blurred by the rain. He looked at the bayonets of the soldiers, at the two big lanterns hanging in the entrance-way, at the sea of heads all around him. Uncontrollable anger welled up within him. He wanted to shout; he was suffocating. The soldiers' attack in the theatre had been too sudden. Although there had been rumours that the authorities were planning some action against the students, no one had guessed it would take the form that it did.

How despicable! "Why are they treating us like this?" he asked himself. "Is love of country a crime? Are pure, sincere young people really harmful to the nation?" He didn't believe it.

A watchman's gong sounded twice in the distance. Ten p.m.!

Why haven't our deputies come back yet? Why is there still

no news? the irritated students wondered. They began to stir uneasily. The rain was coming down hard now, soaking them from head to foot. Chueh-hui could feel the cold seeping into his bones. He shivered. Then he thought—Is a little discomfort like this going to bother me? . . . Placing his hands in his sleeves, he raised his chest.

All around him, students stood with hunched shoulders, their hair plastered on their foreheads by the rain. But they were not dismayed. One was saying to a classmate:

"If we don't get any results, we won't go back. We can be just as brave as the Peking students. When they go out to make speeches, they bring packed suitcases with them—ready to go to jail. You mean to say we can't stand here one night to get our demands?"

Chueh-hui heard these words clearly. He was moved almost to tears. He wanted to take a good look at the speaker, but the mist in his eyes prevented him from seeing clearly. Chueh-hui felt a strong admiration for the boy, although he had said nothing out of the ordinary, nothing different from what Chueh-hui himself might have said. Chueh-hui forgot everything—his well-lit home, his warm bed. He would have been willing to do anything for the boy who had just spoken, even if it meant going through fire and water!

By the third watch—midnight—the deputies still had not returned, and there was no news. It was growing much colder. Cold and hungry, and, most of all, weary of the indecision, boys were beginning to ask, "How much longer do we have to wait?"

The bayonets of the soldiers lined up before the entrance gleamed dully, as if in warning.

"Let's go back. We can decide on our next step tomorrow. Hanging around here won't do any good," a few of the weaker boys suggested.

But none of the others responded. It looked as if the majority were willing to wait out the night.

After a long, uncomfortable period, someone said, "The deputies are coming out." A deep hush fell on the entire field.

"Fellows, the Department Chief is going to say a few words to us," announced one of the deputies.

"Gentlemen, the governor left for home hours ago. I'm sorry we had to keep you waiting all this time," said a crisp unfamiliar voice. "I have already conferred with your deputies, on his behalf, and I have received your demands. Tomorrow I shall present them to the governor. He, of course, will attend to them; you gentlemen may rest assured of that. He will also send a representative to call on the students who were hurt. And now it is getting late. Please go home. We don't want any of you catching cold. You know the governor has the greatest concern for all you gentlemen, so please go home. We wouldn't want anything unfortunate to happen to you."

The voice stopped and, at once, the students began talking among themselves.

"What is he saying? What does he mean by 'unfortunate'?" a classmate asked Chueh-hui.

"He says the governor will attend to our demands; that we should go home. He doesn't take any responsibility himself. Pretty slick!" Chueh-hui retorted indignantly.

"We might as well go home. Standing here won't get us anywhere. . . . And that last thing he said—it's worth thinking over."

Another deputy came forward and addressed the students. "Did you hear what the Department Chief said, fellows? He has received our demands and the governor will attend to them. Why not wait and see? Now that we've got results, we can go home."

"Results? What results?" a number of students demanded hotly. But most of the boys cried, "Let's go home, then." It was not because they believed the words of the Department Chief, but rather because they realized that to stand all night in the open would be a useless sacrifice. The temperature was still falling and the rainfall was growing heavier. Everyone was cold and hungry. They had had enough.

"All right, we'll go home. We can talk some more about this tomorrow," was the feeling of most. Only a few wanted to stick it out, but there were not enough of them to make their view prevail.

The two hundred students began to leave the field.

Large raindrops pelted them without mercy, striking their heads and bodies fiercely, as if intent on leaving an indelible impression on their memories.

IX

Because even the promise that a representative of the governor would call on the students who were hurt was not kept, two days later, the students in all schools called off classes. But actually this was only a gesture since most of the schools were already closed for winter vacation.

The second day of the strike, on the insistence of the Foreign Languages School and the Higher Normal School, the Students' Federation formally issued a strike proclamation, which contained a few disrespectful remarks about the governor. Several days of terror followed. There were frequent clashes between soldiers and students; the citizenry were highly apprehensive that the soldiers might once again turn into undisciplined mobs. Students did not dare appear on the streets alone, but walked only in organized groups of five or six. A student was badly beaten by three soldiers at dusk near the city's South Gate, while a policeman looked on from the sidelines, afraid to intervene.

Disorder reigned everywhere, but the authorities turned a blind eye. The governor seemed to have forgotten the students completely, perhaps because he was busy making preparations for his mother's birthday celebration. Soldiers grew increasingly arrogant, particularly demobilized wounded soldiers. Thrown out on their own, subject to no discipline whatsoever, the "wounded veterans" roved the streets at will. No one dared to interfere.

But the students were not so easily bullied. They launched a heated "Self-Defence Drive to Preserve Respect for Students," they turned out pamphlets, they made speeches. The

Students' Federation went into action with telegrams to leading social organizations all over the country requesting support; it sent representatives to other cities to explain the students' position; most important of all, it enlisted the co-operation of other students' federations. The drive grew to impressive proportions. But there was still no sign of any action by the governor.

Chueh-hui was much more active in all this than Chueh-min, who was occupied helping Chin review her English and was not very interested in anything else.

One afternoon, on returning home from a meeting of the Students' Federation, Chueh-hui was summoned into his grandfather's room.

Well over sixty, the old man lay in a reclining chair. His body looked very long to Chueh-hui. Sparse white stubble sprouted on the jaws of his long, dark face, and there was a fringe of grey hair around his shiny bald head. Lying with eyes shut, the Venerable Master Kao dozed, snoring slightly.

Chueh-hui stood timidly before his grandfather, afraid to call the old man, yet not daring to leave. At first Chueh-hui was very uneasy; the whole atmosphere of this room oppressed him. He stood in silence, hoping that his grandfather would awaken soon so that he could quickly leave. But gradually his fear diminished, and he gazed with interest at the old man's dark face and bald head.

As long as Chueh-hui could remember, there had always been a picture of a stern grandfather in his mind. A severe, forbidding man whom all feared and respected. Chueh-hui seldom exchanged more than a few words with his *Yeh-yeh*. Except for the two times during the day, once in the morning and once in the evening, when he formally called briefly to pay his respects, Chueh-hui had little opportunity to come into contact with him. Chueh-hui avoided him as much as possible, for he always felt awkward and overawed in his presence. The old man seemed to him a person devoid of any affection.

At the moment, his grandfather, lying weakly in the reclining chair, looked very worn-out. *Yeh-yeh* probably wasn't always such an irritable old stick, thought Chueh-hui. He recalled that many of his grandfather's poems had been dedicated to singsong girls, quite a few girls at that. Picturing how the old man probably looked in his youth, Chueh-hui smiled. He must have been a dashing sort then; it was only later he acquired his pious air. . . . Of course that was thirty years ago. As he grew old, he turned into a crusty Confucian moralist. . . .

Yet even now, his grandfather still played around with the young female impersonators in the opera. The old man once invited one of them to the house and had his picture taken with him. The actor had worn his costume for the occasion. Chueh-hui recalled seeing him putting on his powder and woman's wig in their guest room.

Of course nobody looked askance at that sort of thing in Chengtu. Not long ago, a few old-timers who had been officials under the deposed Ching dynasty—pillars of the Confucian Morals Society, too—made a big splash in the local press, publishing a list they had composed of the "best" female impersonators in the opera. Patronizing these actors was considered a sign of "refinement." Chueh-hui's grandfather, as a well-known gentleman who had several collections of poems published, an epicure of ancient books and paintings, could not go against the fashion.

Yet how can you reconcile this "refinement" with the defence of "Confucian Morals"? Young Chueh-hui couldn't figure it out.

His grandfather kept a concubine—Mistress Chen, a heavily made-up woman who always reeked of perfume and simpered when she talked. She was not in the least attractive, but the old man, who bought her after his wife died, seemed to like her. They had been living together for nearly ten years. She had given birth to a son, but he died of illness at the age of five. . . .

Mentally comparing his grandfather's elegant tastes in books and paintings with his fondness for this coarse woman, Chueh-hui had to laugh.

People are certainly inconsistent, he mused. The more he puzzled over it, the less he understood the old man. His grandfather was an unfathomable mystery to him.

Suddenly the old man opened his eyes. He stared at Chueh-hui in surprise, as if he didn't recognize him, and waved at him to leave the room. How strange! Had his grandfather summoned him and let him stand so long only to send him away without a word? About to ask, Chueh-hui thought better of it when he saw his grandfather's irritated expression. But as he walked towards the door, his grandfather called him:

"Come back here. I have something to say to you."

Chueh-hui turned and walked back.

"Where have you been? We've been looking all over for you." The old man's low voice was dry and harsh. He was sitting up now.

The question took Chueh-hui by surprise. He knew he couldn't say he had been at a Students' Federation meeting, but for the moment his quickness of wit failed him and he was unable to think of an answer. His grandfather's stern eyes were scrutinizing him, and Chueh-hui felt his face reddening. "I went to see a classmate," he finally managed, after some hesitation.

The old man laughed coldly. His eyes swept Chueh-hui's face. "Don't lie," he snapped. "I know all about you. People have told me. The students and the soldiers have been brawling the last few days, and you've been in it. . . . School is over, but you're out every day at some students' federation or other. . . . Mistress Chen just told me she heard from one of my sedan-chair carriers that he saw you handing out leaflets on the street. . . .

"You students have been much too reckless right along—checking stores for Japanese goods, seizing merchants and parading them through the streets—completely lawless! The soldiers would be quite right to beat you. Why do you provoke them with such nonsense? . . . I hear the authorities are planning to take strong measures against the students. If you keep rioting around like this you're liable to riot your young fool lives away!"

After each few sentences, the old man paused or coughed. But whenever Chueh-hui tried to answer, he went on with his lecture. Now he concluded his remarks with a veritable fit of coughing. Mistress Chen hastened in from the next room to drum her fists lightly on his back.

Yeh-yeh's coughing slowly subsided. But the old man's anger was again aroused when he saw Chueh-hui, still standing before him.

"You students don't study, you just make trouble. The schools are in a terrible state. They produce nothing but rioters. I didn't want you boys to go to school in the first place. The schools make you all go bad. Look at your uncle Ke-ting. He never went to school, he only studied at home with a tutor. But he reads the classics very well, and he writes better than any of you."

"It's not that we want to make trouble. We've been concentrating on our studies right along. We only started this drive in self-defence. The soldiers attacked us for no reason at all. Naturally, we couldn't let them get away with it," Chueh-hui replied evenly, repressing his anger.

"How dare you argue! When I talk, you listen! . . . From now on, I forbid you to go out brawling again! . . . Mistress Chen, call his Big Brother in." The old man's voice was trembling, and he began to cough again. Gasping, he drew long, shuddering breaths.

"Third Young Master, look at the state you've got your *Yeh-yeh* in! Please stop arguing with him and let him get a little rest," rasped Mistress Chen, her face darkening. Her frown made her long face look even longer.

Though stung by the unfairness of her implication, in the presence of his coughing grandfather Chueh-hui could only hold back his retort and hang his head in silence, biting his lips.

"Call his brother, Mistress Chen," the old man said in a calmer voice. He had stopped coughing.

Mistress Chen assented and went out, leaving Chueh-hui standing alone before his grandfather. The old man did not speak. His misty old eyes stared vacantly around the room. Then he half closed them again.

Chueh-hui gazed at his grandfather stubbornly. He examined the old man's long, thin body. A peculiar thought came to him. It seemed to him that the person lying in the cane reclining chair was not his grandfather but the representative of an entire generation. He knew that the old man and he—the representative of the grandson's generation—could never see eye to

67

eye. He wondered what could be harboured in that long thin body that made every conversation between them seem more like an exchange between two enemies than a chat between grandfather and grandson. Gloomy and depressed, Chueh-hui shook himself defiantly.

Finally Mistress Chen returned, a crafty smile on her heavily powdered face. Chueh-hui saw her high cheekbones, her thin lips, her darkly pencilled eyebrows. She was redolent of perfume. Then Chueh-hsin came in, and the two brothers exchanged unhappy glances. Chueh-hsin realized at once that Chueh-hui was in some sort of fix, but he approached their grandfather calmly.

At the sound of the footsteps, the old man opened his eyes. "Where is Third Elder Master?" he asked Mistress Chen.

"He's gone to his law office," she replied.

"More interested in handling other people's litigation than in the affairs of his own family," the old man fretted. He turned to Chueh-hsin. "I'm entrusting Third Young Master to you. Look after him carefully. He's not to be allowed out of the compound. I'm holding you responsible." Although *Yeh-yeh*'s voice was still stern, it was much milder than a few minutes before.

Chueh-hsin made respectful noises of assent, and shot a glance at Chueh-hui indicating that he shouldn't try to argue. The younger boy's face was expressionless.

"All right, take him along. He's given me enough of a headache," the old man said listlessly, after a pause. He closed his eyes.

Chueh-hsin again murmured his compliance. At a signal to Chueh-hui, the two brothers walked quietly out of the room.

After crossing the great hall, they entered the courtyard. Chueh-hui drew a deep breath and said ironically, "Now at last I feel I'm my own master again." Chueh-hsin gave him a reproachful look, but he was unaware of it. Suddenly, Chueh-hui asked seriously, "Well, Big Brother, what about it?"

"What else can we do? We'll have to carry out *Yeh-yeh*'s orders. You just won't go out for a few days." Chueh-hsin helplessly spread his hands.

"But our students' drive is at its height. How can I stay home

68

quietly at a time like this?" cried Chueh-hui, disappointed. He was beginning to realize that this thing was serious.

"That's what the old gentleman wants. What can we do?" said Chueh-hsin, unruffled. Lately he had been refusing to be upset by anything, big or small.

"There's your 'policy of non-resistance' again. Why don't you become a nice, docile Christian? When someone slaps your left cheek you can offer him your right," Chueh-hui said hotly. He was letting out on Chueh-hsin all the emotion his grandfather's abuse had pent up in him.

"You *are* excitable," Chueh-hsin replied with a calm smile. "Why get angry with me? What's the good?"

"I insist on going out! I'm going to leave here right now! Let's see what he can do about it!" Chueh-hui stamped furiously.

"All that will happen is that I'll be scolded and lectured a few more times," said Chueh-hsin in a melancholy tone. Like his brother, he seemed to be talking more to himself than for others to hear.

Chueh-hui gazed at him in silence.

"Let's speak frankly," urged Chueh-hsin, but his voice was even. "I hope you'll stay home a few days and not make *Yeh-yeh* angry. . . . You're still young and impetuous. When *Yeh-yeh* talks to you, you ought to listen. Just let him talk. After he's finished and calmed down a little, say 'Yes' a couple of times and walk out. Then you can forget the whole thing. It's much easier that way. Arguing with him will get you nowhere."

Chueh-hui did not reply. He raised his head and looked at the blue sky. Though he didn't at all agree with his brother, he didn't want to argue. And there was something in what Chueh-hsin said. What was the point of wasting energy on something from which no good could come? But how could his young mind be for ever weighing fine questions of possible personal profit and loss? Big Brother plainly didn't understand him.

It made Chueh-hui's heart ache to see the clouds drift by. He was torn by conflicting desires. But finally he made up his mind.

"I won't go out for a few days," he said to his brother. "Not because I want to obey *Yeh-yeh,* but to save you trouble."

"Thanks very much," said Chueh-hsin with a smile of relief. "Of course, if you wanted to go out, I couldn't stop you. I'm at the office all day, usually. I just happened to have come home early today, and ran into this business of yours. In all fairness to *Yeh-yeh,* he wants you to stay home for your own good."

"I know that," Chueh-hui replied mechanically. He stood in the courtyard and watched Chueh-hsin walk away, then gazed idly at the potted flowers along the path. A few blossoms still remained on the plum trees; their fragrance drifted to his nostrils. Breaking off a small branch, he snapped it into sections, then plucked off the blossoms and ground them to a soggy pulp between his palms. His hands, stained yellow with the juice, were steeped in perfume.

This act of vandalism somehow satisfied him. Some day, when his hands were bigger, if he could crush the old order between them in the same way, how wonderful that would be. . . .

Then his mood changed, and he grew sad. He couldn't take part in the student movement.

"Contradictions, contradictions," he muttered. He knew contradictions existed not only between him and his grandfather, or between him and his brother. There were also contradictions within himself.

X

You can lock up a person physically, but you cannot imprison his heart. Although Chueh-hui did not leave home for the next few days, his thoughts were always with his schoolmates and their struggle. This was something his grandfather could not have foreseen.

Chueh-hui tried to envisage what stage the student movement had reached; he avidly searched the local paper for news. Unfortunately, there was very little. He was able to get hold of a mimeographed weekly, put out by the Students' Federation, which contained quite an amount of good news and a number of stirring articles. Gradually the tension was subsiding, gradually the governor was relenting. Finally, the governor sent his Department Chief to call on the students who had been injured in the riots, and issued two conciliatory proclamations. Moreover he had his secretary write a letter in his name apologizing to the Students' Federation and guaranteeing the safety of the students in the future.

Next, the local press carried an order by the city's garrison commander forbidding soldiers to strike students. It was said that two soldiers who confessed to having taken part in the theatre brawl were severely punished. Chueh-hsin saw the proclamation posted on the streets, and he told Chueh-hui about it.

With the news improving from day to day, Chueh-hui, a prisoner in his own home, grew increasingly restless. He paced alone in his room, too fretful at times even to read. Or he lay flat on his bed, staring up at the canopy above.

" 'Home. Home, sweet home!' " he would fume.

Hearing him, Chueh-min would smile and say nothing.

"What's so funny!" Chueh-hui raged, on one of these occasions. "You go out every day, free as a bird! But just watch out. Some fine day you're going to end up like me yourself!"

"My smiling has nothing to do with you. Can't I even smile?" retorted Chueh-min with a grin.

"No, you can't. I won't let you smile! I won't let anyone smile!"

Chueh-min closed the book he had been reading and quietly left the room. He didn't want to argue.

"Home, a fine home! A narrow cage, that's what it is!" Chueh-hui shouted, pacing the floor. "I'm going out. I must go out. Let's see what they're going to do about it!" And he rushed from the room.

Going down the steps into the courtyard, he spied Mistress Chen and Aunt Shen (the wife of his uncle Ke-ting) sitting on the veranda outside his grandfather's room. Chueh-hui hesitated, then made a detour around his brother Chueh-hsin's quarters and entered the large garden.

Passing through a moon-gate, he came to a man-made hill. The paved path he was following here forked into two branches. He chose the one to the left, which went up the slope. Narrow and twisting, it led through a tunnel. When Chueh-hui emerged again on the other side, the path started downward. A delicate fragrance assailed his nostrils, and he struck off in the direction from which it seemed to be coming. Moving down slowly through the bushes, he discovered another small path to the left. Just as he was turning to it, the view before him suddenly opened up, and he saw a great sea of pink blossoms. Below was a plum tree grove with branches in full flower. Entering the grove, he strolled along the petal-strewn ground, pushing aside the low-hanging branches.

In the distance, he caught a glimpse of something blue shimmering through the haze of plum blossoms. As he drew nearer, he saw it was a person dressed in blue coming in his direction over the zigzag stone bridge. A girl, wearing a long braid down her back. Chueh-hui recognized the bondmaid, Ming-feng.

Before he could call to her, she entered the pavilion on the isle in the middle of the lake. He waited for her to emerge on the near side. But after several minutes there was still no sign of her. Chueh-hui was puzzled. Finally, she appeared, but she was not alone. With her was another girl, wearing a short purple jacket. The tall girl's back was towards him as she chatted with Ming-feng, and he could only see her long plait, not her face. But as they came closer over the zigzag bridge leading from the near side of the isle, he got a look at her. It was Chien-erh, bondmaid in the household of his uncle Ke-an.

As the girls neared the shore, he hid among the plum trees.

"You go back first. Don't wait for me. I still have to gather some blossoms for Madam Chou," said Ming-feng's crisp voice.

"All right. That Madam Wang of mine is a great talker. If I'm out too long she'll grumble at me for hours." Going through the grove of plums, Chien-erh departed along the path by which Chueh-hui had just come.

As soon as Chien-erh disappeared around a bend, Chueh-hui stepped out and walked towards Ming-feng. She was breaking off a low-hanging branch.

"What are you doing, Ming-feng?" he called with a smile.

Concentrating on her task, Ming-feng hadn't seen him approach. She turned around, startled, on hearing his voice. She gave a relieved laugh when she recognized him. "I couldn't imagine who it was! So it's you, Third Young Master!" She went on breaking the branch.

"Who told you to gather blossoms at this hour of the day? Don't you know that early morning is the best time?"

"Madam Chou said Mrs. Chang wants some. Second Young Master is going to take them over." Ming-feng stretched for a branch that was heavily laden with blossoms, but she couldn't reach it, even standing on tiptoe.

"I'll get it for you. You're still too short. In another year or so you might make it," said Chueh-hui, grinning.

"All right, you get it for me, please. But don't let Madam know." Ming-feng stepped aside to make room for Chueh-hui.

"Why are you so afraid of Madam Chou? She's not so bad. Has she scolded you again lately?" Chueh-hui reached up and twisted the branch back and forth, twice. It snapped off. He handed it to Ming-feng.

"No, she doesn't scold me very often. But I'm always scared I'll do something wrong," she replied in a low voice, accepting the branch.

"That's called—Once a slave, always a slave! . . ." Chueh-hui laughed, but he wasn't intending to deride Ming-feng.

The girl buried her face in the blossoms she was holding.

"Look, there's a good one," Chueh-hui said cheerfully.

She raised her head and smiled. "Where?"

"Don't you see it? Over there." He pointed at a branch of a nearby tree, and her gaze followed his finger.

"Ah, yes. It has lovely blossoms. But it's too high."

"High? I can take care of that." Chueh-hui measured the tree with his eye. "I'll climb up and break the branch off." He began unfastening his padded robe.

"No, don't," said Ming-feng. "If you fall you'll hurt yourself."

"It's all right." Chueh-hui hung his robe over a branch of another tree. Underneath, he was wearing a close-fitting green padded jacket. As he started up the tree, he said to Ming-feng, "You stand here and hold the tree firm."

Setting his feet on two sturdy branches, he stretched his hand towards the blossom-laden branch he was after. It was out of reach, and his exertions shook the whole tree, bringing down a shower of petals.

"Be careful, Third Young Master, be careful!" cried Ming-feng.

"Don't worry," he responded. Cautiously manoeuvring himself into another position, he was able to grasp the elusive branch. With a few twists, he snapped it off. Looking down, he saw the girl's upturned face.

"Here, Ming-feng, catch!" He tossed her the branch. When it was safely in Ming-feng's hand, he slowly climbed down the tree.

"Enough," she said happily. "I've got three now; that's plenty."

"Right. Any more and Second Young Master won't be able to carry them all," laughed Chueh-hui, putting on his robe. "Have you seen him around?"

"He's reciting by the fish pond. I heard his voice," Ming-feng replied, arranging the flowers in her hand. Observing that Chueh-hui had only draped his robe over his shoulders, she urged, "Put it on. You'll catch cold that way."

As Chueh-hui was putting his arms through his sleeves, the girl began walking off along the path. He called after her:

"Ming-feng!"

Stopping, she turned around and asked with a smile, "What is it?" But when he didn't answer, and only stood smiling at her, she again turned and walked away.

Chueh-hui hastily took after her, calling her name. Again she halted and turned. "Yes?"

"Come over here," he pleaded.

She walked up to him.

"You seem to be afraid of me lately. You don't even like to talk to me. What's wrong?" he asked, half in jest, toying with an overhanging branch.

"Who's afraid of you?" Ming-feng replied with a gurgle of laughter. "I'm busy from morning till night. I just haven't the time for talk." She turned to go.

Chueh-hui held out a restraining hand. "It's true. You *are* afraid of me. If you're so busy, how do you have time to play with Chien-erh? I saw you two just now in the isle pavilion."

"What right have I to chat with you? You're a Young Master; I'm only a bondmaid," Ming-feng retorted distantly.

"But before we used to play together all the time. Why should it be any different now?" was Chueh-hui's warm rejoinder.

The girl's brilliant eyes swept his face. Then she dropped her head and replied in a low voice, "It's not the same now. We're both grown up."

"What difference does that make? Our hearts haven't become bad!"

"People will talk if we're always together. There are plenty of gossipers around. It doesn't matter about me, but you should be careful. You have to uphold your dignity as one of the masters. It doesn't matter about me. I was fated to be just a cheap little bondmaid!" Ming-feng still spoke quietly, but there was a touch of bitterness in her voice.

"Don't leave. We'll find a place to sit down and have a long talk. I'll take the blossoms." Without waiting for an answer, he took the branches from her hands. Surveying them critically, he broke off two or three twigs and threw them away.

He set off along a small path between the plum grove and the edge of the lake, and she silently followed him. From time to time, he turned his head to ask her a question. She answered briefly, or responded with only a smile.

Leaving the grove, they crossed a rectangular flower terrace, then went through a small gate. About ten paces beyond was a tunnel. The tunnel was dark, but it was quite straight and not very long. Inside, you could hear the gurgling of spring water. On the other side of the tunnel, the path slanted upward. They mounted about two dozen stone steps, followed a few more twists and turns, and at last reached the top.

In the centre of the small gravelled summit was a little stone table with a round stone stool on each of its four sides. A cypress, growing beside the flat face of a large boulder, spread its branches in a sheltering canopy.

All was still except for the chuckling of a hidden brook, flowing somewhere beneath the rocks.

"How peaceful," said Chueh-hui. He placed the blossoms on the table; after wiping the dust off one of the stone stools, he sat down. Ming-feng seated herself opposite him. They couldn't see each other clearly because of the blossoms heaped between them on the little table.

With a laugh, Chueh-hui shifted the branches to the stool on his right. Pointing to the stool on his left, he said to Ming-feng, "Sit over here. Why are you afraid to be close to me?"

Silently, Ming-feng moved to the place he had indicated. They faced each other, letting their eyes speak for them, letting their eyes say the many things words cannot express.

"I must go. I can't stay too long in the garden. Madam will scold me if she finds out." Ming-feng stood up.

Taking her arm, Chueh-hui pulled her down again to her seat. "It doesn't matter. She won't say anything. Don't go yet. We've just come. We haven't talked at all. I won't let you go!"

She shrank a bit from his touch, but made no further protest.

"Why don't you say anything? No one can hear us. Don't you like me any more?" Chueh-hui teased. He pretended to be very downcast.

The girl remained silent. It was as if she hadn't heard him.

"You're probably tired of working for our family. I'll tell Madam that you're grown up now, to send you away," Chueh-hui said idly, with affected unconcern. Actually he was watching her reaction closely.

Ming-feng turned pale, and the light went out of her eyes. But her trembling lips did not speak. Her eyes glistened like glass, and her lashes fluttered. "You mean it?" she asked. Tears rolled down her cheeks.

Chueh-hui knew his teasing had gone too far. He hadn't meant to hurt her. He was only testing her; and he wanted to pay her back for that cold remark. It had not occurred to him that his words could cause her so much pain. He was both satisfied and regretful over the results of his experiment.

76

"I'm only joking," he laughed. "You don't think I'd really send you away?" But his laughter was forced, for he had been very moved by her emotion.

"Who knows whether you would or not? You masters and mistresses are all as changeable as the winds. When you're displeased there's no telling what you'll do," sobbed Ming-feng. "I've always known that, sooner or later, I'd go the road of Hsi-erh, but why must it be so soon?"

"What do you mean?" Chueh-hui asked gently.

"What you said. . . ." Ming-feng still wept.

"I was only teasing you. I'll never let that happen to you," he said earnestly. Taking her hand and placing it on his knee, he caressed it soothingly.

"But suppose that's what Madam Chou wants?" demanded Ming-feng, raising her tear-stained face.

He gazed into her eyes for a moment without replying. Then he said firmly, "I can take care of that, I can make her listen to me. I'll tell her I want to marry—" Ming-feng's hand over his mouth cut him short. He was quite sincere in what he was saying, although he hadn't really given the matter much thought.

"No, no, you mustn't do that!" the girl cried. "Madam would never agree. That would finish everything. You mustn't speak to her. I just wasn't fated. . . ."

"Don't be so frightened." He removed her hand from his mouth as he said this. "Your face is all streaked with tears. Let me. . . ." He carefully wiped her face with his handkerchief. This time she did not draw back. Wiping the tear-stains, he said with a smile, "Women cry so easily." He laughed sadly.

Ming-feng smiled, but it was a melancholy smile, and she said slowly, "I won't cry any more after this. Working for your family I've shed too many tears already. Here together with you, I certainly shouldn't cry. . . ."

"Everything will be all right. We're both still young. When the time comes, I'll speak to Madam. I definitely will work something out, I mean it," he said comfortingly, still caressing her hand.

"I know your heart," she replied, touched. Somewhat re-assured, she went on, half in a reverie, "I've been dreaming about you a lot lately. Once I dreamed I was running through the mountains, chased by a pack of wild animals. Just as they almost caught me, someone rushed down the slope and drove them away. And who do you think it was? You. I've always thought of you as my saviour!"

"I didn't know. I didn't realize you had so much faith in me." Chueh-hui's voice shook. He was deeply moved. "I haven't taken nearly good enough care of you. I don't know how to face you. Are you angry with me?"

"How could I be?" She shook her head and smiled. "All my life I've loved only three people. One was my mother. The second was the Elder Young Miss—she taught me to read and to understand many things; she was always helping me. Now both of them are dead. Only one more remains. . . ."

"Ming-feng, when I think of you I'm ashamed of myself. I live in comfort, while you have such a hard time. Even my kid sister scolds you!"

"I'm used to it, after seven years. It's much better now, any-how. I don't mind so much. . . . I only have to see you, to think of you, and I can stand anything. I often speak your name to myself, though I'd never dare say it aloud in anyone else's presence."

"You suffer too much, Ming-feng! At your age, you ought to be in school. A bright girl like you. I bet you'd be even bet-ter than Chin. . . . How wonderful it would be if you had been born in a rich family, or even in a family like Chin's!" Chueh-hui said regretfully.

"I never hoped to be a rich young miss; I'm not that lucky. All I want is that you don't send me away, that I stay here and be your bondmaid all my life. . . . You don't know how happy I am just seeing you. As long as you're near me, my heart's at ease. . . . You don't know how I respect you. But sometimes you're like the moon in the sky. I know I can't reach you."

"Don't talk like that. I'm just an ordinary person, the same as everyone else." His low voice trembled and tears rolled from his eyes.

"Be quiet," she warned suddenly, grasping his arm. "Listen. Someone's down there."

They both listened. The sound, when it reached them, was very faint. Mingled with babble of the hidden spring, it was difficult to distinguish clearly. They finally recognized it as the voice of Chueh-min singing.

"Second Young Master is going back to the house." Chueh-hui rose and walked to the edge of the hilltop. He could see a small figure in grey flitting through the pink haze of the plum blossoms. Turning to Ming-feng he said, "It's Second Young Master, all right."

Ming-feng hastily rose to her feet. "I must go back. I've been out here too long. . . . It's probably nearly dinner time."

Chueh-hui handed her the plum blossoms. "If Madam Chou asks why you're so late, make up an excuse—anything will do. . . . Say I asked you to do something for me."

"All right. I'll go back first, so we won't be seen together." Ming-feng smiled at him, and started down the slope.

He walked with her a few steps, then stood and watched her slowly descend the stone stairway and disappear around the face of a bluff.

Alone, he paced the hilltop, all his thoughts devoted to Ming-feng. "She's so pure, so good . . ." he murmured. Walking over to the little table, he sat down opposite the place she had just vacated, and, resting his elbows on the stone surface, supported his head in his hands and gazed off into the distance. "You're pure, truly pure . . ." he whispered.

After a while, he rose abruptly, as if awakening from a dream. He looked all around him, then hurried down the path.

The moonlight was lovely that night. Chueh-hui couldn't sleep. At one in the morning, he was still strolling about the courtyard.

"Why aren't you in bed, Third Brother? It's cold out here." Chueh-min had come out and was standing on the steps.

"With a beautiful moon like this, sleep is a waste of time," Chueh-hui replied carelessly.

Chueh-min walked down the steps into the courtyard. He shivered. "It's cold," he repeated, and raised his head to look at the moon.

There wasn't a cloud in the night sky. A full moon sailed through a limitless firmament, alone, chaste, its beams lulling all into slumber, coating the ground and the roof tiles with silver. The night was still.

"Lovely," Chueh-min sighed. "A perfect example of 'moon-light like frost.' "[18] And he joined Chueh-hui in his stroll. But the younger boy remained silent.

"Chin is really intelligent . . . and brave. A fine girl," Chueh-min couldn't refrain from commenting, a pleased smile on his face.

Chueh-hui still said nothing, for his mind was occupied by another girl. He walked slowly behind his brother.

"Do you like her? Are you in love with her?" Chueh-min suddenly grabbed him by the arm.

"Of course," Chueh-hui replied automatically. But he immediately amended, "Who are you talking about? Sister Chin? I don't really know. But I think *you* love her."

"That's right." Chueh-min was still gripping his arm. "I love her, and I think she could love me too. I haven't said anything to her yet. I don't know what to do. . . . What about you? You said you also love her."

From the sound of his voice and the way his fingers trembled on Chueh-hui's arm, the younger boy could tell that his brother was highly agitated, even without seeing his face. Lightly he patted Chueh-min's hand and said with a smile, "Go to it. I'm not competing with you. I wish you success. I love Chin only like an elder sister."

Chueh-min did not reply. He stared at the moon for a long time. At last, when he had calmed down somewhat, he said to Chueh-hui, "You're really a good brother. I was wrong about you; it got me all upset. I don't know what makes me so jealous lately. Even when I see Chien-yun and Chin talking

[18] From a poem by Li Tai-po (701–762), one of the greatest Chinese poets.

together, I feel annoyed. Do you think I'm silly? Are you laughing at me?"

"No, I'm not laughing at you," Chueh-hui answered sincerely. "I sympathize with you. Don't worry. I don't think Chien-yun will compete with you, either." Then in another tone of voice, "Listen, what's that?"

A sound like quiet, subdued weeping spread softly, pervading every corner of the moonlit night. It was not a human voice, nor was it the cry of a bird or insect. The sound was much too light, too clear, for that. At times it seemed to rise in pitch, a persuasive plaint issued directly from the soul. Then it slowly faded again until it became almost inaudible, like the merest hint of a breeze. But one was still aware of a vibration in the atmosphere, charging the very air with sadness.

"What is it?" Chueh-hui repeated.

"Big Brother playing a bamboo flute. The past few nights, he's been playing only when it's very late. I hear him every night."

"What's troubling him? He wasn't like this before. That bamboo flute has such a mournful sound!"

"I don't know exactly. I think it's probably because he's heard that Cousin Mei has come back to Chengtu. That must be it. He keeps playing those same mournful tunes, and always so late at night. . . . He probably is still in love with her. . . . I haven't been sleeping well the past few nights. I keep hearing his flute. It seems to carry a warning, a threat. . . . I'm in practically the same situation with Chin now as Big Brother was with Cousin Mei. When I hear that flute I can't help fearing I'll go the same road as he. I don't dare to even think about it. I'm afraid I couldn't live if it ever came to that. I'm not like him." Chueh-min's voice shook with emotion. He was almost in tears.

"Don't worry. You'll never go Big Brother's road," Chueh-hui consoled him. "Times have changed."

He looked up again at the full moon, bathing the night with its limitless radiance. An irresistible strength seemed to well up within him as he thought of Ming-feng.

"You're so pure," he murmured. "You alone are as unsullied as the moon!"

81

XI

The storm over the clash between the soldiers and the students gradually subsided. Out-of-town students returned home for the New Year holidays. Among those who lived in Chengtu, a number began reviewing for exams. The student strike dragged on, overlapping into the winter vacation. The school authorities wound up their work for the term and prepared to celebrate the New Year. On the surface, at least, the students had won.

During this period, Chueh-min continued calling at his aunt's house every night to teach Chin English. Chueh-hui continued hanging around the house reading the newspaper. The paper was full of items in which Chueh-hui had no interest. Its coverage of the student strike dwindled steadily until there was no news at all. By that time, Chueh-hui had stopped reading even the newspaper.

"You call this living! A prisoner in a narrow cage!" he would fume. Often he grew so exasperated he didn't want to see any member of his family. To add to his troubles, Mingfeng seemed to be avoiding him. He seldom had an opportunity to speak to her alone.

As usual, he went every morning and every evening to pay his formal respects to his grandfather. He could not avoid seeing the old man's exhausted dark face and Mistress Chen's crafty powdered one. In addition, he also frequently encountered a number of expressionless, enigmatic visages. Chueh-hui felt ready to burst. "Just wait," he would mutter. "The day is coming. . . ."

Exactly what would happen when the day finally came, he wasn't quite sure. All he knew was that everything would be overthrown, everything he hated would be destroyed. Again he looked through his *New Youth* and *New Tide* magazines. He read an article entitled "Impressions of an Old-Style

Family,"[19] and its biting attack pleased him immensely; it was almost as if he had already gained his revenge.

But his joy was only momentary, for when he tossed the magazine aside and came out of his room, he was confronted with all the things he so disliked. Lonely and bored, he returned to his room.

It was mostly in this manner that he whiled away his days.

Although Chueh-min and Chueh-hui shared the same room, the older boy was always busy with his own affairs. Even when he was home, he spent most of his time reading in the garden. He was also quite occupied helping Chin with her lessons. Chueh-hui didn't like to disturb him.

"It's so lonesome here," Chueh-hui would sigh, alone in his room. He had not looked at any of the new periodicals for several days, having lost interest; reading them made him feel even more lonely. Idly he turned through the pages of his diary. He hadn't made any entries in a long time. Taking up his pen he began to write:

> This morning I went to pay my respects to *Yeh-yeh*. He was in the study, telling Uncle Ke-an to write on a pair of scrolls a birthday greeting that Uncle Ke-ting had composed and send it to old man Feng Le-shan who is going to celebrate his sixtieth birthday. After Uncle Ke-an left, with a slight smile on his dark, tired face, *Yeh-yeh* handed me a book and said, "You should read this carefully." "Yes," I said. On my way out, I saw Mistress Chen in the next room combing her hair. I left as quickly as I could. I always feel much better once I get out of *Yeh-yeh*'s room. I don't know why, but somehow it reminds me of a magistrate's inquisition chamber.
>
> I had only to look at the title of that book he gave me and my head ached: "On Filial Piety and the Shunning of Lewdness." I threw the thing on the table and went out for a walk in the garden.
>
> I saw Sister-in-law in the plum grove, picking blossoms with her little son Hai-erh, who is not quite four. It made

[19] By Ku Cheng-wu. Published in *New Tide* in February 1919 and September 1920.

me feel good just to see her healthy affectionate face, and that lively pair of big kindly eyes.

"You're out early this morning, Sister-in-law," I said to her. "If you want blossoms, why not let Ming-feng get them for you?"

She broke off another branch and smiled at me. "Your Big Brother likes plum blossoms. Haven't you noticed his room? He's got vases full of them. . . . I'd rather pick them for him myself than ask Ming-feng to do it. I'm afraid she wouldn't choose the right ones."

Sister-in-law told Hai-erh to greet me and wish me good morning. Hai-erh is very intelligent. He's obedient too. We all like him. But then another thought came to me and I said:

"Big Brother has always loved plum blossoms."

Blushing faintly, she answered, "I sketched a plum blossom design to embroider the side runner of our bed canopy. You must come and see it." She smiled proudly, and two dimples appeared in her cheeks. Her voice is very warm whenever she mentions Big Brother. I know she loves him a lot, but I'm beginning to worry about them. If she knew why he's so fond of plum blossoms, what they signify to him, she'd be terribly hurt.

"Third Brother, you don't look very happy. I know these past few days have been hard on you. They've got you locked up at home and won't let you out. But *Yeh-yeh* must be over his anger by now. You'll be free in another day or two. Don't take it so hard. Brooding too much will make you ill."

Here she was trying to comfort me, while all the time I was thinking—It's because of you I'm brooding. You don't know Big Brother whom you love so dearly is in love with another woman! A woman whose name means "plum blossom"! . . . But seeing her calm, sympathetic face, I didn't have the courage to tell her.

"I must go back and boil an egg for your Big Brother," she said, taking Hai-erh by the hand. She smiled at me. "Come over after a while and we'll play chess. I know you're bored, home all day."

I nodded and watched her walk away. I felt I was falling in love with her. But this would not harm Big Brother, for I loved her like an elder sister. Of course I'd be too embarrassed to tell this to anyone, even Chueh-min—Chueh-min whom I trusted so.

Chueh-min is very partial to Chin; he's told me so. But, from what he says, apparently he still hasn't revealed his feelings to her. He's been turning rather queer lately. He never gives a thought to home. He leaves early in the morning for Chin's place and doesn't even come home for supper. I'm afraid sooner or later the gossipers around here are going to notice, and then. . . .

Whenever he speaks to me now, it's always about Chin. He gives you the impression that Chin belongs to him alone. Well, it's none of my business. He was not very interested in our student strike either. Chin seems to be his whole world. He's much too happy. I'm afraid he's riding for a fall, but I certainly hope it doesn't happen.

I strolled in the plum grove for a long time and Chueh-min came and chatted with me a while. After he left, I remained there until Ming-feng called me to lunch.

She seems to be avoiding me lately, I don't know why. Today, for instance, when she saw me coming, she turned and walked the other way. I ran after her and asked, "Why are you avoiding me?"

She stopped and looked at me timidly, but the light in her eyes was warm. Then she dropped her head and said in a low voice, "I'm afraid . . . I'm afraid Madam and the others will find out."

Very moved, I raised her face and, smiling, shook my head. "Don't be afraid. It's nothing to be ashamed of. Love is very pure." I let her go. Now, at last I understand.

After lunch I went back to my room and started reading the English translation of *Resurrection* that Chueh-min had just bought. Suddenly I grew frightened, and couldn't go on. I was afraid that book might become a portrait of me, even though its hero's circumstances are very different from mine. . . . Lately, I've been daydreaming a lot, wondering how families like ours are going to end. . . .

I'm so lonely! Our home is like a desert, a narrow cage. I want activity, I want life. In our family, I can't even find anyone I can talk to.

That book *Yeh-yeh* gave me—"On Filial Piety and the Shunning of Lewdness"—was still on the table. I picked it up and skimmed through a few pages. The whole thing is nothing but lessons on how to behave like a slave. It's full of phrases like "The minister who is unwilling to die at his sovereign's command is not loyal; the son who is unwilling to die at his father's command is not filial," and "Of all crimes, lewdness is the worst; of all virtues, filial piety is the best." The more I read, the angrier I became, until I got so mad I ripped the book to pieces. With one less copy of that book in the world, a few less people will be harmed by it.

I felt depressed and weighted down with all manner of unpleasant things. Everything in the room is so dull and tasteless; outside my window too, it's always so gloomy. I wished I could sprout wings and fly away, but the silent house engulfed me like a tomb. I threw myself on the bed and began to groan.

"Third Brother, are you coming over for a game of chess?" the voice of Sister-in-law called from the next flat.

"All right, I'll be right over," I answered. I wasn't the least interested in chess, but I knew she was trying to cheer me up, and I couldn't be ungracious. After a few minutes, I went over. I became so interested in the game I forgot everything. Sister-in-law plays a better game than Big Brother, but she's not as good as me. I beat her three games in a row. She didn't mind a bit—just as pleasant and smiling as ever.

The nursemaid brought Hai-erh in, and Sister-in-law played with him, while continuing to chat with me. As I wandered about the room, my eye was caught by the embroidered bed canopy, with its plum blossom design.

"That's a nice design, Sister-in-law," I said. I really liked it, though I don't really know much about art. I thought it was the best sketch she had ever done.

"I don't draw very well, but I took a lot of pains with that one. Your Big Brother pleaded with me several times to do a plum blossom design." A pleased smile appeared on Sister-in-law's face. "I'm very fond of plum blossoms too."

"You mean because Big Brother likes them?" I teased her.

A faint blush coloured her cheeks and she smiled. "I won't tell you now. When you're married, you'll understand for yourself."

"What will I understand?" I pretended to be puzzled.

"Don't press me like that. In the future, you can ask your wife!"

There were sprigs of plum blossom in the small vase on the table and in the big vase on the desk. The golden yellow of the flowers hurt my eyes. I pictured the sad and beautiful face of Cousin Mei—"mei" for "plum blossom"! I wanted to say to Sister-in-law, "Take care that these plum blossoms don't steal a part of Big Brother's love away," but I didn't have the courage.

"It's been a long time since I've done any sketching. The past two or three years I've been so busy with Hai-erh, I've forgotten everything I ever studied," Sister-in-law was groping for words; her eyes shone with memories of dreams past.

I wondered whether she remembered the days before her marriage, days as beautiful as a rainbow. It seems to me she hasn't changed much in appearance, but her manner is much more open now, and her girlish shyness is gone.

I asked her, "Do you ever think of the time when you still lived with your parents?"

She nodded. "Sometimes. . . . It all seems like a dream now. Things were very different then. Aside from my elder brother, I had a sister who was three years older than me. She and I used to practise drawing and writing poetry together. Father was the head of Kuanyuan County then, and we lived in the Official Residence. My sister and I had a room on the upper floor, looking out over a large garden with many mulberry trees. Magpies used to perch in the branches and wake us early in the morning with their chatter.

"At night, the moonlight would shine in through our window and it was very still. My mother always went to bed quite early, but my sister and I loved the moonlight, so we often stayed up quite late. We used to open the window and gaze at the moon, while we chatted or made up poems. Sometimes, in the deep of the night, we would hear the sound of a distant horn. That meant the courier was coming. You know, in those days, all important official documents were always sent by special messenger who changed horses at relay stations. He would blow his horn while he was still a long way off, so that the people at the relay station would get a fresh horse ready for him. The sound of the horn was very mournful. It would wake us in the middle of the night, and we wouldn't be able to fall asleep again. . . .

"My mother raised silkworms, and we girls helped her. We would take a lantern late at night and go down the stairs and out to the breeding shed to see whether the silkworms had eaten all their mulberry leaves and needed more. I was still very young then, but nearly grown up. Those were wonderful days.

"Then the 1911 Revolution came, and father resigned his post as an official for the Manchus and took us all back to Chengtu. We were young ladies by then. Father said our painting was not bad, and arranged for us to do paintings on fans for a fan shop. We used the money we earned to buy more paints and some poetry collections.

"Later, my sister got married. We had been very close to each other and hated to part. The night before she left, we cried together all night. Less than a year later, she had a miscarriage and died. . . . We heard that her mother-in-law treated her badly, and it made her furious. She always had a nasty temper. At home, mother used to pamper and spoil her. She just couldn't learn to accept her in-laws' abuse. It burned her up inside; the aggravation is what finally killed her.

"Looking back on those things now, they all seem to have happened in a dream," Sister-in-law concluded in a sad voice. Her eyes were moist.

I was afraid she was going to cry, but my stupid brain couldn't think of anything to comfort her. "Have you had any news from your mother or brother lately?" I asked.

Sister-in-law's face was unhappy. "Brother writes that they're both well, but they won't be able to come back to Chengtu for another year or two."

We talked a while longer, and then I said I had to review my lessons and returned to my own room. I was still thinking of the things she had told me, but at last I calmed down and began to review *Treasure Island*. After reading more than twenty pages, I was worn out. I lay down on my bed and slept.

When I awoke it was already dark, and I felt cold. The faint glow of the sixteen-watt electric bulb in my room did nothing to warm my heart. Again I was oppressed with the dullness of my family life. Pacing the floor, I thought of the many exciting things going on outside. I can't stand this kind of life any more. There's nothing but oppression for me here in this house. I must fight to the finish.

At dinner I heard my stepmother and Big Brother discussing the battle tactics of Aunt Wang and Aunt Shen. Though they were speaking quite seriously, I couldn't help laughing. Later I talked with Big Brother in his room about filial piety. He's too weak and he's full of reservations. I'm very dissatisfied with him because he's slipping backward day by day. Just as our argument was getting warm, Aunt Shen's maid Hsi-erh called him to play mahjong with the ladies, and he agreed without the least hesitation.

"You mean you're going?" I asked in some annoyance.

"What else can I do?" he replied simply, and walked out with Hsi-erh. Those are his battle tactics.

I have two brothers. One plays mahjong to get on the good side of certain people; the other stays all day at my aunt's house teaching Chin English and doesn't even come home for supper. I must never become like them.

What a life! This is how I spent today. If I keep on like this, I'll have wasted my youth away.

I won't put up with it. I must resist, go against my grandfather's orders. I've got to get out of here.

The above was one day's entry in Chueh-hui's diary. The next morning, he did indeed leave the compound.

XII

The traditional New Year Holiday was fast approaching, the first big event of the year, and everyone, except those who owed heavy debts—which traditionally had to be paid off before the end of the year—was enthusiastically looking forward to it. It slowly drew nearer, with each day bringing a new harbinger of its coming. The whole city bubbled with life. More people than usual were on the streets. Many lanterns and toys appeared. Everywhere the sound of festive horns could be heard.

Although the Kao compound was located on a relatively quiet street, this gentry family, while outwardly calm and reserved, was also beginning to stir. Preparations for New Year ceremonies were being set in motion; a great many things had to be got ready. The servants, of course, were as busy as their masters; they were impatiently awaiting holiday festivities, and the traditional gifts of cash that came their way each New Year.

Every evening, the cook bustled about the kitchen making glutinous rice dumplings. During the day, all the females of the family—young and old—gathered in the room of the Venerable Master and folded gold and silver paper into the shape of ingots—these were to be burned at memorial services, and thus "sent" to ancestors for their use in the next world; the women also cut intricate pictures and designs out of red and green paper—these were to be pasted on the paper windows or on the oil-lamp cups.

The Venerable Master Kao was seldom at home during the day. If not at the theatre, he was visiting friends and playing mahjong. He and his cronies had organized what they called "The Nine Old Men's Club" and each took turns at playing host to the others, displaying his prized books and paintings, his antiques.

Chueh-hsin and his uncle Ke-ming were busy supervising the family's large body of servants, preparing for the New Year. Large red lanterns were hung in the main hall; on each of the side walls were placed panels of embroidered red silk. Portraits of departed ancestors were invited out of the chests in which they had been resting, and carefully hung on the hall's middle wall, there to enjoy the respects that would be paid them during the New Year Festival.

It was the Kao family tradition to have a large banquet two nights before the New Year. The afternoon of the banquet, Chueh-min and Chueh-hui went to call on Big Brother at his office, bringing with them a few new magazines they had picked up at the bookstore. They had also bought a translation of Turgenev's novel *On the Eve*.[20]

[20] Translated into Chinese in 1921.

As they neared Chueh-hsin's door, they could hear the clicking of his abacus counters. Pushing aside the door curtain, they entered.

Chueh-hsin looked up, and was surprised to see Chueh-hui. "You're out?" he asked.

"For several days already. Didn't you know?" Chueh-hui grinned. He was entirely at ease.

"What if *Yeh-yeh* finds out?" asked Chueh-hsin, worried. Again he bent over his abacus.

"I can't be bothered about such details. I don't care if he does!" Chueh-hui said coolly.

Chueh-hsin looked at him silently, then, frowning, continued with his calculations.

"It's all right. *Yeh-yeh* is sure to have forgotten by now," Chueh-min said soothingly. He stretched out on the cane reclining chair beside the window.

Chueh-hui sat down near the wall, and began to read aloud from *On the Eve:*

> *Love is a great word, a great feeling . . . but what kind of love are you talking about?*
> *What kind of love? Whatever kind of love you like, so long as it's love. For my part I confess that there just aren't different sorts of love. If you fall in love—then love with all your soul.*

His two brothers were looking at him in surprise, but Chueh-hui was unaware of it. He continued to recite:

> *It's the thirst for love, for happiness, nothing else.*
> *We're young, we are not monsters, not fools. We'll conquer happiness for ourselves.*

A surge of warmth swept through Chueh-hui's body; his hands trembled with emotion. Unable to go on, he closed the book and took several large swallows from his teacup.

At this moment, Chien-yun slowly entered.

"What were you saying just now with so much passion, Chueh-hui?" he asked in his dry rasping voice.

"I was only reading," Chueh-hui replied with a bitter laugh. Again he opened the book, and read aloud:

Nature awakens the need for love, but it is not capable of satisfying it.

The room was very quiet. Even the sound of the abacus was stilled.

In Nature there is Life and Death. . . .
In Love there is Life and Death.

"What does that mean?" Chien-yun asked in a low voice. No one replied. His face showed doubt, then fear, but the expressions were fleeting.

A nameless terror began to flutter in the small room, but gradually it vanished, and a common misery gripped each of the four young men.

"In this kind of society, what other kind of life can you have!" Chueh-hui burst out angrily. "This kind of existence is simply a waste of youth, a waste of life!"

He had been increasingly tortured by this feeling, of late. Ever since childhood, he had been consumed by a craving to be entirely different from the men of his elder generation. As a boy, he had travelled a great deal with his county prefect father, and had seen many odd things. He often dreamed of running away to distant exotic lands, of pursuing unusual careers. There had been something dreamlike about the life in his father's yamen. Later, when they returned to Chengtu, he was brought into closer contact with reality, and he began to have a new recognition of the world.

In the Kao family, servants and sedan-chair carriers alone came to several dozen. These "underlings," though coming from many different places, were bound together by a common fate. People who originally were strangers to one another, for a pittance of a wage, now served the same masters, living together like some large tribe—peacefully, even affectionately—because they were the same kind of people; they had only to anger their master today, and tomorrow they would not know where their next meal was coming from.

Sympathizing with them, Chueh-hui spent much of his childhood among them, and he earned the servants' love and respect. He would lie on the bed of one of the sedan-chair carriers, watching, in the light of an opium lamp, a lean porter smoking his opium pipe and telling his favourite stories. Chueh-hui loved to sit around a brazier in the servants' quarters and hear tales of bold and masterly swordsmen, dreaming of the day when he would be grown up, when, holding a sword like his heroes, he would rob the rich and give to the poor, a gallant wanderer with no family ties.

Later, when he entered middle school, his world again began to change. From his books, from the words of his teachers, he gradually became inspired with patriotic and reformist sentiments. He became a devoted reader of the agitational articles by Liang Ch'i-ch'ao,[21] who demanded constitutional reforms. He read *The Soul of China* and *The Collected Essays of the Yin-ping Shih,* and supported the proposal advocated by Liang Ch'i-ch'ao in his *Citizens' Guide to Elementary Politics* that national military conscription replace the prevailing practice among the various warlords of hiring mercenaries. Chueh-hui even considered leaving school to become a soldier.

But when the May Fourth Movement erupted in 1919, he seemed to be brought into a new world. He lost his admiration for Liang Ch'i-ch'ao and embraced newer and much more progressive theories. It was then he earned the title his Big Brother ironically bestowed upon him—"The Humanitarian." The main reason for the nickname, so far as Big Brother was concerned, was that Chueh-hui refused to let himself be carried in a sedan-chair. The boy had been influenced by a number of articles in the magazine *New Tide,* such as "The True Meaning of Life"[22] and "The Rudiments of the Problem of

[21] Liang Ch'i-ch'ao (1873–1927) took a prominent part in the Reform Movement of 1898. At the beginning of the century and after the Revolution of 1911, Liang was a leader of the Democratic and later of the Progressive Party. After a trip to Europe in 1919 he revised his former admiration of Western civilization and became a conservative.

[22] By Ch'en Tu-hsiu, published in February 1918. Ch'en Tu-hsiu (1879–1942) took part in the revolutionary movement before

Life,"[23] on the purpose and meaning of life as a member of society, and was starting to think about these things for the first time. In the beginning, Chueh-hui had only the haziest conceptions. But gradually, as he gained more experience—particularly through his recent "imprisonment"—and after much internal struggle and the study of many books, his vision widened and he began to understand the significance of life and how a real man should behave.

And so Chueh-hui was pained by this waste of his youth. But the more he hated the life he was leading, the more intangible barriers he found hemming him in, preventing him from breaking away from it.

"What a cursed life!" he fumed. His eye accidentally caught Chueh-hsin's confused gaze, and he quickly looked away. He observed Chien-yun, melancholy and resigned, then turned to look at Chueh-min. Second Brother appeared engrossed in his magazine. The room was still, deathly still. Chueh-hui felt as if something were gnawing at his heart. He could bear it no longer.

"Why don't you speak?" he shouted. "You all deserve to be cursed too . . . every one of you!"

The others gazed at him in astonishment.

"Why?" Chueh-min asked mildly, closing his book. "We're all trying to get along in an old-fashioned family, the same as you."

"That's exactly the reason!" Chueh-hui retorted hotly.

1911. He was a professor at Peking University, played a prominent role in the New Culture Movement and was a founder of *New Youth*. Ch'en was also among the founders of the Chinese Communist Party and its leader until 1927, when he was blamed for the party's defeat and deposed from leadership. In 1930 he was expelled from the party and soon afterwards organized a pro-Trotsky Communist opposition group. In 1932 he was arrested by the Kuomintang government and spent five years in jail.

[23] By Fu Ssu-nien, published in January 1919. Fu Ssu-nien (1896–1950) was an outstanding historian and philologist, and a leader in the New Culture Movement. He was Director of the Institute of History and Philology at Academia Sinica, and Director of the Academy during the war with Japan.

"You're all so docile. You don't put up the slightest resistance. How much abuse can you take? You talk a lot about opposing the patriarchal family system, but actually you support it. Your ideas are new but your conduct is still the old kind. You're all spineless! You're full of contradictions!"

Chueh-hui forgot for the moment that he was full of contradictions himself.

"Third Brother, calm down a little. What's the good of raising such a row? You're not going to solve anything all in one sweep," Chueh-min asserted. "What can you accomplish alone? You ought to know that the patriarchal family system exists because it has its economic and social foundation." Chueh-min had just read this last sentence in his magazine, and it rolled off his tongue very naturally. "You're not necessarily any worse off than the rest of us," he added.

Again Chueh-hui happened to catch Chueh-hsin's gaze. Chueh-hsin was looking at him in a melancholy and somewhat reproachful manner. Chueh-hui's wrath slowly subsided and he went back to reading his book. After an interval of quiet, he again read aloud in a low voice:

> Let them be! My father was right when he said: "We're not Sybarites, my boy, we're not aristocrats, the spoilt children of destiny, we're not even martyrs—no, we're just workers, workers, workers. Put on your leather apron, worker, and get to your bench in your dark workshop! Leave the sunshine to other people. There's pride and happiness even in our obscure existence."

That could be a description of me, thought Chien-yun. But where is my pride, my happiness? All an illusion!

"Happiness? Where can it be found? Is there actually such a thing?" sighed Chueh-hsin.

Chueh-hui looked at him, then leafed back a few pages to a place he had dog-eared. He read aloud, as though in answer to his brother's question:

> We're young, we are not monsters, not fools. We'll conquer happiness for ourselves!

"Third Brother, please don't read any more," Chueh-hsin begged.

"Why not?" Chueh-hui persisted.

"You don't know how badly I feel. I'm not young—I never had a youth. I never had any happiness, and I never will." Another person might have said these words angrily, but Chueh-hsin's tone was only sad.

"Just because you never had any happiness, are you afraid to hear someone else even talk about fighting for it?" Chueh-hui demanded rudely. He was very dissatisfied with his Big Brother's weak-kneed attitude towards life.

"Ah, you don't understand, your situation is different from mine," said Chueh-hsin, pushing aside his abacus and looking at Chueh-hui with a sigh. "You're quite right. I'm afraid to hear others talk of happiness. That's because I no longer have any hope of attaining it. My life is finished. I don't fight back because I don't want to. I'm willing to be a victim. Once, like the rest of you, I had my beautiful dreams, but they all were shattered. Not one of my hopes was fulfilled. I have no one but myself to blame. I was quite willing to assume the burdens *Tieh*[24] left me. . . .

"I remember the day before he died. He was very ill. That day our little sister passed away; she was only five, and the news hurt him badly. He wept and, holding my hand, said, 'When your mother died she entrusted all you six children to me. But I've let her down. Today I lost one of you.' The tears ran from his eyes, and he said, 'I haven't much chance of recovering. In case anything happens, I'm turning your stepmother and brothers and sisters over to you. Take good care of them for me. I know your character well. You won't disappoint me.'

"I couldn't help bursting into loud sobs. *Yeh-yeh*, who was passing by, thought *Tieh* had died, and he came rushing in. He scolded me for upsetting a sick man, then he gave *Tieh* a few words of comfort. Later, he called me to his room and questioned me in detail on what had happened. When I told him, he wept too. He seemed to want to say something but, what-

[24] *Tieh*—father.

ever it was, he couldn't get the words out. Finally, he waved me away, telling me to take good care of the patient.

"That night *Tieh* summoned me to his bedside to write his will. Stepmother held the candle and Elder Sister the ink box. I wrote as he dictated and, as I wrote, I wept. The next day he died, and his burdens fell on my shoulders. I still cry whenever I think of how he died. I had to sacrifice myself for him. What else could I do? I'm quite willing to be the victim. Even so, I've let him down, for I lost Elder Sister. . . ."

Tears ran down Chueh-hsin's face as he told this story, and he was more and more wracked with sobs. Finally, unable to go on, he lay his head on the desk and wept unrestrainedly.

Chueh-hui was almost weeping too. He held back his tears with an effort. He saw that Chien-yun was mopping his eyes with a handkerchief and Chueh-min had hidden his face behind his magazine.

In the arcade outside the window, footsteps kept approaching, then passing on and fading away.

Chueh-hsin took a handkerchief from his pocket and wiped his tears, as he proceeded:

"There are other things which you do not know. I am now telling the old man's tale again. When I was only five and neither of you were yet born, Father was appointed District Marshal to a certain district. Father and Mother went there with me and Sister. The area was then infested with the Red Lantern Society[25] bandits; the district magistrate Tang had to take off every day with troops and militia for bandit suppression, and Father had to be out every night for night watch over the city. He came home usually after one or two o'clock, and we waited for him to be home before we went to bed. I was then considered by everybody in the house as mature, and every night I would sit up to keep Mother company, cracking melon seeds while talking about this and that with her. Mother would fondly tell me in soft words that I should study hard, in order to be somebody who would make her lot worth while,

[25] One of the many secret societies of Old China. It organized peasant revolts against the landlords in Szechwan at the turn of the century.

97

and then, in tears, she would tell me all the painful experiences of how she had suffered after her marriage into our family. I would then either shed tears in response, or talk to please her until she returned a smile. I would say that I would study hard, so that I could rise to the position of Director of the Censorate and Circuit Inspector, in order to bring upon her honour and glory, and then she would have her vindication. I did indeed study hard soon afterwards, and Magistrate Tang was pleased to hear of it, and often he would send carriers to take Mother to visit their house with me. The whole house would praise and envy Mother's blessedness of having a child under six who excelled in studies and further could console her in times of trial, and all would assure Mother that I would undoubtedly grow up to hold very high positions. Thus Mother was able to begin to feel a little better and forget some of her pains and worries. Another year and more passed by, and the provincial government then sent another appointee to take over Father's position. As we were making preparations to leave the place, Mother took time to tell me, in tears, of all of Father's difficulties. At the time Mother was pregnant with Chueh-min, only a month or two away from delivery. Father was very worried about the hardships the journey was going to inflict on Mother, but we had to take the journey, there was no other way out. Then in less than two months after we got back to Chengtu, Chueh-min was born. This was again a trying period and life was very difficult for Mother. Next year Father went to Peking to wait for an Imperial audience as a candidate magistrate. Mother waited at home for the news of Father's magistracy appointment, and it was then that Chueh-hui came into the world. Soon information came that Father's appointment was withheld because of failure to conform to certain procedural requirements and was therefore kept waiting in Peking for the next turn. Grandfather was dismayed by the news and would often show his anger, while others in the family contributed unkind words. Mother was made to suffer from these, and only Sister and myself were there to cheer her up. Every time a letter came from Father, she would cry for one or two days. It was not until his letter finally came with the information that he had the audience and appointment and would be home after the Harvest Festival, that with a long sigh she let her heart rest in peace. She certainly had enough painful humiliations. In a word, from the time she married into our family to the time of her death, Mother did not have many days of peace and joy. She had loved me so much, expected so much of me! What do I have to repay her with? Whenever I think of Mother, my heart suffers tremendous pain. . . . For her, I would be willing to sacrifice all and everything, even to sacrifice all of my future prospects. If only my brothers and sisters could grow up properly, to bring honour and glory to vindicate Mother, my life's purpose would be fulfilled. This I hope you will understand well . . ."

"Don't feel badly, Big Brother," came the voice of Chueh-min from behind his magazine. "We understand you."

Chueh-hui could no longer restrain his tears, but an instant later he stopped himself. What's past is dead and buried, he thought. Why dig it all up again now? Yet he couldn't help grieving for his departed father.

"Those lines you just read are very apt, Third Brother," said Chueh-hsin with a mournful smile. He had recovered his calm somewhat. "I'm not a wastrel or the spoilt child of destiny. I'm only a worker. I put on my leather apron and work in my own dark workshop. . . . I'm a worker without pride or happiness. I—" Chueh-hsin suddenly paused, a startled look on his face. He had heard a familiar cough outside the window. "*Yeh-yeh*'s coming," he said to Chueh-hui in a low voice. "What are you going to do?"

Chueh-hui felt a brief flurry of panic, but he suppressed it immediately. "Why get excited?" he said coolly. "He won't eat me."

The door curtain was pushed aside and the old man entered, followed by a servant who waited in the doorway. The four young men rose in greeting, and Chueh-min offered the cane chair in which he had been sitting.

"So you're all here," said the Venerable Master Kao, a pleasant smile on his dark countenance. He looked more affectionate when he was cheerful. "You can all go home early. We're having our New Year's banquet tonight." He sat down in the

99

cane chair beside the window, but at once rose to his feet again.

"Chueh-hsin, I want to do some shopping. Come along with me," he directed. Walking sedately in his cotton-padded black cloth shoes, he stepped across the threshold as Chueh-hsin held aside the door curtain. Chueh-hsin and the servant followed him.

The moment they were gone, Chueh-min blew out his breath in relief and grinned at Chueh-hui. "He's forgotten all about you."

"If I were as docile as Big Brother, I'd probably be locked up at home for ever. It's a good thing I had a little courage," said Chueh-hui. "As a matter of fact I was silly not to have come out earlier. Yeh-yeh gets mad, and then it's over and forgotten. How would he remember that I was still suffering, pent up at home? Let's go. There's no need to wait for Big Brother —we're walking and he'll be taking a sedan-chair. Besides if we start back early, we can avoid bumping into Yeh-yeh again."

"Right," Chueh-min agreed. "What about you?" he asked Chien-yun.

"I've got to go back too. I'll walk along with you."

On the way home, Chueh-hui was very happy. He had closed the tomb of the past and sealed the door tight. He said to himself:

"I'm young. I'm not an invalid, not a fool. I'll conquer happiness for myself."

Once again he was grateful that he was not like his Big Brother.

XIII

Dusk had already fallen in the Kao family compound. In the main hall, in addition to the hundred-watt electric bulb which had just been installed, suspended from the central beam was an "eternal flame" lamp that burned vegetable oil, a large kerosene lamp, and four lamps with picture glass panels. Their combined light brilliantly illuminated the pictures on the wall and the portraits of the Ching dynasty ancestors resting on the altar. Even the cracks in the coloured-tile floor were made visible.

Eating utensils had been neatly laid on two large round tables placed in the centre of the hall. The chopsticks were of ivory; the bowls, spoons and plates were silver. Beneath each plate was a red slip of paper on which a place name had been written. Four servants waited on each table; two to pour the wine, two to serve the food. Cooked dishes were brought from the kitchen to a large service table outside the hall, from there passed by an older woman servant to the male servants, who carried the food to the round tables. The bondmaids from all the households were also there to help.

After eight varieties of cold-cuts and two plates of melon seeds and almonds had been set upon the tables, the diners were invited to enter. Led by the Venerable Master Kao, everyone, old and young, gathered in the hall; then, at the old man's signal, found their places and took their seats.

The members of the elder generation all sat at the main table, each according to rank. First was the Venerable Master Kao, then Mistress Chen, Madam Chou, Third Elder Master Ke-ming and his wife Madam Chang, Fourth Elder Master Ke-an and his wife Madam Wang, Fifth Elder Master Ke-ting and his wife Madam Shen, plus the old man's daughter Mrs. Chang, mother of Chin. At the second table were Chueh-hsin, his wife Jui-chueh, Chin, Chueh-min and Chueh-hui, plus the boys' male cousins—Chueh-ying and Chueh-jen of the Third Household; and Chueh-chun, Chueh-shih and Chueh-hsien of the Fourth Household. Also present were the boys' young sister Shu-hua, their fifteen-year-old cousin Shu-ying of the Third Household, seven-year-old cousin Shu-fen of the Fourth Household and twelve-year-old cousin Shu-chen of the Fifth Household. Because the old man wanted all four generations represented at the banquet, Chueh-hsin's wife Jui-chueh held their son little Hai-chen on her lap for a while and let him eat with the grown-ups.

Winecup in hand, the old man gazed around at the smiling

celebrants crowding the tables—his children, his grandchildren, his great-grandson. His wish to see "four generations under one roof" had been fulfilled. A satisfied smile on his face, he drank deeply of his wine. He looked at the younger generation at the next table, laughing, drinking, calling for more wine in their fresh clear voices, the two male servants rushing around, refilling the cups from small wine kettles.

"Not too much wine, don't get drunk," he called with a smile. "Eat more food."

He heard Chueh-hsin's sound of assent, and unconsciously the old man raised his cup again and took another carefree sip. All the winecups at the table of the Venerable Master Kao rose in unison with his; when he placed his cup back on the table, the other diners followed suit. It was quiet and restrained at the old man's table. The Madams and Elder Masters sat stiffly correct. They took up their chopsticks when the old man raised his; they returned theirs to the table as soon as he put his down. They spoke to one another rarely, and then only a word or two. Finally the old man took notice. Slightly tipsy, he urged:

"Don't be so formal. Relax, all of you. Talk, laugh. See how gay they are at the next table. We're much too quiet. There's no need to stand on ceremony. We're all one family." Lifting his cup, he drained it, then said, "I'm very happy tonight."

The old man's unusual high spirits brought a breath of life to his table. Wine began to flow and the food was attacked in earnest.

It did the old man's heart good to see the excited flushed faces, to hear the noisy laughter accompanying the wine-drinking games. He took another sip from his refilled cup. He thought back on the past—his early struggles to get an education, his success as a scholar, his service as an official for many years. Starting empty-handed he had accumulated vast farm-lands, built houses, raised this large family. All had gone well. If the family continued to prosper at this rate, who could tell how affluent the Kaos would be in another generation or two. . . . Smiling, he took another big swallow of wine, then put down the cup and announced:

"I've had enough. It takes only two cups to get me drunk. But the rest of you go on." And he ordered the servants: "Refill the cups of the gentlemen and ladies here."

The second table was indeed, as the old man had said, much more gay. The chopsticks of the diners seldom rested. A new dish had only to appear, and in a few minutes the platter was clean. The little boys Chueh-chun and Chueh-shih, who were still unable to manipulate chopsticks successfully, knelt on their chairs and helped themselves from the platters with their spoons. The young men and women ate and drank and laughed with complete abandonment right up to the very end of the banquet. Most of them were a little drunk by the time it was over.

Chin and her mother left first. Originally, Chueh-min, Chuch-hui, their sister Shu-hua and their cousin Shu-ying had pleaded with Madam Chou to let Chin stay as their guest over the holidays. But Mrs. Chang said they had things to do at home, and took Chin off with her. Jui-chueh went back to her room to look after Hai-chen. Chueh-hsin, Chueh-min and Shu-hua all had drunk too much; they went to their rooms to sleep it off.

By then, the zest had gone out of the party, and the other youngsters had no choice but to return to their own households. Quiet descended on the big compound. Only a few servants remained in the large hall, clearing off the tables and sweeping the floor.

Chueh-hui, also, was feeling the wine he had drunk. His face burned, his heart felt very hot. On the street, firecrackers were bursting like the staccato hoofbeats of stampeding horses. Chueh-hui couldn't sit still. He went out into the cold air of the hall's ante-room. A few sedan-chairs stood waiting, while three or four carriers sat on the high threshold of the gatehouse, talking in low tones. A string of firecrackers rattled in the compound next door.

After standing for several minutes, Chueh-hui started towards the street. Just as he reached the main gate of the compound, the sound of fireworks ceased, except for an occasional scattered burst. The smell of powder filled the air; corpses of

103

exploded firecrackers littered the street. Two large red paper lanterns hung in the gateway, casting only hazy red shadows on the ground in spite of the large candles burning inside.

The streets were quiet. Scattered remains of fireworks lay ignored and disappointed, emitting their last warm, sulphurous breath. From somewhere came the sound of soft weeping.

Why should anyone be crying at a time when everyone else is happy? wondered Chueh-hui. He was growing sober again. Peering around in the darkness, he observed a dark shadow near the large stone vat on the right side of the compound gate. Curious, he approached.

A tattered beggar child was leaning his head on the edge of the vat, weeping, his tousled hair dangling into the water within. The child looked up at the sound of Chueh-hui's footsteps. Although they could not see each other clearly in the darkness, they stood staring, face to face, neither speaking a word. Chueh-hui could hear the child's laboured sobs.

It was like a dash of cold water to Chueh-hui. He could distinctly sense the silver coins clinking in his own pocket. A rare emotion possessed him, and he drew out two silver half-dollars and placed them in the beggar child's moist hand.

"Take these," he said distractedly. "Find yourself some place warm. It's cold out here, very cold. Look how you're shivering. You'll feel better after you've bought a bit of hot food."

Chueh-hui turned quickly and strode back into the compound, as if running from something shameful. Passing through the main gate into the courtyard he could visualize his Big Brother's mocking smile and hear him scoff—"Humanitarian!" As Chueh-hui neared the main hall after going through the inner compound gate, a voice seemed to shout at him in the silence:

"Do you think deeds like that are going to change the world? Do you think you've saved that beggar child from cold and hunger for the rest of his life? You—you hypocritical 'humanitarian'; what a fool you are!"

Terrified, he fled to his own room. Sinking down weakly on to his bed, he kept repeating to himself, "I'm drunk, drunk."

XIV

Next day was the last day of the old lunar year. Chueh-hui woke quite late that morning. Sunlight already filled his window and the room was very bright. Chueh-min, standing by his bedside, said with a teasing smile:

"Just see how you slept last night."

Throwing back the covers, Chueh-hui found that he had not undressed. He grinned at his brother and sat up. The sunlight was painful. He rubbed his eyes. Mama Huang, the boys' maid, came in, carrying a basin of hot water for Chueh-hui to wash his face.

"You were so drunk last night you didn't even take your clothes off," she scolded. "It's very easy to catch a chill in weather like this. When I covered you, you were snoring away, dead to the world. And you slept right through till this morning!" Her wrinkled face was wreathed in smiles. She often berated the boys, but with such motherly affection that they always took it in good grace.

Chueh-min smiled, and Chueh-hui couldn't suppress a grin.

"You do love to chatter, Mama Huang," Chueh-hui teased her. "Everyone was so happy last night. What was wrong with drinking a little? I saw you glaring at me every time I raised my cup. It took all the fun out of it. You ought to loosen up a bit during holidays. You're much stricter with us than Madam Chou!"

"It's because she's not strict enough with you that I have to be so strict," retorted the old lady as she made the bed. "I'm over fifty this year. Been working in this family for more than ten years, looking after you two. I watched you grow up. You've been good to me too. Never a harsh word. I've been thinking of going home for a long time, but I can't bear to leave you. I've seen all sorts of things in this compound. It's not as good now as in the old days. I keep thinking—Leave.

When you're used to living in clear water, it's not worth staying after it gets muddy. . . . But I can't part with you two. Who would take care of you after I've gone? Both you Young Masters are very good—just like your mother. She'd be happy if she could see how well you've grown. I know she's still protecting you, up there in heaven. In another few years, after you've finished school, you'll both become big officials. That will be a great honour for me too!"

Chueh-hui grinned. "If we really become big officials, we'll probably have forgotten all about you by then. How could we think of you at a time like that?"

"I know you'd never forget me. Not that I'd want anything from you. I'll be old and useless by then. All I want is to hear that you've done well in your studies and come up in the world, and I'll be satisfied," the old lady said, gazing at the boys affectionately.

"Of course we won't forget you, Mama Huang," Chueh-min assured her, patting her on the shoulder.

The old lady smiled at him and took up the wash basin which Chueh-hui had finished using. At the doorway she paused to warn them:

"No more drinking tonight."

"A little bit won't hurt," was Chueh-hui's laughing rejoinder. But the old lady was already out of earshot.

"What a nice woman," said Chueh-min. "Servants as good as she are hard to find."

"So you've made the great discovery that servants have feelings and consciences, the same as their masters," Chueh-hui twitted him.

Chueh-min sensed the mild sarcasm, but he made no reply. He started walking towards the door.

"Going to Chin's house again?" Chueh-hui called after him.

Chueh-min, at the threshold, turned and gave his brother a reproachful look. But his reply was moderate.

"No. I'm going for a walk in the garden. Would you like to come?"

Chueh-hui nodded and joined him. Passing the door of Chueh-hsin's flat, they heard Chien-erh, bondmaid of the Fourth Household, apparently looking for their elder brother, calling, "First Young Master!" They walked on into the garden.

"Let's stick to the right. *Yeh-yeh* is in the plum grove, supervising the servants cutting branches," said Chueh-min when they passed through the moon-gate.

The boys followed a winding covered walk, enclosed on one side by a whitewashed wall inlaid with plaques of decorative marble. A bit further on, a number of windows were cut in the wall—behind these was the drawing-room. Running along the outer side of the covered walk was a stone balustrade, beyond which a large man-made hill and a long stretch of garden could be seen. There was also a low terrace where a few bare peony bushes braved the cold. The end of each branch was wrapped in a layer of cotton padding.

"That's the way to be," said Chueh-hui, nodding approvingly at the peonies. "Standing out in the icy breeze, never shivering a bit. We ought to be like them, not like the little grass that falls withered at the first frost!"

"There you go, making speeches again," laughed Chueh-min. "Even though peonies weather the winter, grow leaves and put forth blossoms, in the end they still can't avoid *Yeh-yeh*'s shears."

"What of it? The next year they put out new blossoms all over again!"

Emerging from the covered walk, the boys went down a flight of stone steps into a garden filled with misshapen boulders. Some looked like bent old men, some like crouching lions, some like long-necked cranes. At the other end of the garden, the boys mounted some stone steps to a bamboo fence and went through a gate so narrow that only one person could pass at a time. They were confronted with what at first glance seemed an impassably dense thicket of growing bamboos. Then they entered upon a small twisting path which took them through. Nearing the end of the thicket, they first heard, then saw, a little brook flowing out from beneath the man-made hill. Its waters were very clear—you could see plainly the pebbles and fallen leaves lying on the bottom.

A wooden bridge took the boys to the opposite side, where they entered another garden. Here, in the centre, was a pavilion with a thatched roof before which grew a few cassia trees and camellia bushes. Beyond the pavilion was another whitewashed wall, with a small gate leading through its left corner. As the boys crossed the gateway, the sound of waves struck their ears, and a cold breeze made them shiver, but they pressed on.

They had entered a maze of fences, through which they twisted and turned for a long time before finally finding their way out again. Before them stood a grove of tall cypresses. They could hear the wind moaning through the grove; the sky was darkening. Halfway through, to the right where the trees were not so dense, they could see the gleaming windows of a dull red building. At last they reached a clearing on the other side of the grove. Ahead were the shining waters of a crescent-shaped lake, embracing the opposite bank in its curve. A zig-zag bridge led to a small isle with a pavilion in the lake's middle.

The boys halted at the edge of the lake and stood gazing at the ripples. They picked up stones and tried to fling them across, but each time, although they were at a relatively narrow section of the lake, their throws fell short, and the stones dropped into the water.

"Let's go over to the other side and find a place to sit down," Chueh-min suggested.

The boys traversed a small hump-backed bridge to the opposite shore.

Then, crossing a narrow strip of lawn, they mounted stone stairs to a large garden of magnolia trees. A path paved with stones of different sizes ran through the centre, flanked on each side by a row of four glazed earthen stools. Going up a few more steps, the boys came to the recently repaired building they had seen through the cypresses. Except for its tile roof, its whole exterior had been painted vermilion. It was very attractive. A horizontal plaque over its door bore the building's name—"Fragrance at Eventide." The inscription had been written by their uncle Ke-an.

Chueh-min sat down on one of the glazed earthen stools and gazed appreciatively at the plaque.

Chueh-hui stood on the steps of the building. "Let's climb

the back of the hill," he suggested to his brother with a smile.

The older boy refused to get up. "Suppose we rest a while first," he countered.

"All right. I'm going in to take a look around." Chueh-hui pushed open the door of the building and entered.

He gave only a cursory glance at the room's furnishings and the paintings on the wall. Walking towards the rear, he went up the stairs to the upper storey. There he found Big Brother lying on a brick bed. His eyes half shut, Chueh-hsin looked worn out.

"What are you doing here, all alone?" Chueh-hui asked, surprised.

Chueh-hsin opened his eyes and gazed at him wearily. "I've come for a rest," he replied with a forced laugh. "The last few days have been too much for me. I can't have any peace at home. People are always coming to me for one thing or another. We're going to be up all night again tonight. If I don't get some rest, I won't be able to last."

"Chien-erh was looking for you a while back. I don't know what she wanted."

"You didn't tell her I was here?" Chueh-hsin asked in alarm.

"No. I didn't see her. I just heard her calling you in your room."

"Good," said Chueh-hsin, relieved. "I know Uncle Ke-an wants me for something. I'm glad I was able to get away."

Evidently Big Brother's tactics had changed. Chueh-hui wondered whether his new methods of placating everyone would be any more successful.

"You had quite a lot to drink at dinner last night. You never used to like drinking, and your health's none too good. Why drink so heavily?" Chueh-hui was not one to beat about the bush.

"You're always laughing at my battle tactics. Well, this is one of them," Chueh-hsin sat up and replied with a wry smile. "When things get too much for me I drink some wine, and the world becomes pleasantly hazy. It makes life much easier." Chueh-hsin paused. "I admit I'm a weakling; I haven't the courage to face life. The best I can do is make myself befuddled; it's only in that state that I can get along."

What can you do with a man who admits he's a weakling? thought Chueh-hui bitterly. He began by pitying his Big Brother and ended by sympathizing with him. Afraid that anything more he might say would only add to his brother's unhappiness, Chueh-hui turned to leave.

"Wait a minute, Third Brother. There's something I want to ask you," said Chueh-hsin.

Chueh-hui walked back and faced his brother. Chueh-hsin looked at him, his eyes gleaming.

"Have you seen Cousin Mei?"

"You know she's in Chengtu?" replied Chueh-hui, surprised. "I haven't seen her, but Chin has."

Chueh-hsin nodded. "I've seen her too—a few days ago, at the entrance of the Hsinfahsiang Department Store in the arcade."

Silently, Chueh-hui also nodded, trying to read his brother's face.

"She was coming out with her mother. Her mother stopped to talk to someone inside and Mei stood in the doorway looking at some clothing material. I nearly called out. Mei turned around and looked at me. She nodded in half a greeting, then faced towards the interior of the store. Following her gaze, I saw that her mother was there inside. I didn't dare to come any closer, I just stood looking at her from a distance. Her limpid eyes were fixed on me for a long time, her lips trembling. I thought she was going to say something. But she turned and walked back into the store without so much as another glance."

A peal of children's laughter flew in from outside the building, then subsided. Chueh-hsin continued:

"Meeting her like that brought everything back again. I had already forgotten. Jui-chueh is wonderful to me, and I love her. But now Mei's return is stirring up old memories. Living in these surroundings, how can I help thinking of her? I wish I knew how she felt about me. Perhaps she hates me for having led her on. I know that she married, and that she's a widow now, that she's gone back to live with her mother. . . ." Chueh-hsin's voice was choked with emotion. Pain and regret contorted his face. He sighed.

110

"I'm sure she doesn't hate you after all this time and after everything that's happened. Why do you keep torturing yourself with the past? The past should be buried and done with. It's the present we should be thinking of, and the future. Cousin Mei has probably forgotten all about you by now." As Chueh-hui spoke the last sentence, he knew in his heart he was lying.

"You don't understand." Chueh-hsin shook his head. "How could she have forgotten what happened between us? Women remember everything. If life had been better for her, if she had had a husband who loved her, perhaps she could have forgotten, and I wouldn't worry about her. But Fate had to rule otherwise! Now she's a young widow, a companion for life to her crochety old mother, living like a recluse in a nunnery. How can I help worrying about her?

"But when I think of her, I feel I'm not being fair to Jui-chueh. Jui-chueh loves me. Why must I turn around and love someone else? If I go on like this, I'll hurt both of them. I'll never forgive myself. . . . Life is too cruel; that's why I have to dull my brain, that's why I've taken to drink. But it wears off quickly, so I hide myself away from Jui-chueh after I drink, and quietly weep, for my past sins haunt me even worse then. I curse myself for being such a coward!"

Chueh-hui felt like saying, "You brought it on yourself. Why didn't you fight back? When they wanted to choose a bride for you against your will, why didn't you speak up? You only got what you deserved!" But when he saw his brother's tragic countenance, he only said softly, "It may work out all right. If Cousin Mei falls in love and marries again, everything will be solved."

Chueh-hsin shook his head and smiled bitterly. "That only happens in those new books of yours. You ought to open your eyes and take a look at reality. How could a thing like that happen in a family like hers? Not only would her mother oppose it—she herself would never even consider such a thing."

There seemed to be nothing more Chueh-hui could say. He didn't want to argue with Chueh-hsin; the distance between their ways of thinking was wider than ever. He didn't really understand Chueh-hsin. If a thing was right, why couldn't it

111

be done? It was a useless sacrifice to throw away one's happiness because of conditions, which were capable of being changed. It did no one any good and only served to extend the life of an old-fashioned family a few hours longer. Why couldn't Cousin Mei remarry? Since Big Brother loved her, why did he marry Jui-chueh? After marrying Jui-chueh why was he still thinking of Cousin Mei?

Chueh-hui understood, and yet he didn't. Everything about his patriarchal family was a tangled knot to him; his ardent, direct young mind had no way to unravel it. As he stood gazing at his brother's agonized expression, he was struck by a frightening thought: It was a tragic truth that for people like Chueh-hsin there was not a shred of hope; they were beyond saving. Bringing new ideas to them, opening their eyes to the true aspects of the world only intensified their misery. It was like resurrecting a corpse and letting it view its own putrefying flesh.

This bitter truth tormented his young mind. Everything seemed clear to him now; he had a premonition of a still unhappier future. He could see an unfathomable chasm yawning before people like his Big Brother. They were stepping into it without any hesitation, as if they didn't know it was there. It was just as well that they didn't, for they were beyond redemption.

Though he could see them walking towards the chasm, he was powerless to save them. What a tragedy! Chueh-hui's spirits sagged. He felt trapped in a narrow lane, unable to find his way out. The laughter of the children playing outside seemed to be mocking him.

Enough he said to himself. How many problems can I cram into my one small brain after all? Let everything take its natural course. As long as I behave like a man, that's plenty. That seemed the best solution, and he refused to think any further.

He put his head out of the window and looked around. There were his two boy cousins Chueh-ying and Chueh-chun, his sister Shu-hua, his girl cousins Shu-ying, Shu-chen and Shu-fen. His brother Chueh-min was there too. The children were taking turns kicking up a small feathered pad with the inner side of the foot. The point of the game was to see who could kick it up the most times without letting it fall to the ground.

Chueh-hui hailed them with a cheerful shout. His sister Shu-hua, who was busy kicking the pad and counting at the same time, turned her head instinctively at his call. As a result, in spite of her desperate effort to retrieve it in mid-air with her foot, it thudded to the ground. And she had just reached a score of one hundred and forty-five, too!

Chueh-min and the children had also been counting, growing rather anxious as her score mounted. Now, when she missed, they set up a great cheer. Shu-hua was furious. She stamped her foot and said it was all Chueh-hui's fault.

"Why is it my fault?" teased Chueh-hui. "I wasn't talking to you!" Turning to come downstairs, he discovered that Chueh-hsin was no longer there. Slowly he descended to the ground floor.

He could hear Big Brother's voice. By the time he got outside, Chueh-hsin was already kicking the feathered pad. His awkward gestures were quite funny to behold, and the children hooted with laughter. Although Chueh-hsin kept a straight face, he was obviously enjoying himself immensely.

Chueh-hui watched, marvelling at how easy it was for people to forget. Within a short time, a person could have a complete change of mood. Could it be that this ability to forget is what enables us to bear up under adversity? Chueh-hui was beginning to have some understanding of this Big Brother of his. Chueh-hsin could open the tomb of the past, then close it again and promptly forget all about it.

XV

When darkness fell that day, firecrackers began to pop, first sporadically, then bursting all over the neighbourhood. The quiet street resounded with explosions, the boom of big crackers shaking the earth. There was so much sharp, agitated

113

sound it was impossible to tell which direction it was coming from. The noise was like ten thousand stampeding horses, a roaring tidal wave.

After the evening meal, all the Kaos gathered in the family hall. Everyone wore new clothes. The men stood on the left side of the hall, the women on the right. Lights in the hall were burning bright as day, but the two big doors were wide open. Before the ancestral shrine, stood a rectangular altar table, covered with a red velvet cloth. In a large basin in front of the altar, several dozen chunks of charcoal, piled up like a mountain, glowed hotly with a bright red flame. Two or three balsam branches sizzled noisily in the fire, emitting an acrid smoke that stung the eyes and nostrils. More branches were scattered on the large, deep-yellow carpet spread upon the floor. A large cushion for kneeling had also been placed before the flaming basin; this cushion was covered with a red velvet cloth.

A pair of tall candlesticks and a big incense burner stood near the outer edge of the altar table. Along the inner edge and at both ends of the table were a great many winecups; only a few members of the family knew exactly how many. Because the Venerable Master Kao was too old to conduct the tiring ceremony, his son Ke-ming had been put in charge.

Wearing long gowns and wide-sleeved jackets, Ke-ming and his brother Ke-an slowly filled the cups with fine white liquor, and lit the incense sticks and inserted them in the burner. Then Ke-ming went to the inner room and invited the Venerable Master Kao to come out and start the ceremony.

A hush fell on the assembly when the old man appeared. Ke-ming issued the order to start the fireworks. A servant hurried out to the inner compound gates—also opened wide—and shouted, "Set them off!" A thunderous burst of fireworks shattered the air.

The women then left the hall by a side door and the men lined up with their backs to the altar table. Facing the main door, the Venerable Master Kao knelt and kowtowed his respects to the gods of Heaven and Earth. He was followed by his three sons who knelt in a line and also kowtowed. Chueh-hsin had been out carrying a lighted incense stick to the kitchen, symbolizing the Kitchen God's return after his annual New

Year's report to Heaven on the way the family had been conducting itself. Now Chueh-hsin entered the family hall just in time to join his two brothers and his three male cousins lining up to kowtow to the gods of Heaven and Earth. This done, all the men turned and stood facing the altar table. The women, who had been peeking from the side door, hastily filed back into the hall.

In accordance with custom, the Venerable Master Kao was the first to kowtow to the ancestral shrine, after which he retired from the hall. The others followed in this order: Madam Chou, the boys' uncles and aunts, then Mistress Chen. They all kowtowed leisurely, consuming a full half hour. Next came the male children of Chueh-hsin's generation—nine in all. The ceremony took place only once a year and the youngsters were quite awkward at it. They were supposed to kneel, kowtow three times, rise, then repeat the whole process twice more. But the nine couldn't co-ordinate their movements. The little boys Chueh-chun and Chueh-shih were too slow. Before they finished their first three kowtows, the others had already risen. Chueh-chun and Chueh-shih scrambled to their feet, but the others had already knelt for the second set. Some of the watchers chuckled, and Madam Wang, mother of the two youngsters, kept urging them to hurry. Amid general laughter, the nine young heads quickly bobbed to a finish. They were capable of much greater speed than their elders.

Jui-chueh led four girls to the velvet kneeling cushion—Shu-ying, Shu-hua, Shu-chen and Shu-fen. Their movements, though naturally a little slower, were considerably more orderly than the boys'. Even Shu-fen, though only seven, was quite graceful. Jui-chueh then brought forward her little son Hai-chen, to pay his respects.

The servants removed the velvet cover from the kneeling cushion, and Ke-ming went to the next room to invite the Venerable Master Kao to emerge again. After the old man came out, all the men and women of Ke-ming's generation knelt around him in a circle and kowtowed. They were followed by the grandsons and granddaughters. The old man received their respects with a smiling face, then he retired to his own room.

A festive air filled the hall after the old man left. The men

115

and women of the older generation formed a semicircle on the velvet carpet and kowtowed to one another. Grandchildren kowtowed to their parents, then bent the knee to their aunts and uncles. Finally, at Madam Chou's suggestion, everyone gathered in a large circle, joking and talking only of "auspicious" things. The children and young people then ran off to play, but Chueh-hsin and his wife remained with the elder generation to receive the respects of the servants.

Chueh-min and Chueh-hui ran from the hall through the side door and hurried towards their room to avoid the servants' obeisances. But they were caught as they were passing Madam Chou's flat. First, old Mama Huang made them a very respectful curtsey and wished them well from her heart. Moved, the boys clasped both hands before their faces, and swung them down as they bowed. Three other women servants followed.

Last came Ming-feng. There was a faint sprinkling of powder on her face and the dark braid of her hair shone lustrously. Over her cotton-padded jacket, she wore a new short coat of fine cloth with a rolled edge-trimming. After curtseying to Chueh-min, she turned to Chueh-hui with a smile. "Third Young Master," she hailed him, and bent her body in a brief bow. Happily Chueh-hui returned her greeting.

During that instant as they openly smiled at each other, he forgot the past, and the world seemed a beautiful place. It was quite reasonable that he should feel this way, for everywhere in the compound were the sounds of joy and merriment. As to the broad world beyond the compound walls, young Chueh-hui didn't give it a thought. He even forgot the little beggar child he had seen the night before.

A servant came down the steps outside the family hall and shouted, "Set off the fireworks!" A voice further away relayed his command. From the outer courtyard between the front gate and the inner gate, a dazzling display of pyrotechnics shot into the sky. One burst followed another, eight or nine times in succession. These fireworks had been presented by Chin's mother, Mrs. Chang. The Venerable Master Kao sat on a chair placed for him in the doorway of the family hall. Surrounded by his daughters-in-law, he watched and made critical comment on the show.

Chueh-hui and his young boy cousins went to the main hall in the front courtyard where they could get a better view. The youngsters had already bought some fireworks of their own —"Drops of Gold," "Scurrying Mice" and "Miraculous Book and Arrows"—and were waiting to set them off.

When the display ended, the elders in the family hall departed. Chueh-hsin and his three uncles called for sedan-chairs and left to pay their Year's End respects to socially prominent friends. Chueh-hui stood outside the main hall watching his young cousins set off their fireworks.

In the old man's room a game table was placed, and the Venerable Master Kao, Madam Chou, Madam Chang and Madam Wang played mahjong. The heavily made-up Mistress Chen, who had just removed her pink outer skirt, sat beside the old man, helping him with the game. Women servants and bondmaids stood around to fill the water-pipes and serve tea.

Jui-chueh, Shu-ying, Shu-hua and Madam Shen played mahjong in Chueh-hsin's room. As hostess, Jui-chueh offered to relinquish her place to Chueh-min. But he refused and was only willing to stand behind her and watch her play one game. Then he left.

Instead of returning to his room, Chueh-min joined Chueh-hui and his young cousins outside the main hall. Chueh-hui was setting off a "Miraculous Book and Arrows" for the boys. A fiery ball shot up over the rooftops, where it disappeared in mid-air—a dud. Chueh-min walked up to Chueh-hui and said quietly in his ear:

"Let's go and see Chin."

Chueh-hui nodded and the two brothers walked off, ignoring the pleas of their young cousins that they stay and finish the fireworks.

From the eaves of the front gateway, the large lanterns still shone with a hazy red glow that shimmered in the cold air. The old gatekeeper, seated on an ancient straight-backed wooden armchair chatting with a sedan-chair carrier who sat on a bench opposite, rose respectfully to his feet as the brothers walked by.

Crossing the high iron-bound threshold, they noticed a thin dark face beside the stone lion to the right of the gate. Not

117

recognizing the countenance of their former servant, Kao Sheng, in the dim light of the lantern, they strode on into the street.

Kao Sheng had served in the Kao family for over ten years. Then he became addicted to opium smoking and stole some pictures belonging to the Venerable Master Kao and sold them. When the theft was discovered, he spent a term in jail. On his release, he drifted about from place to place, begging. But at every important holiday he returned to the home of his former master to plead for the small cash gift customarily given to servants at such times. Too ashamed of his tattered clothes to enter the compound, he would wait outside the main gate until a servant who had worked together with him would come out, and beseech the man to relay his request. Because his requests were always very modest, and made at a time when his former master was in good spirits, he usually attained his purpose. As time went on these hand-outs became an established custom.

Today, he had received his small gratuity, as usual. But this time he did not leave immediately. Instead, he remained concealed behind one of the stone lions, rubbing his hand over an icy flank that did not shrink from his caress, picturing the festivities he knew must be going on inside the compound.

When the two brothers emerged, he had recognized them. He remembered Chueh-hui particularly well, for the Third Young Master used to lie on his bed and listen to him tell stories in the light of the opium lamp. He wanted to come forward, to talk with them, fondly. But then, conscious of the shabby state of his clothes, and recalling his disgrace, he drew back, squatting behind the lion to avoid being seen.

Only after the brothers were well down the street did he rise and stare after them, keeping his misty eyes upon them until they were out of sight. He stood in the centre of the street, oblivious of the merciless wind biting through the thin garments covering his bony frame. A loneliness such as he had never felt before gnawed at his heart, and he walked listlessly away, one hand holding the money his master had given, the other clutching his chest.

At this very moment, Chueh-min and Chueh-hui were

striding along, light-hearted and gay, stepping over the remains of fireworks. They walked through quiet streets and noisy, past shops in front of which burned pairs of huge candles, until they finally reached the home of Chin and Mrs. Chang. Their minds were filled with many cheerful things, and they gave never a thought to the man named Kao Sheng.

The Chang home had a cold appearance. A lonely kerosene lamp hung from a beam in the gateway, revealing its bareness.

Although not very large, the compound was shared by three families. The heads of two of these families were widows, and there were only two or three adult men in the entire compound, so that life here was quiet. Even on New Year's Eve the place was only a bit more lively than usual.

And the Chang family was the most quiet of all, for it consisted of only mother and daughter. Chin also had a grandmother who lived in a nunnery, but she seldom came home. The family was served by a man and a woman who had been with the Changs for over ten years.

As the boys entered the east courtyard in which the Changs lived, the man servant came forward to greet them. Outside Mrs. Chang's window, the boys called "Aunt!" and they heard her respond. They then went in and knelt before her, saying, "Our respects to Aunt on the End of the Year." Although she protested that such courtesy was "unnecessary," it was too late to stop them. Chin also came in, and the boys clasped their hands and bowed to her ceremoniously. Mrs. Chang invited them to sit in the family parlour, while the woman servant, Sister Li, went to make some tea.

The boys learned from Mrs. Chang that their brother Chueh-hsin and their uncle Ke-ming had already paid her a formal call, but had left early. They chatted a while with Mrs. Chang and asked her to spend the New Year Holiday in the Kao compound, the home of her childhood. She said she first had to take Chin to visit her grandmother at the nunnery, but that they would come to the Kaos on the second. She herself would stay only a day or so, because she preferred quiet, but she would let Chin remain a few days more. This made the boys very happy. Chin asked them to come to her room for a while. They followed as she led the way.

To their surprise, they found another girl there. Slim, wearing a rust-coloured satin vest over a pale blue silken gown, the girl sat on the edge of the bed reading beside an oil lamp. She raised her head at the sound of their footsteps, then put down the book and stood up.

The boys stared at her, speechless.

"Don't you recognize her?" asked Chin, surprised.

The girl smiled at them, a sad, helpless smile that deepened the furrow on her forehead, a furrow that somehow heightened her beauty and intensified her melancholy air.

"Yes, of course," replied Chueh-hui wryly. This girl had left a permanent impression on the boys. Time had passed quickly, yet here she was before them, as beautiful and as sad as ever, still slim, with the same head of thick fine hair, the same limpid eyes. Only the furrow in her brow was deeper now, her long braid of hair had been done up in a married woman's bun, and her face was slightly powdered. They had never expected to see her here.

"Are you all well? . . . It's been a long time!" Though her words were ordinary, Mei had to make a great effort to speak them.

"We're all fine, Cousin Mei. And you?" Chueh-min replied warmly. He forced a laugh.

"Still the same. Except that the last few years I've become even more sensitive. I'm very easily hurt. I don't know why." Mei knit her brows. She was still the same disturbing personality. "I always have been on the melancholy side," she added.

"Environment makes a difference," said Chueh-hui. "But you don't look any different."

"Why don't you sit down? What are you all standing for?" Chin interrupted. "Just because you haven't seen each other for a couple of years, that's no reason to become so formal."

Everyone sat down, Chin seating herself beside Mei on the bed.

"I thought of you often after we parted. The last few years have been like a bad dream. Well, now it's over, and I'm left with nothing but an empty heart," said Mei. Then she immediately corrected herself: "No, I'm dreaming yet. Who knows when I'll really awake? I have no regrets for myself. I'm only sorry I delayed the happiness of someone else."

"You shouldn't be so pessimistic, Cousin Mei. You're still young. Who can predict what the future will bring? Happiness will come to you too. There's no need for such gloomy talk!" said Chin, patting Mei's shoulder. "We're entering a new age. It may be bringing you happiness." Smilingly, Chin added a few words in Mei's ear.

Mei coloured slightly, and her brows relaxed. A touch of brightness flitted across her face. Looking at Chin, she pushed a lock of hair back into place. But then her features were again overcast, and she said to Chin with a melancholy smile:

"I think there's a lot in what Third Brother says—environment does make a difference. Our circumstances are very different. I can't be like you. I can't keep up with the changing times. All my life I've been a plaything of Fate. I was never allowed to make up my own mind about anything. What hope have I for happiness?" Squeezing Chin's hand, Mei cocked her head to one side and gazed at her friend approvingly. "I certainly envy you. You have courage and strength. You never let yourself be pushed around."

Chin was pleased with Mei's admiration, but her feeling of satisfaction drifted by like a passing breeze. She was left only with the sad smile that some girls use when confronted with an insoluble problem. Though praised for her "courage and strength," Chin had no choice but to resort to that kind of a smile now.

"Circumstances are certainly important, but why can't we change them?" Chueh-hui interjected heatedly. "Circumstances are man-made to begin with, and man must struggle against them constantly. It's only by conquering our environment that we can win happiness for ourselves." There was much more he wanted to say, but didn't.

In Chueh-min, Mei aroused varying emotions—sadness, satisfaction, alarm, pity, fear. Not only for Mei, but for himself as well. Yet seeing the firm expression on Chin's face, he recovered his calm. He was even able to find words of comfort for Mei.

121

"You've had a great deal of trouble the past few years, so you're often downhearted. But in the next few years, things are sure to change, and you'll change too. Actually, Chin's situation isn't much better than yours, except that you've been married—let's say you've had one more bad dream than she. The world is the same, the difference is that you look at the dark side and she looks at the bright. That's why you're so easily hurt, while nothing deters Chin."

"Cousin Mei, why not read more of the new books? Chin has some here," said Chueh-hui. He thought the new books could solve all problems.

Mei smiled sadly. She did not answer at once, but looked at them with her limpid eyes. They couldn't guess what was on her mind. Suddenly she withdrew her gaze and stared at the lamp flame and sighed. . . . She started to speak, then hesitated and silently gnawed her lip. Finally she said, "You all mean well, but it's no use. What's the good of reading new books?" She paused, then went on again, "Everything is beyond redemption. No matter how the times change, my situation will never change."

Chueh-min had nothing more to say. He knew she was right—everything was beyond redemption; she had married and Big Brother now had Sister-in-law. No change in the times could bring them together again. Moreover, their mothers had become enemies.

Even Chueh-hui was beginning to realize that the solution to many problems could not be found in books.

Everyone sat trying to think of an appropriate remark. It was Mei who finally broke the silence.

"I was just looking at some of Chin's *New Youth* magazines. Of course, there are some things in them I don't understand, but there's a lot I do. They have some good articles. I know, because I've suffered. But reading them only makes me feel bad. They talk about another world, a world that has nothing to do with me. Although I admire it, I know I can never reach it. I feel like a beggar standing outside the garden wall of some wealthy home and hearing the laughter inside, or smelling the fragrance of meat cooking as I pass the door of a restaurant. It's sheer agony!"

122

The furrow in Mei's brow deepened. She drew a hand-kerchief from her bosom and coughed into it a few times, then smiled mournfully. "I've been coughing a lot lately. At night I can't sleep. My heart pains me."

"Forget about the past, Cousin Mei," Chin begged. She was close to tears. "Why torture yourself? You should take care of your health more. Our hearts ache too to see you this way."

Mei gave Chin a smile and nodded gratefully, but her voice was still sad. "You know my disposition. I can never forget the past. It seems engraved upon my heart. You don't know how I spend my days. My home is much the same as yours, except that in addition to my mother I also have a younger brother. He's busy preparing for his entrance exams; mother is either playing mahjong or visiting friends. I'm alone in the house. I sit reading poetry, without a single person I can tell my troubles to. . . .

"I see fading flowers and I weep. The waning moon hurts my heart. Everything recalls unhappy memories. It's a year now since I left my husband's family and returned to my mother. There's a tree outside my window that I planted when I went away to be married. It was budding then, but by the time I returned, its branches were bare. I often think—that tree symbolizes me. . . . There was a storm a few nights ago, and I lay on my bed, unable to sleep. The rain beat incessantly on the roof tiles and windows. In the dim lamplight, I thought of the lines of a poem:

> *The wind and rain recalls to my heart*
> *The past, so like a misty dream. . . .*

You can imagine how I felt! Tomorrow, tomorrow—you all have a tomorrow, but what kind of tomorrow have I? I have only yesterday. The events of yesterday are painful things, but they are all I have to console myself with."

Suddenly the tone of Mei's voice changed, and she asked the boys, "How is Big Brother? Is he well?"

The boys had been quite moved, listening to her talk, and this abrupt change of mood took them by surprise. Finally,

Chueh-hui, the more quick-witted of the two, managed a brief reply.

"Not bad. He said he saw you the other day."

Only Mei understood the meaning of this. Chin and Chueh-min stared at Chueh-hui in astonishment.

"It's true, we have already met. I recognized him the moment I saw him. He looks a bit older. Perhaps he's angry with me for avoiding him. I wanted very much to talk to him, but I was afraid of stirring up old memories. He would be hurt and so would I. Besides, my mother was there. He came here a little while ago. I heard his voice, but I was afraid to look at him through a crack in the door. Only when he was leaving did I steal a glance at him as he walked away."

"I'm sure he's not angry," said Chueh-hui.

"Don't talk about those things any more," urged Chin. "I was afraid you'd feel lonely over the New Year. That's why I invited you here. I didn't know it would only make you think of the past even more. It's all my fault for bringing the boys in to see you."

Gradually, Mei's melancholy diminished. Although her brows were still slightly knit, her face brightened and she smiled, "It doesn't matter. Getting all this off my mind has done me good. At home I have no one to talk to. Besides, I enjoy talking about the old days."

Then she asked the boys many solicitous questions about their Big Brother and their Sister-in-law.

XVI

It was past eleven when Chueh-min and Chueh-hui left the Changs, but there was still considerable activity in the streets. Walking along the cobble-stoned thoroughfare and observing the brightly burning lamps in the stores and wine shops that lined the way, they shook off the depression their meeting with Mei had engendered.

Anxious to get home, they walked rapidly and in silence. Their own street, when they reached it, was quiet and littered with the remains of fireworks. But as they neared the stone lions flanking the gateway of the Kao compound, they could already feel the gaiety and activity seething inside.

All of the doors of the gatehouse were open. Servants and sedan-chair carriers were crowded around a dimly lit table, noisily playing a dice game. The doors of the family parlour were open too, and the boys could see their aunts and uncles, or most of them, surrounding a well-lit table, engrossed in a dice game of their own. Uncle Ke-ting and Aunt Wang were the most boisterous of the lot.

Hearing the clatter of mahjong dominoes in Chueh-hsin's room, Chueh-hui stopped in and watched the game for a little while, then left. The clicking of dice, the clink of coins, laughter and chatter, swept after him in gusts of sound. He stood on the steps, like a spectator at a play, and watched the revellers move about, laugh, shout.

Suddenly he felt lonely and far removed from all this festivity. A chill enveloped him and he was weighed down by a nameless despair. No one sympathized with him or cared about him. He seemed completely isolated.

Chueh-hui found these peculiar surroundings increasingly difficult to comprehend. On previous New Year's Eves he had been able to join in the festivities, merrily, whole-heartedly, forgetting everything as he laughed and played with the other young people. But today he stood alone in the darkness listening to the laughter of others. He seemed to be living in another world.

Has this place changed, of have I? he asked himself. Though he had no definite answer to the question, he knew that he and this big family were travelling in two opposite directions. He recalled Mama Huang's remark about "clear and muddy water."

To calm the confusion in his mind, he came down the steps to walk along paths that were unobstructed.

Passing through a corridor, he turned into an inner courtyard. The sound of laughter was gradually left behind him. He stopped, and discovered that he was outside the room of his sister Shu-hua. On the other side of the courtyard the flat of his uncle Ke-an stood brightly illuminated. A wistaria vine clambered over a trellis arbour in the garden separating the two dwellings. Chueh-hui sat down on a straight-backed chair outside his sister's window and gazed dully at the kitchen in the corner diagonally opposite. Through the open door of the kitchen, he could see women servants bustling about.

He heard a low familiar voice in Shu-hua's room say, "I hear they're going to pick one of us two. . . ." The speaker was Wan-erh, bondmaid in the Third Household of Chueh-hui's uncle Ke-ming, a long-faced girl about a year older than Ming-feng, who spoke rather quickly.

The remark came suddenly, and it drew Chueh-hui's attention. Sensing that there was something unusual behind it, he listened with bated breath.

"Needless to say, you'll be the lucky one," said the voice of Ming-feng, with a giggle.

"I'm serious. How can you have the heart to laugh at me?" Wan-erh retorted hotly.

"I congratulate you on your good fortune—does that make me heartless?" laughed Ming-feng.

"Who wants to be a concubine!" Wan-erh's anger mounted, but there was misery in her voice.

"A concubine's life is not so bad. Look at the Venerable Master's Mistress Chen."

"Got an answer to everything, haven't you? Just wait, we'll see who they pick. Your turn is coming sooner or later," Wan-erh replied in agitation. She laughed spitefully.

Chueh-hui's heart pounded. Repressing an urge to cry out, he listened intently, waiting to hear what Ming-feng would say.

Apparently realizing that this was no joking matter, Ming-feng remained silent for a long time. The only sound was the steady ticking of the clock on the wall. Chueh-hui was growing impatient, but he couldn't tear himself away.

"If they choose me, what shall I do?" Ming-feng asked despairingly.

"All you can do is go, cursing your fate," was Wan-erh's bitter response.

"No, no, I can't go, I couldn't. I'd rather die than be that old man's concubine!" Ming-feng cried desperately, as if already faced with the prospect. Her voice shook tragically.

"Maybe it's not true. Maybe someone has only made it up to scare us. If it ever really came to that, we could still think of a way out. We could ask Madam Chou to help us," said Wan-erh, somewhat mollified by Ming-feng's words. She seemed to be trying to console herself as much as to soothe the younger girl.

Chueh-hui sat motionless in the straight-backed chair, oblivious to time and place, deaf to the maids laughing and chatting in the kitchen. Servants carrying platters of food occasionally passed by Uncle Ke-an's window. They never gave Chueh-hui a glance. The laughter in the kitchen grated on his ears; it sounded raucous, mocking.

"I have an idea that you're in love with someone. Am I right?" Wan-erh asked Ming-feng softly. She spoke more slowly than usual.

Ming-feng didn't answer, and Wan-erh gently pressed, "You are in love, aren't you? You've been acting rather strange lately. Why don't you tell me the truth? I won't tell anyone. I'm like your elder sister. You shouldn't hold anything back from me."

Ming-feng whispered a few words in Wan-erh's ear. Though Chueh-hui listened with all his might, he was unable to hear what she said.

"Who is it? Tell me," Wan-erh demanded with a laugh. Electrified, Chueh-hui strained his ears.

"I won't tell you." Ming-feng's voice shook a little.

"Is it Kao Chung?" Wan-erh persisted. Kao Chung was the young servant who worked for Uncle Ke-ting. Chueh-hui released his breath and a weight seemed to drop from his heart.

"Him? Ha! Why should anyone love him! You're the one who's after his heart but you won't admit it," laughed Ming-feng.

"I was asking you in earnest. How can you say such things?" Wan-erh retorted. "Are you sure Kao Chung isn't in love with you?"

"Oh, good sister, no more nonsense!" Ming-feng pleaded. "Let's talk sensibly."

Then in a lowered tone she continued, "You can't guess, and I won't tell you. I'm the only one who knows his name." She felt safe and secure when she thought of him, and happiness crept into her voice.

The girls' voices dropped lower and lower, until Chueh-hui could catch only snatches of it, interspersed with muffled laughter. He gathered that Wan-erh was talking about her own romance. One of the older women servants shouted for her from one of the front buildings, but Wan-erh paid no attention and went on with her story. Only when the calls drew very close and it seemed that the older servant was about to enter the room where the girls were hiding did Wan-erh reply.

"We're at their beck and call all day long. Even on New Year's Eve we can't get any rest," she grumbled as she walked out.

Ming-feng was left alone in the room. She sat silent, motionless.

Chueh-hui knelt on his chair and, poking a small hole in the paper window, peered inside. Ming-feng was sitting on a cane chair, her elbows on the desk, supporting her face in her hands, the little finger of her right hand tucked in the corner of her mouth. She was staring at the pewter oil lamp whose stem was festooned with cedar twigs and clusters of peanuts.

Suddenly she sighed. "What is the future going to bring?" She leaned forward and buried her head on the desk.

Chueh-hui tapped lightly on the small pane of glass in the centre of the window. There was no response. He rapped more loudly, and called in a low voice, "Ming-feng, Ming-feng."

The girl raised her head, and looked around. Seeing nothing, she sighed again. "I must have been dreaming. I thought I heard someone calling me." Listlessly, she pushed herself up from the desk and rose to her feet. The lamplight cast the shadow of her early-ripening young form against the bed canopy.

128

Chueh-hui rapped harder and called her name several times.

When she at last determined where the sound was coming from, Ming-feng hurried over and knelt on the chair beside the window. Leaning against the chair back, she asked, "Who is it?"

"It's me," Chueh-hui replied quickly. His voice was low. "Lift the curtain. I want to ask you something."

"It's you, Third Young Master?" cried Ming-feng, surprised. She raised the paper curtain, painted with grass and flowers, and saw the tense face of Chueh-hui pressed against the pane of glass. "What's wrong?" she asked in alarm.

"I heard what you and Wan-erh were saying just now—"

Blushing, Ming-feng cut him short. "You heard us? We were only joking."

"Don't try to fool me," Chueh-hui replied excitedly. "Suppose there really comes a day when they want to marry you off. What will you do then?"

For several minutes Ming-feng did not speak. Suddenly tears began to roll from her eyes. She did not wipe them away but, taking a grip on herself, said with utmost determination, "I won't go. I'll never go to another man. I give you my vow!"

Chueh-hui hastily pressed his hand against the glass, as if to seal her mouth. "I believe you," he assured her. "You don't have to swear."

Like one awakening from a dream, Ming-feng remembered where they were. Urgently she rapped on the glass, pleading, "Go away, Third Young Master. Someone is liable to see you."

"I won't go until you tell me what's happening."

"All right, I'll tell you. But then you must go, please, dear Young Master. . . ."

Chueh-hui nodded.

"They say your grandfather's old friend Feng is looking for a concubine. Mrs. Feng came here to help him find one among us bondmaids. Wan-erh heard from her mistress that the Venerable Master had agreed, and she told me. As to how we feel, well, you just heard us. . . . Now please go. It would

129

be bad if anyone saw you here." Ming-feng firmly pulled the curtain back into place and refused to open it again, no matter how much Chueh-hui rapped and called.

Defeated, he got down from the chair and stood dully on the steps. His mind was alive with many things. Though his eyes were facing the kitchen, he saw nothing.

Inside, Ming-feng remained kneeling on the chair. Thinking Chueh-hui had gone, she cautiously raised the curtain and peeked out. When she saw him still standing there, she was touched. Unconsciously, she pressed her face against the glass and gazed abstractedly at his back.

XVII

When Chueh-hui returned to his room, the sound of dice rolling in a bowl had already stopped, but many people remained chatting around the game table. Although the mah-jong tiles were still clicking in Chueh-hsin's room, they were not nearly so noisy. The sky was beginning to lighten. The year was ending. The old was disappearing with the darkness, and the new and bright was emerging.

At the hour for prayers to the gods, Chueh-hui went to the family hall. Because young Chueh-chun had let slip an unlucky remark there, the Venerable Master Kao wrote the phrase "A child's words cannot prevent good fortune and prosperity" on a piece of red paper and pasted it on the door post. Chueh-hui couldn't help smiling.

Firecrackers began bursting outside the main hall. Three long strings in succession were set off; they were still popping when the last of the worshippers had entered the hall. It was then already daylight.

Chueh-hsin and his three uncles got into sedan-chairs and went off to pay their New Year calls. The women of the family, stepping over the remnants of exploded firecrackers, walked smilingly through the main gate and out on to the street. This was the women's annual comedy of "going abroad." It was only during this brief interval each year that they were permitted to travel freely in public, other than in closed sedan-chairs. The women feasted their curious eyes on the sleepy little street. Then, fearful of meeting any strange men, they hurried back into the compound. The firecrackers were finished, the laughter was stilled. For a short time, the street again lapsed into silence.

With the important events of the day over, most of the Kao family, having been up all night, went to bed early. Except for people like Chueh-hsin and his uncle Ke-ming, who had many social functions to perform, nearly everyone slept through until the evening prayer service. A few, like Chueh-min and Chueh-hui, didn't even get up for dinner.

The days of the New Year Holiday thus passed smoothly. Each day's programme was arranged in advance, much the same as in previous years. Gambling went on apace; the sound of dice and mahjong almost never stopped. Even Chien-yun, who considered gambling pointless, also took part, unhesitatingly acting against his own desires for the sake of pleasing others. In these intervals he was able to shake off a bit of his melancholy and enjoy a pittance of fun.

On the second day of the New Year, Chin and her mother arrived. Mrs. Chang remained three days, then returned home, permitting Chin to stay on until the sixteenth.

Having Chin with them greatly added to the young people's enjoyment. All day they played games in the garden or told stories. They would each contribute and send one of the servants to buy spicy and salty delicacies which they would take to the foot of the hill behind the "Fragrance at Eventide" building, and heat up picnic lunches on a small stove. The girls Jui-chueh, Shu-ying and Chin were good cooks, and they took turns at preparing the meals, with the rest of the young folks helping out. When the food was ready it would either be brought into "Fragrance at Eventide," or to some other clean, quiet spot, and placed upon a table. Then everyone would set to eating with a will, to the accompaniment of noisy wine-drinking games.

One day they had a visitor—Hsu Chien-ju, a classmate of

Chin. Chien-ju lived in a compound diagonally opposite the Kaos. She was a plump girl of eighteen or so, outspoken, with a free and easy manner, very much the modern schoolgirl. Like Chin, she was dying to get into the boys' school. She was anxious to meet Chueh-hui and Chueh-min and ask when their school was going to life its ban against girls.

Chien-ju's father was active in the Tung-meng Hui Society.[26] In his youth, he had attended a university in Japan. Later, he managed a revolutionary newspaper advocating the overthrow of the Manchus. He now held a post in the Bureau of Foreign Affairs of the Szechuan Provincial Government. He was much more advanced in his thinking than the average man of his day.

Chien-ju's mother, who had also studied abroad, had died two years before, but her father had not remarried. An only daughter, Chien-ju was still looked after by an old nursemaid who had cared for her ever since she was born.

Brought up in this enlightened environment, it was inevitable that Chien-ju should be quite different in personality from Chin. But the two girls were very good friends.

Chien-yun also spent a few days with them. He seemed somewhat happier, and although Chueh-min could not entirely conceal his dislike, the other boys were very good to him.

On the evening of the eighth, after the young people had prepared for two whole days, they invited their elders to the garden to watch some fireworks. Unable to resist the youngsters' ardent entreaties, the grown-ups, with the exception of *Yeh-yeh*, who couldn't take too much of the evening cold, arrived on time.

All the electric lights in the garden were blazing. In addition, small lanterns of red and green and yellow burned on the branches of the bamboo and cypress trees. The illuminated railings of the arched stone bridge joined their reflections in

[26] "Alliance Society," founded in 1905, and a predecessor of the Kuomintang (organized in 1912). This was a revolutionary organization headed by Sun Yat-sen which advocated overthrow of the Manchu (Ch'ing) Dynasty, establishment of a republican government and a broad program of social reforms.

the water to make perfect circles. Big panelled red lanterns with dangling tassels hung from the eaves of "Fragrance at Eventide," casting soft pink shadows that evoked a dream-like atmosphere.

The audience took their seats inside the building beside the widely opened windows. Except for a few faint coloured shadows here and there, outside all was dark.

"Where are the fireworks? You've fooled us," said Madam Chou with a laugh.

"You'll see them in a minute," replied Chin, smiling. She looked around and observed that the boys had already disappeared.

In the inky stillness beyond the windows, suddenly, from a somewhat lighter patch of darkness, came a piercing sound, and a ball of red flame rose high into the black sky, burst into a shower of golden rain, then melted back into the night. Immediately a snow-white thing like a goose egg shot heavenward. There was a shattering explosion, and silver sparks flew in all directions. Then a blue light streaked up into the sky, where it changed colour and came down in droplets of red, quickly turning into a shower of green. The last was so brilliant that even after it vanished, the audience still saw green shadows before their eyes.

"How lovely," said Madam Chou. "Where did you buy them?"

Chin only laughed, but did not reply. In the light of the dazzling fireworks that followed, a small boat was revealed near the opposite shore of the lake.

"So that's where they've been setting them off. No wonder they seemed to rise from a different place each time," Madam Wang remarked to her husband Ke-an. He nodded and smiled.

For a time the lake was absolutely still. The watchers craned their necks, but their eyes couldn't pierce the darkness.

"Is it over?" Ke-ting asked regretfully. As he started to rise, the lake burst into light.

A myriad of fireworks streaked and flowered all over the sky. After a while, darkness again descended. The air trembled and the clear notes of a bamboo flute sailed up from the lake,

133

to the muted accompaniment of a bow on a two-stringed *hu chin*, lulling its listeners with a melody that charmed like an ancient fairy tale, making them forget their petty cares, evoking old dreams, dreams that were never fulfilled.

"Who is that, playing so well?" asked Madam Chou, when the tune was nearly over.

Listening entranced, Chin was a bit shaken by the sudden question. "Cousin Shu-ying," she whispered quickly. "And that's Big Brother on the *hu chin*."[27] She again concentrated on the concluding performance.

The flute stopped, and in the distance there was applause and laughter. Striking the quiet surface of the lake, they were at once swallowed up, and did not float to the surface again. Only a few sounds that had escaped the water reached the audience on the wings of a breeze; and these were already very faint, dying with the lingering echoes of the melody's last few notes.

Then the mellow tones of the flute again soared forth in a lively and cheerful air, and a strong male voice joined in song, penetrating the dark night, driving away the echoes of the earlier melody. The listeners in the building were awakened from their misty reveries; they recognized the voice of Chueh-min.

The singing did not last very long. Soon, together with the sound of the flute, it faded away in the darkness. Then Chueh-min's voice rose again, this time in a popular operatic aria. As he launched into the second line, he was joined by a chorus of mixed voices. But even as these blended together, it was still possible to distinguish the individual singers; the crisp soprano of Shu-ying was not drowned out by the vibrant baritone of Chueh-min. The forceful music struck the audience like a blow in the face. It poured into their ears; overflowing, it flew all around them; it seemed to rock the very building they were sitting in.

Then, just as the audience's tension was at its height, the singing abruptly stopped. But this was immediately followed

[27] An ancient Chinese musical instrument, similar to a violin, with two strings.

by a great roar of laughter—the audience wasn't give a moment's rest. The laughing voices collided with one another in mid-air. Some splintered into thready slivers, shattered beyond repair; a new laugh would rise, pursue one that was still intact, and smash it to bits. To those in the building it seemed as though the laughter was battering, leaping, chasing through the darkness.

Little red and green lanterns began to appear, floating on the lake, one after another. Before long, that patch of water on which the audience was concentrating its attention was covered with lanterns. They moved slowly, reflecting strange colours on the surface of the water, changing, bobbing, but without a sound. Suddenly, there was a flurry of activity, and the lanterns separated to leave a lane in the middle. Again there was laughter—this time more subdued. A small boat loaded with laughter slowly drew near, and stopped beside the bridge. The laughing voices were now much clearer to the people in the building; they could see Chueh-hsin and his brothers coming ashore. The boat then passed under the hump-backed bridge and approached the near bank. To the surprise of the audience, there was another boat behind it. This one remained at the bridge, and several girls got out— Shu-ying, Shu-hua and Shu-chen, all carrying lanterns.

As the young people came into the building, the atmosphere grew lively.

"Well, how did you like it?" cried Chueh-hsin with a laugh.

"Excellent," commended Uncle Ke-ting. "Tomorrow night I'm inviting you all to see a dragon dance. I'm preparing the 'fire tubes' myself."

Chueh-ying excitedly clapped his hands, and the other young people joined in with exclamations of approval.

The performance that night had indeed brightened the lives of the older folks like a rainbow. But in a little while everything returned to its original form, and the garden again stood quietly in the chill darkness.

XVIII

On the ninth day of the New Year, the young boys Chueh-ying, Chueh-chun and Chueh-shih were extremely busy. From early morning, they laboured all through the day, helping the sedan-chair carriers make fireworks and discussing the coming dragon dance.

That morning Uncle Ke-ting's carriers had cut down two thick bamboos and sawed them into segments. With the aid of the other carriers, these were packed with gunpowder, fuses and bits of copper coins—the last because they would stick to the skin of their human targets and burn without dropping off. Everyone worked with a will, and the dozen-odd tubes were soon ready. The tubes were then placed on exhibition in the gatehouse for all to admire. Proudly lined up on a long bench, they stonily awaited their victims.

Time seemed to drag interminably, but dusk came at last. After the prayer services were over, Uncle Ke-ting took charge of the servants in making final arrangements. In the inner compound, a number of tables were set up and chairs placed on top of them to serve as a temporary grandstand. Ke-ting personally sealed the packets of coins to be awarded to the performers. He made several trips to the main gate to see if they were coming, while dispatching a servant to stand on the street corner to keep a lookout for them.

A quarter of an hour later, the whole compound stirred with excitement. By then the entire family, with the exception of the Venerable Master Kao, had taken their seats on the grandstand. The dragon dance troupe, beating drums and cymbals, entered the outer compound. The main gate was promptly closed behind them, to keep outsiders from slipping in under cover of the general tumult.

To the pounding beat of the drums and cymbals, the dragon began to dance. From head to tail, the dragon consisted of nine sections, made of paper pasted over bamboo frames and painted to resemble scales. Each section contained a lit candle, and was manipulated by a dancer who held it aloft by a bamboo handle. Ahead of the dragon pranced a youth twirling a staff with a big ball of coloured paper streamers at one end. The dragon bounded after the ball, rolling on the ground, or wagging its tail or shaking its head as if in great satisfaction, leaping and cavorting like a real dragon, while the beat of cymbals and drums seemed to add to its awesomeness.

A sharp report like the crack of a rifle bullet split the air. Firecrackers began to pop, and the dragon danced more wildly, as if angered. As firecrackers fell and exploded on its body, it dodged and twisted from left to right and made several startled leaps. The drums and cymbals roared more loudly, like the cries of a wounded dragon.

Perched on a ladder against the compound wall, Kao Chung, a young male servant, extended a long bamboo pole with a string of bursting firecrackers dangling from one end, over the dragon's body. A few sedan carriers who had been standing by, waiting with a powder-filled "fire tube," now ignited it and took turns spraying the flying sparks against the bare torsos of the dragon dancers. The maddened dragon rolled desperately on the ground, trembling from head to tail, trying to ward off the shower of hot sparks. People shouted, while the drums and cymbals crashed incessantly. The sedan-chair carriers laughed. The gentry on the grandstand laughed too, though in a much more refined way, of course.

Now the chair carriers attacked the dragon with four or five "fire tubes" from both sides. It was impossible for the dragon to escape. No matter how it writhed and rolled, the sparks streamed against the bare flesh of the dancers, some of the flame adhering to their bodies, making them halt their dancing and cry out loudly. Finally the dancers stood stock-still and, holding the poles by which they had manipulated their segments of the dragon end up like walking staffs, they struck bold poses and let the carriers spray them. Their only defence was to shake their bodies violently to throw off the sparks. The audience laughed approvingly, and the carriers moved in closer with their fire-spitting tubes, determined to make the dragon dancers beg for mercy.

Though strong, powerful men, the dancers made no attempt to defend themselves. In spite of the pain, they uttered fierce defiant cries.

"If you've got any more 'fire tubes,' bring them on!" they yelled.

But the dancers were only flesh and blood. When the flaming tubes came closer and closer, they broke and fled, the awesome dragon disintegrating into nine parts, as each man ran off with the segment he had been manipulating. The dragon's scales had been burned away completely, from head to tail, and all that remained of the segments were the bamboo frames.

Some of the dancers, carrying the empty frames on their shoulders, ran for the main gate. But it was already closed, and they had no choice but to steel themselves and return. At their master's signal, the chair porters again attacked with fresh "fire tubes." The compound was flat, offering no concealment, and several of the dancers ran towards the inner compound gate. But the gateway was jammed tight with spectators, presenting a solid screen of nothing but heads. As the dancers drew near, Uncle Ke-ting suddenly stepped forward with a flaming tube and sprayed, catching the youth who twirled the stick with the ball of coloured paper streamers. Uttering a sharp cry of pain, the boy turned and fled, only to be headed off and driven back by a servant armed with another "fire tube." The boy shook his body violently to ward off the burning sparks; his forehead was beaded with sweat.

Uncle Ke-ting, pursuing the dancer who had manipulated the dragon's tail, suddenly observed the trembling youth. "Are you cold?" he asked with a grin. "Here, this will warm you up a bit!" And he directed the full force of his fire against the boy at close range.

By instinct the youth raised his staff defensively, exposing the ball of paper streamers. The paper burst into flame; in a moment it was demolished by the blaze. Servants and chair carriers with spewing tubes of sparks were closing in now on the youth and the tail dancer, determined to make them beg for mercy. But just then the tubes burned out, and it was discovered that there were no more reserves; so the merry-makers were forced to desist.

The main gate was then opened. Carrying their clothes, the dancers again formed into ranks, took up the skeletal remains of the dragon and, to the bedraggled beat of drums and cymbals, wearily marched out of the compound. The youth who twirled the coloured ball had been hurt. He was muttering under his breath as he limped away.

Uncle Ke-ting had finished handing out the packets of money gratuities to the dancers. "Too bad we didn't have enough 'fire tubes,'" he said regretfully. "Were you satisfied? I'll invite you all to watch another show tomorrow night."

"I've had enough. I don't want to see any more," said Chueh-hui coldly.

Ke-ting looked at him uncomprehendingly. Other people, more polite, added, "It's not necessary."

The three young boys, Chueh-ying, Chueh-chun and Chueh-shih, who had had the best time of all, were already lost in the crowd. The rest of the gentry, well pleased, strolled back to the inner compound, while the servants quickly dismantled the temporary grandstand.

Chueh-min and Chueh-hui lagged behind with Chin. Chueh-hui asked her, "Did you find it interesting?"

"I didn't see anything interesting about it."

"Well, what was your reaction?"

"Nothing in particular."

"It was dull," Chueh-min interposed. "I used to like these shows a lot as a kid; not any more."

"You mean neither of you was the least bit moved?" Chueh-hui demanded sternly.

Chueh-min didn't know what his young brother was driving at. "It's just a low-class carnival act. How could it move anyone?" he protested.

"You didn't feel even a touch of sympathy?" Chueh-hui asked heatedly.

"What has sympathy got to do with it?" inquired Chin. "Uncle Ke-ting and his friends enjoyed themselves, and the dragon dancers got their money. Everybody was satisfied. What's wrong with that?"

"Spoken like a true daughter of the rich!" Chueh-hui laughed coldly. "Why can't an intelligent girl like you understand? Do you really think enjoyment should be based on others' pain? Do you think just paying money entitles you to sear a man's flesh? You talk as if you look at things with your eyes only half open!"

Chin did not reply. It was her habit when confronted with a question she could not answer to remain quiet and think, instead of plunging into an argument. She did not know that this was a problem to which her young girl's mind could never find a solution.

XIX

The weather was exceptionally fine the night of the fifteenth, the Lantern Festival.[28] A lovely full moon like a white jade platter hung suspended in the dark blue sky amid a sprinkling of bright stars and a few whisps of white clouds. Riding slowly through the heavens, the moon spread its rays on the world below.

That evening, the usual prayer service was concluded early. The little boys went out to the street to watch other dragon lanterns being burned up. The young people were gathered in Chueh-hsin's room, discussing how to spend the last night of Chin's visit. The New Year Holiday would end on the fif-

[28] The Lantern Festival began on the eighth day and ended on the seventeenth of the first month of the lunar calendar. During the Festival, houses, streets and shops were adorned with colorful lanterns in various forms, and firecrackers and fireworks were set off. The fifteenth day of the first month, when the full moon shone for the first time in the New Year, was the main day of the Festival. Special cakes called *yüan-hsiao* were eaten on that day.

teenth day of the first lunar month, and though Chin lived nearby they seldom had an opportunity to visit together for several full days at a time. They all agreed with Chueh-hsin's suggestion that they go rowing on the lake.

Originally, Jui-chueh was also going, but the baby began to cry just as they were leaving, and she stayed behind to look after him. The party consisted of Chueh-hsin and his two brothers, their sister Shu-hua and her two girl cousins, and Chin, with Ming-feng bringing a small hamper of food.

Slipping into the garden one after another, like a school of fish, they travelled along the covered walk. Shu-chen, the most timid of the girls, stuck close to Ming-feng. It was very quiet, and the scattered electric bulbs glowed dim and lonesome. A swath of moonlight in the long garden was mottled over with dark shadows.

The young people moved on slowly, chatting as they walked. As they reached the flower terrace, they suddenly heard a strange noise, and a dark shape leaped from the artificial hill to the tile roof of the covered walk, terrifying Shu-chen so that she shrank behind Ming-feng.

"What was that?" cried Shu-hua in a startled voice.

Everyone stood still. In the surrounding darkness nothing moved. Chueh-hui stamped his foot, but there was no response. He stepped across the railing, walked over to the flower terrace, picked up a few pebbles and tossed them on to the tile roof of the covered walk. A cat miaowed, then was heard scampering away.

"Only a cat," laughed Chueh-hui. Vaulting the railing back into the promenade, he noticed Shu-chen cringing behind Ming-feng. "Aren't you ashamed?" he twitted her. "Scared of nothing at all."

"My ma says there are ghosts in the garden," the girl replied in a quavering voice. She was clutching Ming-feng's hand tight.

"Ghosts? Who ever saw a ghost? Your mother was only teasing you, and you fell for it. What a simpleton!" Chueh-hui laughed.

"Why did you come with us if you're afraid of ghosts?" asked Chueh-hsin.

Shu-chen dropped Ming-feng's hand. "It's fun to be with you," she replied timidly. "I just had to come."

"Well said, dear. That's the way to talk," Chin commended with a smile. "Come on, I'll protect you. Don't worry. With me at your side, no ghost will dare come near you." Chin took her by the hand, and the two girls walked on together.

"Old Master Chiang, the famous ghost exorcizer, is here. All spirits disperse!" cried Shu-hua sarcastically, and everybody laughed.

They entered the bamboo grove. Although there were no electric lights here, the moonlight illuminated a small winding path. The grove was not very dense, and the sky was bright overhead. The bamboos rustled slightly in the breeze. From somewhere came the sound of running water; near the end of the grove the young people discovered a little brook.

To show his contempt for ghosts, Chueh-hui deliberately lagged behind, walking with Ming-feng. Suddenly he dashed into a bamboo thicket. At the noise, everyone turned around, and Chueh-min asked:

"Third Brother, what are you up to?"

Chueh-hui made no reply, but uprooted a young bamboo and, breaking off the thin end, shaped it into a staff. He rapped it experimentally against the ground, and said with satisfaction, "This will make a good walking stick." Then he rejoined Ming-feng.

The others laughed. "Is that all?" grinned Chueh-min. "I thought you had gone crazy and rushed off to dig for buried treasure!"

"Treasure? You are thinking of treasure all the time! I can see that before you have learned how to play *Treasure Island*, you have already been bewitched by the treasure," Chueh-hui retorted.

In high spirits, the group entered a grove of pines. Little of the moonlight filtered through the dense pine needles, and in the deepest part of the grove the path seemed to vanish completely. But they all knew the way well. With Chueh-hui in the lead, feeling out the twists and turns with his bamboo staff, they were able to proceed. The soughing of the pines somehow gave them a feeling of terror, a fear of the unfathomable darkness. Tensely, they moved slowly forward, Chin holding Shu-chen closely to her.

Gradually, the path ahead lightened, and then they saw the lake, silver and glistening in the moonlight. The reflection of the full moon, floating on the surface of the water, was pulled at times into an oval shape by the spreading ripples. Occasionally, a leaping fish splashed. Not far to the right was the humpbacked bridge. In the distance on the left, the twisting stone bridge leading to the pavilion in the centre of the lake was vaguely discernible.

Halting at the water's edge, the young people relaxed in the cool tranquillity. A stone, flung into the water, broke the moon's reflection, rippling it out into a large circle. Although the mirrored moon quickly resumed its original appearance, the ripples continued to widen until they vanished.

Chueh-min turned around to see Chueh-hui standing behind them, grinning.

"So it's you again," Chueh-min snorted.

"What are you all hanging around here for? The boat's over there." Chueh-hui pointed to a small craft moored to a willow on the opposite side of the bridge.

"No need for you to tell us. We saw it long ago," said Shu-hua. She pulled her long braid around from behind her. Toying with it, she looked up at the moon and began to sing an old tune.

Just as she had sung the first line, "When is the moon at its brightest," Chueh-min's vibrant voice joined in, then Chin and Shu-ying sang too. Chueh-hsin began to accompany them on his flute. At this point, Shu-ying borrowed Chueh-min's piccolo, saying:

"That flute's too reedy. This is sharper." Then the long clear notes of the piccolo pressed down on the thin, weakly piping flute. But some of the flute's mournful tears seeped through, and could still be heard.

Chueh-hui slowly strolled along the lake's edge towards the bridge, after beckoning Ming-feng to come with him. They exchanged a few brief words as they walked a distance, then Ming-feng turned around and rejoined the others. It wasn't until Chueh-hui had almost reached the bridge that he realized he was alone. He turned and went back to the group.

The beautiful surroundings suddenly irritated him. He felt he was somehow different from his brothers and his girl relatives. It seemed to him that under this peaceful exterior, his family harboured a smouldering volcano.

The song concluded, Shu-ying raised the piccolo to her lips to begin another. Chueh-hui stopped her.

"Let's wait till we get in the boat. What's the rush?"

With Chueh-hui in the lead and Ming-feng bringing up the rear, the young folk walked along the lake to the bridge and went across.

Chueh-hsin untied the boat and held it while everyone got in. Then, pushing off, he jumped into the stern and, taking up the tiller oar, started the boat moving.

Slowly passing under the hump-backed bridge, the boat entered the broad bosom of the lake. In the prow, Ming-feng opened the small hamper she had brought, and took out some salted vegetable bits, melon seeds and peanuts. She also produced a bottle of rose wine and some little winecups. She passed all these to Shu-ying and Shu-hua, who laid them on the small round table in the middle of the boat. Chueh-min pulled the cork from the bottle and poured the wine. In the direct rays of the moonlight, the young people set to eating and drinking.

Moonlight draped the now distant hump-backed bridge like shimmering gossamer, and the electric lights at the bridge's either end could be seen only dimly. Imperceptibly, the boat had slowly turned. The young people had been gazing up at the moon, and when they next looked around they discovered quite a different section of the lake. On one side was a sharp towering cliff; on the other, a building stood overlooking the water. The pavilion on the isle in the centre of the lake was now entirely visible, etched against the moonlight.

Chueh-hui's heart was bursting with things he wanted to say. To relieve the pressure, he let out an exuberant shout that rang and echoed against the cliffside.

"You certainly have a big voice," laughed Chueh-hsin, and he launched into a Peking opera aria.

Rounding the cliff, the boat passed the fishing pier. The

building overlooking the water was now screened by a dense growth of low trees.

"Big Brother, come over and have a drink, leave the boat alone, it will take care of itself," Shu-ying called from the other side.

"It's nice here, lots of room all by myself," Chueh-hsin answered, as he stopped rowing, took a drink, and had a few peanuts. The boat was steady, moving a little bit. As he finished his peanuts, he said as if to himself, "Let's moor the boat at the fishing pier, I have to go ashore." Thus, without waiting for any consensus, he edged the boat towards the fishing pier, which he succeeded in doing with some effort. He took the stone steps that led from the lower surface to the top, and in no time his head appeared over the stone balustrade, grinning at the group.

Shu-ying seized some melon seeds and threw them at Chueh-hsin, but he disappeared in no time, singing Peking opera lines as he left, his voice fainter and fainter, until it could not be heard any more.

"What a shame that we do not have another person here with us tonight," said Chin as if complaining.

"Sister-in-law, right?" Shu-hua offered in a hurry while still cracking melon seeds.

Chin shook her head.

"I know, it is Cousin Mei." But before Chueh-hui could finish Chueh-min checked him with a reproachful glance and the remark, "You are really impertinent, lower your voice lest Big Brother hears it."

"What if he hears it? He has already seen her anyway," argued Chueh-hui with nonchalance.

"He has seen Cousin Mei . . . ?" Shu-hua declared in surprise.

"Young Master," came Ming-feng's loud call from the prow. Everybody looked up to discover Chueh-hsin's head perched over the balustrade listening to them with attention. Silence reigned over all.

Chueh-hsin walked slowly down to the stone steps and then to the boat, sat himself again at the stern, and said to them, "Why did you stop talking when I got here?" His voice had in it a touch of anguish and pain.

"We forgot our subject as you came, but anyway it has nothing to do with you," Chueh-min tried to cover up.

"No use covering up, I heard clearly that you were talking about Cousin Mei and about me," Chueh-hsin replied with a bitter smile, while slowly moving the boat towards the middle of the lake.

"True, what Chin has in mind is, the night would be a much more enjoyable one if Cousin Mei were here." It was the straightforward Chueh-hui who burst it out. The boat was now passing the centre of the lake, drifting forward somewhat.

"Cousin Mei will never be here any more all her life long," Chueh-hsin said with a heavy sigh as he raised his head towards the sky. In so doing he tilted the boat, splashing water into it, and then instantly steadied it and restored its balance.

Clusters of white clouds appeared in the sky, the brilliant moon disk edged smoothly towards them. But everybody's attention was on Chueh-hsin, and the sky went unnoticed.

"In fact what we should have here tonight is not only Cousin Mei, but also Cousin Hui and Cousin Yun, of Grandma Chou. They used to come to visit us, what fun we had! Now they have been gone from Chengtu for three years already, how time flies!" Shu-ying said to Chueh-hsin with a tone half nostalgic and half emotional. She then turned to Chin: "Tomorrow you will be leaving us, if we were to come here boating tomorrow night, wouldn't it be still another one less? How true it is that there is no party that would never break up."

"If there's to be breaking up anyway, let it be in good time. If after such reluctant and grudging anticipation the end is still the same breaking up, it is too much for me!" Chueh-hui said with passion.

"You ought to know that when the tree falls, the monkeys each go their own way; the tree has not fallen yet!" Chueh-hsin said with resignation.

"There will be a day that it will fall, let the break-up come sooner, so that each will have time to go his own way." So

146

saying, Chueh-hui felt that he had given vent to all the pent up hostile feelings he had had for a long time.

"Chin, I do not want to break up, to be left all by myself, what loneliness," Shu-chen, sitting between Chin and Shu-ying, suddenly raised her head and said imploringly towards Chin, in the clear and sharp voice of a youthful girl. In this there was embedded the seeds of tragedy. At the sound of these words there arose before Chueh-hui's eyes the image of tiny bound feet in tiny embroidered scarlet satin shoes, and in his ears the sobs of agony and pain. The tragedy of this little girl's lot forcefully oppressed everyone, made everyone automatically sympathetic. But this sympathy was temporary, ephemeral, because in front of everyone towered the unknown future, with its sombre presence, forcing each to think of his or her own self, to have doubts and apprehension for his or her own future.

The surface of the lake suddenly turned dark, everything became wrapped in grey, without a single ray of light. The moon had hidden itself in a huge mass of clouds, which totally enveloped its brightness for a little while. Stillness reigned over the lake surface, broken only by the rhythmic splash of the oar.

"Row a little slower," Chueh-hsin said to Ming-feng who was at the bow.

Shu-chen clung to Chin, and Chin held her tightly. The sky opened up, brightness suddenly descended on all sides, for the moon had dashed out of its dark enclosure, leaving the dark clouds behind, and sailing straight ahead into the immense azure. The Lake Centre Pavilion and bending stone bridge lay vividly ahead, the moon had cast their shadow on the lake surface, and the serene beauty rendered the scene picturesque. On the left was the plum grove, the blossoms were no more, leaving the unadorned boughs proudly displaying themselves under the moon, with probably some left-over scent, and an occasional long horizontal shoot casting its shadow over the water. On the right was a spreading slope, with a few scattered willows, while beyond it a dyke encircled part of the lake to form a little pond, with an arched opening on the dyke to let in water.

"Don't be scared, take a look, the moonlight is all out again, how beautiful it is!" Chin patted Shu-chen on the shoulder to cheer her up.

Shu-chen drew herself away from Chin, sat in an upright posture, looked at the sky, looked around at everybody, and finally fixed her eyes on Chin and asked in puzzlement, "Chin, why break up, wouldn't it be nice to be together all the time?"

Everybody laughed, and Chin fondly patted Shu-chen on the shoulder and said with a smile, "Poor girl, everybody has his own things to do, how could they be together all the time?"

"In time we will all break up and each go his own way. The same with you, you will get married when you grow up, and you will go away with your young master consort, you will be in his company every day, and you will forget all of us," said Chueh-hsin, half sarcastic and half emotional.

Why must a girl be married into some other family, forsaking those she loves to be in the company of somebody else? Shu-chen had asked her mother this question several times, but she never got a comprehensible answer. Now that the term young master consort was mentioned, she blushed instinctively and felt bashful for something that she did not even comprehend.

"I will not marry, I will not be married to anybody," she gave a straight answer.

"Are you then to remain at home to be an old maid?" remarked Chueh-min who sat diagonally across from her, while Chueh-hui quickly added, "If you don't want to get married, why do you let Aunt bind your feet?"

Shu-chen was not able to find an answer to this one. She pouted and bowed her head, silently touching her bound feet which still ached somewhat, and her mother's words came back to her in quick response. Certainly Mother did tell her that when Big Sister-in-law first came to the family, she was ridiculed behind her back because of her unbound natural-sized feet. It went so far that on her first entrance into the wedding chamber, as she walked in and sat on the wedding couch, someone willfully came across the room to raise her skirt to take a look at her large feet. In this way from Mother's words she learned of the misfortunes of those with unbound feet,

148

and at the same time from under Mother's whip she acquired the fortunes of those with bound feet. After many whippings, a long period of excruciating pain, countless days in which tears washed her face, and endless nights which aching rendered sleepless, she had succeeded in mauling her feet into a pair of such odd shaped things. And what did she gain from it? On the one hand she became the object that Mother could show off with pride, but on the other she became the target of brothers' and sisters' ridicule. The praise and glory promised by Mother did not come true, but ridicule and pity which Mother least expected were heaped upon her. She was only thirteen, so young, so tender, yet she was already a victim, an object of sacrifice. With such a pair of crippled feet, aching all the time, she had fallen behind in all aspects compared to her cousins. The crippled body even made her a weaker person, thinking that her only hope of vindication and revenge would lie in her hour of wedding. Touching and caressing her traumatized feet, did she still have the courage to say that she did not want to marry? Yet hope in the future is uncertain and vague, while reality of the present has rendered things different now. Right here in this tiny boat there were unmistakably three pairs of unbound natural feet, how could she then be sure of the successful realization of her moment of revenge?

When her thoughts had come to such a pass, she could not help letting herself fall into Chin's lap and cry.

Nobody was aware of the cause of this, and all ascribed it to her emotions related to parting, and therefore tendered consolations along that line. But she kept on crying even more, which made the others give up their vain attempts. Chueh-min even said, "Look, you have soiled Cousin Chin's dress," which still failed to make her raise her head. Shu-ying therefore took up the piccolo and played the tune of "autumn sorrows," which produced sad and wailing music, as if relating in tears a sad story of the past. The vibrating sound from the instrument floated over the lake surface, falling and again rising, spreading and again condensing, bringing everybody to the verge of tears.

Suddenly a heavy sigh rose from the stern, making its impact felt on all sides, even on the surface of the water. Everybody looked astern and found Chueh-hsin embracing his knees to his bosom, lifting up his head, staring at the sky. The boat silently floated on, the Lake Centre Pavilion was right ahead, appearing massive and solemn, as if it were a place of some clandestine concealment.

"Why are we still here after such a long while?" Chueh-hui questioned in surprise.

Nobody gave an answer. Chueh-hsin started to manage the boat so that it would spin towards the right to pass under the bridge. The bridge was low and not much room was left above their heads, so everybody instinctively moved to the left to lower themselves, causing the boat to tilt violently. When they regained balance, the effusive moonlight from above was pouring over their faces again, and the bridge was already behind them.

"What was the matter?" Shu-chen set herself straight and timidly asked Chin, but before Chin could manage a reply, Shu-hua could not suppress a chuckle.

The boat was on a wider expanse of water, the lake surface displayed a grand patch of even reflection, not ruffled by the slightest ripple. The water moved slowly forward under the moonlight with a lovely shining smoothness. The boat followed the flow of water, steady and serene, not disturbing in the least the general tranquility.

"Look at the water, it is like satin!" Chueh-min exclaimed in admiration. He was dazed by the sight.

"The moon night is indeed lovely. The pity is, it is not autumn, it is a little too cold, also it does not have the aromatic scent of an autumn night," Chin claimed.

"Women are hard to please, when you have this, you begin to demand that. As a matter of fact the present evening has its winning points. Look, the mist is descending," said Chueh-hsin, as he then turned to give orders to Ming-feng. "Ming-feng, row faster, it is late now."

As the waters of the lake turned and narrowed, the trees and house gradually disappeared. On both sides were manmade hills, a small hut leaning out from the hilltop on the right. The water flowed more rapidly here, and the boat soon drifted through the narrow passage. With Chueh-hsin cautiously operating the oar which he had taken over, the boat described a wide circle to the rear of one of the artificial hills. Here the span of water was short. On one side was a low wall; on the other, the man-made hill, looking extremely tall and blocking out some of the moonlight.

Mist, creeping over the lake, cast a veil over everything. It was beginning to get chilly. The young folk finished the wine in their cups and sat closer together. A gong, clashing faintly in the distance, seemed to be in another world. Chueh-hsin and Ming-feng plied the oar vigorously.

"Has the question of your schooling really been settled?" Chin asked Shu-chen. "I hear your teacher is coming tomorrow."

The past few days, with Chin's encouragement, Shu-hua and Shu-chen had been bombarding their mothers with pleas that they be allowed to study. The women finally consented to let them join the class conducted by the private tutor of their young boy cousins.

"It's settled," Shu-chen replied promptly. "I'm all ready."

"I didn't think you'd succeed so easily," remarked Chin.

"There's nothing strange about that," Chueh-hui interposed. "It's not costing her parents a penny—the tutor gets the same fee no matter how many pupils he teaches in one family. With other people's daughters learning how to read and write, you can't be very proud of yourself when your own daughter's practically illiterate. As long as Shu-chen's mother agreed, her father doesn't care; he never bothered about such things anyhow. *Yeh-yeh*'s always worried that he'll lose face by some female member of our family doing something conspicuous in public, but he doesn't mind them studying at home, particularly since they only read the 'works of the sages'. . . ." Just mentioning the "works of the sages" caused Chueh-hui's flesh to creep; he couldn't suppress an uncomfortable laugh.

Chueh-hui's recital made the whole thing as clear as day to the others. They had no need for further explanation.

White-capped waves tossed and a mist covered the lake as the boat neared the hump-backed bridge, seen dimly through the fog. The electric bulbs on the shore gleamed red and yellow

151

in the mist. The young people had made a complete circuit of the lake.

From the slowly moving boat, they found the picture of the moon shining through the fog intriguing. As they silently gazed around them, their craft sailed past the "Fragrance at Eventide" building. Chueh-hsin asked whether they wanted to go back.

"It's getting late," said Chueh-hui, "and there are sweet dumplings waiting for us at home."

Since no dissenting opinion was expressed, Chueh-hsin steered for the bank. When the boat was again moored to the willow tree and everyone was ashore, the group walked across the bridge.

"I never enjoyed an evening more in my life," Chueh-min commented, and several of the others voiced their agreement.

But Chueh-hsin was thinking—If only Mei had been here with us. . . .

And Chin was saying to herself—I must bring Mei to join one of our outings some time. . . .

As the group emerged from the garden, the two young boys, Chueh-ying and Chueh-chun, puffing hard, came running to meet them. To Chueh-hsin, Chueh-ying cried excitedly:

"Have you seen the newspaper 'extra,' Big Brother? They've started to fight!"

Chueh-hsin was mystified. "Which extra? Who's started to fight?"

"Here, see for yourself," said the boy, proud to be the bearer of such important tidings. He thrust a "Special Edition" of the *National Daily* into Chueh-hsin's hand.

"The governor has ordered a punitive campaign against General Chang," Chueh-hsin read with a growing feeling of tension. "Hostilities have already commenced."[29]

[29] The next two chapters describe the experiences of the family Kao at about 1920–23 in the city easily recognizable as Pa Chin's native Chengtu. It was the time of the civil war between the warlords in the North supported by conservatives and reactionaries, and liberal and nationalist forces in the South rallied around the Kuomintang and its leader Sun Yat-sen.

Beginning in 1915 the Szechuan province and its capital Chengtu

XX

"Is there any news?" Jui-chueh asked Chueh-hsin as he entered the house. There was a worried look on her face.

"The situation has worsened," he replied, shaking his head despondently. "The provincial troops suffered another bad defeat. They say the attacking General Chang has already reached the city's north gate." Chueh-hsin walked over to the window and sat down on a wicker chair.

"I hope there won't be any street fighting," Jui-chueh said in alarm.

"Who knows? That depends on whether the governor is willing to step down." Chueh-hsin was worried, but to soothe Jui-chueh he added, "But I think they'll be able to solve this thing peacefully." Actually he hadn't the faintest idea how it would end.

Jui-chueh walked into the adjoining room and listlessly seated herself on the edge of the bed where little Hai-chen was sleeping. There was a faint smile on his face. She lightly caressed his rosy cheeks with her fingers. He seemed espe-

---

had more than their full share of civil war, since the domination of this rich province was important in the struggle between North and South. From March 1918 Szechuan was ruled by the governor-general Hsiung K'e-wu installed by the Southern army. But at the beginning of 1920 Hsiung allied himself with his former rival general Liu Ts'un-hou and together with him fought against the Southerners. In July 1920 the Southern army won a victory and for a while controlled Chengtu and the province. In September, however, the Southerners were defeated. But by the end of the year the generals Hsiung and Liu began to fight and in July 1921 they were ousted by General Liu Hsiang. Yet Liu Hsiang's rivals were not completely subdued and the civil war in the province continued to inflict great calamities on the people. Pa Chin here presents a condensed picture of events and uses fictitious names for the generals.

cially precious to her at this moment. It was as if someone wanted to snatch him away from her. She couldn't bear to let him go and sat guarding him, her eyes staring blankly at the window. The compound was very still, and the rhythmic ticking of the clock struck her heart like little blows.

Rapid footsteps hurried into the next room. Obviously someone was bringing an urgent message. Frightened, Jui-chueh rose to her feet, and hastened to see who had come. She found Chueh-min standing beside the desk talking to Chueh-hsin.

"What is it?" she asked from the doorway, very upset.

"I just saw them carrying wounded soldiers into the city, two and three at a time. I don't know how many there are," said Chueh-min excitedly. "It's simply terrible. They're on stretchers, all bloody, some with shattered hands, some with broken legs, dripping blood and groaning. I saw one fellow with a gash an inch long in his temple. His face was as white as paper. It's really terrible. . . ." Chueh-min paused, then went on, "The battlefield can't be far from the city. If they lose another battle, we're sure to have fighting in the streets."

"Will we be all right here?" Jui-chueh asked quickly, frightening pictures flashing into her mind.

"Maybe. Let's hope the routed soldiers don't set fire to everything like they did the last time!" retorted Chueh-min.

"We've only had two or three years of peace, and now this had to happen. They just won't leave you alone! What kind of life do you call this?" Chueh-hsin suddenly burst out, rising to his feet. He strode from the room, leaving Chueh-min and Jui-chueh alone and frightened.

Then Chueh-hui and Shu-hua came in.

"The circus has begun again." Chueh-hui's bright voice broke the silence.

"Aren't you afraid, Third Brother?" Chueh-min asked fretfully. "You seem quite happy."

"What's there to be afraid of?" replied Chueh-hui breezily. "It's been much too quiet around here. A little military acrobatics will liven things up a bit. I'm afraid our school will have to suspend classes tomorrow, though."

Jui-chueh was surprised. "How can you be so brave!"

"When you've seen this same show often enough, even the

timidest person becomes brave. They've been fighting for years, but I'm still me. Why should I be afraid?"

But Chueh-hui's words couldn't drive away their fears. When Ming-feng, who raised the door curtain just then, called them to dinner, none of them had any appetite.

"I'm not hungry," Jui-chueh replied apathetically.

"Me either," said Shu-hua.

"You girls are really useless creatures, scared of your own shadows. Hear a little news and you can't even eat," laughed Chueh-hui, as he left for the dining room.

After dinner, the three brothers decided to go out and see if they could pick up any news. But they found the big doors of the compound gate closed and bolted with a great wooden bar. It was very dark in the gateway. The old gatekeeper told them the streets were already closed to traffic.

As they turned and walked back into the interior of the compound, they discussed the relative strength of the two contending military forces.

"We're sure to hear gunfire tonight," said their uncle Ke-ting, meeting them at the entrance to the inner courtyard.

The compound was much quieter than usual that night. Everyone seemed afraid to speak in a normal tone; people even walked more softly. The least sound was enough to set hearts to pounding. The kitchen fires had been banked early; no one felt much like eating. The women wrapped their valuables and hid them in the basement or concealed them on their persons. In every room parents and children, staring at one another with tired, frightened eyes, sat in vigil through the long, long night.

A serious-visaged Ke-ming went from room to room, announcing the instructions of the Venerable Master Kao. Everyone was to act with caution. It would be best for all to wear their clothes to bed so as to be able to flee at a moment's notice.

These orders heightened the tension even more, as if some tremendous calamity was just about to happen. Chueh-hui began to lose a bit of his self-assurance.

"Flee? Where to?" he asked himself. A picture suddenly appeared in his mind: A rifle bullet ricocheting off the cobbled street hits a servant standing beside a stone vat. The servant clutches his wound, utters a piercing cry, falls writhing to the ground and dies in a pool of blood. This was something Chueh-hui had seen with his own eyes. Although several years had elapsed since, the scene was still etched in his memory. He too was full of life; but, like all the people around him, he was only flesh and blood. Chueh-hui felt uncomfortable and a little frightened recalling that terrible day. The glaring light of the electric bulb irritated him. He wished it would vanish and leave him buried in the darkness.

At about ten o'clock, a clear sharp report rang out, the air vibrating briefly with its trailing echo.

"They've commenced firing." Chueh-min raised his head from the desk. He spoke in a hushed voice. His eyes were dull in an ashen face.

Three or four more shots sounded, this time much closer.

"From the look of things, the situation isn't too serious yet. That was just soldiers on the city wall firing to scare off the enemy." Chueh-hui forced himself to speak calmly. But before he had finished, more shots were fired, loudly and rapidly. Then another brief silence, followed by very heavy firing, like a squall of rain. Bullets sang over the rooftops, a few striking and smashing the tiles. Hai-chen, awakening in the next room, began to cry. Outside, a tragic voice wailed someone's name.

"Awful, it's awful," sighed Jui-chueh in the adjoining room. Hai-chen stopped crying. The old man, in his room in the central building, coughed loudly.

"Boom!" A tremendous sound like a clap of thunder shattered the air, followed by a grave hissing. The whole house shook with the explosion.

"They're firing shrapnel shells!" Jui-chueh's low voice trembled.

"Boom! Sssh! Sssh!" Three times in succession, and with the last a huge crash somewhere behind the Kao compound, like a wall collapsing. The house shuddered long and violently.

"We're finished. They're using such heavy artillery—we're all goners!" Chueh-hsin, in the next room, could be heard stamping his foot in anguish. "That last crash sounded like a wall coming down. I'd better go to the back and see if Uncle Ke-ming and the others are all right."

"Don't go. It's even more dangerous outside. I won't let you go!" cried Jui-chueh tearfully.

Chueh-hsin sighed. "The three of us together like this—one shell can finish us all off."

"Shells have no eyes. You can be killed outside just as easily as in here. If we have to die, I'd rather we die together," sobbed Jui-chueh. Hai-chen began to cry again, loudly, and the artillery shells again commenced to boom.

"This is torture! Let's die and get it over with!" Chueh-hsin's voice was tragic, hopeless, frightened.

Chueh-hui couldn't bear to listen to it any longer. He covered his ears with his hands, pressing hard to blot out every bit of sound.

A piercing mournful wail cut through the air, as if intent on tormenting the weak of heart. Suddenly, the electric lights went out, and the whole compound was plunged into darkness.

"Light the oil lamps!" The cry seemed to rise from every building simultaneously. There was much confusion and scrambling about in the rooms.

But Chueh-hui lay on his bed; Chueh-min sat beside the table. Neither of them moved.

There was a momentary lull in the pounding of the artillery, but rifle fire was still quite heavy. Suddenly, many people were heard shouting in the distance. Were they uttering cries of joy, or of warning, or of sorrow? To the brothers the noise evoked a terrible picture: Soldiers running down the streets, driving gleaming bayonets into the backs of fleeing citizens, who dropped dead to the ground as the bloody blades were ripped out again; in a fury of sparks from burning buildings, the mad soldiers, howling like animals that had tasted blood, savagely searching for more victims. . . .

In the compound there was only darkness and terror. Everyone waited in silence for the decision between death and survival. On the fields and hills outside the city, thousands were locked in mortal combat, fighting, struggling, dying. This thought would not let the brothers rest for a

157

moment. In the darkness of their room, red and white shadows danced constantly before their eyes.

"What a terrible age we live in," Chueh-hsin sighed bitterly in the next room, his cry evoking a sympathetic echo in his brothers' hearts.

"Isn't there anything we can do?" moaned Jui-chueh. "We must think of something!"

"Don't talk like that. You only make me feel worse," Chueh-hsin pleaded. "Try to sleep a little. You look exhausted."

"How can I close my eyes at a time like this? A shell might land on us at any moment."

"Calm yourself, Jui-chueh. If we're fated to die, there's nothing we can do about it. You must try and get some sleep." Chueh-hsin forced himself to speak in a soothing voice.

Next door, Chueh-min struck a match and lit the oil lamp. Its small wick flickered weakly, illuminating only a small part of the room. When his lacklustre eyes fell on Chueh-hui's white face, Chueh-min cried in surprise:

"What's wrong? You look awful!"

Chueh-hui lay motionless on his bed. "You don't look so good yourself," he replied softly.

The two brothers gazed at each other in silence. Bullets continued flying over the roof, while thundering artillery shook the house to its foundations. Hai-chen again began to cry.

"There's no use just waiting around like this. Let's get some sleep, I say," said Chueh-hui with determination, rising to his feet and starting to unbutton his clothing.

"That's a good idea, but we'd better keep our clothes on," advised Chueh-min.

But the younger boy had already removed his outer garments and slipped between the covers. He pulled the comforter over his head; sure enough, before long the sound of the firing began to fade from his ears.

The next day dawned bright and clear, and the new rays of the sun, radiating up from the horizon, revealed that the Kao compound was quite unharmed—except for a few broken roof tiles and a piece that had been knocked off the roof of the left wing. There was only desultory firing now, and the general atmosphere was fairly peaceful.

Chueh-min and Chueh-hui went to see their stepmother, Madam Chou, and found Uncle Ke-ming's wife and daughter Shu-ying there with her, looking weary and rather bedraggled. The room was very messy, with four square tables pushed together in the centre over a thick carpet. The two women and the girl had slept beneath the tables the previous night, tightly barricading themselves on all sides with quilt comforters, hoping that this would protect them from bullets. Madam Chou said Shu-ying and her mother had moved over after a shell had landed in the garden behind their house, knocking down a section of the courtyard wall.

"It must have been about three o'clock in the morning. A shell seemed to have struck the roof of your wing and broke many tiles. Jui-chueh came running over here, crying, carrying Hai-chen," Madam Chou said to the boys. "I was afraid your room had been hit, and I called and called to you, but nobody answered. Bullets were flying thick and fast. No one dared to go out and look. Finally, Ming-feng went over and found your door locked but your room undamaged. It was only then we knew you were all right and stopped worrying. Don't go to sleep like that again tonight whatever you do. You must be ready to run at any minute."

Madam Chou ordinarily spoke quite quickly, and this speech she uttered without stopping for breath. The words came sliding out of her mouth like pearls rolling down a smooth surface.

"I usually wake at the least noise. With all that racket going on outside, I don't understand why I slept so soundly," laughed Chueh-min.

At this point Chueh-hsin and Ke-ming came in. Their calm appearance soothed Madam Chou.

"Is everything all right now?" she asked them.

"It's probably all over," replied Ke-ming in his usual measured tones. "The streets are passable again. There isn't a soldier in sight. Things are quiet outside. They say the attacking troops took the arsenal last night and the provincial authorities asked the British Consulate to act as intermediary. They asked him to say that they were willing to make concession and that the governor would resign. I don't think there will be any more fighting. Last night we all had a needless scare."

Turning to his wife, Ke-ming urged her to go home and get some rest. "You were up all night," he said. "You look worn out. . . ." And to Madam Chou he courteously added, "You ought to rest too. We put you to a lot of trouble last night."

After a few more words, Ke-ming and his wife and daughter departed. The two brothers remained to chat with their step-mother.

The day passed uneventfully. Everyone assumed that the trouble was over. But towards evening, the situation suddenly changed again.

Except for the Venerable Master Kao, the whole family was sitting in the courtyard, discussing the happenings of the previous night. A servant rushed in, out of breath, and announced tensely:

"Madam Chang has come."

A moment later, Madam Chang, Chin and another young woman entered through a side gate. They were dressed in the ordinary clothing that women wore around the house, rather than in the more formal dress for making calls. Although their expressions were different, they all appeared rather frightened.

Everyone rose and greeted them in turn. But just as Mrs. Chang was about to explain the reason for their sudden arrival, there was a noise like a clap of thunder. A fiery streak flew across the sky, followed by a tremendous explosion, then several more. Men, women and children hastily left the courtyard for the shelter of the family hall.

After four or five rounds, the artillery fire stopped, and rifle bullets began to sing. These came from the north-east corner of the city, thick as a squall of rain. The chatter of machine-guns joined the fray, and it was soon impossible to distinguish this sound from the rapid popping of rifles. Suddenly, the noise grew in intensity, like the wild rush of a large army, and the cannon mounted on the city walls commenced firing. The racket was no less deafening than the night before, with over a dozen big guns, quite nearby, roaring simultaneously. The ground shook and the windows rattled as if the compound had been struck by an earthquake.

Inside the family hall, frightened speechless, people turned pale and looked at one another distractedly. They knew that their lives were hanging by a thread, and they waited silently —without a sigh, without a groan, without a struggle. The fear of extinction overrode all other emotions. They simply did not react to Chueh-hsin meeting Mei again, to her coming to this compound again with Mrs. Chang after several tumultuous years. Their only thought was of the fiery harbingers of death streaking through the sky above them.

Slowly, the daylight faded. There was a lull in the artillery barrage, although the heavy rifle fire continued. People began to worry: "How are we going to get through this night?" Just then an enormous explosion made the walls tremble. A noise followed like the sputter of firecrackers and the smashing of tiles.

"Finished, we're finished!" cried Madam Chou in a quavering voice, instinctively rising to her feet. Walking to the door that led to her room, she almost collided with Ming-feng who came running in.

"What is it? What's happened?" several voices demanded at once.

Ming-feng's face was bloodless. She was gasping so hard, she couldn't speak.

The door curtain was pushed aside and the Venerable Master Kao entered, followed by Mistress Chen. Everyone rose.

"What's wrong?" the old man asked.

"I was in Shu-ying's room . . . a big shell landed . . . and knocked a hole in the eaves. . . . It broke all the windows too. . . . The courtyard was full of smoke . . . I ran. . . ." Ming-feng stammered, very frightened.

"Crowding together like this won't do at all. One shell in here could finish off the whole family. We'll have to think of something better," the old man warned. He started coughing.

"I say it's best for us to separate, leave the compound. Each household can go and live with relatives in other parts of the city. *Tieh* can move in with the Tang family. It's quite safe there," suggested Ke-ming.

"There's no way to get through to the East Gate section. But the sections near the South Gate and West Gate might be a bit better," said Mrs. Chang. She and the girls had fled by way of the East Gate after her house had been taken over by the military. Mei, who was visiting the Changs, was intending to go home, but when the road was cut, she had come with them to the Kao's, instead.

Before Mrs. Chang had finished speaking, another shell howled over the roof. It exploded somewhat further off than the previous one—probably in the next compound.

Everyone rushed towards the entrance; but they were stopped by servants at the main hall, who explained that the big gate was already bolted—the streets were full of soldiers and all traffic had been halted.

There was no choice but to return. For the want of a better shelter, at Chueh-hsin's suggestion, everyone went into the large garden.

It was like entering another world. They could still hear the firing, but their surroundings helped them forget their terror. Green grass, flowers of red and white—everywhere expressions of gentle life. Veiled in the twilight mists, the garden had an air of mystery. Although people were overwrought, they could not help noticing these beauties of nature.

Passing through the grove of pines, they came to the edge of the lake. The sunset clouds, the colour of the rambling rose, were reflected in the pale blue water, which was already draped with twilight mists. Without pausing, they followed along the edge of the grove where it skirted the lake and proceeded towards the "Lakeside Retreat" building.

Thickets of slim bamboos screened the dark grey tiles of the building's roof. A few magnolias, in the clearing before the front door, were in full blossom, and their white flowers gave out a heady fragrance.

Ke-ming, opening the door, invited the Venerable Master Kao to enter first; the others filed in behind him. A servant lighted a hanging kerosene lamp. The old man was exhausted. He lay down on a bed, while everyone else found chairs and benches. Besides this middle room, the "Lakeside Retreat" also had two side-rooms which the servants now quickly set in order, preparing one for the men and one for the ladies.

By this time the big guns were silent, and the rifle fire dwindled and then finally stopped altogether. In these peaceful quiet surroundings the recent terror seemed merely a bad dream. From the windows overlooking the lake, people gazed at the clear water. The fresh breeze drifting in seemed to blow away much of their anxiety. A new moon cast pale silver beams on the surface of the lake, adding to its coolness. Opposite, the "Fragrance at Eventide" building rose chastely in the moonlight; before it spread a swath of white flowers. The man-made hills, the cliffs, the plum trees, the willows—each with its own distinctive colour and shape—when touched by the moon's silvery rays, became clothed in an air of the deepest secrecy.

"I came here once about five years ago." Mei, who had been worrying about her mother and brother at home, now relaxed a bit in these pleasant surroundings and sat staring at the "Fragrance at Eventide" building on the opposite shore as if in search of something there. After a while her gaze shifted to the line of willows along the bank and, with a sigh, she addressed this remark to Chin.

Standing beside Mei, Chin was silently watching the moon sail slowly through clouds resembling billowy white waves. She turned and looked at Mei, who pointed at the willows and said:

"Those trailing willow strands are knotted around my heart. . . . And now spring has come again."

Changing the subject, Chin tugged at Mei's sleeve and said cheerfully, "We all went boating here on the first full moon of the New Year. Everyone said what a pity it was you couldn't be with us. Who would have thought that you could come so soon. . . ."

But Mei's response was still sad. With tears in her eyes she took Chin's hand. "I'm very grateful for your good intentions. But what's the good of my coming here? Don't you know how I feel? Nothing has changed here. Every tree, every blade of grass, brings back painful memories. Even though my heart has turned to cold ashes, I can't forget the past completely."

Chin gave Mei a startled glance, then looked around quickly to see whether anyone had overheard her. "You shouldn't talk that way here," Chin whispered. "They might hear you. Even if it is hard to forget, you shouldn't torment yourself like this."

Just then, Chin heard footsteps behind her. She turned quickly to see Jui-chueh approaching, leading little Hai-chen.

"What were you two whispering about that was so secret?" Jui-chueh asked with a laugh.

Mei blushed and made no reply. Chin said jestingly, "You've come just at the right moment. We were finding fault with you!"

Even Mei laughed at this. "Don't you believe her," she said to Jui-chueh.

"Of course I can't compare with Chin," smiled Jui-chueh. "She's read many books, she goes to a new-type school, she's good-looking, courageous—"

"And what else?" Chin demanded, with mock sternness.

"And, and . . . oh, and lots more!" Jui-chueh burst out laughing. Then, in a more serious tone, she said to Mei, "I've been wanting to meet you for a long time—I've heard so much about you—but I never had the good fortune. What lucky wind brings you here today? I can't tell you how glad I am. But haven't I seen you somewhere before?"

"Her photograph perhaps?" Chin suggested.

"No. I'm sure I've seen her somewhere. I just can't remember where. . . ."

Mei moved her lips in a tight little smile. "I haven't been fortunate enough to have known Sister-in-law before," she said courteously. But she immediately added in a friendly voice, "You're a bit plumper than your picture, though." Taking the little boy by the hand, she asked, "And this must be Hai-chen?"

"Yes," smiled Jui-chueh. To Hai-chen she said, "Say hello to aunty."

The little boy, his eyes fixed on Mei, promptly responded.

Mei smiled at the child fondly and bent to embrace him. Patting his cheek, she remarked, "He looks just like Big Brother, especially his bright eyes. How old is he? Four?"

"Not yet."

Mei pressed her cheek against Hai-chen's, kissing him and

calling him "darling" several times before finally returning him to Jui-chueh. "You're really fortunate to have such a wonderful son," she said quietly, in a somewhat different tone of voice.

Sensing the change, Chin quickly began to talk of something else. As the three young women chatted, Jui-chueh suddenly realized that she was attracted to Mei, in spite of the fact that this was the first time they had met.

That night everyone went to bed early. Ke-ming and Chueh-hsin returned to their own quarters so as to be able to keep an eye on the compound. Chueh-min and Chueh-hui felt very restricted occupying the same room as their grandfather; they too went back to their own room where they could have more freedom. Having already been through a few shellings, they were much braver now.

XXI

No one slept well that night. As the sky was turning light, the Venerable Master Kao began to cough. He coughed loudly and incessantly, waking the others, who decided they might as well get up early too.

Chin and Shu-ying, after washing their faces and combing their hair, took Mei on a tour of the grounds, pointing out the changes that had been made during the years she had been away. The girls also talked of some of the events in their own lives in that period.

The garden had not been damaged much by the bombardment. Only two pine trees had been knocked down by a shrapnel shell.

Outside, the streets were still not open to traffic, but the restrictions were a bit more relaxed than the day before. Although soldiers remained on duty at every intersection and sentries stood at regular intervals along the streets, individual pedestrians, if not stopped by the sentries, could travel within limited areas.

The Kao family cook could find little in the vegetable market. Because all the city gates had been closed for two days, peasants had been unable to bring in their produce from the surrounding countryside. Although the cook exercised all his ingenuity, the meals that day were necessarily rather skimpy.

Lunch was served in the "Lakeside Retreat." Two large round tables were set up in the middle room, with the elder generation sitting at one and the younger folks at the other. Although no one had eaten well for two or three days, the few dishes which now appeared on the table looked so uninspired that most people lost their appetite. After a couple of listless mouthfuls, they put their bowls down again and left the table.

Only Chueh-min and Chueh-hui did justice to the food. Chueh-hsin stole glances at Mei, seated diagonally opposite, and their eyes met several times. Mei quickly lowered her head or looked away, blushing, her heart beating fast. She didn't know whether the surge of emotion she felt was joy or sorrow. Fortunately, everyone was so engrossed watching the voracious way the two younger brothers were cleaning out their bowls that no one noticed her reactions.

"Your appetites aren't bad at all," Shu-hua twitted her brothers after her grandfather had left the room. She addressed her remark to Chueh-min. "The food is gone, but you're still holding on to your rice bowls."

"Naturally we're not the same as you girls," Chueh-hui retorted, swallowing a large mouthful of rice and putting his bowl down. "You have to have chicken or duck or fish or meat at every meal. Do you know what our lunch at school consists of? Green vegetables, cabbage, beancurd, bean paste. . . . Now you have to suffer too. I hope we're cut off another few days just to see whether you can take it."

He was preparing to go on, but Chueh-min joggled his elbow, signalling him to be quiet. Chueh-hui, also noting the displeased expressions on the faces of some of his elders, lapsed into silence. He pushed back his chair and got up.

"I was talking to Second Brother," snapped Shu-hua. "Who

asked you to butt in?" Turning her head, she refused to pay any more attention to him.

The meal over, the three brothers went out to the street to see whether there was any news. They also intended to have a look at the house of Mrs. Chang, if they could get there.

Few pedestrians were abroad. People were gathered in groups of four or five at the front gates of their compounds, craning their necks to look up and down the street and engaging in earnest discussion. Every ten yards or so, a soldier in full battle dress stood beside the wall or paced slowly back and forth, holding his rifle. But none of the sentries challenged the brothers, and they strode on freely.

Beside a barrier at a fork in the road, they came upon half a dozen men reading an announcement posted on the wall. It was the governor's resignation. As the governor modestly expressed it, his "virtues were insufficient to serve the people and (he) lacked the talent to alleviate their distress." As a result, a battle took place which "brought suffering to my officers and men and hardship to the people." He had therefore decided to retire, so as to avoid "prolonging the fighting and bringing devastation to the land."

"Now that the enemy soldiers are camped outside the city walls, he makes pretty speeches," Chueh-hui laughed. "Why didn't he resign long ago?"

Chueh-hsin hastily looked around. Fortunately no one was standing nearby, and the remark had not been overheard. He tugged at Chueh-hui's sleeve and warned in a low voice, "Be a little more careful in what you say. Don't you want to live?"

Chueh-hui made no reply. With his two brothers he passed through an opening in the barrier. In front of an old temple, a dozen soldiers, their faces expressionless, stood near their stacked rifles. Next door, the little general store had a few copies of that day's newspaper on sale. The boys picked up a copy and glanced through it. The paper's attitude had already begun to change. Although it still had kind words for the retiring governor, it no longer referred to the enemy army as rebels. Enemy leaders whom it formerly had designated as "insurrectionists" and "bandits" it now described politely as General this or Commander that. The same Merchants' Association, the same Society for the Preservation of Ancient Morals, which had previously published denunciations of the "vile bandits," in today's paper announced their welcome to the officers and generals about to enter the city.

"It looks like the trouble is over," said Chueh-hsin. By then the boys had already walked two blocks and were entering the intersection of a third.

The barrier ahead of them was shut tight, guarded by two armed soldiers. The boys had no choice but to turn back. They tried to make a detour through a back lane, but they again found themselves confronted by a sentry where the lane rejoined the main street.

"Where do you think you're going?" the thin-faced soldier demanded savagely.

"We want to visit a relative who lives a few blocks beyond here," Chueh-hsin replied courteously.

"You can't get through." The sentry clamped his mouth tight. He looked with satisfaction at the rifle in his hands and the bright blade affixed to the end of it. "If you come one step nearer," he seemed to indicate, "I won't waste any more words. I'll let this bayonet do the talking."

Silently turning away, the three brothers retraced their footsteps through the small lane and sought another entrance to the main street. But all their efforts were in vain. Sentries blocked every intersection.

They decided to go home. Worried that the road back might be cut off, they walked quickly. There were few people on the streets. Shops and homes were silent, their doors shut. It was much quieter than when the boys had set out, and this increased their apprehension. Each time they passed a sentry their hearts pounded, fearful that he would stop them. Luckily, this did not happen, and they finally arrived home.

Most of the family were in the garden. The brothers hurried to join them. They found their grandfather and their aunts playing mahjong at two tables in the Lakeside Retreat. Chueh-hui marvelled at their interest in the game at a time like this. Noticing that Chueh-min had disappeared, he slipped out too. Chueh-hsin remained standing beside his grandfather's chair where he reported what little news they had been able to obtain.

This news naturally pleased the older folks considerably. Mrs. Chang was still rather uneasy that Chueh-hsin was unable to tell her the condition of the house she had been forced to abandon, but then she drew a good hand and promptly forgot about her worries.

When the older people became engrossed in their game, Chueh-hsin took the opportunity to depart. He stood a while beneath a magnolia tree, feeling rather silly, as if longing for something he knew he couldn't attain, though it was right in front of his eyes. Life seemed empty, futile. Leaning against the tree trunk, he gazed at the greenery stretching before him.

Birds sang in the trees. A pair of grey thrushes fluttered on a branch above, bringing a shower of snow-white magnolia petals down on Chueh-hsin's head. He watched the thrushes fly off to the right. He would have given anything to change into a bird and soar with them aloft into the vast firmament. An intoxicating fragrance assailed his nostrils; when he bent his head to look around, magnolia petals dropped from his head and shoulders. One still adhered to his chest. He gently picked it off with two fingers and, releasing it, watched it sail languidly to the ground.

A woman's figure came rounding the artificial hill. She walked slowly, head lowered, a willow branch in her hand. Suddenly, she looked up and saw Chueh-hsin standing beneath the tree. She halted, her mouth trembling a little, as if about to speak. But no sound came from her lips, and she silently turned and walked away. Over a jacket of pale green silk she wore a black satin vest. It could be no one but Mei.

Chueh-hsin felt chilled all over, as if drenched with a bucket of cold water. Why was she avoiding him? He had to know. He set off in pursuit, walking softly.

As he rounded the artificial hill, he saw flowers and shrubs, but there was no sign of Mei. Strange. Then, off to the right, through a cleft of the adjoining man-made hill, he observed her black satin jacket. Making a circuit of that hill too, he came to a small oval-shaped lawn fringed with a few peach trees. She stood beneath one of the trees, her head down, looking at something in the palm of her hand.

"Mei!" The cry escaped him as he walked quickly towards her.

She looked up. This time she did not turn away, but gazed at him blankly, as if she didn't recognize him.

Coming up to her, he demanded in an agitated voice, "Mei, why are you avoiding me?"

She lowered her head and gently stroked the dying butterfly cupped in her hand. It was still feebly moving its wings. Mei made no reply.

"Haven't you forgiven me yet, Mei?" he asked painfully.

She looked up and gazed at him steadily, then replied coldly, "You haven't injured me in any way, Big Brother."

Only those few words.

"That means you won't forgive me." His tone was almost tragic.

She smiled. But it was a sad, not a happy, smile. Her eyes, softening, caressed his face. She placed her right hand on her breast and said quietly, "Don't you know what's in my heart? Could I ever have hated you?"

"Then why do you avoid me? We've been parted so long, but now, at last, when we're able to meet again, you're hardly even willing to talk to me. How do you think I feel? How can I help thinking you still hate me?" Chueh-hsin demanded tearfully. He drew out a handkerchief and mopped his eyes.

Mei did not weep. She only bit her lips, and the furrow in her brow deepened. "I never hated you," she said slowly, "but it's better that we don't see much of each other. There's no use stirring up the past."

Chueh-hsin, sobbing, was unable to speak. Mei bent and gently placed the butterfly on the grass. "What a shame," she said in a voice filled with love and pity. "Who could have put you in such a state?" Although this might be taken in two different ways, Mei had not intended any hidden meaning. She walked away in the direction of the Lakeside Retreat.

When Chueh-hsin looked up, through the tears that filled his eyes he could see the bun on the back of Mei's head and the pale blue woollen cord that held the hair in place. She was about to disappear behind the hill. A cry burst from his lips.

"Mei!"

She paused and waited for him to catch up.

"What is it?" she asked, assuming a cool air.

"Are you really so cruel? You have pity to give a butterfly. Don't I deserve any pity at all?" He was sad and disappointed.

Mei remained silent. Head down, she leaned against the face of the man-made hill.

"You may be leaving tomorrow. We may never have a chance to see each other again, living or dead. We seem to be in two different worlds. Can you really walk off from me like this without a word of farewell?" sobbed Chueh-hsin.

She still did not reply, but her breathing was rapid.

"Mei, I've wronged you, hurt you . . . though I couldn't help myself. After I got married, I forgot about you. . . . I didn't think of how you must be suffering." His voice was still low but broken with agitation. Though he held a handkerchief, he did not wipe his eyes, and tears coursed down his cheeks.

"Later, I heard what you've been through these last few years, all because of me. After that, how could I live in peace? I've been suffering too, Mei. Can't you even say that you forgive me?"

This time when Mei looked up tears stained her face and her eyes glistened. She was weeping softly after all. "My heart is tangled like flax. . . . What do you want me to say?" she kept repeating. She pressed her hand to her breast and began to cough.

Her distress wrenched Chueh-hsin's heart. Forgetting himself, he drew near to her and dabbed her tears with his handkerchief.

For a moment she permitted this. Then she pushed him back. "Don't," she said miserably. "You mustn't arouse any suspicion." She started to walk away.

He grasped her hand. "Who can suspect anything? I'm a married man already, the father of a child. I shouldn't make you suffer so. You must take care of your health." He wouldn't release her. "You can't go back looking like that. So many tears," he said tenderly. Chueh-hsin forgot his own unhappiness completely in his pity for Mei's tragic fate.

Gradually her weeping subsided. She took the handkerchief from him and wiped her tears, then returned it to him. "I've thought of you every minute these past few years," she said

171

sorrowfully. "You don't know what a comfort it was getting a glimpse of you at Chin's house the day before New Year. I was very anxious to see you after we came back to Chengtu, but I was afraid. That day at the Hsinfahsiang Store I avoided you. Later I was sorry. But I couldn't help it. I have my mother. You have Sister-in-law. I was afraid recalling the past would only hurt you. I don't care about myself. My life is already over, but I don't want to cause you any pain. . . .

"At home, my mother doesn't know how I feel. She only sees things from her own viewpoint. She loves me, but she doesn't think of me as a person. To her I'm just a soulless thing. She can't possibly understand my tragedy." Mei sighed. "I'd rather die early than go on like this."

Chueh-hsin massaged his chest. His heart pained him terribly. They stood looking at each other. Chueh-hsin smiled mournfully and pointed at the grass.

"Do you remember as children how we used to roll on this lawn? When an insect bit my hand, you sucked the bad blood out. We used to chase butterflies here and dye our fingernails with the juice of red balsam flowers. The place is still the same, isn't it? . . . Once when there was an eclipse of the moon, we took a bench and sat in the garden. We offered to accept the pain so that the moon wouldn't have to suffer while it was being eaten. . . . Remember? . . . And those days when you studied together with us at our house. How happy we were then. Who would have believed that we'd end up as we have today?"

He spoke as if in a reverie, as if straining to recapture the joy of the past.

"I live almost entirely on my memories now," Mei said, softly. "Memories sometimes can make you forget everything. I'd love to return to those carefree days. Unfortunately, time cannot flow backwards. . . ."

Footsteps were heard approaching, then the voice of Shu-hua spoke. "We've been looking for you all over, Cousin Mei. So this is where you've been hiding!"

Mei quickly stepped back a bit from Chueh-hsin and turned around.

Chin, Shu-ying and Shu-hua were coming her way. As the

172

three girls drew near, Shu-hua noticed Mei's face and cried in mock alarm, "Has Big Brother been picking on you? Why are your eyes all swollen with crying?" Then she peered at Chueh-hsin who hastily drew back. But she had already seen.

"Oho, you've been crying too? Meeting again after so many years you both ought to be happy. Instead you hide here and weep at each other. Very peculiar."

Mei blushed, while Chueh-hsin looked away muttering something about "my eyes hurt."

Shu-ying laughed. "That's strange. They never hurt you before. Why should the pain start just when Cousin Mei arrives? Funny you should both be suffering together!"

Chin was tugging at her sleeve, indicating that she should be quiet for Jui-chueh was approaching, leading the baby. But Shu-ying couldn't stop in time, and Jui-chueh overheard her.

Jui-chueh didn't know what to make of it. Smiling, she brought little Hai-chen to Chueh-hsin and asked that he carry him. To Mei she said, "Don't feel badly, Cousin Mei. Let's go for a walk. I'm afraid you take things too seriously." Affectionately, she took Mei by the arm and led her away to the other side of the hill.

Shu-ying and Shu-hua wanted to follow, but Chin stopped them. "They probably have something private to discuss," she admonished. "I think they'll become good friends. Sister-in-law is very fond of Cousin Mei." Although addressing the girls, Chin intended her remark for the ears of Chueh-hsin.

XXII

Two days later, the streets were opened to traffic again. The invading army, under General Chang, was encamped outside the city walls. It was rumoured that the governor was departing from the city that day, leaving the newly appointed garrison commander temporarily in charge of public security. Although the fighting had ceased, the city was badly disorganized, and people were very uneasy.

Small groups of soldiers of the defeated army roved the streets. They were a sorry sight—minus their hats, their leg wrappings undone, their uniforms unbuttoned. Some had torn off their unit designation. Their rifles they carried in their hands, on their shoulders, across their backs—any old way. But they hadn't lost their usual insolence. Their scowling, belligerent manner was a constant reminder of the evil they had done before under similar circumstances; it intensified the atmosphere of fear hanging over the city.

Early in the morning Chang Sheng, man-servant of Chin's mother Mrs. Chang, came to the Kao compound. He reported that the soldiers who had been quartered in the Chang compound had departed, except for two or three who, it was said, would be leaving soon too. None of the soldiers had been billeted in any of the women's rooms, so nothing of value had been damaged. Chang Sheng added that Mei's family had sent someone to inquire about her, and he had told the man that she was staying at the Kao's.

Mrs. Chang and Chin were very relieved to learn that everything was all right, and they said no more about returning home.

In the afternoon Mei's mother Mrs. Chien sent a servant with a note to Madam Chou, thanking her for her kindness in looking after Mei. Mrs. Chien said she was extremely grateful and that in a few days, when things were more peaceful, she would come to offer her thanks in person. The servant also brought a message to Mei from her mother saying that all was well at home, she needn't worry. There was no necessity for her to come home immediately; she could stay at the Kao's a few more days if she wished.

At first Mei was going to return with the servant but, unable to resist the importunities of Madam Chou and Jui-chueh, she finally agreed to remain.

In spite of the tense atmosphere on the streets, it was quiet and serene in the Kao's garden. A few walls seemed to mark the separation between two different worlds. Time passed

174

quickly in this peaceful environment. Soon, before anyone was aware of it, evening came.

A half-moon hung in the sky, and the air was filled with the fragrance of dusk. Gradually, as the blue of the sky deepened, the rays of the moon grew richer. It was a warm, beautiful night.

Suddenly, the tranquillity was shattered. The parents of Fourth Household's Madam Wang sent someone to bring her home immediately. The man said there were many rumours. It was feared there might be looting that night. The Kaos were the richest family in the North Gate neighbourhood; their compound was bound to be one of the first invaded. . . . Madam Wang and her five children quickly departed in three sedan-chairs.

Next, the family of Madam Shen of Fifth Household sent for her and her daughter Shu-chen, for the same reason.

This alarmed Madam Chang of Third Household. Without waiting to be called, she departed for her mother's house with her three children, Shu-ying, Chueh-ying and Chueh-jen.

Only Madam Chou and Jui-chueh remained of the Kao family womenfolk. Their parents did not live in Chengtu and they had no place to go. There were a few distant relatives with whom they might have sought refuge, but they didn't know them very well. Besides, by the time Madam Chou and Jui-chueh heard of the danger, the streets were already deserted. Except for the soldiers, no one dared to venture out.

The Venerable Master Kao had gone to call on a cousin that morning. His concubine, Mistress Chen, was visiting with her old mother. Ke-an and Ke-ting had quickly disappeared, though their brother Ke-ming remained, writing letters in his study. The only intact household was Chueh-hsin's. In time of crisis, this old rich family, which depended on ancient morality to sustain itself, revealed its inner emptiness. No one cared about anyone else. Each was concerned solely with his own personal safety.

Mrs. Chang had always been partial to Chueh-hsin's household. Even if she had been able to go home—which she was not—she would not have been willing to abandon them.

"I'm not so young any more," she said to Chueh-hsin, "and

I've seen many things in my time. But I've never seen good people suffer evil retribution. Your father was a good man all his life. No calamities could ever happen to his children. I know that Heaven is just. Why should I be afraid to remain with you?"

But the others were unable to share her confidence, and as time passed she herself grew worried. Although the night was still young, the streets outside were completely silent. A dog began to bark. Usually, they seldom heard him, but this night his barking sounded particularly loud.

Time dragged on with unbearable slowness. Every minute seemed a year. At the slightest sound, they imagined pillaging soldiers had broken in. Immediately they pictured all that this entailed: bayonets, knives, blood, fire, naked female bodies, money scattered on the ground, strong-boxes ripped open, corpses lying in pools of blood. . . . With hopeless desperation they struggled against this irresistible, shapeless force. But terror was closing in on them and they were weakening steadily.

They wished they could close their eyes to everything, end all sensation. As it was, even the feeble glow of the lamp hurt their eyes. It reminded them of the dilemma they were in. They prayed that time would pass quickly, that the sun would rise a little earlier. Yet they knew that the quicker time passed, the sooner the things they dreaded might occur. They were like prisoners awaiting execution. Although they were men and women with different personalities and ideas, in their fear of death they were the same. It was worse for the women, who faced an anguish more terrible than death.

"Cousin Mei, if the soldiers really break in, what shall we do?" asked Chin. They were all gathered in Madam Chou's room. When Chin uttered the words "what shall we do," her heart trembled. She didn't dare let herself think any further.

"I have only this one life to lose," retorted Mei coolly, but there was a note of sadness in her voice. She quickly covered her face with her hands. Her mind was growing hazy. Before her eyes there seemed to be a vast stretch of water, rolling on and on, without end.

176

"What shall I do?" Jui-chueh asked herself in a low voice. She knew what Mei meant. She felt it was the only way out for her too. But she didn't want to kill herself. She didn't want to leave those she loved. As she looked at little Hai-chen, playing at her feet, a dozen knives seemed to plunge into her heart.

Chin silently rose to her feet and began slowly to pace the room, fighting against her rising fear. "You could never do it," a voice inside her said. Although she could think of no other alternative, she felt there must be one. All her new ideas, her new books and periodicals, Ibsen's social dramas, the writings of the Japanese author Akiko Yosano[30]—had vanished from her mind. She could see only outrage and humiliation, leering at her, mocking her. The shame would be something she could not live with. She had her pride.

Chin looked at Mei, seated on the reclining chair, her hands over her face. She looked at Jui-chueh, holding Hai-chen's hand and weeping. She looked at her mother. Mrs. Chang was standing with her back to the lamp, sighing. Chin looked at Shu-hua, at Chueh-min, at the others. It was hopeless; none of them could save her. Yet they all were infinitely precious to her; she couldn't bear to leave them. Weary, despondent, for the first time Chin began to think she was no different from women like Mei and Jui-chueh. She was just as weak, after all.

She sat down and lay her head on the tea table and wept softly.

"Chin, what is it?" cried Mrs. Chang. "Do you want Ma to feel any worse than she does already?" Tears sprang to Mrs. Chang's eyes.

The girl didn't answer, but continued to sob with her head on the table. She wept for herself, for the shattered dream she had fought so hard and long to attain. Now, just as she was beginning to see a glimmer of hope that she might become a strong and self-reliant woman, a "human being," like Nora in Ibsen's *A Doll's House,* she had collapsed, weak

[30] A well-known Japanese romantic poet (1878–1941), and an advocate of individual and women's rights. Her poems, published in Chinese in *New Youth,* were very popular in the 1920s.

and frightened, at the first real danger she had to face. What was the use of all her fine ringing phrases? She used to think she was brave, and others had praised her for her courage, yet here she was, waiting like a lamb to be slaughtered, without even the strength to resist.

Her mother couldn't understand what was going on in her mind, nor could the others, even Chueh-min—who believed he knew her best. They assumed she was weeping because she was afraid. They too were tormented by fear, and they could find no words of comfort for her, though her sobbing cut them to the quick. Chueh-min wanted to take her in his arms, but he didn't have the courage.

Unable to sit still, Chueh-hui got up and went out. He was shocked to see a pale red glow in the sky to the east, a glow that was slowly spreading, accompanied by occasional sparks shooting heavenward.

"Fire!" The shout escaped him, and his blood seemed to congeal in his veins. He stared stupidly at the sky, unable to move a step.

"Where?" several voices in the room cried in alarm. "Where's the fire?" Chueh-hsin was the first to come rushing out, followed by Shu-hua. Soon they all were standing outside on the steps.

The sky was blood-red. Each of them suddenly had the feeling that his life was fading, as if something were eating it away.

A cloud hid the moon, and the brightness of the flames was accentuated in the ensuing darkness. The crimson glow now covered half the sky, reddening the stone flaggings and the tiles on the roofs. Sparks flew wildly. Viewing this holocaust, they gave up any hope of living.

"Those must be pawn shops on fire," said Mrs. Chang. She sighed. "After they've looted them clean why can't they at least leave people a place to live?"

"What's going to become of us?" cried Jui-chueh, stamping her foot frantically.

"Why don't we change into old clothes and make a run for it?" suggested Chueh-min.

"Where would you run to? And who would look after the

compound? If no one in charge stays here and the soldiers come, they'll burn the place to the ground," countered Chueh-hsin. He didn't know what to do either.

Suddenly, sharp rifle reports broke the silence. Dogs began to bark wildly. There was shouting too, but it seemed to come from a distance.

"We're finished. This time we'll never get away," cried Chueh-hsin. Then he said loudly, "Must we all wait around to die? We've got to think of some way to get out of here."

"But where can we go?" Madam Chou queried tearfully. "If we run into any deserters on the streets, we're sure to die. We're better off to remain at home."

"If we're staying here, we still have to find places to hide. If we can save even one of us, it will be better than none. Our household must leave someone to continue the family line," said Chueh-hsin in a voice filled with sorrow and anger. After a pause, in a different tone, he addressed Chueh-min and Chueh-hui.

"Second Brother, Third Brother, take the womenfolk into the garden. Hurry. There are places to hide there. If all else fails, there's always the lake. Your Sister-in-law knows how to preserve her honour." He looked longingly at Jui-chueh, then gave a glance to Mei. Chueh-hsin trembled violently and tears rained from his eyes. Although he seemed to have made up his mind, he was struggling desperately to control himself.

"What about you?" the others demanded.

"Chueh-hsin was silent for half a minute. Finally, regaining some semblance of calm, he said, "Never mind about me. Just go. I can take care of myself."

"Nothing doing. If you don't go, we won't go either," retorted Chueh-hui decisively.

Rifles again cracked, but the intensity of the firing had not increased.

"Third Brother, why are you only concerned about me? The women are important!" Chueh-hsin stamped his foot with anxiety. "If no one in charge stays here and the soldiers come, they'll be sure to search the garden."

Jui-chueh, who had been sitting holding Hai-chen without a word, now placed the child down and walked over and firmly took a stand beside Chueh-hsin. "You'd better hurry and take the other women into the garden," she said to the younger brothers. "Please take the baby for me, too. I'll stay here with Big Brother. I know how to look after him."

"You—you'll stay here with me? What's the meaning of this?" Startled, Chueh-hsin lightly pushed her away. In a worried voice he added, "What would be the good? Go quickly, before it's too late!"

Jui-chueh grasped his arm. "I won't leave you," she sobbed. "If you're going to die, I want to die with you."

Little Hai-chen came over and tugged at Jui-chueh's jacket, beseeching, "Mama, let me stay too."

Chueh-hsin was nearly beside himself. He clasped his hands and swung them repeatedly in obeisance. "For the sake of our child, please leave me," he begged. "What purpose is served in our dying together? Besides, I may not die. If they come, I know how to deal with them. But if they should see you here, who knows what they'd do. You must preserve your purity. . . ." Chueh-hsin couldn't go on.

Jui-chueh stared at him dully, blankly, as if she didn't recognize him. She stood before him and let his anxious gaze caress her face a moment longer, then said in a mournful and tender voice, "Very well, I'll do as you wish. I'll go."

At her instructions, Hai-chen said, "Good-bye, Papa." Then mother and child turned and walked away.

That night, everyone except Chueh-hsin slept in the Lakeside Retreat. Through the open windows they could see the chill moonlight shining on the water. The red glow in the sky was gradually fading. Everything was the same as before, only the barking of the dogs was unusually frightening. All was the same, but to the dull eyes of the watchers the waters of the lake, rippling slightly in the moonlight, appeared more mystic, colder. They wanted to plumb its depths. Some even wondered: What would it be like to sleep far down beneath its surface?

They looked at one another, but could think of nothing to

say. Finally, Madam Chou, observing how tired Chueh-hui looked, told him to go to sleep.

Chueh-hui got into bed. Just as he was dozing off, Madam Chou came and opened the mosquito netting. Leaning her round face down, she whispered into his ear.

"The firing has started again. It seems to be very near. You must be careful. Whatever you do, don't sleep too soundly. If anything happens, I'll call you."

Her breath warmed his cheek, and there was a concerned, affectionate look on her face. She tucked him in, closed the netting, and softly walked away.

Although the news she had brought was not good, Chueh-hui was very comforted. He felt he had a mother again.

After three or four days of tension, order was restored on the streets, and everyone felt much better. Those who had left for places of safety in other parts of the city began to return. The compound was once again alive and bustling.

Mrs. Chang's man-servant, Chang Sheng, came to take her and Chin home. Mei also wanted to go back, but Madam Chou prevailed on her to remain a few days longer. In the afternoon, Mei's mother, Mrs. Chien, arrived in a sedan-chair to pay her respects to Madam Chou.

Elderly women are naturally inclined to be forgetful. Besides, Madam Chou and Mrs. Chien were distant relatives. In the few years since they had last seen each other they had completely forgotten their differences. Madam Chou received Mrs. Chien with the fullest cordiality, and the two women had a long chat. Later, they sat down for a game of mahjong, in which Mei and Jui-chueh joined.

When Chueh-hsin returned, Jui-chueh relinquished her place at the table to him. He found himself sitting opposite Mei. They spoke very little. Occasionally they exchanged a mournful glance. Chueh-hsin's heart wasn't in his game, and he made several bad plays. Jui-chueh came and stood behind him, to try to help. He turned his head and smiled at her. He and Jui-chueh were both entirely natural and quite affectionate in their manner to each other.

Mei, observing, felt a pain in her heart. If she had only

told her mother how she felt about Chueh-hsin before he became engaged to Jui-chueh, perhaps she, not Jui-chueh, would be standing behind him now. Ah, how wonderful it might have been. But today it was too late.

She saw the close bonds between Chueh-hsin and Jui-chueh, and thought of her own unhappy life and the lonely years ahead. The mahjong tiles blurred before her eyes. Her heart ached unbearably.

She stood up and asked Jui-chueh to take her place, saying there was something she had to attend to. Jui-chueh gave her a friendly look, then sat down on her vacated chair. As Mei walked slowly from the room, Jui-chueh gazed after her thoughtfully.

Mei went to Shu-hua's room, which she was sharing with the younger girl. Fortunately, no one was there, and she lay down on the bed and reviewed her past, carefully, in detail. The more she thought, the worse she felt, until finally she burst into tears. Muffling her sobs for fear of being overheard, she cried a long time. She felt better then, although she still couldn't see even a thread of hope. Her past, her present, were crushing her like a weight. She felt weak, unable to stir. At last, she drifted off into slumber.

"Cousin Mei," a warm voice called her. She opened her eyes. Jui-chueh was standing beside her bed.

"Aren't you playing mahjong, Sister-in-law?" Mei asked with a weary smile. She tried to sit up, but Jui-chueh gently held her down and sat beside her on the edge of the bed while gazing at her affectionately.

"I let Aunt Shen take over for me." Then, surprised, Jui-chueh said, "But you've been crying! What's the matter?"

"No, I haven't," said Mei, trying to smile.

"Don't pretend. Your eyes are all swollen. Tell me what's troubling you," Jui-chueh insisted, squeezing her hand.

"I had a bad dream, that's all," replied Mei airily, but the hand which Jui-chueh held was trembling.

"Don't try to fool me. There must be something wrong. Why won't you tell me the truth? Don't you believe I really care about you? I want to help you." Jui-chueh's voice was full of sympathy.

Mei made no reply. Fixing her mournful gaze on Jui-chueh's friendly visage, she frowned slightly and shook her head. Her eyes glistened suddenly and she blurted, "You can't give me any help." She lay her head on the pillow and wept softly.

There was a lump in Jui-chueh's throat. She patted Mei's quivering shoulder. "I understand, Cousin Mei," she said sorrowfully. "I know what's in your heart." Jui-chueh wanted to cry too. "I know he loves you, and you love him. You would have made a fine couple. . . . He shouldn't have married me in the first place. . . . Now I know why he loves plum blossoms so—because that's what your name means. I love him too, I love him more than life. . . . But, Mei, why didn't you marry him? . . . You and I—he too—we've done wrong, we've fallen into a tragic muddle. I've been thinking. I ought to step out of the way and let you two have your happiness. . . ."

Mei had already stopped her tears. She looked around when she heard Jui-chueh weeping. With one hand pressed against her chest, she listened intently to what Jui-chueh was saying, then immediately turned her head, not daring to look at Jui-chueh's tear-stained face. But at those last few sentences, she quickly sat up and covered Jui-chueh's mouth with her hand.

Jui-chueh buried her head on Mei's shoulder and sobbed.

"Sister-in-law, you're wrong. I don't love him," said Mei, then promptly contradicted herself. "No, I do love him. I don't have to fool you. . . . Our mothers wouldn't let us marry. Fate must have ordained it that way. We just weren't meant for each other. . . . We separated, and that's the end of it. Suppose you gave him up, what would be the use? He and I will never be together again in this life. . . . You're still young, but I, emotionally, am already old and feeble. Haven't you seen the wrinkles on my forehead? They show what I've been through. . . . I'm tired of this world. I'm fading, while you are only beginning to blossom and bear fruit. I truly envy you, Sister-in-law. . . . I no longer live; I just exist. My life is only a burden to others."

Mei smiled bitterly.

"You know the saying, 'There is no greater tragedy than the death of the heart.' Well, my heart is already dead. I shouldn't have come to your compound again. I only upset people. . . ."

Her voice had changed. Jui-chueh could feel her trembling.

"How can I possibly feel at ease here?" she cried despondently. But then she went on quietly with a mournful smile, "If there ever was a case of 'woman's wretched fate,' I'm a perfect example. No one understands me at home. My mother is interested only in her own affairs. My brother is still very young. Who can I pour out my bitterness to? . . . Sometimes, when the misery is more than I can bear, I hide alone in my room and cry, covering my head with the bedding so that no one will hear. . . .

"You shouldn't laugh that I weep too easily. It's only the past few years that I've become this way. It began when my mother quarrelled with his stepmother and broke us up. Later, after we left Chengtu, I cried many times. It was all fated, but sometimes I think things might have been different if his own mother hadn't died. She was related to my mother, and they were good friends. . . . But who wants to hear my complaints? No one understands me. The best thing for me is to swallow my tears. . . ."

Mei paused, pressing her handkerchief to her mouth to smother a few coughs. "Later, I married, much against my will. I had no choice in the matter. I lived for a year with my husband's family. It was simply awful. Even today I still don't know how I managed to exist. If I had to spend another year or two in that house, I'm afraid I wouldn't be here today. . . . Weeping was an actual pleasure for me then. I wasn't permitted to do a thing. Everything was forbidden, but weeping—that was all right. . . . I don't cry nearly so much now. Maybe my tears are running dry. Tu Fu said, 'Though you weep till the bones show through your eyes, there is no mercy in heaven or on earth.' But what other consolation have I except to weep?

"You mustn't feel badly because of me, Sister-in-law. I'm not worth your pity. I didn't intend to ever see him again. Something seems to have drawn us together. Yet, at the same time, something is driving us apart. Even though I know there's no hope for me in this life, the last few days I've been acting as if there might be. Please don't hold it against me. Anyhow, I've decided to leave. You can treat the whole thing as a bad dream. Just forget about me. . . ."

Tears of blood were running into her heart, but Mei did not weep. She only smiled sadly.

Every word of this tragic tale weighed heavily on Jui-chueh's tender feminine heart. She listened intently, unwilling to miss a single syllable, gazing quietly at Mei's mournfully smiling face. The tear-stains on Jui-chueh's lightly powdered cheeks in no way detracted from her beauty.

When Mei finished speaking, Jui-chueh shook her head, for all the world like a mischievous little girl. Her dimples deepened and she smiled, a sad, moved smile. She forgot her own misfortune completely. Placing both hands on Mei's shoulders, she said in a clear affectionate voice:

"Cousin Mei, I didn't know you were suffering so. I shouldn't have led you to talk about it. I was too selfish. Your situation is much worse than mine. Promise me that you'll come here often. I like you very much. Cousin Mei—it's the truth. You say no one understands you. I hope you'll let me be the one. I had a sister once, but she died. If you won't refuse me, I hope we can be sisters. I can comfort you. I'll never be jealous. As long as you're happy, I'll be pleased from the bottom of my heart. You must come to visit with us often. Promise that you'll come. That's the only way to prove you don't dislike me, that you've forgiven me."

Gazing at Jui-chueh with loving tenderness, Mei removed Jui-chueh's hands from her shoulders and pressed them tightly, then leaned wearily against her. For a moment she was too moved to speak. Finally she said:

"I don't know how to thank you, Sister-in-law." She kept stroking Jui-chueh's plump ripe hands. She coughed several times.

Jui-chueh looked at her in concern. "Do you cough very much?"

"Sometimes. Mostly at night. I've been a little better lately, but my chest always pains me." Mei's voice was melancholy.

185

"Are you taking any medicine? That kind of ailment it's better to cure in the early stages."

"I was taking some medicine. It helped a little, not much. Now there are some pills; I swallow a few every day. My mother says it's nothing to worry about—I'll be all right with a tonic and a good rest at home."

Overwhelmed with pity, Jui-chueh looked avidly at Mei's face, while tightly squeezing her hand. Both young women were gripped by an emotion that would have been difficult for them to describe. They put their heads together and talked softly for some time.

Finally, Jui-chueh rose to her feet. "We'd better be going back." She went to the mirror, combed her hair and powdered her face, then helped Mei do the same. Hand in hand, the two young women walked from the room.

XXIII

Tension quickly subsided in the city. The battle soon became only a memory. Peace was again restored. At least on the surface people once more lived in peace. The fighting seemed only a bad dream.

Some real changes began to be put into effect. General Chang was chosen military commander of the combined conquering forces, after which he became civil administrator. With the administrative power in his hands, he indicated that he was willing to institute reforms.

In this new atmosphere, the students came to life and put out three new periodicals. Chueh-min, Chueh-hui and some of their classmates published a weekly magazine which they called *Dawn*, containing news of the new cultural movement, introducing new ideas and attacking all that was unreasonable of the old.

Chueh-hui enthusiastically took part. He wrote many articles for the magazine. Of course most of his material came from the new periodicals published in places like Shanghai and Peking. He had not yet made either a really thorough study of the new theories or a careful analysis of society. All he had was a little experience in life, some knowledge derived from books, and the ardour of youth.

As to Chueh-min, he was busy with his classes at school all day; in the evening he went to tutor Chin. That left him little time for anything else. Except for writing a short article once in a while, he wasn't of much help to the magazine.

The magazine was very well received by the young people. Its first issue of a thousand copies sold out in less than a week. The second issue did the same. By the time the third issue was published, the magazine already had nearly three hundred subscribers. The backbone of the magazine's staff were three of Chueh-hui's best friends, and their fine work earned his deepest admiration.

With the advent of the magazine Chueh-hui's life became more interesting and active. For the first time he found an outlet for his pent-up energies. His ideas were put into print and a thousand copies were distributed at a time. People everywhere knew what he was thinking; some of them even wrote in expressing agreement. In his ardent eyes the fanciful, lofty joy he experienced was something precious to the extreme. But although he was more than willing to devote his free hours to the magazine, he was afraid his grandfather would find out, or that his participation would get his Big Brother into trouble. And so he was compelled to conceal his connection with it.

But in the end he was discovered. One day his uncle Ke-ming came across an issue of the magazine in Chueh-hui's room containing one of his articles. Ke-ming made no comment; he only smiled coldly and walked out. Though Ke-ming did not report the matter to *Yeh-yeh*, from that time on Chueh-hui increased his caution. He considered the majority of his relatives to be his enemies and was wary of them. His activities, his work, his desires were things he revealed to no one in his family. He didn't even confide in Chueh-hsin. He knew his Big Brother was weak, and not necessarily in sympathy with what he was doing.

As his interest mounted in his new life, Chueh-hui's youthful fervour knew no bounds. In a short time a group for the study and propagation of the new culture had been built up around the magazine. They met every Sunday in the park, twenty of them, sitting around a few tables under a big mat canopy, drinking tea and heatedly debating every conceivable social question. Or they would gather in small groups in the homes of various students and discuss plans to help others—for they had become inbued with the spirit of humanitarianism and socialism. They had already taken on their shoulders the burden of reforming society and liberating mankind.

The galley proofs, the rhythmic motion of the printing press, the beautiful printed pages, the many letters from people he had never met—these were all wonderfully new and stimulating to Chueh-hui. They were things he had never dreamed of, yet today they were all reality, tangible, forceful, meeting his young thirst for action.

Chueh-hui gradually became more deeply immersed in his new environment; at the same time the distance between him and the members of his family widened. He felt they were incapable of understanding him. His grandfather's visage was eternally stern; the powdered face of Mistress Chen never lost its crafty expression. His stepmother remained courteous and cool. Big Brother continued to practise his "compliant bow" philosophy. Sister-in-law, pregnant again, was beginning to lose her blooming vitality. Behind Chueh-hui's back his aunts and uncles complained that he was too proud; he showed them none of the respect due from a nephew. They protested to his stepmother, demanding that she scold him. Yet whenever he met them, they greeted him with hypocritical smiles.

The only one in the family Chueh-hui was close to was his brother Chueh-min. But Chueh-min had his own aspirations, his own work. Even in his thinking, he was different from Chueh-hui.

There was one other person. Every time Chueh-hui thought of her, his heart melted with tenderness. He knew at least one person in the compound loved him. The girl's selfless devotion was a source of constant happiness to him. Whenever he looked into her eyes—more expressive than any pair of lips, burning with the clean flame of love—hope surged in his breast. All the world was in those eyes; in them he could find his life's purpose. At times he was so overcome by emotion, he wanted to cast everything aside for their sake; he felt they were worth any sacrifice.

But when he walked out into the world, entered his new environment, met with his new friends—his vision widened. He could see the great world before him; there was room for his smouldering fire; it was there he should concentrate his energies. Life was not so simple; he knew that well. Comparing the wide world with a girl's eyes was really too silly. How could he give everything up for them?

Recently he had read a forceful article in *Journal*, a semi-monthly published in Peking. The writer had said that the youth of China must not be idlers living only for enjoyment; they ought to lead a Spartan existence. Chinese society was dark, and their responsibility was a heavy one. It was up to them to face the social problems and solve them. Naturally this would require all their energies. In conclusion, the writer warned his young readers: "You must guard against falling in love. Don't become emotionally involved."

Although the theoretical basis of the article was weak, at the time it influenced many of the young people who read it, especially those who were anxious to devote themselves to the service of society.

It made a strong impression on Chueh-hui too. He read it with a trembling heart. It moved him so, he was ready to vow that he would be exactly the kind of youth the author demanded. His mind was filled with the vision of an ideal society. He forgot completely the pure love of the young girl.

But his forgetfulness was only temporary. True, he did forget her when he was busy outside. But as soon as he returned home, when he again entered that compound silent as the desert, he was bound to think of her. And thinking of her he was sure to feel troubled. Two thoughts struggled for supremacy in his mind—or perhaps we could say the struggle was between "society" and Ming-feng. But since the girl was alone, and pitted against her were the whole system of feudal morality and the Kao family clan, in Chueh-hui's mental battle, Ming-feng was doomed to defeat.

Of course Ming-feng herself knew none of this. She still loved him, secretly but unreservedly. She was happy for his sake. She waited, praying that one day he would rescue her from the miry pit of her existence.

Her life was somewhat easier than before. Her masters were much kinder to her. She was sustained by her love. It brought her beautiful daydreams in which she could take refuge. Yet she remained very humble. Even in her dreams she did not conceive of living with Chueh-hui as equals; she wanted only to be a faithful slave, but the slave of him alone. It seemed to her that this would be the greatest possible happiness.

Unfortunately, reality is often the exact opposite of what people desire; it smashes their hopes, mercilessly, swiftly.

One evening, after the fourth issue of the *Dawn* was sent to the press, Chueh-hui went with Chueh-min to visit Chin.

Her mother, Mrs. Chang, was sitting on the elevated stone pavement outside the window, chatting with her. As the Kaos approached, she ordered chairs to be brought and asked the brothers to join them.

"I have read the third issue of your Weekly. The article attacking traditional family must be yours. Why do you use such an odd pen-name as Jen-ming?"[31] Chin asked Chueh-hui with a smile.

Chueh-hui was startled. Casting a glance at his aunt and finding no responsive expression, he felt assured and replied laughing, "How do you know it's mine? I insist that it isn't."

"I don't believe you. I am sure the mood and style are all yours. If you don't admit it I will ask Second Cousin!" So saying, she turned to look at Chueh-min, who couldn't help but nod and smile in return.

"Well, then, would you write some articles for our Weekly?" Chueh-hui took the opportunity to press a request.

[31] *Jen* literally means to slaughter with a sword.

190

"You know very well that I am not good at it, why allow me to disfigure your paper? Just let me be one of your readers," Chin replied modestly.

"The fourth issue of the Weekly has just been sent to the press. There is in it an article promoting short hair for women, only it is written by a man. This is a problem that has been discussed in Shanghai papers, and in big cities like Peking and Shanghai women have started to put it into practice. But here nobody has broached the subject yet. It would be better if you women would come forward with some opinion of your own; the Weekly will be pleased to publish it."

His eyes swept over Chin's face, which immediately flushed with lustre. Her beautiful big eyes turned glowingly toward Chueh-hui, while she replied ardently but without raising her voice, "The subject has been fervently discussed at our school. No doubt the majority of us favor short hair. There are two or three of us seriously thinking of cutting our braids, but we didn't do so for fear of certain eventualities. Nobody has the courage to do it. Hsu Chien-ju has made up her mind, but hasn't taken action yet. It is indeed not easy to be a vanguard. What we should do is to promote it vigorously in the papers . . ."

"How about you?" Chueh-hui asked laughingly, as if deliberately pressing the opportunity upon her.

Chin glanced at her mother, who was reclining on a rattan lounge with her eyes shut, but the smile on her face indicated that she seemed not to be listening to what the young people were saying. This was her usual way of carrying herself, of which the brothers were quite aware, and therefore they didn't pay much attention to her.

"You just watch me," Chin replied with a smile, which masked the real expression on her face. Chueh-hui couldn't help from thinking, What a sly girl, giving a non-committal answer without betraying the slightest cowardice.

"Well, how about an article?" Chueh-hui pressed further.

She smiled, thought for a while, and then said in a low voice, "All right, I promise you an article. . . . I would like to dwell on the advantages of short hair for women, which are indeed numerous, for example, sanitary, economic, convenient, and the removal of one source of discrimination against women. . . . These can all be discussed at length, but didn't the article just published in the current issue cover the same ground? If so, there is no need for me to write another one."

Chueh-hui was overjoyed with her promise, and quickly said, "Not all the same, please do write yours, and we will publish it in the next issue."

There was a pause, and then suddenly Chin asked Chueh-min, "When is the Students' Day of Performances and Entertainments at your school to be? The term is almost over now."

"Most probably there won't be any, nobody is talking about it now," Chueh-min said apologetically. "We did spend a lot of time and effort last year to get the play *Treasure Island* quite well rehearsed, and now we don't even have a chance for a single performance, what a shame! This is all due to the war. I still remember how Chueh-hui and I were so worried that the Western suits wouldn't fit us on the opening night, or that we wouldn't be used to them. Besides Teacher Chu, who is English and therefore always in Western dress, in our school there is only our president who owns a Western suit, which he invariably puts on once every year on the Students' Day."

"It's not only the performances that suffered, even the measures for women's liberation were knocked out of existence by the war. The term is drawing to its end, the admission of girl students is not heard of anymore, it's no longer mentioned by the president. Most likely it will again evaporate like a dream. The president is always a man of words and promises," Chueh-hui said with resentment and indignation. Chueh-min looked at him askance, as if blaming his brother for breaking the bad news.

Indeed Chueh-min's apprehension was well founded, for Chueh-hui's words darkened Chin's face, made her bite her lips as if to suppress something inside. She suddenly turned to Chueh-min and asked him in a subdued voice, "Is it true?" She was impatient for an answer, entertaining the hope that Chueh-hui might only be kidding.

Chueh-min dared not look her in the eye, lest he should see her depression when she learned the truth, so he replied with bowed head and dejected voice, "The outcome is not definite yet. But as of now the prospect is very poor. Anyway, to initiate a new measure is not easy, it takes outstanding courage." Anticipating her disappointment, he consoled her, "Chin, our school isn't good, it's not an irremediable loss that you were not admitted. I advise you to go to Peking or Shanghai for your advanced study. You still have a year before graduation, although the admissions policy at our school would take in students based on evidence of qualifications equivalent to high school graduation. But you will pass the admissions examination much easier in a year's time when you are graduated; furthermore, in a year's time the admission of girl students probably will have been introduced." He said this in spite of the fact that he didn't have the slightest idea how much probability there was in it.

Chin knew the implications, so she simply let the subject drop. . . .

In three days Chin got her article written. Chueh-hui took the manuscript, noticing the beautiful grace of her feminine calligraphy, and admiring her pioneering spirit and manly courage. He valued the article immensely and immediately had it published in the fifth issue of the Weekly, with a laudatory comment of his own. Following this an article by Hsu Chien-ju appeared in the sixth issue, and successively more than twenty girl students sent letters to the Weekly to announce their support. Thus in a short time the subject of short hair for women became a fervently debated reform issue in Chengtu. But the one who dared to face all eventualities and conquer all hindrances, and who stood out as the foremost vanguard to put words into deeds and set a real and bold example for all, was Hsu Chien-ju.

One day as Chin got to school, she saw Hsu Chien-ju standing under a willow tree on the fringe of the sports field, chatting with a group of girls around her. Chin edged in and found that all eyes were on Chien-ju's head, where her own eyes naturally followed. She was startled by the extraordinary beauty of Chien-ju's head today. As Chien-ju was turning to talk to a girl behind her, the back of her head seemed to glisten with a bright belt. Chin found that it was a ring of snow white skin, bared above the collar of her blouse, and falling underneath a band of evenly cut hair just covering her ears. The shining braid of hair flowing down to the back was no more! The head now carried with it freshness of style and beauty in simplicity, which added greatly to its loveliness. Concomitant with Chien-ju's ease and composure when she was conversing in high spirit, it looked all the more befitting and becoming.

Before this, although Chin supported short hair for women, she couldn't help worrying lest her hair would look awful when cut. Now that she had seen it in Chien-ju's demonstration she felt assured. Yet at the same time a sudden feeling was aroused in her by the same picture in her mind, that of her own inferiority standing at Hsu Chien-ju's side. She looked at Chien-ju's head with envy and adulation, and as she talked to Chien-ju with great intimacy, she felt proud to be her friend. She even began to imagine that the braid behind her own head was no more, gone she knew not when. But as her hand inadvertently reached back, there it was, the smooth greasy stuff.

"How did you do it?" Chin asked admiringly with a dreamy smile.

Chien-ju, smiling, looked back at Chin. Letting her glowing and exalted smiling features dominate her face, she spoke, gesturing with her hands at the same time, in a crisp, clear voice, "A pair of scissors, a pair of hands, and—the braid fell."

"I don't believe it's that simple," one girl said pouting. "Say, who cut it for you?"

"Who else," Chien-ju laughed, "besides my old sweet wet nurse? There is no one else in my family. My father wouldn't do this for me."

"Your old wet nurse, indeed she agreed to do it for you?" Chin declared in surprise.

"Why not? When I asked her to do it, she did it. She always complies with my wishes. My father sympathizes with the cause, naturally he would not object to it. As a matter of fact, it would be futile even if he opposed it. I do what I want, nobody is going to stop me," Chien-ju said with a firm tone, and a smile of self-approval.

"Well said. I am going to cut off my braid tomorrow," a girl of miniature stature said, blushing.

"Wen, I know you have such courage." Chien-ju nodded at the girl, whose name was Wen, indicating her praise and approval. Then she let her sharp and forceful glance sweep over the faces of all the girls there, and she was dismayed that no one accepted Wen's challenge and declared the same. She asked them a little sarcastically, "Who else has the courage to cut her hair?"

"I do," responded a shrill voice, and a girl with a thin face emerged from the back rows. She was one of the oldest girl students of the school, and the others had nicknamed her Old Miss. She was usually very active, and was known for always substantiating her words with deeds.

Chien-ju was pleased. She turned towards Chin, and asked, "How about you, Chin?"

Chin was suddenly unable to meet Chien-ju's eyes. Blood rushed to her face, and she bowed her head unable to say a word, for at the moment she was really uncertain of whether she did have the courage to cut her hair.

"I understand, Chin, your situation is very difficult." Chien-ju spoke in loud and clear words, which made Chin unsure of whether they were sarcastic or sympathetic. "In your families of the gentry society, the only proper things to do are a few lines of poetry, a few rounds of drinks, some card games, or certain intramural plotting, and so on. To have sent you to school was an extraordinary and exceptional commitment. If you step still beyond to such a new-fangled venture as cutting your hair like a man's, there will be a furor of condemning voices of full opposition from all sides. There are indeed too many moralistic souls in your family."

A guffaw broke out from the group, and all eyes began to converge on Chin, who found herself submerged in shame and humiliation. Tears gushing uncontrollably from her eyes, she walked away in resigned silence.

The group regained its composure, and Chien-ju continued, "To cut your hair at the present moment does indeed require

195

unlimited courage. When I walked to school a little while ago, I was followed by a number of students and young rogues who heaped jeers and insults on me, calling me such names as 'little nun'[32] or 'duck's behind,' as well as other unspeakable vulgarisms. Besides, everybody on the street cast looks of hatred or curiosity my way. Although I put up a front of looking completely unperturbed, and walked straight forward without the slightest hesitation, I found my heart beating faster and faster. When I left for school, my old nurse tried to persuade me to take a sedan-chair to avoid being bothered by people on the street. But I wasn't afraid, I would rather have tested my courage. Why should I be afraid of them? I am human also, what have my affairs to do with other people? I will do whatever I want to do. What can they do to me? I am at school right now, no harm was done to me!" Chien-ju said this with the air of a brave warrior triumphantly coming through a trial combat unintimidated by formidable challenges.

In class, Hsu Chien-ju and Chin sat side by side sharing the same desk. A teacher in his late forties, with convex glasses, was conducting a Chinese language class, expounding a lesson in the *Models of Classical Prose Essays,* a copy of which he was holding in his hand. Chien-ju found that Chin was staring dazedly at a copy of the book spread on the desk in front of her. Tearing a page from an exercise book, Chien-ju wrote a few lines on it and pushed it in front of Chin. What she wrote was as follows: "You resent it? I was not trying to hurt you when I said that. If I had known that it would cause you such misery, I definitely would not have said it. Please forgive me."

Chin read the note, slowly added something to it and passed it back, and Chien-ju read, "You misunderstood me, I did not resent it at all. Instead I praise you, envy you. You have courage, but I don't. My hopes, my goals, you know them all. You know my situation too well. What am I going to do? Do you think that I can continue resolutely towards my goals?" The notes were passed to and fro:

"Chin, I know that you are not a girl lacking courage. Do

[32] The Buddhist nuns had their hair cut.

196

you remember that you said we should struggle ahead with the greatest resolution, disregarding all eventualities, in order to open up a new road for our sisters who come after us?"

"Chien-ju, I didn't know myself until this moment. I am indeed a girl without courage. I created a hope for my future, and resolved to proceed towards this goal in spite of all difficulties. Yet when I got close to it, I became disheartened, my worries and concerns grew, and I lost my courage to go on."

"Chin, don't you realize that this will lead you to misfortune and disaster?"

"Chien-ju, I have fallen into it already. I love my future, but I love my mother too. I love light, but for the sake of my mother, I would remain in darkness to keep her company. Ideas like co-education and short hair for women are unacceptable to her. Some time ago I made up my mind that I should do what I want, irrespective of mother's opposition and relatives' condemnation. But when the time comes when I can do what I want by a single movement of my hand, my thoughts turn to my mother, to what a blow it would be to her, and my courage wanes, my resolve is shaken. I think of her toiling through miserable years of widowhood to bring me up, all the while loving me, caring for me, and it is now my turn to make her happy. Yet instead I would be bringing her heavier miseries, the collapse of her hopes, the mockery of society, the reproaches of relatives—it is indeed too heavy a blow for her to take. For her I will have to sacrifice my own future."

"Chin, don't you know that such sacrifice is meaningless? If we are to sacrifice, we should not sacrifice for one person. We should sacrifice for our multitudes of sisters of the future. If we sacrifice so that they will have happiness in the future, such sacrifice would be worthwhile and meaningful." Here the penmanship turned into the cursive style, done with running hand and high speed, indicating that Chien-ju was quite emotionally upset and intense. To this Chin replied:

"Chien-ju, this is where the two of us differ. Your reason can conquer your feeling, but my reason is often conquered by feeling. I can't say that in theory your words are wrong. But in practice I am unable to follow your words. Once I

197

think of my mother, my mind becomes pliant. In reality, as I see it, to sacrifice for our sisters whom we will never even meet is far less realistic than to sacrifice for the mother who loves me and whom I love."

"Chin, are these words coming from deep down in yourself? Let me ask you, if your mother arranged for you to marry an illiterate vulgar businessman, or a middle-aged bureaucratic government man, or a good for nothing wealthy playboy, would you not resist it? Would you sacrifice for her sake and accept that too? Answer me. Don't be evasive!" More cursive speed writing, to which the answer was:

"Chien-ju, don't ask me this, I beg of you, do not bring up this question." The paper bearing these words also bore a tear-drop.

"Chin, let me ask you then: I know that you are very friendly with your cousin. Suppose your cousin were from a poor family, and another young man from a house of wealth and position proposed to your mother for your hand. If you then insisted on marrying your cousin, your mother would say to you in great earnest and sincerity: 'I brought you up through all kinds of difficulties with the hope that you would marry into a rich family to live a happy life, so I would be able to feel satisfied and rest assured. If you do not take my advice, and insist on marrying into a poor family to lead a life of suffering, you are not a worthy daughter of mine.' What would you do then? Would you give up the man you love and offer yourself to someone else to be the entertainer of his sex life? Sure, I know, every mother at the time of selecting a son-in-law would ask her daughter the question: 'Do you wish to marry for a happy life, or for suffering?' The mother's choice is invariably for enjoying a happy life. As to marriage without love, prostitution for life, and spiritual punishment and suffering—the mother does not take these into consideration at all. Does the mother indeed have the right to ask such a sacrifice? No, she does not have the right. For instance, you have told me about your Big Cousin and Mei. . . . If your mother has arranged for you the same fate as that of Mei, are you going to comply with her wish? Are you willing to accept her lot of having a whole life left at the wanton disposal of others?" The end was punctuated not by one question mark, but by several.

"Chien-ju, don't ask me this question, I beg you, my mind is in complete disarray, let me have time to think."

"Chin, what a time this is, will you still not open your eyes wide? Don't procrastinate any more. I can see that you have lived in the traditional family for too long a time, and have been too deeply contaminated by old ways. If you do not make up your mind soon enough to shake off all of these, you will quite possibly end up being the second Cousin Mei. . . ."

Her note got no reply from Chin, so Chien-ju turned to look at her. She found that Chin's eyes were filled with glistening tears. Her heart immediately softened. Her anger and indignation also gradually melted away. She extended her hand to hold Chin's hand that was resting on her thigh. She felt Chin's hand trembling, and tightened her grasp. If they had not been in class, she would have taken Chin in her arms. She looked at the platform and found that the teacher was writing on the blackboard, with his back to the class. She then put her lips up to Chin's ear and whispered, "Chin, maybe I have been hammering at it too hard, but I love you and care for you, I want you to be a courageous modern girl, I don't want you to follow Cousin Mei's lot. I strongly persuade you to brace up your spirit and fight on. Those who can march on with the times will eventually be rewarded. Only those falling behind will drink the potion of bitterness the rest of their lives, and that is the real tragedy. I hope this is crystal clear in your mind." Her lips almost kissed Chin's face.

Chin gave no answer, but turned to look at Chien-ju with a glance of deep gratitude, and then nodded in silence.

In the afternoon, when Chin and Chien-ju were through with classes and ready to go home, Wen and Old Miss got hold of them and asked Chien-ju to help cut off their braids.

A dozen or so girls crowded into Wen's room in the dormitory. They bolted the door, and Wen sat under the light from the window, and in one move of the scissors her braid was gone. Scissors in hand, Chien-ju felt elated. She went on to brush Wen's hair with great ease, until Wen looked in the mirror and expressed her satisfaction. Old Miss was not so meticulous as Wen, and Chien-ju was able to finish hers in a much shorter time. Thus in the room there were three short-haired girls.

Suddenly they heard a knock on the door which signalled the approach of the dorm supervisor. The girls quickly left the room and went home.

Chien-ju and Chin walked home together. At the crossroad where their ways parted, Chien-ju was about to say goodbye, but Chin begged Chien-ju to accompany her home. She said walking alone seemed frightening as she had just shared Chien-ju's experience of having insulting looks and words coming their way.

Actually Chin had something else in mind too. She wanted to find out what her mother's attitude was towards short hair for women, and she hoped that Chien-ju's fluent tongue and ready arguments could help convince her mother. But this was to no great avail, for Mrs. Chang would not say anything while Chien-ju was there, and from her words and attitude it could be surmised that she was against short hair for women.

After Chien-ju left that evening, Mrs. Chang lamented, "Such a nice girl, why does she go after these new-fangled ideas, making herself look neither a maiden nor a nun? There isn't a bit of the big family high principles left in her. She is really a pleasant girl, what a pity that her mother died early and she was left without adequate family principles in her, so that she was spoiled by having everything her way. Where this is going to lead in the future is indeed a lamentable situation. What a pity!" Mrs. Chang uttered deep sighs after she had said this. She felt that the world was now more bizarre every day, there was no way to imagine what it would become at the end. She tried to recapture the golden age of the past, and lamented that this golden age would never reappear. Then, her eyes caught Chin in an imploring mood, as if she had something to say but was not saying it, so she asked in surprise, "Chin, what is it?"

"Ma, I want to cut my hair like Chien-ju did," said Chin; then she timidly lowered her head.

"What did you say? You want to be like Chien-ju? You want people to ridicule me for being devoid of family principles?" Mrs. Chang said in great surprise, as if an unexpected blow had hit her with great impact. She couldn't believe her own ears.

"There is nothing wrong with wanting to be like Chien-ju!" Blood rushed to Chin's face, and although she knew that her hope was already half gone, she still braced up her courage and said, "Many girls in school have cut their hair. Short hair is more convenient, better looking, besides having a number of other advantages . . ." She was about to go on with it but was stopped by her mother.

Mrs. Chang showed a look of impatience, waved her hand and said, "I wouldn't want to hear your statement of righteous causes. I could not vie with you in making such statements, you command a great number of causes. You also have a great number of schemes and contrivances, today you want this, tomorrow you will want that. I am of the opinion that in a few days you will tell me that you want to fly high up into the sky. . . . One more thing I want to tell you. A few days ago Aunt Chien came to arrange a match for you, she said it is with the Cheng family, which is very wealthy. The boy is handsome, though he didn't go very far in his schooling, but the family wealth is more than enough to supply plentifully for his whole life, and marrying him would therefore ensure you lifelong happiness. Aunt Chien tried to persuade me to accept the match. But I thought that you wouldn't like it, so I turned it down. I said that you are still young, and I have only one daughter, and therefore we plan to think of marrying you off a few years from now. . . . But as it looks now, come to think of it, it really would be better to marry you off earlier, to avoid the trouble of new scheming every day, lest some day your reputation will be completely destroyed, and no one will come to ask for your hand anymore." Mrs. Chang spoke slowly, without any expression on her face, except that thin smile of weariness, making it hard to tell whether she had really made up her mind to take such action.

But in spite of this unknown quality, her words had already brought down a terrific blow on Chin. Now it was not only that the previous hope was totally gone, but at the same time a new source of terror had descended to bring tremendous pressure upon her. "The family is wealthy," "the boy is handsome," "didn't go very far in schooling," "it would really be better to marry you off earlier," these lines alternately rang in her ears. Before her eyes there suddenly appeared a lengthy highway stretching to infinity, upon which were lain spreading corpses of young women. It became clear to her that this road was built thousands of years ago; the earth on the road was saturated with the blood and tears of those women. They were all tied and handcuffed and driven to this road, and made to kneel there, to soak the earth with their blood and tears, to satiate the sex desire of wild animals with their bodies. When they first came they still groaned, wailed, prayed, hoping that someone would save them from this road. But before long their hope was shattered, their blood and tears were exhausted, they fell down and breathed their last breath. From several thousand distant years ago to the present day, this road had cut short the youthful lives of no one knows how many young women, and exhausted from them no one knows what measure of blood and tears. Indeed, buried there are millions and millions of heartbreaking, painful and tragic life stories.

Now there was aroused in Chin an emotional urge to appeal her case to justice. There were several questions whirling around in her head: "To whom would such sacrifice bring happiness?" "Is it the case that since for thousands of years this road has been soaked with the blood and tears of numberless young women, present day and future women would therefore still have to give up their youth and exhaust their blood and tears here?" "Is it the case that women will always be only the play things of men, the instruments for the satisfaction of their animal desire?"

Then, last but not the least: "Are you willing to give up the one you love, and hand yourself over to be the instrument of sexual satisfaction to some stranger?" She felt that at this very moment she was already kneeling on that road, groaning and wailing filled her ears, blood and flesh filled her eyes. What courage was left in her to search for answers to these questions? Justice was so dim, remote and uncertain. Her hope was completely dashed. She could not stand it any longer, she held her face in her hands and wept bitterly.

"What is the matter, my Chin? Did I say something that hurt you so much?" Mrs. Chang was startled. She stood up and came over to Chin's side and tenderly consoled her.

Chin cried with more abandon, she forcefully drew away from her mother's hand, as if she were fighting against someone, and muttered in a tragic voice, "I will not take that road. I want to be a human being, a human being like a man. . . . I don't want to go that way, I want to take a new road, I will take a new road."

XXIV

One night, after the electric lights in the compound had been turned off, Ming-feng was called to the apartment of Madam Chou. The fat face of the older woman was expressionless in the feeble glow of an oil lamp. Although she could not guess what Madam Chou was going to say, all day Ming-feng had a premonition that something bad was about to happen to her. She stood before Madam Chou with trembling heart and gazed at her unsteadily. They both were silent. The fat face seemed to swell gradually into a large, round object that wavered before Ming-feng's eyes, increasing her feeling of fear.

"Ming-feng, you've been with us for several years. I think you've worked long enough." Madam Chou began very deliberately, though still speaking more quickly than most people. After these first few words, her speed increased, until the syllables were popping from her lips like pearls.

"I'm sure you also are quite willing to leave," she continued. "Today, Venerable Master Kao instructed me to send you to the Feng family. You are going to be the concubine of the Venerable Master Feng. The first of next month is an auspicious day; they will call for you then. Today is the twenty-seventh. That still leaves four days. From tomorrow on, you needn't do any work. Take things easy for the next few days, until you go to the Feng family. . . .

"After you get there, be sure to take good care of the old man and the old lady. They say he's rather strange; his wife's temper is none too good either. Don't be stubborn; it's best to go along with their whims. They also have sons and daughters-in-law and grandchildren living together with them. You must respect them too.

"You've been a bondmaid in our family for several years, but you haven't gained anything from it. To tell you the truth I don't think we've treated you very well. Now that we've arranged this marriage for you I feel much better. The Feng family is very rich. As long as you remember to act according to your station, you'll never want for food or clothing. You'll be much better off than Fifth Household's Hsi-erh. . . .

"I'll think of you after you leave. You've looked after me all these years and I've never done anything to reward you. Tomorrow I'll have the tailor make you two new sets of good clothing, and I'll give you a little jewelry." The sound of Ming-feng's weeping interrupted her.

Although every word cut the girl's heart like a knife, she could only let them stab. She had no weapon with which to defend herself. Her hopes were completely shattered. They even wanted to take away the love she depended upon to live, to present her verdant spring to a crabbed old man. Life as a concubine in a family like the Feng's could bring only one reward: tears, blows, abuse, the same as before. The only difference would be that now, in addition, she would have to give her body to be despoiled by a peculiar old man whom she had never met.

To become a concubine—what a disgrace. Among the bondmaids "concubine!" was one of the worst imprecations they would think of. Ever since she was very small Ming-feng felt that it was a terrible thing to be a concubine. Yet after eight years of hard work and faithful service that was her only reward.

The road ahead looked very black. Even the thread of light which her pure love had brought her, even that was snapped. A fine young face floated before her. Then many ugly visages leered at her, horribly. Frightened, she covered her eyes with her hands, struggling against this terrifying vision.

Suddenly she seemed to hear a voice say, "Everything is decided by Fate. There is nothing you can do about it." An irresistible disappointment took possession of her, and she wept broken-heartedly.

Words were flying from Madam Chou so fast it was difficult for her to stop at once. But when she heard the girl's tragic weeping, she paused in surprise. She couldn't understand why Ming-feng was so upset, but she was moved by her tears.

"What's wrong, Ming-feng?" she asked. "Why are you crying?"

"Madam, I don't want to go!" sobbed Ming-feng. "I'd rather be a bondmaid here all my life, looking after you, and the young masters and the young mistresses. Madam, don't send me away, I beg you. There's still a lot I can do here. I've only been here eight years. I'm still so young, Madam. Please don't make me marry yet."

Madam Chou's maternal instincts were seldom aroused, but Ming-feng's impassioned pleas struck a responsive chord. The older woman was swept by a feeling of motherly love and pity for the girl.

"I was afraid you wouldn't be willing," she said with a sad smile. "It's true, the Venerable Master Feng is old enough to be your grandfather. But that's what our Venerable Master has decided. I must obey him. After you get there, if you serve the old man well, things won't be so bad. Anyhow you'll be much better off than married to some poor working man, never knowing where your next meal is coming from."

"Madam, I'm willing to starve—anything but become a concubine." As Ming-feng blurted these words, the strength drained from her body, and she fell to her knees. Embracing Madam Chou's legs, she begged, "Please don't send me away. Let me stay here as a bondmaid. I'll serve you all my life. . . . Madam, have pity, I'm still so young. Pity me. You can scold me, beat me, anything—only don't send me to the Feng family. I'm afraid. I couldn't bear that kind of life. Madam, be merciful, pity me. Madam, I've always been obedient, but this—I can't do it!"

Endless words were welling up from her heart into her throat, but something seemed to be stopping her mouth, and she could only swallow them down again and weep softly. The more she cried the more stricken she felt. The tragedy was too overwhelming. If only she could cry her heart out, she might have some relief.

Looking at the girl weeping at her feet, Madam Chou was reminded of her own past. Sadly, maternally, she stroked Ming-feng's hair.

"I know you're too young," she said sympathetically. "To tell you the truth, I'm against your going to the Feng family. But our Venerable Master has already promised. He's the kind who never goes back on his word. I'm only his daughter-in-law. I don't dare oppose him. It's too late. On the first, you must go. Don't cry. Crying won't do any good. Just gather your courage and go. Maybe your life will be comfortable there. Don't be afraid. People with good hearts always get their just rewards. Get up now. It's time for you to be in bed."

Ming-feng hugged Madam Chou's legs tighter, as if they were the only things that could save her. With her last strength she cried despondently, "Don't you have even a little pity for me, Madam? Save me. I'd rather die than go to the Feng family!"

Raising her tear-stained face, she looked into Madam Chou's eyes and stretched forth her hands pleadingly. "Save me, Madam!" Her voice was tragic.

Madam Chou shook her head. "There's nothing I can do," she replied sadly. "I don't want you to go, myself, but it's no use. Even I can't go against the decision of the Venerable Master. Get up now, and go to bed like a good girl." She pulled Ming-feng to her feet.

Ming-feng offered no resistance. All hope was gone. She stood dazedly before Madam Chou, feeling that she was in a dream. After a moment, she looked around. Everything was dim and dark. She was still sobbing soundlessly. Finally, she brought herself under control. In a dull, melancholy tone she said, "I'll do what you say, Madam."

Madam Chou rose wearily. "Good. As long as you're obedient I won't have to worry about you."

Ming-feng knew it was no use to remain any longer. She had never been so miserable in her life. "I'm going to bed, Madam," she said listlessly. She slowly walked from the room, her hand pressed to her breast. She was afraid her heart would burst.

Madam Chou sighed as she watched the girl's retreating back, sorry that she was unable to help her. But, half an hour later, this comfortable, well-fed lady had forgotten all about Ming-feng.

The courtyard was dark and deserted. Feeble lamplight gleamed in Chueh-hui's window. Originally Ming-feng had intended to return to the servants' room but now, seeing the light, she walked softly towards Chueh-hui's quarters. The light was seeping through the tiny openings in the curtain, casting a pretty pattern on the ground. That curtain, the glass windows, that room, now seemed particularly adorable to Ming-feng. She stood on the stone porch outside the window and gazed unwinking at the white gauze curtain, holding her breath and being as quiet as possible so as not to disturb the boy inside.

Gradually, she imagined she could see colours on the white curtain; they became even more beautiful. Beautiful people emerged from the maze of colour—boys and girls, very handsomely dressed, with proud and haughty bearing. They cast disdainful glances at her as they passed, then hurried on. Suddenly, the one she thought of day and night appeared in their midst. He gazed at her affectionately and halted, as if he wanted to speak to her. But crowds of people came hurrying and pushing from behind him, and he disappeared among them. Her eyes sought him intently, but the white gauze curtain, hanging motionless, concealed the interior of the room from view.

Ming-feng drew closer, hoping to get a look inside, but the window was higher than her head, and after two unsuccessful attempts, she stepped back, disappointed. As she did so, her hand accidentally bumped against the window-sill, making a slight noise. From within the room came a cough. That meant he wasn't asleep. She stared at the curtain. Would he push it aside and look out?

But inside it became quiet again, except for the low sound of a pen scratching on paper. Ming-feng rapped softly against the window-sill. She heard what sounded like a chair being shifted, then the scratching of the pen again, a bit faster. Ming-feng was afraid if she rapped any harder, she might be overheard. Chueh-min slept in the same room. Clutching a final hope, she again tapped, three times, and called softly, "Third Young Master." Stepping back, she waited quietly. She was sure he would come out this time. But again there was nothing but the rapid scratching of the pen and the low surprised remark, "Two a.m. already? . . . And I've a class at eight in the morning. . . ." And the sound of the writing resumed once more.

Ming-feng stood dully. Tapping again would be no use. He wouldn't hear it. She didn't blame him, in fact she loved him all the more. His words were still in her ears, and to her they were sweeter than music. He seemed to be standing beside her —so warm, so very much alive.

He needed a girl to love him and take care of him, and there was no one in the world who loved him more than she. She would do anything for him. But she also knew there was a wall between them. People wanted to send her to the Feng family, soon, too, in four days. Then she would belong to the Fengs; she'd have no opportunity to see him again. No matter how she might be insulted and abused, he'd have no way of knowing. He wouldn't be able to save her. They'd be separated, for ever separated. It would be worse than if they had been parted by death.

Ming-feng felt that a life of that kind was not worth living. When she had said to Madam Chou, "I'd rather die than go to the Feng family," she had meant it. She was really considering death. The Eldest Young Miss had often told her that suicide was the only way out for girls who were the victims of Fate. Ming-feng believed this fully.

A long sigh from the room broke in on her wild thoughts. Mournfully, she looked around. All was still and very dark. Suddenly she remembered a similar scene of several months ago. Only that time he had been outside her window, and the conjecture he had overheard then had today become a reality. She recalled all the details—his attitude towards her, how she had said to him, "I'll never go to another man. I give my vow."

Something seemed to be wringing her heart, and she was blinded by tears. The lamplight from the window shone down on her head pitilessly. Eagerly she gazed at the beams, a hope slowly forming in her breast. She would cast all caution to winds, rush into his room, kneel at his feet, tell him her whole bitter story, beg him to save her. She would be his slave for ever, love him, take care of him.

But just then, everything went black. The lamp had been turned out. She stared, but she could see nothing. Rooted to the spot, she stood alone in the night, the merciless night that hemmed her in from all sides.

After a few moments, she finally was able to move. Slowly she groped her way through the disembodied darkness towards her own room. After a long time, she reached the women servants' quarters. She pushed open the half-closed door and went in.

A wick was sputtering feebly in a dish of oil. The rest of the room was all darkness and shadows. Beds on both sides of the room were laden with corpse-like figures. Harsh snores from the bed of the fat Sister Chang struck out in every direction in a very frightening manner. They halted the startled Ming-feng in the doorway, and for a moment she peered anxiously around. Then with dragging feet she walked over to the table and trimmed the wick. The room became much brighter.

About to take off her clothes, Ming-feng was suddenly crushed by a terrible depression. She threw herself on her bed and began to cry, pressing her head against the bedding and soaking it with her tears. The more she thought, the worse she felt. Old Mama Huang, awakened by the sound of her weeping, asked in a fuzzy voice, "What are you crying about?"

Ming-feng did not answer. She only wept. After offering a soothing word or two, Mama Huang turned over and was soon fast asleep again. Ming-feng was left alone with her

209

heartbroken tears. She continued to cry until sleep claimed her.

By the next morning Ming-feng had changed into a different person. She stopped smiling, she moved in a leaden manner, she avoided people. She suspected they knew about her; she imagined they were smiling disdainfully, and she hurried to get away. If she saw a few servants talking together, she was sure they were discussing her. She seemed to hear the word "concubine" everywhere, even among the masters and mistresses.

"Such a pretty girl," she thought she heard the Fifth Master say. "It's a shame to make her a concubine of that old man."

In the kitchen she heard the fat Sister Chang angrily comment, "A young girl like that becoming the 'little wife' of an old man who's half dead! I wouldn't do it for all the money in the world!"

It got so that Ming-feng was afraid to go anywhere for fear of hearing contemptuous remarks. Except when she had to join the other servants for her two meals a day, she hid in her room or in the garden, alone and lonely. Once in a while, Hsi-erh or Chien-erh came to see her. But they were both very busy, and they could only steal out briefly for a comforting word or two.

Ming-feng wanted very much to speak to Chueh-hui, and she was constantly seeking an opportunity. But lately he and Chueh-min were busier than usual. They left for school very early each morning and came home late in the afternoon. Sometimes they had dinner out. But even when they ate at home, they would go out again immediately after the evening meal and not return until nine or ten at night. Then they would shut themselves in their room and read, or write articles. On the one or two occasions she happened to meet Chueh-hui, he gave a tender glance or a smile, but did not speak to her. Of course these were signs of his love, and she knew he was busy with serious affairs; even though he had no time for her, she did not blame him.

But the days were passing quickly. She simply had to speak

to him, to pour out her troubles, to seek his help. He didn't seem to have any inkling of what was happening to her, and he gave her no chance to tell him.

Now it was the last day of the month. Not many people in the compound knew about Ming-feng. Chueh-hui was completely in the dark. He was all wrapped up in the weekly magazine. Even the hours he spent at home were devoted to study and writing; he had no contact with anyone who might have told him about Ming-feng.

To Chueh-hui the thirtieth was the same as any other day. But for Ming-feng it was the day of reckoning: Either she would leave him for ever or serve him for ever. The latter possibility was very slim, and Ming-feng knew it. Naturally she was hopeful that he would be able to save her and that she could remain his devoted servant always. But between them was a wall which could not be demolished—their difference in status.

Ming-feng knew this very well. That day in the garden when she had said to him, "No, no. I just wasn't fated," she already knew. He had replied that he would marry her. But his grandfather, Madam Chou and all the elders were arrayed against them. What could he do? Even Madam Chou didn't dare go against a decision of the Venerable Master Kao. What chance would a grandson stand?

Ming-feng's fate was irrevocably decided. But she couldn't give up the last shred of hope. She was fooling herself, really, for she knew there wasn't the slightest hope, and never could be.

She waited to see Chueh-hui that day with trembling heart. He came home after nine in the evening. She walked to his window. Hearing the voice of his brother, she hesitated, afraid to go in but unwilling to leave. If she gave up this last opportunity, whether she lived or died, she would never be able to see him again.

At long last Ming-feng heard footsteps. Someone was coming out. She quickly hid in a corner. A dark figure emerged from the room. It was Chueh-min. She waited until he was some distance away, then hurried into the room.

Chueh-hui was bent over his desk, writing. He did not look up as he heard her enter, but continued with his work. Ming-feng timidly approached.

"Third Young Master," she called gently.

"Ming-feng, it's you?" Chueh-hui raised his head in surprise. He smiled at her. "What is it?"

"I have to speak to you." Her melancholy eyes avidly scanned his smiling face. Before she could go on, he interrupted.

"Is it because I haven't talked with you these last few days? You think I've been ignoring you?" He laughed tenderly. "No, you mustn't think that. You see how busy I am. I have to study and write, and I've other things to do too." Chueh-hui pointed at a pile of manuscripts and magazines. "I'm as busy as an ant. It will be better in a day or two. I'll have finished this work by then. I promise you. Only two more days."

"Two more days?" Ming-feng cried, disappointed. As if she hadn't understood, she asked again, "Two more days?"

"That's right," said Chueh-hui with a smile. "In two more days I'll be finished. Then we can talk. There's so much I want to tell you." He again bent over his writing.

"Third Young Master, don't you have any time now, even a little?" Ming-feng held back her tears with an effort.

"Can't you see I'm busy?" said Chueh-hui roughly, as if reproving her for persisting. But when he observed her stricken expression and the tears in her eyes, he immediately softened. Taking her hand he stood up and asked soothingly, "Has someone been picking on you? Don't feel badly."

He really wanted to put aside his work and take her into the garden and comfort her. But when he remembered that he had to submit his article by the next morning, when he recalled the struggle the magazine was waging, he changed his mind.

"Be patient," he pleaded. "In another two days we'll have a long talk. I definitely will help you. I love you as much as ever. But please go now and let me finish my work. You'd better hurry. Second Young Master will be back in a minute."

Chueh-hui looked around to make sure that they were alone, then took her face in his hands and lightly kissed her lips. Smiling, he indicated with a gesture that she should leave quickly. He resumed his position at the desk, pen in hand, but his heart was pounding. It was the first time he had ever kissed her.

Ming-feng stood dazed and silent. She didn't know what she was thinking or how she felt. Her fingers moved up to touch her lips—lips that had just experienced their first kiss. "Two more days," she repeated.

Outside, someone was heard approaching, whistling. "Go, quickly," Chueh-hui urged. "Second Young Master is coming."

Ming-feng seemed to awake from a dream and her expression changed. Her lips trembled, but she did not speak. She gazed at him longingly with the utmost tenderness, and her eyes suddenly shone with tears. "Third Young Master," she cried in an anguished voice.

Chueh-hui looked up quickly, only to see her disappearing through the doorway.

He sighed. "Women are strange creatures." He again bent over his writing.

Chueh-min came into the room. The first words out of his mouth were, "Wasn't that Ming-feng who just left here?"

"Yes." Chueh-hui continued writing. He did not look at his brother.

"That girl isn't the least bit like an ordinary bondmaid. She's intelligent, pure, pretty—she can even read a little. It's a shame that *Yeh-yeh* is giving her to that old reprobate for a concubine. It's a real shame!" sighed Chueh-min.

"What did you say?" Chueh-hui put down his pen. He was shocked.

"Don't you know? Ming-feng is getting married."

"She's getting married? Who said so? She's too young!"

"*Yeh-yeh* is giving her to that shameless old scoundrel Feng to be his concubine."

"I don't believe it! Why, he's one of the main pillars of the Confucian Morals Society. He's nearly sixty. He still wants a concubine?"

"Don't you remember last year when he and a couple of his old cronies published a list of 'Best Female Impersonators' and were bitterly attacked by *Students' Tide?* His kind are capable of anything. He gets away with it, too—he's got money, hasn't he? The wedding day is tomorrow. I certainly am sorry for Ming-feng. She's only seventeen."

"Tomorrow? Why wasn't I told before? Why didn't anyone tell me?" Chueh-hui jumped to his feet and hurried out, clutching his hair. He was trembling all over.

"Tomorrow!" "Marry!" "Concubine!" "Old Feng!" The words lashed against Chueh-hui's brain till he thought it would shatter. He rushed out; he thought he heard a mournful wail. Suddenly he discovered a dark world lying at his feet. All was quiet, as if every living thing had died. Where was he to go in this misty space between heaven and earth? He wandered about, tearing his hair, beating his breast, but nothing could bring him peace.

Suddenly a torturing realization dawned upon him. She had come to him just now in the utmost anguish, to beg for his help. Because she believed in his love and because she loved him, she had come to ask him to keep his promise and protect her, to rescue her from the clutches of old man Feng. And what had he done? Absolutely nothing. He had given her neither help nor sympathy nor pity—nothing at all. He sent her away without even listening to her pleas. Now she was gone, gone for ever. Tomorrow night, in the arms of that old man, she would weep for her despoiled springtime. And at the same time she would curse the one who had tricked her into giving her pure young love and then sent her into the jaws of the tiger.

It was a terrifying thought. Chueh-hui couldn't bear it. He had to find her, he had to atone for his crime.

He walked to the women servants' quarters and lightly tapped on the door. Inside it was pitch dark. He called "Ming-feng," twice, in a low voice. There was no answer. She must be asleep, he thought. Because of the other women, he couldn't very well go in.

Chueh-hui returned to his room. But he couldn't sit still. Again he came out and went to the servants' quarters. Pushing the door open a trifle, he could hear only snoring inside. He walked into the garden and stood for a long time in the dark beneath the plum trees. "Ming-feng!" he shouted. Only the echo replied. Several times he bumped his head against the low-hanging plum branches, scratching his forehead and drawing blood. But he felt no pain. Finally, disappointed, he slowly walked back to his own room. As he entered his room, everything began to spin.

Actually, the girl he sought was not with the women servants, but in the garden.

When Ming-feng left Chueh-hui's room she knew that this time all hope was gone. She was sure he loved her as much as ever; her lips were still warm with his kiss, her hands still felt his clasp. These proved that he loved her; but they were also symbols of the fact that she was going to lose him and be cast into the arms of a lecherous old man. She would never see him again. In the long years ahead there would be only endless pain and misery. Why should she cling to a life like that? Why should she remain in a world without love?

Ming-feng made up her mind.

She went directly to the garden, groping her way through the darkness with a great effort until she reached her objective —the edge of the lake. The waters darkly glistened; at times feeding fish broke the placid surface. Ming-feng stood dully, remembering many things of the past. She recalled everything she and Chueh-hui had ever said and done together. She could see every familiar tree and shrub—so dear, so lovely—knowing that she was going to leave them all.

The world was very still. Everyone was asleep. But they were all alive, and they would continue living. She alone was going to die.

In the seventeen years of her existence she had known nothing but blows, curses, tears, toil in the service of others. That plus a love for which she now must perish. Life had brought much less happiness to her than to others; but now, despite her youth, she would leave the world first.

Tomorrow, others had their tomorrow. For her there was only a dark empty void. Tomorrow birds would sing in the trees, the rising sun would gild their branches, countless pearls would bubble on the surface of the water. But she would see none of it, for her eyes would be closed for ever.

The world was such an adorable place. She had loved everyone with all the purity of a young girl's heart, wishing them all well. She had served people without pause; she had brought harm to no one. Like other girls she had a pretty face, an intelligent mind, a body of flesh and blood. Why did people want to trample her, hurt her, deny her a friendly glance, a sympathetic heart, even a pitying sigh?

She had never owned nice clothes, nor eaten good food, nor slept in a warm bed. She had accepted all this without complaint. For she had won the love of a fine young man, she had found a hero whom she could worship, and she was satisfied. She found a refuge.

But today, when the crisis came, reality had proved it was all an illusion. His love couldn't save her; it only added to her painful memories.

He was not for her. His love had brought her many beautiful dreams, but now it was casting her into a dark abyss. She loved life, she loved everything, but life's door was closing in her face, leaving her only the road to degradation.

Thinking of what this meant, she looked at her body in horror. Although she could not see clearly in the darkness, she knew it was chaste and pure. She could almost feel someone casting her into the mire. Painfully, pityingly, she caressed her body with soothing hands.

Ming-feng came to a decision. She would hesitate no longer. She stared at the calm water. The crystal depths of the lake would give her refuge. She would die unsullied.

About to jump, a thought came to her, and she paused. She shouldn't die like this. She ought to see him once more, pour out her heart to him. Perhaps he could save her. His kiss still tingled on her lips, his face still shimmered before her eyes. She loved him so; she couldn't bear to lose him. The only beauty in her life had been his love. Wasn't she entitled even to that? When everyone else went on living, why did a young girl like her have to die?

She pictured an idyllic scene in which she chatted and laughed and played with rich girls her own age in a beautiful garden. In this wide world she knew there were many such girls and many such gardens. Yet she had to end her young life—and there was no one to shed a sympathetic tear, or offer a word or two of comfort. Her death would bring no loss to the world, or to the Kao family. People would quickly forget her, as if she had never existed.

Has my life really been so meaningless? she thought, stricken. Her heart filled with an unspeakable grief, and tears spilled from her eyes. Strength draining from her body, she weakly sat upon the ground. She seemed to hear someone call her name. It was his voice. She halted her tears and listened. But all was quiet; all voices were stilled. She listened, hoping to hear the call again. She listened for a long, long time. But there was no sound in the night.

Then she knew. He was not coming. There was a wall eternally between them. He belonged to a different sphere. He had his future, his career. He must become a great man. She could not hold him back, keep him always at her side. She must release him. His existence was much more important than hers. She could not let him sacrifice himself for her sake. She must go, she must leave him for ever. And she would do so willingly, since he was more precious to her than life itself.

A pain stabbed through her heart, and she rubbed her chest. But the pain persisted. She remained seated on the ground, her eyes longingly roving over the familiar surroundings in the dark. She was still thinking of him. A mournful smile flitted across her face and her eyes dimmed with tears.

Finally, she could not bear to think any longer. Rising tottering to her feet, she cried in a voice laden with tenderness and sorrow, "Chueh-hui, Chueh-hui!"—and she plunged into the lake.

The placid waters stirred violently, and a loud noise broke the stillness. Two or three tragic cries, although they were very low, echoed lingeringly in the night. After a few minutes of wild thrashing, the surface of the lake again became calm. Only the mournful cries still permeated the air, as if the entire garden were weeping softly.

217

XXV

Chueh-hui slept badly that night and got up late the next morning. He and Chueh-min hurried to school, but classes were in session for over ten minutes by the time they arrived.

Mr. Chu, their tall, thin English teacher, was reading aloud from *Resurrection*. Chueh-hui and the other students listened carefully, preparing to answer questions that would be asked on the passage being read.

But Chueh-hui's mind kept going back to Ming-feng, and thinking of her made him tremble inwardly. Not that he had determined to hold on to her. No. After pondering the matter all night, he was ready to let her go. It was a painful decision, but he felt that he could carry it through. There were two things in the back of his mind with which he was already consoling himself for Ming-feng's loss. One was that he wanted to devote himself entirely to serving society. The other was that a person of his position could never really marry a bondmaid —his petty bourgeois pride would not permit it.

The day at school passed quickly. On the way home, Chueh-hui was again torn by conflicting thoughts. Though he said nothing, his brother could tell from his face that something was troubling him, and did not try to draw him into conversation.

Just as they were going through the inner gate of their compound, they saw the sedan-chair the Feng family had sent for Ming-feng departing, accompanied by two servants. Tragic weeping came through the sedan-chair curtains. Although it was barely audible, it went straight to Chueh-hui's heart. She was leaving, and she would never return.

Servants who had seen the sedan-chair off were still gathered in the garden. Chueh-hui was sure they were discussing Ming-feng. He didn't dare to look at them. Hurriedly, he walked on. A mournful voice greeted him as he entered the inner compound:

"You're home early today." The speaker was Chien-yun. His long thin face was cast in its usual melancholy lines. He had been standing on the steps talking with Chueh-hsin, but came towards the two younger brothers when he saw them approaching. Chueh-hsin silently turned and went back to his own apartment.

"We've been having only one class in the afternoon lately, because we're getting ready for exams," replied Chueh-min.

Chien-yun followed them into their apartment and sat down on a cane chair. He sighed deeply.

"Why are you always so gloomy, Chien-yun?" Chueh-min asked him. As for Chueh-hui, he tossed his books on the desk and lay down on his bed without a word to anyone.

"Life is too cruel!" Chien-yun sadly shook his head.

Chueh-min was about to twit him for having such easily wounded sensibilities. But then he remembered Chien-yun's remark about his bad health and how he had lost his parents at an early age, and he changed his mind. Instead, he urged kindly:

"Don't take everything so hard, Chien-yun. Why must you always dwell on things that make you unhappy?"

"Too cruel, too cruel!" Chien-yun didn't seem to have heard Chueh-min. "I just happened to drop in, and there she was, struggling, weeping, as they forced her into the sedan-chair. I cried too. After all, she's a human being. Why should she be treated like some lifeless object and sent to that old—"

"Who do you mean? Are you talking about Ming-feng?" Chueh-min asked sympathetically.

"Ming-feng?" Chien-yun looked at Chueh-min in surprise. "I'm talking about Wan-erh," he said heatedly. "The sedan-chair just left. Didn't you see it?"

Chueh-hui sat up quickly on the bed. "Then Ming-feng didn't go?" he asked delightedly.

"Ming-feng. . . ." Chien-yun's voice trailed off. He turned his hazy eyes on Chueh-hui and said quietly, "Ming-feng . . . drowned herself in the lake."

"What? Ming-feng killed herself?" Chueh-hui leaped to his

feet in horror. Clutching his hair, he paced the room distractedly.

"So they say. Her body has already been carried out of the compound. I didn't see it. Well, she's probably better off than Wan-erh. . . ."

"Ah, so that's it. Ming-feng killed herself, and *Yeh-yeh* sent Wan-erh in her place. Bondmaids aren't persons in *Yeh-yeh*'s eyes, just things he can hand out as gifts," Chueh-min cried, half in anger, half in pity. "I didn't realize that Ming-feng was a girl of such strong character. To do a thing like that!"

"The result is that Wan-erh is out of luck," said Chien-yun. "It would have made anyone weep to see the way she struggled. I think she might have chosen the same path as Ming-feng, but the thing happened too suddenly. She had no idea they were going to send her. And they watched her every minute. . . ."

"I never thought *Yeh-yeh* could do such a thing! One is dead, so he sends another. These girls are people's daughters. How can they be treated so brutally?" Chueh-min demanded hotly.

"Tell me, how did Ming-feng kill herself?" Chueh-hui suddenly walked up to Chien-yun, grabbed his arm and shook it savagely.

Startled, Chien-yun looked at him, unable to comprehend his passion. In his usual emotional tone, he replied: "I don't know. I'm afraid nobody knows. One of the servants discovered her body. He called a few others and they fished her out, then they carried her away, and that was the end. . . . This life, this world . . . it's too cruel."

Chueh-hui stared at Chien-yun's gaunt visage, ravaged by long years of grief. His own face was expressionless. Roughly, he dropped Chien-yun's arm, turned without a word and ran out.

"What's wrong with him?" Chien-yun was confused.

"I'm beginning to understand," Chueh-min nodded.

"Maybe you do, but I don't!" Chien-yun again lowered his head and lapsed into his own thoughts. He was eternally timid, eternally humble.

"Can't you see that love is at the bottom of it?" Chueh-min

shouted. There was no answer. The room was still. Occasional footsteps outside seemed to be stamping on his heart.

After some minutes, Chien-yun again slowly raised his head. His misty eyes travelled about the room, and he said to himself in a shaking voice, "I . . . understand."

Chueh-min rose and paced the floor with large strides. Suddenly he sat down on the chair beside the desk and fixed his gaze on Chien-yun's face. The eyes of the two young men met, exchanging some unhappy thoughts. Chien-yun was the first to lower his head.

"It was all for love," Chueh-min said bitterly. "Third Brother and Ming-feng. . . . I suspected they were interested in each other. . . . Who knew it would come to this? I never dreamed that Ming-feng could be so strong-willed! . . . What a pity. She was a fine girl. If only she had been born in some rich family. . . ." Chueh-min couldn't go on. His internal struggle was reflected on his face.

It was some time before he could say in a shaken voice, "Love, all for love. . . . Big Brother is much thinner lately. The last few days, his spirits have been very low. . . . And isn't it love that's making him that way? . . . I used to think that love brought happiness. Why does it cause so much misery? . . ."

There were tears in Chueh-min's trembling voice. Thinking of his own love affair, he was ready to weep. He could see dark shadows lying ahead. The fate of Big Brother was a terrible example of what might happen to him too.

Chien-yun did not know the cause of Chueh-min's grief, and thought it was solely for sympathy, while at the same time the melancholies of his own heart had also come to be aroused by Chueh-min's words of grief. The grief that had filled his life was more enormous than anybody else's, and he needed sympathy more than anybody else. For a long time he had this heart full of grief in him, unable to find somebody to unload it on, to hear him out. He had always considered himself too unimportant, too incompetent, inferior to everyone else. He had always led a life of humility, and had been truthful towards everyone, but what he got in return was contempt and indifference. Sometimes he was treated with a little sympathy, and although it was only superficial and very thin, to him it was an unmerited favour. Having grown up constantly being stepped on by others, he had never complained of life, and had in fact tolerated contempt and indifference with sobriety or, it might even be said, timidity. This was the kind of life he had lived for all these years.

Now suddenly a possible chance to be heard appeared before him. He would not complain, but only pour out before a man of great sympathy, a man capable of sympathizing with him, the traumatic grief and despair which his crushed and forlorn love had brought upon him all this time. He felt that Chueh-min was such a person, for he had just witnessed Chueh-min being emotionally involved to such an extent for the misfortune of somebody else. Thus the words that he had stored in his heart all this time became an urge forcing him to go ahead. After a few timid false starts he eventually managed to begin. "Chueh-min, I have something to tell you, but I do not know whether I should bother you with my affairs." He stopped here, timidly casting a glance at Chueh-min, and feeling assured by Chueh-min's benignant response, he was able to find courage to go on. "Now that I have recovered from my illness, I do not know why death should cross my mind all the time. Under the conditions of my life, indeed to live is worse than to die, yet in a way I am also afraid to die. Just imagine, to live is so miserable and lonely, to die would be so much more miserable and lonely! There would not be anybody to come to see me, to shed tears over me, all alone, all the time all alone, how lonely it is! . . . You brothers have kindly visited me several times in my illness. These visits shall always be in my heart. What gratitude I have for you brothers! . . ."

"Do not mention these," Chueh-min said, feeling somewhat embarrassed by Chien-yun's words and wanting to change the subject.

"Yes, I must say it. Chueh-min, if my life is worth your sympathy, would you promise that after I die you would come every spring and fall to see me at my grave?" He stopped, to stifle his sobs.

"Chien-yun, why should you say such cheerless things, don't you see that we have had enough miseries." These words from

Chueh-min, though a reproach, were lodged in a tone of great warmth, so they did not check Chien-yun from continuing.

Chien-yun went on after rubbing his eyes, "I have to say it. I have to let you hear the whole of my story, I want you to understand me. Right now only you will be able to hear me out . . . for Big Brother has his own griefs, Chueh-hui also has his own griefs, and I cannot add mine to theirs. . . . You have just brought up the question why love imposes upon us so much suffering, this is a question that I have long asked . . . because I have forlornly loved a woman. I understand quite well that this love is not mine to have, for I know that she will not love me, and that I cannot marry her. I have always told myself, 'Don't dream anymore, why should you love her? Is one like you worthy of anybody's love? Give up this forlorn love, and go bury yourself in nonentity and darkness.'

"Yet in reality I wasn't able to do it. Her presence remains always in my memory. I cannot stop thinking of her. Hearing her name mentioned would quicken the beats of my heart; having a glance at her face amounts to a great blessing. I always call out her name by myself, many times the very name would comfort me, encourage me, but again many times the very name could bring me immeasurable pain. For once I call out her name, my yearning for her is more impassioned, and I have the urge to be with her right away, to pour out the feelings of my bosom to her. Yet such courage I do not have. How could such a petty imbecile like me dare to bare my thoughts to a person of such nobleness and purity like her? . . .

"Whenever I saw her, I would try to get to talk to her. I would do my utmost to search for proper things to say, I would exhaust my wits to search for words that would please her. . . . But once I opened my lips, my heart would fail me, I would lose my concentration; my mind would fail me, I am at my wit's end. It made me feel that I was utterly inferior, in no position to be with her. I would turn remorseful, I got bitter, I became intense: I have only myself to blame. The result was that I would always say things to her that I would not comprehend myself. I knew that she would despise me. Although she would still courteously talk to me with earnestness and concern, how would I dare to go deeper to unfold myself. There is so much distance between us, she is high above in heaven, and I am down below in the trodden earth. . . . I don't know why a man grown up among contempt and treading like I am should possess the instinct of love. And why should I fall in love with her of all women? And why is she so noble and pure that I dare not raise the word love before her? . . . Such love, such forlorn love, how painful it is! . . . Of course this is all my own fault, I can't blame her, she was not aware of it at all! . . . But day after day I have been inflicted with the painful suffering born of such forlorn hope, I have become thinner and thinner in constitution and weaker and weaker in strength. . . .

"Time and again I would go over to take a look at her window. Sometimes she would be in, and I would see the white window curtains, which would allow me a great deal of imagination, beautiful imagination. It would appear to me that I could see her there, her every move inside her room, as if I were close beside her. But such comfort was only transitory, for before long I would become aware of what I am myself, and right then and there I would fall straight down to the bottom, to the filth. . . . When she was home, I would hear her cough, hear her talk, what beautiful sounds they were! I would then have to exert myself to the fullest to be able to bring myself to books, to the teaching of my pupils. . . . Sometimes she was in school and still not home, and the absence of her voice would make me feel the oppression of loneliness too, and I would have to make the same kind of exertion to calm myself from my distracted and distorted feelings. . . . To her I have dedicated every bit of my love, every drop of my blood; more than that, I have reduced my physical self to such a carcass, but she was totally unaware of it, not a single soul knows about it. Even if she were aware of it, what would she have done? She would have some pity on me at the most, she would not love me . . . I understand quite well that no woman at all would ever love me. I am only a lowly good-for-nothing! In this world there is so much light, there is so much love, but they are not for me. I am a man forsaken by blessings and happiness . . ." He halted. Chueh-min did not make any effort to say anything, and in the room only the quickened breathing of the two could be heard.

Chien-yun wiped his eyes with a handkerchief, swept his humble and melancholy glance once again over Chueh-min's face which was evidently moved by his words, and then, forcing a bitter smile, he slowly went on, "Chueh-min, you would ridicule me for my unworthiness, I am indeed utterly devoid of any self-respect. Sometimes I really did forget what kind of a man I am. Sometimes in utter despair I would even blame my parents for letting me live under such conditions. If only I could have better conditions, for example, if I were in your place, I would not have become as despondent and unworthy as I am now . . . Chueh-min, I envy you, I have always wished, or even prayed, that I could be in your place, to be able to see her and talk to her with freedom and ease like you do. I would be willing to give up ten years of my life. . . .

"I often stay sick, sometimes because of her. I would think of her even in my illness, think of her with even more passion. I would pray all the time, wishing that she would come to visit my sick bed just once. I would steadily call out her name in an undertone. I expect that there will be a day when she will hear it. . . . Whenever I hear footsteps I think they must be hers. But I can distinguish her footsteps very easily. Her foot steps right on top of my heart all the time. But she has not come to visit me even once. . . . I remember that you brothers came to see me, and when I saw you, it was like seeing her. For you brothers have been with her very often. When I overheard her name mentioned in your conversation, how fast my heart would beat! I would feel that I was much better right away. But soon you left, and I didn't know when you would come again. When I was overwhelmed by the quietude and loneliness that confronted me when you left, I felt as if I were going to die immediately. You didn't know how eagerly I was expecting you or with what feelings I expressed my gratitude towards you. I was thinking of asking you to forward a few words to her, or of inquiring about her from you. But I was afraid that you would discover my secret feelings, ridicule me, reproach me, so I did not dare say a single word. . . . When you brothers came the second time to

225

see me, I saw the issue of *Dawn* in Chueh-hui's hands, with her article in it and with the title and author's name unmistakably there. I was tempted to borrow the issue from Chueh-hui so that I could read it carefully. But I don't know why I was unable to do it. I was afraid that once I made the request, you would immediately divine my secret, and reproach me and not want to see me anymore. Although in hindsight I understood very well that my apprehension and overdone discretion were ridiculous, at the time it occurred to me that way. . . . After you brothers left, I recited the title of that article I don't know how many times." He halted, pressed his hand on his breast and massaged for a few strokes. His eyes remained focused on the floor. Chueh-min suddenly coughed.

"I was about to come to my conclusion," Chien-yun continued. "I shouldn't have wasted your time by imposing my petty troubles on you, but besides you, there is not a single soul in the world that would care to hear out my words . . . I think you might be in love with her, but naturally you would not be jealous of me. Who would be jealous of someone like me? I envy you and hope you will be able to marry her in love and fulfillment. . . . You do understand me, I take it for granted. Could you promise me that you will visit my grave after I die? If you marry her, and the two of you could come together to see me, how grateful I would be to you both from my final resting place! Will you promise me? Would you promise me to bestow upon me this only blessing of my whole unworthy existence?" He looked at Chueh-min with beseeching eyes.

Chueh-min could not take it, he avoided Chien-yun's eyes. While Chien-yun was talking, Chueh-min changed his facial expression from time to time, but he kept his lips tight without uttering a single word. But towards this last moment he was greatly moved, he could not bear it anymore, he was overwhelmed by an onrush of emotions of sympathy and pity. In spite of himself he said to Chien-yun in a tone of sorrow and agony, "I promise you, whatever you ask I promise you." He was unable to say anything more. Of course he meant what he said, yet at the same time the words he said could not bear his own scrutiny; for if at this moment Chien-yun should ask him to give up Chin, although it was not within his power to hand Chin over to Chien-yun, nevertheless the answer he would give would be a definite no, no matter under what circumstances.

"I don't know what to say to you to express my thankfulness," said Chien-yun as tears of gratitude ran along the contours of his thin, bony face, sweeping over a glimpse of joy rising from its basic characteristics of submissiveness and melancholy. It was only an offhand promise, but to his minimized existence it was a consolation of the greatest magnitude.

At the moment, in the great expanse of the human world, there was a great deal of brightness, a great deal of happiness and blessing, a great deal of love. Yet for this humble man who was deprived of everything except his uncle's dilapidated family, there was only this offhand promise.

XXVI

After Chueh-min saw Chien-yun off, he walked to the garden with excited and agonized emotions, knowing that Chueh-hui would be there. He found Chueh-hui by the side of the lake.

With lowered head, Chueh-hui walked along the lake front. At times he stopped and stared at the calm surface of the water, or, heaving a long sigh, turned to walk with large strides in the other direction. He was quite unaware of the approach of Chueh-min.

"Third Brother," Chueh-min called as he emerged from the plum grove.

Chueh-hui halted and gazed at him silently.

Coming near, Chueh-min said in a moved voice, "You look terrible. Is something troubling you?"

Chueh-hui did not answer and began to walk away. Chueh-min hurried after him and grabbed his sleeve.

"I know all about it," Chueh-min said in a trembling voice.

227

"But since things have come to this, what can you do? The best thing is to forget."

"Forget? I'll never forget," Chueh-hui retorted angrily, his eyes flashing. "Many things in this world are hard to forget. I've been standing here looking at the water for a long time. This is her grave; it's here that I've been searching for a last trace of her. But the water shows me nothing at all. How hateful! After swallowing her body how can the lake look so peaceful?"

He threw off his brother's restraining hand, and raised a clenched right fist as if to strike the water. "She can't be gone without a trace. Every shrub and blade of grass can tell me how she ended her life. I don't dare to think what was in her heart when she died, but I must. I'll remember it for ever, for I am her murderer. But not I alone. There's also our family, the society we live in!"

Taking Chueh-hui's hand and pressing it, Chueh-min said sincerely, "I understand you, Third Brother, and I sympathize with you. These days I've been thinking only of my own happiness, my own future, my own love. That was wrong. I remember when we were small and took lessons with a tutor in our library. We did everything together then. Whoever finished his lesson first always waited for the other. Everyone praised us for being such devoted brothers. It was the same when we entered middle school and, later, the School for Foreign Languages. At home, we helped each other prepare our lessons. We shared our joys, we shared our sorrows. But the past half year, I've been so involved in my own affairs, I've grown away from you. Why didn't you tell me about Ming-feng earlier? Together, we might have worked something out. Two heads are better than one. Isn't that what we always used to say?"

There were tears in the corners of Chueh-hui's eyes. He laughed bitterly. "I remember too, Second Brother. But it's too late. A person is always short of courage, acting alone. I never thought she'd take that road. I truly loved her. But under the circumstances, how could I marry her? Maybe I was too selfish. Maybe I was dazzled by other things. Anyhow, I killed her. She ended her life in the waters of the lake, and another girl, weeping, went to the Feng family to bury her youth, to satisfy the passions of a lustful old dog. With that always in my mind, do you think I'll ever be able to live in peace?"

A look of hatred and regret appeared on Chueh-min's face, and tears rolled down from behind his gold-rimmed spectacles. "Too late," he muttered painfully. He gripped Chueh-hui's hand hard.

"Second Brother, do you remember the night of the fifteenth of the first lunar month?" Chueh-hui asked in an agitated tone. When Chueh-min silently nodded, he continued, "How happy we were that night! It seems only yesterday. But where is she now? . . . Her voice, her face—where can I seek them? She was sure I could save her, but I let her down. I didn't have the courage. . . . I used to blame you and Big Brother for being spineless. Now I know I'm not any different. We're all sons of the same parents, raised in the same family. None of us have any courage. . . . I hate everyone. I hate myself!"

Chueh-hui was too agitated to go on. He was panting, his body was hot as fire. There was a lot more he wanted to say, but the words stuck in his throat. His heart seemed to tremble. He punched himself in the chest, and when Chueh-min grabbed his wrist to restrain him, he struggled like a madman to extricate himself. He didn't know what he was doing; he struggled blindly. Only with the greatest effort was Chueh-min able to hold him and finally push him to the plum grove beside the path. There he stood, leaning limply against a tree, gasping for breath.

"Why carry on like this?" Chueh-min, his face flushed with exertion, stood on the path gazing at him pityingly.

"This family! I can't live here any longer!" Chueh-hui said, more to himself than to his brother. Head down, he was wringing his hands.

Chueh-min's expression changed. He wanted to speak, but couldn't. He looked from Chueh-hui to the grove of plum trees. A magpie was calling from a branch. Gradually, Chueh-min's eyes brightened, and a smile returned to his face. But there were tears in that smile, tears which rolled from his eyes.

"Why don't you trust me like you used to?" he asked. "You

used to talk everything over with me. We shared the bitter with the sweet. Why can't we still be that way today?"

"Because we've both changed. You have your love. I've lost everything. What is there left for us to share?" Chueh-hui was not trying to hurt Chueh-min, he was only releasing some of his pent-up emotion. He felt he was separated from his brother by a damp and dripping corpse.

Chueh-min opened his mouth as if to make a loud reply, then stopped himself. After a long silence, he said in a voice that was almost a plea, "Haven't you forgiven me yet? Can't you see how sorry I am? Let's help one another again, just like before, and stride down life's road together. I promise I'll never leave you."

"What would be the use? I don't want to walk down life's road any more." Chueh-hui seemed to have cast off his armour. His anger was gone. Only despondency remained.

"Can this be you speaking? Would you really throw everything aside because of a girl? That's not like you at all!"

"No, I don't mean that," Chueh-hui started to argue. Avoiding Chueh-min's eyes he said slowly, "It's not only because of her." With sudden anger, he added, "I'm just sick of this kind of life."

"You have no right to say that. We're still young. We don't really know what life is all about yet."

"I suppose we still haven't seen enough! Just wait. The worst is yet to come! I predict it!" Chueh-hui's face was red with anger.

"You're always so excitable! The thing is over with. What can you do about it? Can't you think of the future? It's strange that you should have already forgotten those lines you liked so much."

"Which lines?"

"We're young, we are not invalids, not fools. We'll conquer happiness for ourselves."

Chueh-hui made no reply. The rapidly changing expressions on his face reflected the struggle raging within him. Frowning, he said heavily to himself, "I am young." Then he repeated angrily, "I am young!" After a moment, he asked tentatively, "I am young?" And he added with conviction, "I am young! No question about it, I am young!"

He grasped Chueh-min's hand and gazed into his brother's eyes. That affectionate grasp, that firm gaze, told Chueh-min what was in Chueh-hui's heart. Reassured, he returned the pressure of his young brother's handclasp. They understood each other again.

After an early dinner that evening, the two brothers went out for a walk. As they strolled along the street, they talked animatedly of many things. It was over six months since their last good talk together.

Dark clouds gathered in the evening sky. It was quite cool. Only a few people were abroad on the lonely streets, but at some compound gates servants and sedan-chair carriers stood around in groups, chatting idly.

Two or three blocks further on, the brothers came to a corner compound enclosed by a brick wall. Beside the gate a large yellow placard with green lettering read: "Law Office of Kao Ke-ming."

"How did we ever wander in this direction?" asked Chueh-min.

They turned off into a small twisting lane. It was paved with cobble-stones that were hard on the feet. Tall locust trees in the compounds hung their branches over the earthen walls lining the lane. Here and there were elms. Unfortunately, blossom time was already over. Only a few withered pomegranates remained on the green leafy branches of pomegranate trees.

This section of the town was very quiet. Most of the small black lacquered compound gates were shut. Rarely did anyone emerge.

"Let's go back. It's too dull around here. Besides, it looks like it's going to rain," said Chueh-hui, observing the black clouds piling up in the sky.

"It's raining already," said Chueh-min, as a drop of water struck his forehead. The boys quickened their steps.

"We'd better hurry. It's going to pour in a minute," urged Chueh-hui, breaking into a trot.

231

The brothers ran for home, but the rain caught them. By the time they reached their compound, they were soaked.

"Ming-feng, bring some hot water," Chueh-hui shouted, outside the window of the women servants' quarters.

"You're calling Ming-feng? But she's—" Chueh-min stopped himself.

Chueh-hui turned and looked at him, his face suddenly falling. After a moment, he called in a despondent voice, "Mama Huang!" When she answered he said, "We want to wash our faces." Dully he entered his room and changed his wet clothes, his high spirits completely gone.

Mama Huang soon came with a basin of hot water. When she saw what the boys looked like, she began to scold. She was close to tears.

"If your mother were still alive, she'd never let you run wild like this. For her sake, you two ought to take better care of your health. If it weren't for you boys, I would have left this place long ago. Now that Ming-feng is gone, I'm the only one left to look after you. I don't know who could take care of you if I should die too. The waters here have become muddy. I really don't want to live in this compound any longer."

The old lady said all this in a heartsick voice. Her words so upset the boys that they did not dare to answer for fear of weeping.

Having had her say, and after seeing to it that the brothers put on dry clothes, Mama Huang sighed and left the room.

Chueh-hui went out into the garden. The rain had stopped, and the air was fresh and cool. He paused on the steps to look around at the lights burning in the other apartments, then walked towards the main hall. He could hear young voices intoning lessons from the ancient feudal philosophers:

Children should not live in the best section of the house, nor sit at the centre of the table, nor walk in the middle of the road. . . . That was Chueh-ying's voice.

Of all the major crimes, the worst is violation of filial piety. . . . That was Chueh-chun's voice.

If you laugh, do so quietly. Do not raise your voice in anger. When seated, do not show your knees. When walking, do not sway your body. . . .[33] That was Shu-chen's girlish voice.

Chueh-hui couldn't stomach it. He turned and started to walk back, the voices following him. After two paces he halted, miserable. Gazing around, he doubted his own eyes. All he could see was false and empty shadows. All he could hear was false and empty voices. He didn't know where he was.

"That's what they call education!" a harsh voice abruptly broke upon his ears.

Startled, Chueh-hui turned to see his brother standing beside him. Chueh-hui clutched him with the joy of a man in the trackless desert suddenly meeting an old friend. Chueh-min was a bit mystified by the fervent reception.

Thus, in silence, the brothers returned to their room, two lonely hearts alone in the great wide world.

XXVII

The death of Ming-feng and the marriage of Wan-erh were quickly forgotten in the spacious confines of the Kao family compound. Neither of these events had any effect on the daily life of the family. Two bondmaids were gone, that was all, and the masters quickly bought new ones to replace them. Chi-hsia took the place of Ming-feng; Tsui-huan filled Wan-erh's job. Numerically, there was no change. (Chi-hsia became a waitress. She was from the country. Tsui-huan was the same age as her young mistress, Shu-ying. She had been sold after the death of her father—her last remaining close relative.) Before long, people stopped even mentioning Ming-feng's name.

[33] Quote from *Li Chi* (*The Book of Rituals*), one of the "sacred books" of China, containing the rules of good behaviour as well as ethical and political precepts. It was compiled in the second century B.C., but many parts of it are considerably older.

But in the hearts of Hsi-erh, Chien-erh, Mama Huang and a few others, the girl was a constant unhappy memory.

Chueh-hui never spoke of her either. He appeared to have forgotten her. But she left a wound that would never heal. He had little time to mourn her, however, because of something new which developed.

After the sixth issue of *Dawn* was published, a rumour started that the officials were going to close the progressive weekly down. It was said that the Confucian Morals Society was behind the move. This story naturally aroused Chueh-hui and his friends but, being inexperienced, they didn't take it very seriously. What's more, they didn't believe that General Chang, the new governor, would permit his subordinates to do such a thing.

The seventh issue appeared as usual. There were some new subscribers. The magazine had rented an upstairs shop in the market arcade, and members of its staff met there every night. During the day (with the exception of Sunday) they kept the place shut, so that even Chueh-hsin, whose office was in the same arcade, didn't know that Chueh-hui was a frequent visitor.

The more important enterprises occupied the ground floor shops; most of the upper stories were empty. The magazine office had no neighbours; all of the surrounding rooms were vacant.

Every evening, two or three young students would take down the shutters, turn on the light and set the office in order. Soon there would be half a dozen of them, mostly boys, though girls like Hsu Chien-ju also dropped in once or twice. They would sit around and talk. Anything they could not mention at home, here they discussed without reservation. They were smiling, relaxed. The office was their club.

Chueh-hui came often, sometimes accompanied by Chueh-min. Tuesday evenings, Chueh-hui was sure to come, because the magazine went to press Wednesday mornings. On Tuesday, he, Chang Hui-ju and Huang Tsun-jen edited the final copy.

The day the copy of the eighth issue had to be prepared for press was the day after Ming-feng's death. That evening,

Chueh-hui went to the office as usual. He found Hsu Chien-ju reading a newspaper item aloud to the others. It was a Police Department proclamation prohibiting girls from bobbing their hair. Short hair was considered much too "modern" and "rebellious."

Chien-ju flung the paper down angrily and threw herself into a wicker armchair. "Of all the piffle!" she cried.

"Why don't we print it as it is, in the 'About Face!' column of our next issue?" suggested Tsun-jen, with a grin.

"Fine!" said Chien-ju.

The others agreed. Hui-ju thought there ought to be a critical article to go with it. Everyone asked Hui-ju to write it himself, but he passed the job over to Chueh-hui. For Chueh-hui, it was a chance to give vent to the bitterness filling his heart over Ming-feng's death. He took up his pen and began writing without a word.

He soon finished; the article was rather short. He read it aloud to the others, and they said it would do. Tsun-jen made a few small changes, then announced that the piece would appear on page one of issue number eight. Only one of the older boys sounded a note of caution: "This is going to make a real noise."

"Let it," said Hui-ju jubilantly. "The louder the better!"

The eighth issue of *Dawn* appeared in print on Sunday morning. In the afternoon, Chueh-hui and Chueh-min paid their customary visit to Chueh-hsin's office. They didn't stay long. Chueh-hui soon slipped away to the magazine's headquarters. Hui-ju, Tsun-jen and two or three others were already there. Chueh-hui asked them how the issue was selling; they said they had checked at one or two outlets and were told the magazines were being bought almost as quickly as they appeared on the stands.

"You haven't paid your dues," Tsun-jen suddenly said to Chueh-hui.

Chueh-hui felt through his pockets. "I'll have to do it tomorrow," he said apologetically. "I didn't bring any money with me."

"Tomorrow at the latest, then!" smiled Tsun-jen.

"He's great at squeezing money out of people. He's been

after me too," Hui-ju interjected, walking over to them. There was a grin on his impish face. "This morning, before I left home, I put on a new padded gown. My sister thought I was crazy to wear anything so warm in this weather. I insisted I was cold and walked out. . . ."

Everyone laughed, and Hui-ju laughed with them. He continued:

"I nearly fried in the sun with that gown on. Luckily the pawn shop isn't far from my house. I left the gown there. I was much cooler and lighter when I came out, and I had money to pay my dues with, too!"

"What will your sister say when you get home?" Chueh-hui asked.

"I've got it all figured out. I'll just say I felt too warm and left the gown at a friend's house. If she doesn't believe me, I'll just tell her the truth. Maybe she'll give the money to get it out of pawn!"

"I certainly admire your nerve—" Chueh-hui laughed. Before he could finish, he was interrupted by the entrance of two policemen.

"Do you have any more copies of the latest issue?" asked the older one. He had a moustache.

Tsun-jen handed him a copy. "Three cents apiece."

"We don't want to buy them. We have orders to take them with us," the younger policeman said. He picked up two bundles of magazines that were resting on the floor.

"You boys will have to come along with us to the station. Not all of you—two will be enough," said the older policeman. His tone was not unfriendly.

The startled boys looked at one another. Then they all stepped forward, each insisting that he wanted to go.

"That's too many. Two is all we need." The older policeman looked rather distressed. Finally, he selected Hui-ju and Chueh-hui. The two boys left the room with the policemen, the others trailing behind. When they reached the head of the stairs, the older policeman suddenly changed his mind.

"Forget it," he said to Chueh-hui. "We don't need you two. You can go back."

"What's going on anyway?" Hui-ju demanded hotly. "By what right are you confiscating our magazines?"

"We've got our orders," retorted the younger policeman, continuing down the stairs with the bundles. The older man, about to follow him, paused to give the boys some friendly advice:

"You're young and don't understand much. Better stick to your studies. Don't put out any magazines and bother with things that don't concern you."

He slowly descended the stairs. The boys returned to their office.

They began a heated discussion, with no two opinions alike. While they were still arguing, another policeman arrived and brought them a letter from the police authorities. It was unusually polite, but very firm:

> Because the agitational nature of your periodical disturbs public order and security, we regret that we must ask you to cease circulation immediately. . . .

The life of *Dawn* was thus abruptly brought to an end.

A mournful silence followed. The announcement came as a severe blow to the boys. They had put a lot into the magazine, pooling their feeble resources in an attempt to show the average person a glimmer of light. Working together had also brought them friendship, comfort and strength. Was it all over after only two short months?

"I know now—they're all hypocrites!" cried Hui-ju. "And the new governor is no different from the rest!"

"The old reactionary forces have powerful roots." Tsun-jen stood up and scratched his close-cropped hair irritably. "There's no use expecting anything from Governor Chang. Ten like him wouldn't make any difference!"

"That's just what I'm saying," Hui-ju continued. "All his talk of wanting reforms is a fake. The only 'new' thing he's done is to hire a couple of men who studied abroad as his advisers, and pick up a few girl students for concubines!"

"Yet, last year, before he took office, he invited a lot of people with advanced ideas from Shanghai and Nanking to come and give talks," mused Tsun-jen.

237

Hui-ju laughed scornfully. "Have you forgotten his speech at the meeting to welcome them? His secretary wrote it all out for him, but he memorized it so badly that his meaning came out the exact opposite of his script. He's pulled plenty of boners like that!"

Tsun-jen said nothing. As to Hui-ju, not only did his outbursts fail to solve the present main problem, they didn't even relieve his anger. He was furious. There was a great deal more he wanted to say to the world.

"Let's change the name and put out another magazine with exactly the same content!" Hui-ju proposed. "How can they stop us?"

"I'm for it!" Chueh-hui, who had been silent until now, suddenly spoke up.

"But we have to plan our moves carefully," said Tsun-jen, raising his head. He had been deep in thought.

The boys again began a long discussion. This time they arrived at a decision: They would send out a circular notifying their subscribers of the suspension of *Dawn*. At the same time they would prepare the publication of their new magazine. They also would convert the office to a public reading-room, to which the boys would contribute all of their progressive books and periodicals. Anyone could come in and read, free of charge. This would help spread the new culture.

With a new programme mapped out, everyone promptly sloughed off his gloom and set to work. What a wonderful thing enthusiasm is! It enabled the boys to conquer their difficulties in a very short time. By the following day, they had already set up the reading-room. Two days after that, the preparatory work of the new magazine, *For the Masses*, was well advanced.

There were no classes on Monday, for the final examinations were about to begin. Chueh-hui and Chueh-min went together to attend the opening ceremonies of the Li-chun Newspaper reading-room. When they came back home, it was late, and they arrived just in time for dinner. The day's activities strongly impressed Chueh-hui, nothing had ever so moved him before. Conversation, friendship, enthusiasm, trust . . . never had these been so beautiful as they had been on this day. This tea party of a dozen or so young men was indeed a get together of a close knit family. But the members of this family were bound together not by blood relationship, nor by property inheritance, but by the common possession of equally good intentions and the same high ideals. Within the group, he felt that the heart to heart contact was always between hearts of absolute purity and sincerity, completely free from restraints of considerations of interest. He felt that among them he was not a stranger, an isolated loner. He loved those around him, and those around him all loved him. He understood them and they understood him. He trusted them and they trusted him. He took part as fervently as everybody else in setting up the party and when the preparations were over and the party took place, he enjoyed the refreshments and shared the delights of the group as much as everybody else. They talked about things pleasant and agreeable, and all dark and painful things seemed non-existent at the time.

"How fine it would be if life could always be like this!" Chueh-hui had said excitedly to Chueh-min at the party. The older brother had nodded emotionally.

The boys talked of many things on the way home. Chueh-hui's heart was still warm and glowing. But the moment he set foot in the family hall, he was plunged into despair. Here the old society was all around him. There was virtually no one of the new generation here, no one to whom he could talk.

"How lonely! How insufferably lonely!" he sighed. His bitterness increased.

The faces around the table at dinner that night also bore the scars of bitterness. His stepmother was complaining about the strife between Aunt Shen and Aunt Wang. Somewhere in the rear, Aunt Wang was upbraiding her bondmaid, Chien-erh. Aunt Shen and Mistress Chen were cursing each other in the courtyard.

Chueh-hui finished eating quickly, threw down his chopsticks and ran out, as if pursued by something fearful.

Chueh-min left the dining room at the same time. The two of them agreed to take a walk outside.

"How about going to see the Kao Residence of Ching-ling again?" suggested Chueh-min with a smile.

"All right," Chueh-hui curtly replied. They proceeded along the streets in silence, and soon they arrived at a quiet lane in which the Residence was located.

It was a fine day, the sky was clear, without any clouds. The moon rose from the boughs of a tree, gradually plating the evening streets with a coat of silver. Not a single human voice was heard around. The cicadas sang pensively from the trees inside the walls. As they proceeded, they stepped on their own shadows cast on the cobble road which led to the door of the Kao Residence. The black lacquered gate was tightly shut. They passed the place and walked ahead, until they got to the exit of the lane, from which they turned to walk back. When they passed under the locust tree again, they heard the crying of crow chicks, and they stopped to see what was the matter. They saw a crow's nest on the main branch of the big tree, and two chicks crying with their heads stretched far out.

This quite ordinary scene exceptionally moved the two young men. They couldn't move their eyes from the nest and their feet from the spot. They unconsciously moved closer to each other. The elder brother, his hand trembling a little, took the younger brother's hand and held it, and said in a lamenting voice, "We are just like these motherless little crows." Tears fell from his eyes. The younger held on to his brother's hand without saying anything.

Soon they heard the sound of loud crowing above their heads, the fanning of wings, a dark shadow dashed past their eyes, and the mother crow was back in the nest. The two fledglings lunged forth towards the body of the mother with happy cries, and the mother caressed them with her bill, and the nest was filled with the sounds and movements of togetherness and joy.

"Now they have their mother," Chueh-min said in a husky voice, and lowered his head to look at the younger brother by his side, whose eyes were still glistening with tear drops.

"Let's go home," said Chueh-min as if exhausted.

"No, let me stay a little longer," Chueh-hui replied in a mournful voice, and looked back at the nest.

Suddenly from the house came the sound of a piccolo playing an ordinary love song. It was soft and melodious with a note of sadness, indicating suppressed grief and sorrow which had never been expressed or noticed with justice and sympathy. Their imaginations conjured up a picture of a girl looking at the half moon from her window, thinking of her lover far away, and confiding her thoughts to this slender bamboo pipe, making it produce this moving music of tender emotions, in which is held this heart-breaking love story, and in which vibrates this sadness of a lonely life. This was a popular folk song, which the brothers knew very well. In their house there were occasions when the sing-song blind man was called in to sing, and such folk songs were the ones that he sang with a falsetto voice, impersonating a female. Although the lyrics were vulgar, it represented the voice of life, giving vent to pent up human feelings.

"Someone's coming," Chueh-min said alertly and dragged Chueh-hui along. He knew who it was.

Chueh-hui turned his head and saw his Uncle Ke-ting's sedan-chair turning the corner toward them, with Kao Chung running along panting. "Why be scared, we'll just turn our backs on him and pretend not to see him," said Chueh-hui while doing the same, indicating that he was not budging to follow his brother and forcing Chueh-min to stay too.

In no time the sedan-chair passed them by. They heard Kao Chung go ahead to announce at the gate, which readily opened up. The sedan-chair bearers' footsteps soon faded inside the gate, which was shut right after the group got in. Immediately, the piccolo music playing the love song stopped short and was heard no more.

"Damn, that's what happens. Let's go home," said Chueh-hui who turned and walked on.

The brothers walked slowly. While they were still in the lane, another sedan-chair came towards them. Surprised, they watched it pass them by.

"Strange, is Uncle Ke-an going there too?" Chueh-min was saying to himself as he emerged from the lane.

"Why not?" said Chueh-hui with a sarcastic chuckle, "didn't he create so many ridiculous scenes at home?" He remembered a number of stories about Uncle Ke-an, from an affair with a maid servant to bringing home a falsetto female impersonator to take pictures with make-up and costumes, scene after scene coming in succession like a motion picture show. "They are all the same. I say that they are all the same! Yet they have the audacity to call themselves our elders, and reproach us for not behaving in accordance with the duties of sons and nephews!" Chueh-hui spoke with great vehemence. Again he recalled what Ming-feng had told him, and he went on, "Only Big Brother is afraid of them, only Big Brother would try to placate them. I am not afraid."

"But Big Brother has his difficulties too," Chueh-min said placatingly, and then dropped the subject.

They returned home, and Chueh-min started to study for his final examinations. This was Chueh-min's style. He was an optimist and amnesia easily came by to help him many a time, so that if unpleasant things happened to him he soon forgot them, and opening his text enabled him to concentrate on that. But Chueh-hui was different. He was more passionate and impetuous than his brothers. He came home intending to study for his examinations too, but when he had his books opened before him, his mind became more restless. The feeling of loneliness oppressed him. The unsuppressible bitterness haunted him. The chair under him felt scorched by a burning fire, he wasn't able to stay on it for another moment. He sighed, shut his book and stood up.

"Where are you going?" Chueh-min asked with concern.

"I want to walk around a little. I feel awful."

"All right. But come back soon," said Chueh-min soothingly. "Our exams start the day after tomorrow. You'd better do some reviewing."

Chueh-hui nodded. He went into the big garden. With the change in surroundings, his heart eased a trifle. He strolled slowly in the moonlight.

Crickets chirped mournfully. A fragrance spread through the night like a soft net, enveloping all in its folds. Everything was blurred, illusory, secretive. It was like walking in a world of dreams.

Gradually, Chueh-hui calmed down. He strolled, enjoying the scenery, following the same path he and the other young folks had taken the night they went boating on the lake.

On the hump-backed bridge, he halted and leaned on the railing, gazing at his dark reflection in the waters below. The lake was a deep blue sky in which a half-moon rode, shimmering. Suddenly a lovely face appeared in the water, a face that he adored. Chueh-hui turned and fled.

Crossing a lawn at the edge of the lake, he came upon a rowboat moored to a willow tree. This too recalled memories. He hastily recrossed the hump-backed bridge and returned to the opposite shore.

He followed the path that skirted the grove of cedars near the bank until he came to "Lakeside Retreat." About to go in and rest a while, he suddenly observed a glow of flame from behind the artificial mountain. He almost cried out in surprise. Pausing by the magnolia tree, he watched. There was a steady glow, but it did not grow any larger. Gathering his courage, Chueh-hui walked forward softly to investigate.

Rounding the artificial mountain, he found nothing. The glow was coming from behind another man-made hill, diagonally opposite. Again he advanced. Behind the second hill, he saw a girl kneeling on the ground, burning "ingots" of gold and silver paper.[34]

"What are you doing here?" he demanded loudly.

Startled, the tall girl quickly rose to her feet. When she recognized Chueh-hui, she saluted him respectfully, "Ah, Third Young Master!"

It was Chien-erh, bondmaid in the Fourth Household.

"So it's you," said Chueh-hui. "You nearly scared the life out of me! Why are you burning sacrifice money here?"

"Please don't tell anyone, Third Young Master. My mistress would be sure to scold me if she knew."

"But why are you doing it?"

Chien-erh lowered her head. "Today is the seventh day after Ming-feng's death. . . . She died so pitifully. I thought I'd send her a little money, so she won't go cold and hungry in the next world. . . ." Chien-erh was almost crying.

"Go ahead," said Chueh-hui. "I won't tell anyone." He

---

[34] The paper money, also called "spirit money," was believed to be the currency in the Nether World. The burning of this money was meant as a gift to the spirits, which would encourage them to be benevolent to the deceased.

pressed a hand against his chest. There was a pain in his heart. He watched Chien-erh burn the "money" expressionlessly. She couldn't guess what was going on inside him.

"Why are you burning two piles?" he asked.

"This one is for Wan-erh."

"Wan-erh? But she's not dead!"

"She asked me to. As she was getting into the bridal sedanchair, she said to me, 'Sooner or later, I'm going to die too. Even if I live, my life will be worse than death. Consider me dead. When you burn money for Ming-feng, burn some for me too.' And that's what I'm doing."

Hearing Chien-erh's tragic voice and recalling those two unhappy events, could he simply laugh at her superstitious ceremony? Of course not. Chueh-hui struggled to control his emotions. Finally, he wrenched out:

"Burn it! You're doing the right thing!" He staggered away, not daring to turn his head for a last look.

"Why is there so much misery in the world?" he muttered. Rubbing his aching heart, he came out of the garden.

As he passed Chueh-hsin's flat and saw the lights burning in the windows, and heard the warm human voices, he felt as if he had returned from another world. He remembered what his French teacher had said the other day: "In France, youngsters your age don't know the meaning of tragedy."

But he was a youth of China, and already tragedy was weighing him down.

XXVIII

It was summer holiday time. Chueh-min had much more opportunity to meet Chin. Chueh-hui had much more time to spend with his young friends, to talk and work together. With renewed strength, the boys put out the new magazine, won new readers. All was going well.

That summer a big event was celebrated in the Kao family

compound—the sixty-sixth birthday of the Venerable Master Kao.

Preparations began early. It was to be a gala occasion. At the suggestion of Ke-ming, who handled the accounts, and with the approval of the old man, a large sum of money was allotted from the family funds. As Ke-ming put it: "We collect such a huge amount of rent every year, we have more money than we know what to do with. What difference if we spend a little extra!"

Naturally, no wealthy family would let slip such a good opportunity to show off its affluence.

The festive day was fast approaching; gifts flowed in like a tide. A special office had to be set up to accept them and issue invitations. Many people were kept busy day and night. Chueh-hsin took a fortnight's leave from his office to help out. The gardens were hung with lanterns and bunting; extra electric lights were added. In the main hall, a stage was built, and the best actors in the city were hired to perform three days of opera. The dramas to be presented were chosen by Ke-ting, who was an expert in such matters.

Everyone was busy except Chueh-min and Chueh-hui, who spent most of their time away from the compound. They were home only the three days of the formal celebration, when they had no choice.

Those three days were a new experience for them. Although they ordinarily disliked their family compound, at least they were familiar with it. Now, during the celebration, it changed beyond recognition. It became a theatre, a market-place—crowded with people, noisy, full of unnatural grinning faces. Even their own room was given over to some guests whom they knew only slightly. Here a band of zither-playing blind musicians chanted birthday greetings; there another group sang lewd verses to the accompaniment of two string fiddles. Still a third group performed behind a curtain; the leering tones of the male and female voices were highly erotic; young people were not permitted to listen.

The operas began in the afternoon of the first day. Except for a few special birthday plays, the rest were all pieces which required skilful and subtle interpretation and were not originally included on the programme. These had been specially requested by several of the honourable guests. Whenever a portion was performed that brought blushes to the women and the young folks in the audience and smirks to the grown men, a servant with a stentorian voice would come out on the stage and read from a festively red slip of paper: "The Honourable Mr. So-and-so presents to such-and-such an actor the sum of so-much!" And the lucky actor (invariably a female impersonator) would at once profusely thank his donor, while the beneficent gentleman beamed with pompous satisfaction.

But even this did not satisfy the honourable guests. When an opera was over, the actors who had been rewarded had to drink with them at their tables, still wearing their make-up and costumes. The honourable gentlemen fondled the performers and filled them with wine; they behaved with such crass vulgarity that the younger guests were shocked and the servants whispered among themselves.

Venerable Master Kao, the shining light of all these festivities, sat up front. He gazed around briefly at what was going on, and smiled, then turned his eyes back to the stage, for the old man's favourite female impersonator had just made his entrance.

Ke-ming and the other two sons of the Venerable Master Kao circulated among the guests, looking after their wants with fawning solicitude, while Chueh-hsin trailed in their wake.

To Chueh-min and Chueh-hui it was all absolutely sickening. In this family, in these surroundings, they felt like strangers. The noisy, riotous, drunken sots seemed to them some strange species. A few faces looked vaguely familiar, yet closer examination made the boys wonder whether they had ever really seen them before. They felt completely out of place, but they were not allowed to leave because they were supposed to be acting as hosts. Like the supernumeraries in an opera, they were placed at a table with lesser guests, where they were expected to smile and drink and eat, more like machines than human beings.

Chueh-hui stuck it out the first day; that night he had bad

dreams. The second day was just too much. He stayed away all afternoon between lunch and dinner. The young friends whom he visited first laughed at him, then consoled him. He finally worked up enough courage to go back and receive fresh insults (the word was Chueh-hui's). But the third day, he was unable to escape.

Mei had come with her mother, Mrs. Chien, but had gone home early because of illness. She was growing thinner by the day, and although her frailty was not yet extreme, sensitive people were touched by it, for they knew it was a sign that this lovely star would soon fall.

There were few enough sensitive people in the Kao family, but Chueh-hsin certainly was one of them. He was perhaps the most concerned about Mei. Yet there were so many invisible barriers between them—at least he thought there were—that they could only gaze at each other and converse wordlessly at a distance. They avoided all opportunities to speak together in private, thinking they could thus diminish the pain. The result was just the opposite. Chueh-hsin lost weight steadily and Mei's illness became worse; she began to cough blood.

Madam Chou was very fond of Mei, but because she didn't know what was in Mei's heart, she had no way of comforting her. Actually, there was no one who could comfort Mei—not even Jui-chueh, who recently had grown very close to her and knew her best.

Chin had also come to the party, and also gone home because of illness—though hers was feigned. The next day she secretly sent a note to Chueh-min, asking him to call.

Chueh-min stole away at the first opportunity, and he and Chin had a long talk. On the way home, he was very happy. Chueh-hsin met him at the entrance to the main hall and, to Chueh-min's surprise, asked:

"You've been to Chin's, haven't you?"

Chueh-min could only nod, mutely.

"I saw her servant slipping you a note; her illness wasn't real. I know all about you two." Chueh-hsin spoke in a low voice, a wry smile on his face.

247

Chueh-min said nothing. He too was smiling, only his was a smile of satisfaction.

Chueh-hsin saw Ke-ming approaching. He exchanged a few words with the older man. When his uncle had walked on, he again turned to Chueh-min.

"You're happy," he said softly. "You can do the things you want. I'd like to visit a sick person too, but I don't even have that much freedom. She's very ill. I know she needs me. . . ." His face twisted into an odd expression that could have been either a smile or a grimace of pain.

Moved, Chueh-min didn't know what to say. "Why don't you forget Mei?" at last he blurted awkwardly. "You're only torturing yourself. And what about Jui-chueh? You love her too, don't you?"

Chueh-hsin's face drained of colour. He stood looking at his brother in stricken silence. Suddenly he became angry. "So you too want me to give her up? You're the same as the others! You can still talk that way at a time like this! . . ." Chueh-hsin tore himself away and walked off quickly.

Chueh-min realized that he had not given Chueh-hsin the answer he was seeking. But what other answer could he have given? Chueh-hsin said one thing, but did another. Chueh-min couldn't understand the discrepancy between his Big Brother's words and his deeds. For that matter the whole family was a puzzle to him.

His eyes wandered to the stage, where a short clown and a tall, stately beauty were engaging in a subtle exchange of dialogue. The guests burst into guffaws at some filthy innuendo—the honourable, the not-so-honourable, and the completely dishonourable, guests. Chueh-min laughed scornfully.

He forgot about Chueh-hsin. Slowly, he paced back and forth, his mind filled with his own affairs. For the first time, his prospects looked bright.

Of course it all had to do with Chin. He was very optimistic; she gave him courage and confidence. Not only did she trust him—she had already made it plain that she would not disappoint him. They were progressing smoothly.

At first, when they finished studying English together every day, they had chatted about things in general. Gradually their

248

talk had become more personal, until they understood one another completely, until they had grown so close together that they felt unable to part. Cautiously they spoke of love— the love affairs of their relatives and friends, of Mei and Chueh-hsin. Only much later did their conversation get around to their own emotions. Chueh-min remembered how Chin had blushed and toyed with the pages of a book, trying to appear calm, when she told him how much she needed him. She said she had determined to take the new road, but that there were many obstacles in her path; she needed someone like him, someone who could understand and help her.

He and Chin already knew what was in each other's heart. All that was lacking was on open declaration. When she sent for him today, he felt his chance had come, and he told her what he had never dared say before, announcing heroically that he was willing to sacrifice everything for her sake.

Then she had replied. Actually, one of them had only to speak ten per cent and the other understood the remaining ninety. They had faith in one another, faith in their future. Their latest meeting had parted a curtain; they had made their relationship plain. And this wonderful thing, thought Chueh-min, had happened only today, practically just a minute ago!

His dreams for the future were very rosy and, of course, quite exaggerated. Blinded, he could see none of the difficulties ahead. Standing on the stone platform outside the main hall, he glanced again at the flirtatious actors on the stage inside. Now the short clown and the stately beauty had been replaced by a handsome hero and a pert young maid. Again the audience roared with laughter at some vulgar sally. Chueh-min smiled contemptuously. People like this couldn't stop him.

He gazed off into the distance, picturing an ideal life. A slap on the shoulder from a familiar hand brought him back to reality. Chueh-min turned to find his younger brother, Chueh-hui, standing grinning behind him.

"So you've run out on them too," said Chueh-min.

"Naturally," replied Chueh-hui with a satisfied laugh. "And you . . . have another chance to sneak out!" He had guessed

249

what Chueh-min was contemplating from the expression on his face.

Chueh-min reddened slightly. He nodded. "It's all settled between me and Chin. We've taken the first step. The problem now is the next one." His somewhat weak eyes peered happily at Chueh-hui from behind his gold-rimmed spectacles.

A fleeting smile crossed Chueh-hui's face. Even though he had told Chueh-min he thought of Chin only as a sister, even though he had loved another girl who had died for his sake, even though he had hoped that one day Chueh-min might make Chin his sister-in-law, yet when he heard that she now belonged to another, he couldn't help feeling a stab of jealousy—for he had secretly been in love with her. But at once he berated himself for harbouring such an emotion, particularly where his brother was concerned.

"Be careful. Don't take too much for granted." Though there was reason in Chueh-hui's words, they were still motivated a bit by jealousy.

"Everything's fine." Chueh-min was not in the least discouraged. "You're usually very bold. What makes you so cautious all of a sudden?"

Plainly Chueh-min had no inkling of what he was thinking. Chueh-hui immediately felt ashamed. He laughed. "You're absolutely right. I wish you luck."

From the stage came a deafening uproar of cymbals and drums, as bare-torsoed warriors somersaulted about in a battle scene. This was followed by a fight between three generals with painted faces. Chueh-hui could see his grandfather, seated up front, chatting with a grey-bearded old man beside him. The sight of the guest's mottled, wrinkled face and his sausage-like nose infuriated Chueh-hui. Clenching his fists, he grated through his teeth:

"So he had the nerve to come!"

"Who?" asked Chueh-min, surprised.

Chueh-hui pointed. "That murderer—old man Feng!"

"Not so loud! People will hear you!" said Chueh-min agitatedly.

"So what? I want them to hear! Don't you admire boldness?" Chueh-hui laughed coldly.

While Chueh-min tried desperately to think of a way to quiet him, an interruption distracted Chueh-hui's attention. The boys' younger sister Shu-hua and their young girl cousin, Shu-chen, arrived breathlessly with a bit of news. "Old man Feng's new concubine is here," said Shu-chen, tugging at Chueh-min's sleeve. "Let's go see her!"

"But I don't know her. How can I speak to her?" replied Chueh-min, surprised.

"Do you mean Wan-erh?" queried Chueh-hui. Suddenly he understood. "Where is she?" he demanded, as if asking about someone who had just come back from the grave.

"In my room. No one else is there. Do you want to go?" asked Shu-hua with a conspiratorial smile.

"Yes," said Chueh-hui. He went off with the girls. Chueh-min remained behind.

They found Wan-erh alone—alone except for Jui-chueh, Shu-ying and half a dozen bondmaids. Wan-erh was beautifully dressed, but her face was pitifully haggard. She was telling them something, and Jui-chueh and Shu-ying were crying. As soon as Wan-erh saw Chueh-hui enter, she stood up and greeted him, trying to smile.

"Third Young Master has come."

Chueh-hui nodded and smiled. "Why are you standing? You're not our servant any more; you're a concubine of the Feng family." Though he jested, Chueh-hui felt miserable. Wan-erh was suffering the fate Ming-feng had died to escape.

Wan-erh silently hung her head. Jui-chueh, seated on the edge of the bed, reproved him gently, "Look what they've done to her, Third Brother. How can you have the heart to laugh?"

"I'm sorry. I didn't mean anything." He remembered what Chien-erh had told him in the garden when he found her burning sacrifice money, and he felt very sorry for Wan-erh. He wanted to do something to make amends.

"You're a fine one to scold!" he said to Jui-chueh. "Instead of you all sitting around crying the first time she comes back, why don't you take her out to see some of the operas?"

251

"Who can out-talk that sharp tongue of yours?" said Jui-chueh, pretending to be angry. Shu-hua and Shu-chen laughed.

"If you can't out-talk him, let me try!" Shu-ying interrupted. Noticing that Wan-erh was still standing, she urged, "Please sit down. You needn't be so polite to him." By then Chueh-hui had already seated himself on a stool, so Wan-erh silently resumed her seat. Shu-ying addressed herself to Chueh-hui.

"Those operas aren't fit to be seen. Some of our guests ought to be ashamed of themselves—choosing nothing but dirty plays. Wan-erh has very little chance to visit here. She wanted to talk to Chien-erh and some of her other friends privately, so we arranged for them to meet in this room. Now, just as they're getting started, you barge in. Who asked you to come along and play the young master anyhow?"

"I gather that you'd like me to get out," grinned Chueh-hui, but he made no move to go.

"You needn't feel so cocky, Third Brother. They've already picked a bride for Second Brother. Your turn is next," Shu-hua inserted.

"What? Who's picked him a bride?" Chueh-hui demanded sceptically.

"The Venerable Master Feng. I hear it's his grandniece. They say she's got a fierce temper, and she's not so young either," said Shu-ying.

"Why, that old bastard!" Chueh-hui stood up. "I'm going to tell Second Brother!" He cast a final glance at Wan-erh, as if bidding her goodbye for ever, and hurried from the room.

As he passed the main hall, Chueh-hui saw something that depressed him exceedingly. There was Chueh-min standing before his grandfather and old man Feng. The Venerable Master Feng was smilingly questioning him and Chueh-min was answering respectfully.

"How can you be polite to that old murderer?" Chueh-hui fumed to himself. "Don't you realize he's your enemy, that he's going to drag you and Chin apart!"

Chueh-min finally heard the news not only from Chueh-

252

hui but also from his Big Brother. Chueh-hsin, acting under their grandfather's orders, had approached him to learn his reaction. Inquiring how Chueh-min felt about the matter was not the old man's idea—he issued commands and, naturally, they had to be obeyed. Chueh-hsin thought so too, although he did not approve of his grandfather's methods.

While shaken by the blow, Chueh-min was not afraid. His reply was simple. "I will decide whom I am to marry. Right now, I'm too young. I still have to finish my studies. I don't want to get married." There was a good deal more he wanted to say, but he kept it to himself.

"I can't very well tell *Yeh-yeh* that you want to make your own decisions. It's better to stress the youth aspect. But I'm afraid that won't convince him either. In our family nineteen isn't considered too young for marriage," Chueh-hsin said doubtfully. It was difficult to tell what he really advocated.

"According to you, it's hopeless, then!" said Chueh-min angrily.

"I didn't mean that," Chueh-hsin said quickly, but he had nothing to add.

Chueh-min stared at him fixedly, as if trying to read his mind. "Don't you remember what you said to me this afternoon?" the younger brother demanded. "Do you want me to re-enact your tragedy?"

"But *Yeh-yeh*. . . ." Chueh-hsin agreed with Chueh-min completely, yet he felt their grandfather's orders had to be obeyed.

"Don't talk to me about *Yeh-yeh*. I'm going to walk my own road," Chueh-min snapped. He turned and went into his room.

Chueh-min and Chueh-hui discussed the problem far into the night. Finally they agreed upon a plan of action: Resist. If that fails, run away. In any event, never give in.

Chueh-hui encouraged him, first because he sympathized with Chueh-min, and second because he wanted him to set a precedent, to blaze a new trail for other young men like him.

Fired with enthusiasm, Chueh-min immediately wrote a note to Chin, intending to send it to her the following day, secreted between the pages of a book. The note read:

Chin:

No matter what you may have heard, please do not believe a word of it. People are trying to make a match for me, but I have given my heart to you and I will never go back on my pledge. Please have faith in me. You will see how courageously I can give battle, how I will fight for and win you!

Chueh-min

Chueh-min read the note over twice. This is an important memento in the annals of our love, he thought. He showed the note to Chueh-hui. "How's that?" he asked proudly.

"Splendid," replied Chueh-hui sarcastically. "Straight out of the middle ages!" And to himself he mocked: We'll soon see how courageously you "give battle"!

Now that the Venerable Master Kao's birthday celebration was over, old man Feng sent a matchmaker to formally propose the marriage of his grandniece to Chueh-min. The Venerable Master of course was entirely in favour. Madam Chou was only his daughter-in-law and Chueh-min's stepmother, not his mother; she did not think it proper to express an opinion. Chueh-hsin felt the marriage would be a serious mistake, ruining the life of another young couple. But he hadn't the courage to oppose his grandfather. He could only pray that some miracle might occur.

The matchmaking was done secretly, without Chueh-min's knowledge. Such matters were always conducted in secret; the persons involved were mere puppets. Those who had been puppets in their youth, today were making puppets out of others. That was how it had been in the past, and that was how it always would be—or so people like the Venerable Master Kao thought. But they were mistaken in Chueh-min's case. He wasn't the type to submit to being a puppet.

In contrast to the older generation, Chueh-min took active measures concerning his marriage. Without the least shyness, he made inquiries about the proposed match. Chueh-hui became his scout. Together with Chin the two brothers formed a committee of three. They discussed tactics—how to block the match with old man Feng's niece, how to publicize the relationship between Chueh-min and Chin.

As the opening stage of the battle, Chueh-min made his attitude plain to his Big Brother. Chueh-hsin replied that it was not up to him. Chueh-min requested his stepmother to cancel the match. Madam Chou said the decision rested with his grandfather. But Chueh-min couldn't approach the old man directly and he could find no one with influence to help him. In this family, the Venerable Master Kao passed final judgement.

A few days later, Chin's mother requested him to stop calling. Mrs. Chang was the old man's daughter. Although she sympathized with Chueh-min, as a member of the Kao family she could not and would not help him. There was already a rumour going around among the Kaos that Chueh-min was being supported in his actions by his aunt Mrs. Chang because she wanted her daughter to marry him. Chin was so furious when she heard this, she cried.

After the preliminary skirmish ended in total failure, Chueh-min began the second phase of his tactics. He spread the story that unless the family respected his wishes, he would take drastic measures. Since this threat was never permitted to reach the old man's ears, it did not produce any results either.

Then Chueh-min learned that his horoscope and that of his proposed bride were about to be exchanged, after which a date would be set for the engagement. He heard this news only two weeks after the Venerable Master Kao's birthday celebration.

It was then that Chueh-hsin had given the old man some indication of Chueh-min's feelings, but to no avail.

"How dare he disagree?" the patriarch had retorted angrily. "What I say is final!"

Chueh-min paced the garden for hours that day. His determination wavered a bit. If once he decided to run away from home, there would be no turning back. Sustaining himself alone would be a big problem. He was very comfortable at home; he was well provided with food and clothing. But on the outside, how would he live? He had not made any preparations for such a move. Yet now the problem was upon him; he had to make up his mind.

Seeking out Chueh-hsin, he came directly to the point. "Is there any hope of changing *Yeh-yeh*'s mind?"

"I'm afraid not," said Chueh-hsin mournfully.

"Have you really tried to think of every possible way?" asked Chueh-min, disappointed.

"I really have!"

"What do you think I ought to do?"

"I know what's on your mind but, honestly, there's nothing I can do to help you. The best thing is to do what *Yeh-yeh* wants. In this day and age, we're fit only to be sacrificed," said Chueh-hsin sadly. He was almost weeping.

Chueh-min laughed coldly. "Still the same old policy of non-resistance! A compliant bow philosophy!" He turned on his heel and left.

XXIX

The following morning when Chueh-hsin went to pay his respects to his grandfather, the old man announced triumphantly that the marriage with the Feng family girl was all arranged. The Venerable Master said it could take place after two months and selected an auspicious day in his almanac. He told Chueh-hsin to go ahead with exchanging the horoscopes. Mumbling an assent, Chueh-hsin left, just as Chueh-hui was entering, a cryptic smile on his face.

No sooner had Chueh-hsin reached his quarters than a servant came after him with a summons from the Venerable Master Kao to return at once. Hurrying to his grandfather's study, he found the old man, seated on a sofa, berating Chueh-hui, while Mistress Chen, dressed in a light green, wide-sleeved blouse in crepe silk, her face heavily powdered and her hair smoothly done, sat perched on the arm of the patriarch's chair, and massaged his back with drumming fists. Chueh-hui stood before the old man not saying a word.

"The rebel! That such a thing could actually happen! You

find Chueh-min and bring him back!" shouted the Venerable Master Kao when he saw Chueh-hsin enter. Big Brother was mystified.

The old man burst into a paroxysm of coughing and Mistress Chen increased the tempo of her drumming. "Calm yourself, Venerable Master," she pleaded. "At your age you shouldn't get yourself all worked up. They're not worth it!"

"How dare he disobey me? How dare he oppose me?" gasped the old man, red in the face. "Doesn't like the match I made for him, eh? Well, he'll have to! You bring him back here. I'm going to punish him."

Chueh-hsin murmured an assent. He was beginning to understand.

"Going to school has ruined him. I wanted you boys to take private tutoring at home, but you wouldn't listen to me. Now look what's happened! Even Chueh-min has gone bad. He actually dares to rebel. From now on, no son of the Kao family is permitted to attend an outside school! Do you hear that?" The patriarch began to cough again.

Chueh-hsin stood flustered, his grandfather's words crashing about his head like thunder.

Chueh-hui, lined up beside his Big Brother, was quite unperturbed. Roar away, he thought, smiling inwardly. You'll soon be exposed as a paper lantern!

The old man's coughing finally ceased. Worn out, he lay back and closed his eyes. For a long time he did not speak. He looked as if he were asleep. The brothers continued standing before him respectfully, waiting. Only when Mistress Chen signalled for them to go did they tiptoe out of the room.

"Second Brother left a note for you," Chueh-hui said to Chueh-hsin when they got outside. "It's in my room. Come and read it."

"What in the world did you say to *Yeh-yeh?* Why didn't you tell me first, instead of running to him? How could you be so stupid!"

"I wanted him to know! I wanted him to realize that we're human beings, not lambs that anyone can lead to the slaughter!"

Chueh-hsin knew the barb was directed against him. It

struck home, but he could only bear the pain in silence. No matter how sincerely he explained, Chueh-hui would never believe him.

In Chueh-hui's room, the boy handed him the letter. It was hard for Chueh-hsin to find the courage to read it, but at last he did:

Big Brother,
I'm doing what no one in our family has ever dared to do before—I'm running out on an arranged marriage. No one cares about my fate, so I've decided to walk my own road alone. I'm determined to struggle against the old forces to the end. Unless you cancel the match, I'll never come back. I'll die first. It's still not too late to save the situation. Remember our brotherly love and do your best to help me.

Chueh-min
Written at 3 in the morning.

Chueh-hsin turned pale. The note dropped from his trembling fingers to the floor. "What shall I do?" he stammered. "Doesn't he understand my position?"

"It has nothing to do with your position," said Chueh-hui stiffly. "The question is what are you going to do about it?"

Chueh-hsin rose quickly, as if he had received a shock. "I'm going to bring him back," he said simply.

"You'll never find him," said Chueh-hui with a cold laugh.

"Never find him?" echoed Chueh-hsin, confused.

"No one knows where he's moved to."

"But surely you know his address. You must know. Tell me, where is he? Please tell me," Chueh-hsin begged.

"I do know. But I certainly won't tell you," said Chueh-hui firmly.

"Don't you trust me?" Chueh-hsin angrily demanded.

"It doesn't matter whether I trust you or not. Your 'policy of non-resistance,' your 'compliant bow' philosophy would be sure to bring Second Brother to grief. In a word—you're too weak!" said Chueh-hui hotly. He paced the floor with large strides.

"I must see him. Tell me his address."

"No, absolutely no!"

"You'll have to reveal it. They'll make you. *Yeh-yeh* will make you."

"I won't tell them! Even in this family, I don't think they'd resort to torture," said Chueh-hui coolly. He was aware only that he was achieving some measure of vengeance against his family. He gave no thought to what his Big Brother might be suffering.

Despondently, Chueh-hsin walked out. Before long he came back and had another talk with Chueh-hui, trying to evolve a plan. But he failed. He could offer no compromise that would satisfy both Chueh-min and his grandfather.

Later that day, a small family council was held in Madam Chou's room. Present were Madam Chou, Chueh-hsin, his wife Jui-chueh, his sister Shu-hua, and Chueh-hui. Chueh-hui stood on one side; the others arrayed themselves opposite him. They urged him to reveal Chueh-min's whereabouts; they wanted him to persuade Chueh-min to come home. They made many attractive promises—including an assurance that if Chueh-min returned a way would be found, in time, to call off the match.

But Chueh-hui was adamant.

Since no information could be obtained from Chueh-hui, and since Chueh-min's demands could not be accepted, Madam Chou and Chueh-hsin could only worriedly seek out Ke-ming and ask him to delay the exchange of the horoscopes a few days, without letting the old man know. At the same time they sent people out to try and discover where Chueh-min was hiding.

The search proved fruitless. Chueh-min was well concealed.

Ke-ming called Chueh-hui to his study and gave him a lecture—to no avail. He offered friendly guidance—to no avail. He tried argumentative exhortation—to no avail. Chueh-hui insisted he knew nothing.

Madam Chou and Chueh-hsin worked on Chueh-hui next. They pleaded with him to bring Chueh-min back. They said all Chueh-min's conditions could be met—provided he returned home first. Chueh-hui was firm. Unless he got guarantees in advance, he didn't trust anyone.

Madam Chou scolded Chueh-hui, then she wept. Although she usually left the boys to their own devices, she was genuinely interested in their welfare. The situation was serious. She didn't want anything bad to happen to them, but she was even more concerned with her reputation if this scandal should leak out. She disapproved of Chueh-hui's disrespectful attitude towards his elders, and was very dissatisfied with Chueh-min's flying in the face of the decision of the head of the family. But no matter how she tried, she couldn't think of any solution.

Confronted with a difficult problem, Chueh-hsin's only recourse was to weep. He knew that Chueh-min was right. Yet not only couldn't he help him—he had to help their grandfather oppress him. And now Chueh-hui considered him an enemy. Unless he brought back Chueh-min, he would be unable to placate the old man. But if he did make him return, he would be wounding Second Brother grievously.

No, that was something he could not do! He loved Chueh-min. His father had entrusted his two younger brothers to him on his death-bed. How could he go back on his pledge to love and cherish them? Chueh-hsin broke into sobs. He wept so bitterly that tears also came to Jui-chueh's eyes.

The Venerable Master Kao knew none of this. All that interested him was that his orders had to be obeyed, his face preserved. What others suffered as a consequence meant nothing to him. He demanded that Chueh-min be produced. He swore at Chueh-hsin. He swore at Ke-ming. At times he even swore at Madam Chou.

But all of his ranting evoked no sign of compliance from Chueh-min. His pressure was useless; Chueh-min wasn't there to be subjected to it. By now the scandal was known to everyone in the compound. Great effort was made to keep it from spreading outside.

The days passed. The Venerable Master Kao was in a perpetually bad temper. A pall of gloom hung over Chueh-hsin's household, while the other households sneered privately at his misfortune.

One day, Chueh-hui returned home after a secret meeting

with Chueh-min. Leaving his desperately struggling brother was like leaving the world of light. The Kao compound depressed him dreadfully. The place was a desert; or perhaps it would be more accurate to call it a bastion of reaction, the main base of his enemy. Chueh-hui immediately sought out Chueh-hsin.

"Are you willing to help Second Brother or not?" he demanded irritably. "A whole week has already gone by."

"What can I do?" Chueh-hsin spread his hands despondently. *Now you're the one who's anxious*, he said to himself.

"Are you just going to let the thing drag on like this?"

"Drag on, nothing! *Yeh-yeh* says if Chueh-min doesn't return in another half month, he can stay away for ever. He'll put an announcement in the papers disowning him," said Chueh-hsin unhappily.

"Do you think *Yeh-yeh* would have the heart to do a thing like that?" Chueh-hui asked bitterly. He was still angry.

"Why wouldn't he? He's absolutely furious. He won't allow his orders to be disobeyed. Second Brother's resistance can't win."

"So you say that too. No wonder you won't help him!"

"But how can I?" Chueh-hsin considered himself the unluckiest man in the world. He had no strength whatsoever.

"When our father was dying, didn't he tell you to look after us? He'd be very disappointed in you today!" There were angry tears in Chueh-hui's eyes.

Chueh-hsin made no reply. He began to sob.

"If I were in your position, I'd never be so weak and useless, I tell you that! I'd cut the match with the Feng family with one slash of the knife, that's what I'd do!"

"But what about *Yeh-yeh?*" Big Brother asked, finally raising his head.

"*Yeh-yeh*'s era is over. Are you going to let Second Brother become a sacrifice to *Yeh-yeh*'s prejudice?"

Chueh-hsin again lapsed into silence.

"You *are* a weakling!" Chueh-hui stalked out angrily.

Alone in the room, Chueh-hsin was weighted down with misery. His "compliant bow" philosophy and his "policy of non-resistance" had failed him; he had not been able to make peace in the family. In an effort to satisfy everyone, he had given up his own happiness, but it had not brought him peace. He had willingly accepted the burden entrusted to him by his dying father; he had made every sacrifice for his younger brothers and sisters. The result was that he had driven one brother away, while the other cursed him for a weakling. What could he say to comfort himself?

After brooding thus for some time, he took up his pen and wrote an earnest letter to Chueh-min, vivisecting his own sincerity, and setting forth all his difficulties and tragic circumstances. He spoke of his love and friendship for his brothers, concluding with a plea that Chueh-min return, for the honour of their departed father, for the sake of peace in the Kao family.

Then he went to Chueh-hui and asked him to deliver the letter to Chueh-min.

Chueh-hui read the letter and wept. Shaking his head unhappily, he placed the missive back in the envelope.

Chueh-min's reply, of course, was brought by Chueh-hui. This is what it said:

After waiting so long, I frankly was very disappointed to get a letter like this from you! All you can say is—Come back, come back! As I write this, I am sitting in a little room, like an escaped prisoner, not daring to go out for fear of being caught and brought back to my jail. The jail I mean is our home, and the jailers are the members of our family— they have banded together to destroy me without mercy.

Yes, you all want me to come home. That would solve your problems. There would be peace in the family and another victim would be sacrificed. Of course you would all be very happy, but I would be sunk in a sea of bitterness. . . . Well, you can just forget it. I won't come home unless my demands are met. Home is nothing to me but a lot of unpleasant memories.

Perhaps you wonder what makes me so bold? I wonder myself sometimes. It's my love that sustains me. I'm fighting for the happiness of two people—hers and mine.

I often think of our garden, how we played there as children together. You are my Big Brother. You must help

262

me, for the sake of our father. For Chin too. And don't forget Cousin Mei. There's been enough heartbreak over her. Please don't let Chin become another Mei.

Tears coursed down Chueh-hsin's cheeks, but he was not aware of them. He was plunged into a dark abyss, without a ray of light, without a shred of hope. "You don't understand me," he kept mumbling. "No one understands me."

Chueh-hui stood watching him, torn between anger and pity. He not only had already read Chueh-min's letter—he had helped him write it. He had hoped the letter would move Big Brother, stir him into action, yet this was the result. He wanted to berate Chueh-hsin, but then he thought—What would be the use? Big Brother had become a man with no will of his own.

"This family is absolutely hopeless. The sooner I get out of here the better," Chueh-hui said to himself. From that moment on, he was no longer pessimistic over the chances of Chueh-min's success. This new idea intrigued him. It was a sprout that had just emerged into his consciousness, but it might grow very, very quickly.

Quite a number of people were suffering because of Chueh-min's escapade, Chueh-min himself among them. He was hiding in the home of his schoolmate, Tsun-jen, and although he was comfortable enough and Tsun-jen was very good to him, he hated being cooped up in a small room. Unable to do the things he wanted to do, unable to see the people he wanted to see, tormented by fear and longing, Chueh-min found life very difficult.

All day long he waited for news, but the only news Chueh-hui had been able to bring him so far was bad. Gradually, his hope dwindled. But it was not yet completely extinguished, and he still had the courage to go on. Chueh-hui constantly encouraged him with a promise of final victory. Chin's love, her image, gave him strength. He was sticking it out; he had no intention of surrendering.

Chin was always in his mind; he dreamed of her day and night. The more depressed he felt, the more he thought of her. And the more he thought of her, the more he longed to see her. But although she lived quite near to Tsun-jen's house, he couldn't visit her because her mother was home.

He wanted to send her a note via Chueh-hui. But when he took up his pen he found he had too much to say—he didn't know where to start. At the same time he was afraid if he didn't write her in detail, she would become worried. He decided to wait for an opportunity to talk to her face to face.

It came sooner than he expected. Chueh-hui arrived one day with the news that Mrs. Chang had gone out; he took Chueh-min to see Chin.

Leaving Chueh-min waiting outside the door, Chueh-hui went in first. "I've brought you something good, Cousin Chin," he announced cheerfully.

Chin had been lying down, reading, half-asleep, but she sat up quickly. Adjusting her hair, she asked listlessly, "What is it?" She looked pale, too tired even to smile.

"How thin you are!" Chueh-hui exclaimed in spite of himself.

"You haven't seen me in several days." Chin smiled wryly. "What about Second Brother? Why haven't I received even a single letter from him?"

"Several days? Why, I was here only the day before yesterday!"

"You don't know how time is dragging for me. Tell me quickly. What's happening with him?" Chin stared at him with large, worried eyes.

"He's given in!" Chueh-hui succumbed to an irresistible impulse to tease her.

"No! I don't believe it!"

Just at that moment, a young man stepped into her room, and Chin's eyes lit up.

"You!" she cried. Whether it was doubt, or surprise, or joy, or reproach that she felt, she didn't know herself. She rushed towards him, then checked herself abruptly and stood gazing at him, her eyes aglow.

"Yes, Chin, it's me." There was both joy and sorrow in his voice. "I meant to come much sooner, but I was afraid of running into your mother."

"I knew you'd come, I knew you'd come," she said, weeping tears of happiness. She looked reproachfully at Chueh-hui. "How could you try to fool me like that, Third Brother? I knew he'd never give in. I have faith in him." She gazed at Chueh-min lovingly, with no trace of shyness.

Chueh-hui was favourably impressed. He hadn't realized that Chin had grown so mature. Smiling, he looked at Chueh-min, who plainly was feeling very heroic at the girl's exaggerated praise. Chueh-hui acknowledged to himself that he was wrong. He had expected their meeting would be attended with tears and weeping and all the other trappings of tragedy. Such scenes were common in families like theirs.

But contrary to his expectations, they seemed to fear nothing, sustaining each other with an all-powerful mutual faith. He was delighted with them. They were a gleam of light in a dark world; they gave him hope. They didn't need his encouragement any more. Chueh-min would never bend the knee.

How easy it was for an ardent youth like Chueh-hui to believe in people!

"All right, you can quit talking like a couple of stage actors and get down to business. If you've got anything to say, say it quickly. We haven't much time." Chueh-hui grinned. "Would you like me to step out a minute?"

They both laughed but didn't answer. Ignoring Chueh-hui, they sat down on the edge of the bed, holding hands and talking affectionately. He idly picked one of Chin's books from the shelf. It was a collection of Ibsen's plays, dog-eared and underscored in places. Apparently, she had recently been reading *An Enemy of the People*.[35] She must have found encouragement in it. Chueh-hui couldn't help smiling.

He stole a glance at Chin. She and Chueh-min were engrossed in a lively conversation. Her face was radiantly beautiful. Chueh-hui felt rather envious of his brother. He turned back to *An Enemy of the People*.

After reading the first act he looked up. They were still talking. He read the second act. They still hadn't finished. He read

[35] A drama by Henrik Ibsen published in *New Youth* in July–October 1918.

265

the play through to the end. Chin and Chueh-min were chattering away, with no sign of a let-up.

"Well, how about it? What a gabby pair you two are!" Chueh-hui was growing impatient.

Chin looked up at him with a smile, and continued talking.

"Let's go, Second Brother," Chueh-hui urged, half an hour later. "You've said enough."

"Just a little longer," Chin pleaded. "It's early yet. What's your hurry?" She was holding Chueh-min's hand tightly, as if afraid he would leave.

"I must go back," said Chueh-hui, with mock stubbornness.

"Go ahead, then," Chin pouted. "My humble home isn't good enough for an aristocrat like you!" But when she saw him actually begin walking out, she and Chueh-min, in chorus, hastily called him to wait.

"Must you go, Third Brother? Can't you help me out a little?" Chueh-min asked earnestly.

Chueh-hui laughed. "I was only fooling. But you two are much too cold to me. Chin, you haven't spoken to me, or even asked me to sit down. Now that Second Brother's here, you've fogotten me completely."

The other two also laughed.

"I've only got one mouth. I can only speak to one person at a time," Chin defended herself. "Be good now, Third Brother. Let me talk to him today. Tomorrow, you and I can talk to your heart's content." She coaxed him, as if he were a child.

"Don't try to fool me. I haven't Second Brother's luck!"

Chueh-min opened his mouth to say something, but Chin cut in. "How's your luck going with Hsu Chien-ju?" she asked slyly. "Chien-ju's got it all over me. Do you like her? She's a really modern girl."

"Maybe I like her, and maybe I don't. But what's that got to do with you?" Chueh-hui retorted mischievously. He loved this kind of banter.

"They are well matched. I was thinking the same thing, myself," Chueh-min interposed.

Chueh-hui laughed and waved his hand in refusal. "No thanks. I don't want to become like you two—secret rendezvous and Shakespearean scenes!" In his heart he was thinking: What I want is you, Chin! . . . But this first thought was immediately driven away by a second: I've already sent one girl to her death. I've had enough of love. Outwardly he smiled, but it was a bitter smile.

Chueh-min's conversation with Chin at last came to an end. Now they had to part. Chueh-min hated to leave. Thinking of his lonely life in that little room, he hadn't the courage to go back. But Chueh-hui's impelling look told him that he must; there was no other way.

"I have to go," he said sadly, a note of struggle in his voice. But he didn't move. He cast about in his mind for some words to comfort Chin; all he could manage in that instant was: "Don't think about me too much," although that wasn't his meaning at all. As a matter of fact, he hoped she would think about him a great deal.

Chin stood before him, her big, luminous eyes fixed on his face, listening carefully, as if expecting him to say something out of the ordinary. He didn't. She waited, but he spoke only briefly. Disappointed, she clutched his sleeve, urging:

"Don't go yet. Stay a little longer. I still have a lot to tell you."

Chueh-min gulped down these wonderful words like the tastiest of morsels. He stared at her animated face. "All right, I won't go yet," he said with a smile—a smile so tortured that Chueh-hui, watching from the side, really thought he was going to cry.

To Chin, Chueh-min's tender gaze seemed to be gently laving her eyes, her face. "Speak," they seemed to say. "Speak. I'm listening to every word, every syllable." But she couldn't think of anything to say, and she was frantic for fear that he might leave at any moment. Still holding on to his sleeve, she blurted out the first thing that came into her mind:

"Cousin Mei has become pitifully thin lately. She coughs blood every day, though not very much. She's hiding it from her mother, and she doesn't want me to tell anyone, because she doesn't want to be given medicine. She says every day she lives is another day of misery—she'd be better off dead. Her mother is always busy entertaining and playing mahjong;

she doesn't pay much attention to Mei. Yesterday I finally found the chance to tell her how sick Mei is; only now she's begun to worry. Perhaps Mei is right. But I can't stand by and watch her die. Don't say anything to Big Brother. Mei begged me not to let him know."

Suddenly Chin noticed the tears glistening behind Chueh-min's glasses. They were beginning to trickle down his cheeks. His lips trembled, but he could not speak. She understood. He was frightened that their love, too, might end in tragedy.

"I can't say any more!" she cried. She fell back a few paces, buried her face in her hands and wept.

"I really must go now, Chin," said Chueh-min unhappily. He hadn't imagined that their joyous meeting would terminate with both of them in tears. And they called themselves the new youth, the brave! . . .

"Don't go! Stay!" Chin took down her hands from her tear-stained face and stretched them towards Chueh-min.

Only Chueh-hui's restraining grasp kept Chueh-min from rushing to her. Chueh-min looked at his younger brother. Chueh-hui's eyes were dry, and they burned with a strong, steady light. Chueh-hui jerked his head in the direction of the door.

"Don't cry, Chin, I'll come again," Chueh-min said in a stricken voice. "I'm living not very far from here. I'll come as soon as there's a chance. . . . Take care of your health. I'll be sending you good news soon."

Steeling himself, he turned and walked out with Chueh-hui. Chin followed as far as the door of the main hall. There she halted and stood with her back against the frame of the door-way. Wiping her eyes, she watched them go.

The brothers reached the street with the sound of Chin's weeping still in their ears. They walked on quickly in silence, and soon arrived at Tsun-jen's house. Chueh-hui abruptly stopped in the middle of the street.

"You and Chin are bound to succeed," he said in a bright, strong voice. "We don't need any more sacrificial victims. We've had enough." Chueh-hui paused, then went on firmly, almost cruelly. "If any more sacrifices have to be made, let *them* be the victims this time!"

XXX

Chueh-hsin's conscience had been bothering him a lot of late. He knew that unless he helped Chueh-min, he'd regret it all his life. After talking it over with his wife and stepmother, he went to the Venerable Master Kao and circuitously suggested that the marriage be postponed until Chueh-min was self-supporting. Naturally, he made no reference to the affair between Chueh-min and Chin. Chueh-hsin spoke quite movingly—he had been preparing for several nights; he had even written his speech out. He was sure he could sway the old man.

But Chueh-hsin was wrong. The patriarch was furious. He knew only that his authority had been attacked and stern measures were needed to restore it. A parent's order, the word of a marriage sponsor, the bride chosen by the head of a family—none of these could be questioned by a member of the younger generation. That was an unshakable principle; going against it demanded severe punishment. As to young people's happiness and aspirations, he never gave them a thought. Chueh-hsin's plea only increased his rage. He swore the engagement would not be broken. Unless Chueh-min returned by the end of the month, he would place an announcement in the newspapers publicly disowning him and compel Chueh-hui to marry the girl in Chueh-min's place.

Chueh-hsin didn't dare to argue. Humbly leaving his grandfather's room, he hurried to Chueh-hui and told him what the old man had said. He thought that this might frighten Chueh-hui into urging his Second Brother to return. But Chueh-hui had learned wisdom; what's more he was prepared for something like this. He made no comment, he only laughed coldly. . . . They're certainly not going to make me the victim! he thought.

269

"You'd better persuade Second Brother to come back," Chueh-hsin urged, when Chueh-hui remained silent. "Otherwise you'll be the marriage victim."

"If that's what *Yeh-yeh* really wants, let him go ahead. He'll be sorry. I'm not afraid. I've got some ideas of my own," retorted Chueh-hui proudly.

Big Brother could hardly believe his ears. He had thought he knew Chueh-hui thoroughly.

"I don't understand why you're so weak, so useless!" Chueh-hui mocked him.

Chueh-hsin blushed, then turned pale. He trembled, speechless with anger. At that moment a servant rushed in and breathlessly announced:

"A messenger has just come from Mrs. Chien. Miss Mei is dead!"

"Mei is dead? When did she die?" cried Jui-chueh, emerging hastily from the inner room.

"About seven this morning," the servant replied.

The clock on the wall struck nine. A heavy silence filled the room. No one could speak.

"Get a sedan-chair ready for me immediately," Chueh-hsin directed, his face falling.

"I want to go too," said Jui-chueh, weeping. She sat down in a wicker chair.

"What are you waiting for?" Chueh-hsin said to the servant. After the man had left, he turned to Jui-chueh and said soothingly, "Don't go. Jui, you're with child. It's bad for you. You'll get too upset."

"I want to see her. . . . That day after I visited her in Chin's house . . . as I was getting into my sedan-chair, she took my hand. She said I must come to see her often. She kept repeating that the next time I must bring Hai-chen. Her eyes were filled with tears. Who knew that she'd never see us again. I want to go. . . . It's the last time. . . . She was so good to me . . . it's the least I can do."

"Jui, don't carry on so. You must think of your health. You're all I have left. If anything should happen to you, it would be the end of me," said Chueh-hsin dismally.

Chueh-hui stood beside the desk, staring at the white gauze curtains. The news hadn't come to him as a surprise. He remembered Chin telling him about Mei: "She says every day she lives is another day of misery—she'd be better off dead." Still, the death of this fragile, lovely young woman was hard to bear. Bitterness and fury seethed in Chueh-hui's breast. Controlling himself, he said coldly:

"Another sacrificial victim!"

He knew Chueh-hsin would understand his meaning. He turned to see Big Brother gazing at him with suffering eyes. "The trouble is far from over," Chueh-hui added. "The worst is yet to come." This too was for Chueh-hsin's benefit.

Chueh-hsin could hear weeping as he got out of his sedan-chair at the door of the Chien family. He hurried directly to Mei's room.

Mei's mother, Mrs. Chien, was there, and Mei's younger brother, as well as Chin and a bondmaid. They were grouped around the body, crying. All looked up when Chueh-hsin came in.

"What am I going to do, First Young Master?" wailed Mrs. Chien. Her hair was dishevelled and tears stained her face.

"We'll have to start arranging for the funeral immediately," said Chueh-hsin in a tragic voice. "Has the coffin been bought?"

"I sent Old Wang out to buy one. He hasn't come back yet." (Old Wang was their servant.) Mrs. Chien began to weep again. "Mei's been dead for over two hours, but not a thing has been done. We've no grown men in the family, and Old Wang has been busy notifying people. What am I going to do? Look at the state this house is in!"

"Don't worry, Aunt Chien. Just leave everything to me."

"You're a good man, First Young Master. Mei will be grateful to you in the next world."

The word "grateful" was like a needle through Chueh-hsin's heart. He didn't know what to say. He wished he could cry. Why should she be grateful to me? he thought. It was I who brought her to this! He walked to her bedside. She was lying with her eyes closed, her hair spread upon the pillow. Her thin face was white, her lips slightly parted, as if she had been about to speak when she died. She was draped with a coverlet from the waist down.

"I've come to see you, Mei," he said in a low voice. Suddenly he was blinded by tears. Is this how we part for ever? he wondered. You've gone without a word. You've never forgiven me! Why didn't I come earlier? I could have seen your lips move, heard your voice. I would have known what was in your heart. Silently he beseeched her: Mei, I've come. If you've anything to tell me, say it quickly. I can hear you!

Chueh-hsin wiped his eyes. Mei lay like an icy stone. She wouldn't really be able to hear him even if he shouted himself hoarse; she would remain motionless. All hope was gone. They were separated now by eternity, and they would never be able to bridge the gap. Heartbroken, torn by remorse, he wept hopeless tears.

His crying started Mrs. Chien sobbing again. Chin came over to him impatiently.

"This is no time for weeping. You ought to help make the final arrangements. She's dead. Crying won't bring her back again. Aunt Chien is nearly beside herself as it is. Your crying only makes her feel worse. If Mei has any consciousness after death, you're hurting her too."

I've hurt her so many times already, he thought bitterly, what difference will one more time make! Restraining his tears with an effort, he sighed deeply.

"You shouldn't blame First Young Master," said Mrs. Chien. "He and Mei were very dear to each other. There were people who proposed that they marry. It's all my fault for not agreeing. If I had, we wouldn't have come to this, today!" Mrs. Chien wept as she spoke. She was incapable of doing anything. Her mind was in a whirl.

"Hurry and make the arrangements, Cousin," Chin urged Chueh-hsin. "Don't leave her exposed so long." She knew Mrs. Chien's remark had upset Big Brother, and she used this prod to distract him.

"All right," sighed Chueh-hsin. He discussed the details with Mrs. Chien. Then Mei was dressed in burial clothes and placed in the coffin. Chueh-hsin wanted to lift her out in his arms and run with her to some distant, deserted place. But he didn't have the courage.

Finally, steeling himself, he gave the order to close the coffin. Mrs. Chien grasped the edge of the casket and began to wail:

"Mei, I was blind, I didn't know what was in your heart. I broke up your match with Chueh-hsin. I made you suffer till you died. I'm sorry, Mei. Can you hear me? Why don't you answer? Do you hate me? Take your revenge on me in your next life. Hurt me as I've hurt you. Only don't leave me. We must be mother and daughter again. Do you agree, my poor darling? Mei, Mei, let me go with you. . . ."

She tried to climb into the coffin, deaf to all exhortations to be calm. They had to pull her away.

The lid was placed on the coffin and sealed tight. Mei was gone from the room. Only the coffin remained, and even that was to be removed the same day.

One by one, the few visitors departed. Madam Chou had come with Shu-hua. Chin's mother, Mrs. Chang, had also come, and two or three other women. They had sat for a while and departed. Except for Mei's mother and young brother and their servant, Old Wang, the only ones to accompany the body to the funeral hall outside the city were Chueh-hsin, Chueh-hui, Shu-hua and Chin. Chueh-hui had arrived quite late, but he was in time to take part in the funeral procession.

The funeral hall was in the wing of a large dilapidated temple whose courtyard was overgrown with weeds. Each of the wings flanking the main temple building contained a series of small rooms. Most of these housed coffins and funereal equipment, much of it in an old and neglected condition. Ordinarily a coffin was left in a funeral hall until the family could arrange to transport it back to the deceased's native place for burial. But here, in one room, for instance, were four coffins that had been brought in almost twenty years ago; no one remembered to whom they belonged.

Mei's room was a relatively modest one. They soon set it in order. The coffin was carried in; an altar was placed beside it; Mei's "spirit tablet" was stood upon the altar. Old Wang squatted on the stone platform outside the door and burned paper "money." Mrs. Chien leaned against the coffin and wept, her young son sobbing beside her. Chin tried to comfort Mrs. Chien, but when she remembered what good friends she had been with Mei and thought of what had become of Mei now, she herself burst into tears.

Chueh-hsin stood dazedly before the altar. He could hear the others weeping. He was crying too, though he hardly knew why. It seemed to him that the one in the coffin wasn't Mei, but someone else. She was still alive, looking at him with a mournful expression, telling him of her sad life. Through his tears the red paper inscribed in black ink and pasted on the "spirit tablet" gradually came into clear focus. "Our Deceased Sister . . . Mei. . . ." The words were merciless, unmistakable. She was dead. Behind the altar, Mei's mother wept and beat upon the coffin; her young brother cried, "Sister, sister. . . ." Chin pillowed her head on her right arm and lay against the coffin, weeping quietly—Chin whose love was menaced by the same fate as Mei's.

Chueh-hsin's tears flowed freely. This time he knew why. He wiped his eyes with his handkerchief. He couldn't bear to look any more. Striding out of the door, he paused on the stone platform and watched Old Wang burning sacrifice money. Chueh-hui was just coming out of the main temple; he walked firmly. In spite of his youth, he was the only one who could bolster Chueh-hsin's strength in such surroundings. That certainly was how it seemed to Chueh-hsin at the moment.

"Let's go back," said Chueh-hui, walking up to Chueh-hsin. Old Wang had finished burning the "money." Only a pile of embers and black ashes remained. The wind lifted the flaky ashes, and let them sail down, scattering in all directions.

"All right," replied Chueh-hsin listlessly. He turned and went back into the funeral hall. With tears in his eyes, he urged the others not to cry. Chin was sobbing; Mrs. Chien had wept her eyes dry. Only the little brother was still calling, "Sister, sister. . . ."

Each made an obeisance before the altar. As they were leaving, the little boy suddenly burst out:

"We're going, sister, and leaving you all alone! How lonesome you'll be!"

Tears came to everyone's eyes. Chin pressed the child's hand and, comforting him, led him outside. Mrs. Chien had just

274

calmed down a bit, but her son's cry again plunged her into misery. Standing before the altar, she gazed at the candles, the incense, the "spirit tablet."

"Your brother is right, Mei," she moaned weakly. "This place is too cold, too desolate. Come home tonight; surely you remember your own house. From now on, I'll leave a lamp burning in your room every night, to help you find your way. I won't change anything . . . Mei . . . my dear. . . ."

It was a great effort for her to speak. She wanted to say more, but her chest ached and there was a lump in her throat. She trailed out after the others.

Chueh-hsin was the last to get into his sedan-chair; he turned his head many times to look back as they departed. But the last to leave was Chueh-hui—he wouldn't let any man carry him. He never rode in sedan-chairs; he walked.

Chueh-hui returned to the small room and made a circuit around the coffin. He too wanted to bid farewell to Mei. But he didn't weep; he felt no sorrow—only a furious anger. In a voice that shook with pity and rage, he said:

"To the accompaniment of weeping and words and tears, a sweet young life has been put to rest. Ah, Cousin Mei, if only I could pluck you from your coffin and make you open your eyes, I would prove it to you—You didn't die; you've been murdered!"

XXXI

The following afternoon, Chueh-hui went to see Chueh-min and told him about Mei. Chueh-min wept. They talked for less than an hour, then Chueh-hui left. Chueh-min saw him to the door. Chueh-hui had already crossed the threshold when Chueh-min suddenly called him back.

"What is it?" asked Chueh-hui, returning to the door.

Chueh-min only smiled, but did not speak.

"You're lonely, aren't you?" said Chueh-hui sympathetically. "I am too. Nobody at home understands me. Mama Huang and Sister-in-law and the girls are always hanging around, asking me about you. But their way of thinking is so different from yours and mine. I feel quite isolated. But I know I must be patient, and so must you. You're sure to win."

"I'm a little afraid. . . ." Tears glistened in Chueh-min's eyes.

"Afraid of what? You can't lose." Chueh-hui forced an encouraging smile.

"I'm afraid of the loneliness. I'm very lonely!"

"But don't you remember—you have two people fighting on your side?" Chueh-hui struggled to maintain his cheerful expression.

"It's because you're both so dear to me that I'm always wanting to see you. But she can't come, and now you're leaving. . . ."

Chueh-hui's eyes smarted. He turned his head so that his brother might not see the moisture in his eyes, and clapped Chueh-min on the shoulder. "Be patient. It won't be much longer. You're bound to win."

"Why don't you fellows talk inside?" Tsun-jen had come out and was standing beside them. "You shouldn't be too careless," he added with a smile.

Chueh-hui greeted him and said, "I'm going." As he walked away he heard Tsun-jen saying to Chueh-min, "We'd better go in."

"You're bound to win," he had assured Chueh-min, but now he wondered bitterly—Is victory really possible? How long would it take to finally attain it? . . . But by the time he reached Chin's house, he made up his mind—Never mind all that. We'll fight to the end, come what may!

After paying his respects to his aunt, he went to Chin's room. "I've just seen Chueh-min," he said, coming directly to the point. "He's asked me to tell you—He's fine."

Chin had been writing a letter. She quickly put down her pen and said, "Thank him, and thank you, too. I was just writing to him."

"Needless to say, I'll deliver the letter for you," Chueh-hui smiled. He glanced at the letter and noticed that the words

"Cousin Mei" appeared in several places. "You're writing about Cousin Mei? I've already told him. Tell me, what's your reaction to her death?"

"As I've said in this letter, under no circumstances am I going to be a second Mei. My mother won't permit it either. She told me that after seeing all the heartbreak at Mei's funeral yesterday, she was very shaken. She's willing to help me, now." Chin spoke firmly. She had none of the despondency of a few days before.

"That's good news. You should let him know right away." Chueh-hui urged her to finish the letter. They chatted for a few minutes, then Chueh-hui went back to Tsun-jen's house.

Of course both Chueh-min and Tsun-jen were delighted with the news. They and Chueh-hui talked optimistically for almost an hour. Only then did Chueh-hui return home.

In the compound, he found a small crowd gathered outside his grandfather's window, craning their necks and listening. This sort of thing was very common in the Kao family, and Chueh-hui paid no attention. Walking into the main hall, he was about to enter his grandfather's room, when he heard a woman crying inside. He recognized her voice. It was Madam Shen, wife of his Uncle Ke-ting. Following came the sound of his grandfather swearing and coughing.

I knew there'd be a farce like this sooner or later, Chueh-hui said to himself. He remained outside the door.

"Bring him back immediately! You'll see how I punish him! . . . I've had enough of his insolence!" The old man's voice trembled with rage. He lapsed into a fit of coughing, which was interspersed with the weeping of Aunt Shen.

A man's voice servilely murmured "Yes" several times. Then the door curtain was pushed aside and Uncle Ke-ming, red-faced, emerged. By then Chueh-hui had already left the hall.

Among the audience outside the window was his younger sister Shu-hua. When she saw Chueh-hui, she walked over to him and asked, "Do you know about Uncle Ke-ting, Third Brother?"

"I've known for some time," Chueh-hui nodded. In a low

voice he asked, "How did they find out?" He pointed with his lips towards his grandfather's room.

"Fifth Uncle has been keeping a concubine on the outside," the girl replied dramatically. "He rented an apartment for her. Nobody in the family knew. He took all of Fifth Aunt's gold and silver jewelry; he said he loaned it to someone who wanted to copy the designs. When Fifth Aunt pressed him to return it, he said he lost it. The last few months, he's been out every day; at night he comes home very late. Fifth Aunt has been so busy with her mahjong games that she didn't notice anything. Yesterday morning she found a woman's picture in his pocket. When she questioned him, he refused to say who it was. By coincidence, Fifth Aunt went shopping yesterday afternoon and saw a woman getting out of Uncle Ke-ting's sedan-chair in front of the arcade, with Uncle Ke-ting's servant Kao-chung right behind her.

"Today, Aunt Shen found an excuse to keep Kao-chung at home, and she forced him to tell the truth—Uncle Ke-ting has pawned some of her jewelry; some of it he's given to the woman. Now Aunt Shen has complained to *Yeh-yeh*. . . . Uncle Ke-ting's concubine is a prostitute. Her name is 'Monday'! . . . Oh yes, they say Uncle Ke-ting has begun smoking opium; he's got the habit. His concubine smokes it too. . . ."

Shu-hua rattled on as if she would never stop, plainly relishing the scandal. Chueh-hui was neither much interested nor surprised. He knew the family was hollow and that it was bound to collapse. No one could prevent it—his grandfather or anyone else. The old man himself was already deteriorating rapidly. It seemed to Chueh-hui that he alone was on the threshold of brightness. His moral strength far exceeded that of his tottering family.

Today he was uplifted by enthusiasm as never before. The so-called struggle between parent and child for the right to freedom, love and knowledge was going to conclude happily. The era of tragedies like Mei's would soon be over, giving way to a new era, an era of girls like Chin, or perhaps the still more modern Hsu Chien-ju. It would be Chueh-min's era, and his own. The youth of this era could never be defeated by cor-

278

rupt, weak, and often criminal, old-fashioned families. Victory was assured, of that Chueh-hui was confident.

He shook himself vigorously, as if to cast off the burden of years of bitterness and pain. Proudly, fiercely, he gazed around him, and he thought: Wait and see, old family. Your end is coming, soon!

Naturally, Shu-hua had no inkling of what was going on in Chueh-hui's mind. He didn't answer her, and she could see that he was bored. She hurried back to her listening post outside the window.

Chueh-hui went to his room. Not long after, through his window he observed Ke-ming returning with Ke-ting in tow. Next, from his grandfather's room, came the sound of thunderous swearing, obviously directed at Ke-ting. Finally, it stopped, and the crowd outside the old man's window stirred with excitement, as if over some unexpected development.

"I always said our family loves a farce," Chueh-hui muttered.

The voices of the people outside rose, and men and women ran breathlessly to spread the news.

"*Yeh-yeh* is hitting Uncle Ke-ting!" Chueh-chun, one of Chueh-hui's little boy cousins, went tearing across the courtyard, then halted abruptly to announce this news to Chueh-ying, another young boy cousin.

"Really? Then why are you running away?" asked Chueh-ying.

"I've got to get Sixth Brother to come and see this. . . . A big man like Uncle Ke-ting getting a beating!" Chueh-chun laughed, and he rushed off.

His interest aroused at last, Chueh-hui walked to his grandfather's apartment. Three people, watching surreptitiously through the door-curtain, blocked the doorway. Not wanting to squeeze past them, Chueh-hui went outside to the window. Many people were gathered there, listening. A few had brought chairs and were kneeling on them, peering through small holes in the paper panes.

But there was no sound of any beating, only the furious tones of the old man.

"A man of your age, with a daughter growing up—you still

279

haven't learned to behave! A fine example you give to your child! Be ashamed of him, Shu-chen. He's not fit to be your father!"

Chueh-hui couldn't help laughing to himself.

The old man coughed and, after a pause, resumed his angry lecture.

"You're absolutely shameless. What has been the good of your schooling? Fooling your wife into lending you her jewelry and then pawning it! I give you three days to bring it back!" The Venerable Master Kao went on cursing Ke-ting, and finally he said, "You animal, I pampered you because you were a clever child. I never thought you'd turn out to be such a disgrace. How have you returned my kindness? By deceiving me! Scoundrel! Slap your face! Slap your own face!"

There came the sound of a hand smartly striking a cheek. Chueh-hui walked back quickly to the door of his grand-father's room. "Let me see," he said softly to his sister Shu-hua who was leaning forward, peeking through the door-curtain. He edged past her and stood in the doorway.

Ke-ting was kneeling upright, slapping his cheeks, left and right. His usually thin sallow face was quite red from the blows. Although his wife and daughter were before him, he showed no sign of shame. He continued hitting himself.

But this humiliation didn't satisfy the Venerable Master. He demanded that Ke-ting tell his whole dirty story—how he got into bad company and began sliding downhill, his rela-tions with the prostitute, the apartment he rented for her, how he pawned his wife's jewelry.

Cursing himself, Ke-ting revealed all, including things his father had never suspected. He had incurred many debts, some of them debts for gambling, obtaining credit on the old man's name. What's more, he was helped in all this by his brother Ke-an; in fact, Ke-an was partly responsible for his getting into debt in the first place.

The patriarch was astonished. Even Chueh-hui had not guessed that matters had gone so far.

Chueh-hui couldn't help being impressed by the contrast between his Fifth Uncle, Ke-ting, and his brother, Chueh-min. Chueh-min, nineteen years old, surrounded by enemies, sustained only by his faith and enthusiasm, was fighting on bravely, the family helpless against him. Ke-ting, over thirty, the father of a thirteen-year-old daughter, knelt on the floor, slapping his own face, insulting and reviling himself, implicating others, offering no resistance by word or deed. He did his father's bidding without hesitation, although he didn't really agree with what the Venerable Master said. In the face of the menace of the stubborn old man, what a difference in reaction between these two different generations! Chueh-hui was proud of his own generation. Looking at Ke-ting, he thought contemptuously: Your type can be found only among people of your generation; they'd never be found in ours. He walked away.

Coughing violently, the patriarch ordered Shu-chen to fetch Ke-an. The girl returned in a few moments, saying her uncle was not at home. The old man cursed and pounded the table. "Where is your Fourth Aunt?" he said to Shu-chen. "Bring her to me."

Madam Wang of the Fourth Household had been listening outside the window. When she saw Shu-chen coming for her, although she was afraid, she had no choice but to take a grip on herself and go in.

The old man asked her in a loud voice where her husband Ke-an had gone. Madam Wang said she didn't know. He then asked when Ke-an would return. She replied she didn't know that either.

"Why don't you?" yelled the Venerable Master, slapping the table. "Muddle-head!"

Angry and embarrassed, Madam Wang hung her head. She thought she saw Mistress Chen making an ugly grimace at her, and she felt like telling the long-faced old concubine a thing or two. But in the presence of the Venerable Master, she didn't dare to move. She didn't even dare to weep.

The old man again broke into a violent fit of coughing. Mistress Chen diligently drummed on his back. "Don't make yourself ill over them," she urged. "They're not worth it!"

Gradually, the patriarch calmed down. His anger was replaced by a depression he had never experienced before. Exhausted, he closed his eyes and lay back on the sofa. He didn't want to see any of them.

"Go away, all of you," he sighed with a weak wave of the hand. "I can't bear to look at you."

Everyone had been longing to be dismissed; they exited quickly. Ke-ting got up off the floor and tiptoed out. The Venerable Master was left alone with Mistress Chen. He didn't want to see her either. All he wanted was a little peace and quiet. He sent Mistress Chen away and lay on the sofa, panting slightly.

He opened his eyes. He seemed to see many forms and faces drifting before him. Not one of them looked at him with any affection. There were his sons, indulging themselves in women and wine, sneering at him, cursing him behind his back. There were his grandsons, proudly going their own new road, abandoning him, old and weak and powerless to stop them.

Never had he felt so lonely and despondent. Had all his hopes been nothing but idle dreams? He had built up the family until it was large and prosperous. Ruthless, dictatorial, he had controlled everything, satisfied in the conviction that the family would continue to flourish. Yet the results of his strenuous efforts had brought only loneliness. Though he was taxing his waning strength to the utmost to keep a grip on things, it was obvious he could not.

No question about it—the family was sliding downhill. He already had some premonition of how it would end. It probably would happen very soon. He had no way to prevent it. Viewing the large wealthy family he had spent so many years in the building, the Venerable Master Kao could feel only futile, empty.

Weakly he rested on the sofa, ignored, bitter, lonely. For the first time he became aware of his true position in the family. Not only had he lost his pride—even the people he relied upon to maintain the daily life of the family had proved worthless. For the first time he felt disappointed, disillusioned, sunk in despair. It occurred to him, also for the first time, that he must have made mistakes; but he didn't know what they were. Even if he could discover them, it was already too late.

He seemed to hear Ke-ting wrangling with his wife, Mistress Chen cursing someone. Everywhere were quarrelsome, discordant, grating sounds. He covered his ears, but he couldn't shut them out. He had to find some quiet place to hide! Struggling to his feet, he tottered towards his bed. Suddenly, the room began to spin. He swayed; his eyes went black. He knew nothing more until awakened by the terrified screeching of Mistress Chen.

XXXII

The Venerable Master Kao was ill.

He lay groaning upon his bed, attended by several famous physicians, dosed by dark and bitter potions. The first two days, the doctors said his ailment was not serious. The old man dutifully drank his medicines, but he became worse. The third day, he refused to drink any more, and only relented under the combined pleading of Ke-ming and Chueh-hsin.

Ke-ming sat with the old man all day, leaving the affairs of his law office in the hands of his secretary and another lawyer. Ke-an was at home part of the time, but he also went to the theatre and to the private apartment he kept outside.

Ke-ting took advantage of his father's illness to visit his "love nest" where he drank, played mahjong and bantered with his female friends. He saw the old man only in the morning and in the evening when, as usual, he paid his formal respects.

No one in the family was particularly inconvenienced by the patriarch's illness. People laughed, cried, quarrelled and fought as before. Even the few who were concerned about him didn't think his condition was serious, in spite of the fact that he grew weaker day by day.

When medication proved ineffective, the family turned to superstitious quackery. Some people, when they begin to lose confidence, seek the aid of the supernatural. This may take very complicated forms—forms contrived by weak-minded people and believed in only by other weak-minded people.

Yet the ceremony proposed by Mistress Chen, and approved by the other ladies in the family, also obtained the full support of the grown men, gentlemen allegedly "well versed in the books of the Sages."

It began with a number of Taoist monks beating drums and cymbals in the main hall, and chanting prayers. At night, when all was still, Mistress Chen prayed in the courtyard. Chueh-hui watched her curiously through his window. Formally attired in a pink skirt, she knelt before a pair of candles and an incense burner, in which nine sticks of incense smouldered, and mumbled prayers under her breath. She kept rising, then falling to her knees—time after time, night after night. But the old man did not improve.

"Stupid woman!" Chueh-hui raged to himself. "All you're fit for is to put on an idiotic show!"

The next device was for the Venerable Master's three sons —Ke-ming, Ke-an and Ke-ting—to offer a sacrifice. Mistress Chen's burner was replaced in the middle of the night by an altar bearing tall candles, thick incense and sacrificial implements. The ceremony was conducted seriously, but the solemnity of the three sons was so exaggerated it appeared ludicrous. Although they too knelt and kowtowed, they finished in a much shorter time than it had taken Mistress Chen. Chueh-hui felt the same scorn for them as he had for the old concubine. He knew that only a few hours before Ke-an had been at the theatre, dallying with his favourite female impersonator, and Ke-ting had been gambling and drinking in his "love nest." It was sheer hypocrisy for them to kneel and pray that they be allowed to die in their father's place.

Just when Chueh-hui thought the family had exhausted its ingenuity, a new programme was contrived. A witch doctor was invited to "drive out the devils."

One night, shortly after dark, Ke-ming ordered that all doors be shut tight. The compound was converted into a weird and ancient temple. A thin-faced witch doctor with flowing locks arrived. Dressed in peculiar vestments, uttering shrill cries, he scattered burning resin, exactly like an actor impersonating a devil upon the stage. He ran about the courtyard making all sorts of frightful noises and gestures. Entering the patient's apartment, he leaped and yelled and flung things to the floor, even throwing burning resin beneath the bed. The loud groans of the old man—induced by the clamour and terror—in no way deterred the witch doctor. His performance gained in frenzy. He made such wild menacing thrusts that the old man cried out in alarm. The room was filled with thick black smoke and the glare and odour of sputtering resin.

It went on for an hour. Then the witch doctor, still yowling, departed. After a period of complete silence, normal voices were again heard in the compound.

But there was more to come. The devils had only been driven from the patient's room. That wasn't enough. The compound was full of devils; there were devils, many devils, in all the rooms. It was decided to have a general clean-out the following evening. Only in this way, said the witch doctor, could the old man recover.

Not everyone believed this; some, in fact, were opposed to a second drive against the devils. But not one person had the courage to express his opposition openly. Although Chueh-hui was not afraid to speak his mind, no one paid any attention to him.

The second farce commenced on schedule. Every room was subjected to a ridiculous, yet frightening, treatment. People got out of the witch doctor's way. Children bawled, women sighed, men shook their heads.

Chueh-hui sat in his room, listening to the racket and unearthly howls coming from his sister-in-law's apartment on the other side of the wall. He muttered angry curses. A weight seemed to be crushing him down; he wanted to leap up and cast it off. He couldn't become a party to this preposterous show. Chueh-hui made up his mind. He locked his door, sat down, and waited.

Before long, the witch doctor came to Chueh-hui's flat. Finding the door locked, he rapped sharply; servants helped him knock. No answer. They began to push against the door, calling, "Third Young Master!"

"I'm not going to open!" shouted Chueh-hui. "There are

no devils in here!" He lay down on his bed and covered his ears with his hands.

Suddenly, someone shook the door violently. Chueh-hui sat bolt upright, his face scarlet with rage. He seemed to see Ming-feng's tousled hair, her tear-stained face.

"Quit that racket!" he yelled. "What are you trying to do, anyway?"

"Chueh-hui, open the door," he heard his uncle Ke-ming call.

"Third Young Master, open the door," came the loud voice of Mistress Chen.

So you've brought up reinforcements, he thought. "I will not!" he retorted crisply, and walked away from the door. His brain felt ready to explode. "I hate them, hate them! . . ." he muttered.

But they wouldn't let him go. Their angry voices pursued him, louder and louder.

"Don't you want your grandfather to get better? Open the door! . . . Where's your sense of duty!" The shrill voice of Mistress Chen, which Chueh-hui always found so irritating, now struck him like a threatening blow, wounding him and adding fuel to his rage.

"You must be reasonable, nephew," said Ke-ming. "We all want *Yeh-yeh* to get well. You're a sensible boy—"

Another voice cut his words short: "Open the door, Third Brother. I want to talk to you." It was Chueh-hsin.

You too, thought Chueh-hui bitterly. It's not enough that you're a coward yourself. . . . His heart was breaking.

All right, if that's what you want, he said to himself. He swung open the door. Confronting him were red, furious visages. People pushed towards him, the witch doctor, naturally, being the first to advance.

"Not so fast." Chueh-hui stood in the doorway, his cheeks flushed, his voice trembling with anger. "What exactly do you think you're doing?" he asked contemptuously. He swept their faces with hate-filled eyes.

The question stopped them, cold. Ke-ming muttered something about "driving out devils" in a tone that indicated plainly he had no faith whatsoever in what he was saying.

"We are eradicating devils for your grandfather," said Mistress Chen, reeking of perfume and holding herself very erect. She indicated to the witch doctor that he should enter.

"You're out of your mind!" Chueh-hui virtually spat the words in her face. "You're not chasing devils, you're hurrying *Yeh-yeh* to his grave. You're afraid his illness won't kill him soon enough, so you're trying to exasperate him to death, scare him to death!"

"You—" That was all Ke-ming could say. He was livid with fury.

"Third Brother!" Chueh-hsin cried warningly.

"As for you, you ought to be ashamed of yourself!" Chueh-hui fixed his gaze on his Big Brother. "An educated man like you. How can you be so stupid? A man is sick, and you call in a witch doctor! It's all right if you people enjoy this sort of idiocy, but you shouldn't make *Yeh-yeh*'s life the butt of your games. You say you respect him. Why don't you let him rest? I saw the way the witch doctor terrified him last night. But you're still not satisfied; tonight you're at it again. I say you're not driving out devils—you're trying to kill him! I'm warning you—the first person to set foot in my room gets a punch in the jaw! I'm not afraid of any of you!"

Ordinarily, such intemperate words might have created a situation ending badly for Chueh-hui. But tonight, it was the very intensity of his attack that brought him victory. He stood grimly blocking the door, his eyes gleaming proud and righteous. They were his elders and he was heaping them with scorn. But, he felt, they had brought it on themselves by their contemptible behaviour!

Ke-ming, ashamed, was the first to drop his head. He knew Chueh-hui was right. He knew that the devil-eradication performance could only do harm. But for the sake of giving friends and relatives the impression he was a "dutiful" son, Ke-ming was reluctantly taking part. Unable to face Chueh-hui, he walked away without a sound.

Chueh-hsin felt angry and humiliated. Tears ran down his cheeks. When he saw Ke-ming leave, he turned and followed.

Mistress Chen was a woman with no courage of her own. She relied entirely on the other people's power. Ke-ming's departure left her without support, and she was afraid to open her mouth. But she really believed in the efficacy of driving out devils, and was genuinely concerned about the old man's illness. She couldn't understand Chueh-hui's attitude. She hated him. He had insulted her openly, before many people. But in the absence of the Venerable Master, and now that even Ke-ming had gone, she didn't dare to oppose Chueh-hui. Humiliated, she left the scene, cursing in her heart the grandson who didn't respect his grandfather.

The remainder of the crowd broke up too. No one offered the witch doctor any help. Although the sorcerer grumbled, and some of the ladies of the family privately expressed dissatisfaction, this time Chueh-hui won a total victory. He himself had never expected it.

XXXIII

Chueh-hui slept exceptionally well that night. He went to visit his sick grandfather the following morning, expecting a scolding, at least.

Half of the bed curtain had been pulled back, revealing the old man from the waist up. He lay with his bald head propped against high-piled pillows, his face bloodless and thinner than ever, his mouth slackly open. Above high cheekbones, his large eyes were sunken; from time to time he closed them wearily. To Chueh-hui, his grandfather looked weak and pitiful; he no longer resembled the awesome and frightening Venerable Master Kao.

Yeh-yeh was breathing with difficulty. He opened his eyes wide to gaze at Chueh-hui as he entered. An affectionate smile slowly appeared on the old man's face, a smile that was without strength, pathetic.

"Ah, you've come," he said. He had never greeted Chueh-hui so warmly before. Chueh-hui couldn't comprehend this change in him.

"You're a good boy," the old man said, making a great effort. He forced a smile. Chueh-hui leaned closer to him.

"You're very good," *Yeh-yeh* repeated weakly. "They say you have a peculiar disposition. . . . Study your books well."

"I understand things better now," he continued slowly. "Do you ever see your Second Brother? I hope he's well." Tears shone in the corners of his eyes. It was the first time Chueh-hui had ever seen him look kind.

Chueh-hui said, "Yes."

"I was wrong. I want to see him again. Bring him home, quickly. I won't make any more trouble for him." The old man wiped his eyes with his hand.

Mistress Chen, who had just finished combing her hair, rouging her face and pencilling her brows, observed this scene as she emerged from the next room. She addressed Chueh-hui reproachfully. "Third Young Master, you're old enough to know better. You shouldn't upset your *Yeh-yeh* when he's so ill."

"Don't blame him," said the old man quickly. "He's a good boy." Mistress Chen turned away, angry and resentful, while the old man urged Chueh-hui, "Bring your Second Brother back. I haven't seen him in a long time. Tell him I'll say no more about the match with the Feng family. I'm afraid I won't live much longer. I want to see him again. I want to see all of you."

On leaving his grandfather, Chueh-hui went directly to Chueh-hsin's room. Big Brother and Sister-in-law were talking about something, and they both looked worried. Chueh-hsin, recalling the previous night's fiasco, dropped his eyes in embarrassment when he saw Chueh-hui approaching.

"*Yeh-yeh* wants me to bring Second Brother back. He admits he was wrong," crowed Chueh-hui, the moment he entered the door.

Surprised and pleased, Chueh-hsin raised his head. "Really?" He could hardly believe his ears.

"Of course. *Yeh-yeh* is sorry now," Chueh-hui said, his face glowing with satisfaction. "I told you we would win. You see—we've won after all!"

"Tell me—what exactly did he say?" Smiling, Chueh-hsin

walked over and took Jui-chueh's hand. She tried, unsuccessfully, to pull it away, being unaccustomed to public displays of affection. Husband and wife were both very glad to hear this news. It seemed virtually a miracle to them that such a big problem could be solved so easily. They thought this miracle would bring them good fortune.

Chueh-hui told them the details of his conversation with his grandfather, growing more elated with every word. Before he could finish, a maid came in and announced:

"The Venerable Master wants to see the First Young Master." Chueh-hsin left immediately.

Chueh-hui remained to chat with Jui-chueh. The nursemaid brought Hai-chen back from outside, and Chueh-hui played with the little boy for a while.

Then he ran to where Chueh-min was living. He literally ran. At home he hadn't felt any need for haste; he had spent quite some time gaily talking with Sister-in-law. But as soon as he left the compound it seemed to him he had delayed too long. He should have brought the good news to Second Brother as quickly as possible.

Chueh-min, of course, was overjoyed when Chueh-hui told him their grandfather's decision. After a few minutes of conversation with Tsun-jen, in whose home Chueh-min had been hiding, the two brothers quickly left.

First, they went to see Chin. She was extremely happy with their news, just as they had expected. The prospect of a bright future seemed more likely than ever to these three young people; they could almost reach their hands out and touch it. It was coming to them not by any accident of fate, but through their own strenuous efforts. And so it appeared to them particularly precious.

Relaxed and cheerful, they talked for a long time. After lunching together with Chin and her mother, the brothers strolled home. On the way, Chueh-min prepared little speeches —what he would say to his grandfather, to his stepmother Madam Chou, to his Big Brother. He was very happy. He was returning home like a conquering hero.

Chueh-min walked through the main gate, entered the inner courtyard, then went into the main hall, then walked still deeper into the compound. He was rather surprised that everything still looked the same.

But suddenly, he became aware of a change. People were hurrying in and out of his grandfather's apartment. They all appeared very alarmed, and spoke in hushed voices.

"I wonder what's wrong," said Chueh-hui. He took his brother by the arm and hastened him forward. His heart sank with a dark premonition.

"Maybe *Yeh-yeh.* . . ." Chueh-min dared say no more; he dared think no more. He was afraid the bright future which had seemed so close at hand had flown away.

The two brothers entered their grandfather's room. It was filled with people. They couldn't see their grandfather. The people blocked their view. They could hear only a low strange sound. No one paid any attention to them. Finally, they managed to push their way forward. Their grandfather was seated in a large armchair before the bed, his head down, gasping for breath. That was the strange sound they had heard.

Overcome with emotion, Chueh-min wanted to throw himself on his grandfather, but his uncle Ke-ming restrained him. Ke-ming looked at Chueh-min in a startled manner, and shook his head.

"*Yeh-yeh* told me to bring him here," Chueh-hui explained. "He said he wants to see him."

Sadly Ke-ming shook his head. "It's too late," he said in a low voice.

"Too late!" The words struck Chueh-hui like a blow. He didn't seem to understand them. But when he heard his grandfather's painful gasping, he knew indeed that it was too late. The old man was going to depart, with the gap between grandfather and grandson unbridged for ever.

Chueh-hui couldn't stand it. He rushed up to his grandfather, took the old man's hand and cried, "*Yeh-yeh, Yeh-yeh!* I've brought Second Brother back to you!"

The old man said nothing. He only continued to fight for breath. People tried to pull Chueh-hui away, but the boy threw himself at the old man's knees and shook him, crying tragically, "*Yeh-yeh!*" Chueh-min stood watching.

Suddenly the old man sighed and opened his eyes wide. He

looked at Chueh-hui without recognition. "Why are you making such a row?" he asked in a low voice. He waved his hand weakly, indicating that Chueh-hui should go.

Then the haziness slowly vanished from the old man's thin face. His lips moved, but no sound came out. He looked at Chueh-min, and his lips moved again. *"Yeh-yeh!"* Chueh-min called. The old man didn't seem to hear him. Turning his eyes to Chueh-hui, the patriarch grimaced slightly in what evidently was an attempt at a smile. Tears rolled from his eyes. He patted Chueh-hui on the head and whispered, "You've come. . . . You're a good boy. . . . Your Second Brother? . . ."

Chueh-hui pulled Chueh-min forward and said, "Here he is."

"Yeh-yeh," said Chueh-min respectfully.

"You've come back. Good! We won't talk about the match with the Feng family any more. . . . You boys must study diligently. . . ." The old man took a deep breath and went on slowly, "Remember—bring honour to the family name. . . . I'm very tired. . . . Don't go. . . . I'm leaving. . . ." His voice grew weaker and weaker, and he slowly dropped his head. At last he closed his mouth completely.

Ke-ming walked up quickly and called to him, but his father did not respond. He grasped the old man's hand. With tears in his eyes he cried, "His hand is cold!"

Everyone crowded closer, all exclaiming loudly. Then the noise gradually stilled; someone dropped to his knees. Others followed suit, and the room was filled with weeping.

News of a death spreads more quickly than any other. In a matter of minutes, the whole compound knew that the old man had passed away. Servants hurried to the homes of the Kao's relatives to deliver the sad tidings. Guests soon began to arrive. Women guests helped add volume to the weeping, bewailing their own unhappy fate at the same time.

Then the work commenced. A division of labour was made between the men and the women. Three or four female relatives were assigned to sit by the body and weep. The old man was laid out on the bed, from which the canopy was removed.

The work advanced rapidly; many people were busy. The ancestral tablets, the altar and other equipment were moved

292

to a chamber in the rear of the main hall. Then the coffin was carried in. It had been bought several years before and stored away. The price was reported to be quite reasonable —only a little over one thousand ounces of silver.

The Taoist priest who was to "open the road" to the next world, arrived. By divination, he decided on the propitious hour and minute for encoffining the body. The old man was bathed and dressed in his burial clothes, then laid comfortably in the coffin. All the objects the Venerable Master Kao had loved best in life were packed in beside him, filling the casket to the brim.

By now it was almost nightfall. A troupe of Buddhist monks were next called in. Each of these shaven-pated men —one hundred and eight of them—carried a stick of lighted incense. They wandered through the compound, going in and out of rooms, up and down stairs. Behind them trailed Chueh-hsin and his three uncles, also holding incense sticks. Chueh-hsin walked in the lead, because he was the "first son of the first son."

At ten o'clock in the morning of the following day, the sealing of the coffin took place. This hour, too, had been divined by the Taoist priest. The weeping reached its maximum intensity then; some of it was genuine.

The death of the Venerable Master brought everything in the family to a stop. The family hall became a funeral parlour, hung with mourning bunting; the main hall became a temple of prayer. Women wept in the funeral parlour; monks intoned prayers in the temple. The funeral parlour was hung with eulogy scrolls and odes to the departed; in the temple were Buddhist idols and ten scenes from the Palace of the Afterworld.[36]

Everyone was busy with the final rites for the deceased. Or perhaps it would be more accurate to say everyone was busy using the occasion to maintain face and display his own affluence.

[36] The Grandfather considered himself to be a Confucian. Nevertheless the family, as was customary in China, let the Taoist and Buddhist priests participate in the performance of the funeral rites.

Three days later, the Mourning Period officially commenced. Innumerable gifts came pouring in, dozens of ceremonies were conducted, droves of condolence callers arrived. This was what everyone had been looking forward to, and now the activities were at their height.

Even Chueh-min and Chueh-hui could not help becoming involved. They didn't want to be, but they felt it didn't matter much. They were set to work "returning courtesies." In other words, whenever a visitor kowtowed to the spirit of the departed, they were required to do the same, while a Master of Ceremonies intoned, "Thanks from the Filial Sons and Grandsons." Then all would rise to their feet and grin at each other sheepishly at the silliness of it all.

The boys couldn't help smiling to themselves, too, when they saw their elder brother and their uncles decked out in mourning clothes—a hempen crown with a long "filial" streamer trailing behind, a white mourning gown covered by a wide hempen vest, straw sandals—holding a mourning staff and walking with solemn tread. To the younger brothers it was like an act from a farce.

After lunch the following day they were able to escape. Chueh-hui left first, and went directly to the reading-room the students had set up. He worked there all day and did not come home until evening. Chueh-min had not yet returned.

Chueh-hui found the main hall empty. The monks had already departed. The pair of tall candles in front of the coffin of the deceased had burned far down; their wicks were sputtering in pools of tallow. Even the sticks of incense had burned out.

Why is it so quiet? he wondered. Where has everyone gone? . . . He adjusted the candle wicks with a pair of tongs and lit another bundle of incense stick.

"Nothing doing! Just sharing the land and the property without touching the antiques and pictures isn't a thorough division!" The voice of Chueh-hui's uncle Ke-ting suddenly declaimed loudly from the old man's room.

"They were the things he loved best. He spent his whole life collecting them. As his sons we shouldn't simply parcel them out among ourselves!" This was Ke-ming speaking. He was panting angrily.

"Antiques and pictures mean nothing to me. But if we don't divide them, someone will nab them all." Ke-an laughed coldly. "I say anything that belonged to the old man, we ought to share equally."

"All right. If that's what you all want, we'll make a division tomorrow!" Ke-ming gave a fretful cough. "But, honestly, I never intended to keep them for myself."

There was a stir in the room, followed by the sound of the voices of several women. Then Ke-ting came stalking out. "Testamentary order, testamentary bequest—they're all trumped up!" he was muttering. "That kind of division isn't fair!" He walked outside.

A little later Chueh-hsin, looking very downcast, also emerged.

"Dividing up the family property, eh?" Chueh-hui greeted him mockingly. "Not wasting much time, are you?"

"Stepmother and I are being moved around like puppets. *Yeh-yeh* left me three thousand shares of West Szechuan Mercantile Corporation stock, but our uncles don't want to recognize the bequest," said Chueh-hsin bitterly.

"What about Mrs. Chang?" asked Chueh-min, who had just then returned home. He of course was concerned about the woman who was both their aunt and Chin's mother.

"She only got five hundred dollars' worth of stock, and a few other things—and these only because it was in the will. But Mistress Chen got a residence and compound. Our household is the only one that cares anything about Mrs. Chang. None of the others would say a word for her," Chueh-hsin sighed.

"Why didn't you speak up?" asked Chueh-min reproachfully.

"Here comes Uncle Ke-ming," warned Chueh-hui in a low voice.

Coughing irritably, Ke-ming strode slowly from the apartment of the Venerable Master Kao.

XXXIV

It was almost time for Jui-chueh to give birth, and Mistress Chen and other women of the family were deeply disturbed. At first they only discussed the matter privately. Then, one day, with stern visage, Mistress Chen talked to Ke-ming and his brothers about "the curse of the blood-glow."

There was a superstition that if, while the body of one of the elder generation was still in the house, a birth should take place at home, the glow of the blood emitted by the mother would attack the corpse and cause it to spurt large quantities of blood. The only means by which this could be prevented was for the pregnant woman to leave the compound and move outside the city.

Nor was that enough. The big city gates weren't strong enough to keep the blood-glow from returning—she had to move across a bridge.

Even that was not necessarily fool-proof. The coffin had to be covered with a layer of bricks and earth. Only thus could it be protected from "the curse of the blood-glow."

Madam Shen of the Fifth Household was the first to approve of these preventive measures; Madam Wang of the Fourth Household quickly seconded her. Ke-an and Ke-ting agreed next, followed finally by Ke-ming and Madam Chou. Of the elder generation only Madam Chang of the Third Household expressed no opinion. In any event, it was decided to act according to Mistress Chen's recommendation, and the elders wanted Chueh-hsin to move his wife out immediately. They said the interests of the Venerable Master Kao should transcend all.

Although the decision struck Chueh-hsin like a bolt from the blue, he accepted it meekly. He had never disagreed with anyone in his life, no matter how unfairly they may have treated him. He preferred to swallow his tears, suppress his anger and bitterness; he would bear anything—rather than oppose a person directly. Nor did it ever occur to him to wonder whether this forbearance might not be harmful to others.

Jui-chueh made no complaint when he informed her. She expressed her unwillingness in tears. But it was no use. She hadn't the strength to protect herself. Chueh-hsin hadn't the strength to protect her either. She could only submit.

"You know I don't believe in this, but what can I do?" Chueh-hsin helplessly spread his hands. "They all say it's better to be on the safe side."

"I'm not blaming you. I blame only my unhappy destiny," Jui-chueh sobbed. "My mother isn't even in town to look after me. But I can't let you get the reputation of being unfilial. Even if you were willing, I wouldn't agree."

"Jui, forgive me, I'm too weak. I can't even protect my own wife. These years we've been together . . . you know what I've been suffering."

"You shouldn't . . . talk like that," Jui-chueh said, wiping her eyes with her handkerchief. "I know . . . what you've been through. You've . . . suffered enough. You're so good to me. I'm very grateful. . . ."

"Grateful? You're going to give birth any day now, and I'm sending you to a lonely place outside the city where there are no conveniences and you'll be all alone. I'm letting you down. What other man would let his wife be treated so badly? And you still say you're grateful!" Chueh-hsin wept miserably.

Jui-chueh stilled her crying, rose quietly and walked out. Soon she returned, holding little Hai-chen by the hand and followed by the nursemaid.

Leading the child to the softly weeping Chueh-hsin, she instructed him to call his *"Tieh-tieh,"* to take his father's hand and tell him not to cry.

Chueh-hsin embraced the little boy and gazed at him with loving eyes. He kissed the child's cheek several times, then put him down and returned him to Jui-chueh. "There's no hope for me," he said hoarsely. "But rear Hai-chen well. I

297

don't want him to be like me when he grows up!" Chueh-hsin left the room, wiping his eyes with his hand.

"Where are you going?" Jui-chueh called after him in concern.

"Outside the city to look for a house." He turned around to face her, and his eyes again were blinded by tears. After wrenching these words out, he hastily walked away.

That day Chueh-hsin returned very late. Finding a house was not easy, but in the end he had succeeded. It was a little place in a small compound, ill-lighted, with damp walls and an earthen floor. The rent was cheap enough, but that wasn't the reason Chueh-hsin took it. He had been concerned with only two things—"outside the city" and "across a bridge." Such matters as comfort and convenience were secondary.

Before Jui-chueh moved, Mistress Chen and few other ladies of the family went to inspect the house. They could find no objections.

Chueh-hsin insisted on doing all the packing for Jui-chueh. He made her sit in a chair and supervise. Before putting anything in the suitcase, he would hold it up and say, "What about this?" and she would smile and nod her head, whether she really wanted it or not. When the packing was done Chueh-hsin declared proudly, "You see, I know exactly what you like."

Jui-chueh smiled. "You do indeed. The next time I go on a trip I'll be sure to ask you to pack for me again." She hadn't intended to make the last remark, but it slipped out.

"Next time? Of course I'll go with you next time. Where will you be going?"

"I was thinking of visiting my mother. But we'll go together, naturally. I won't leave you again."

Chueh-hsin changed colour, and he hastily dropped his head. Then he raised it again and said with a forced laugh, "Yes, we'll go together."

They were fooling each other and they knew it. Though they smiled, they wanted to cry. But they masked their true feelings behind a cheerful countenance. Neither was willing to give way to tears in the presence of the other.

The girls, Shu-hua and Shu-ying, came in, then Chueh-min

298

and Chueh-hui. They could see only the pleasant expressions on the faces of Chueh-hsin and Jui-chueh, and could not guess the turmoil that was in their hearts.

Chueh-hui couldn't keep silent. "Big Brother, are you really going to let Sister-in-law go?" he demanded. Although he had heard something about this, at first, he had thought people were joking. But when he had come home, a few minutes before, he had met Yuan Cheng, Chueh-hsin's middle-aged servant, at the gate to the inner courtyard. The man had greeted him affectionately, and Chueh-hui stopped to chat with him.

"Third Young Master, do you think it's a good idea for Mistress Jui-chueh to move outside the city?" Yuan Cheng had asked with a frown, his thin face darker than usual.

Chueh-hui was startled. "Of course not. But I don't believe she'll really go."

"Third Young Master, you don't know. First Young Master has ordered me and Sister Chang to look after her. They've already called in a mason to make a false tomb for the old man's coffin. I don't think she ought to go, Third Young Master. Even if she must, it ought to be to some place decent. Only rich people have all these rules and customs. Why doesn't First Young Master speak up? We servants don't understand much, but we think her life is more important than all these rules. Why don't you talk to First Young Master, and Madam Chou?"

There were tears in Yuan Cheng's eyes. "We ought to think of the Young Mistress. Everyone in the compound wishes her well! If anything should go wrong. . . ." Yuan Cheng couldn't continue.

"All right. I'll speak to First Young Master immediately. Don't worry. Nothing's going to happen to the Young Mistress," Chueh-hui had said, agitated, but determined.

"Thank you, Third Young Master. But please don't let anyone know I told you," Yuan Cheng said in a low voice. He turned and went into the gate house.

Chueh-hui had immediately sought out Chueh-hsin. Although the appearance of the room already proved the truth of Yuan Cheng's words, Chueh-hui demanded to know whether Big Brother was sending Jui-chueh away.

Chueh-hsin looked at him vaguely, then silently nodded his head.

"Are you crazy? Surely you don't believe in all this superstitious rot!"

"What difference does it make what I believe?" cried Chueh-hsin, wringing his hands. "That's what they all want. . . ."

"I say you should fight back," said Chueh-hui angrily, his eyes gleaming with hatred. He didn't look at Chueh-hsin. "This is the last act of their farce." His gaze was fixed outside the window.

"Third Brother is right," said Chueh-min. "Don't send Sister-in-law away. Go and explain your reasons in detail. They'll understand. They're reasonable people."

"Reasonable?" echoed Chueh-hsin fretfully. "Even Third Uncle who studied law in a Japanese university was forced to agree. What chance have I? I couldn't bear it if I became known as unfilial. I have to do what they want. It's just hard on your Sister-in-law. . . ."

"What's hard about it? It will be much quieter outside the city. . . . I'll have people to look after me and keep me company," said Jui-chueh with a forced smile. "I'm sure it'll be very comfortable."

"You've given in again, Big Brother! Why do you always give in? Don't you realize how much harm you do?" Chueh-hui demanded hotly. "Your weakness nearly wrecked the happiness of Chueh-min and Chin. Luckily, Second Brother had the courage to resist. That's why he won."

Chueh-min couldn't repress a smile of satisfaction. He agreed with Chueh-hui. His happiness had been won through victory in battle.

"Certainly, you've triumphed." Chueh-hsin suppressed his anger. He seemed to be ridiculing himself. "You resist everything, you have contempt for everything, and you've won. But your victory has deepened my defeat. They heap upon me all their resentment against you. They hate me, curse me behind my back. You can resist, go away. But can I run away from home like Second Brother? There are many things you don't know. How much abuse I had to put up with on account of

300

Second Brother. The trouble I had over Third Brother working on that magazine and mixing with those new friends. I took it all, without a word. I kept my bitterness inside me. No one knew. It's all very well for you to talk about resistance, struggle. But who can I say those fine-sounding words to?"

Gradually his anger abated. An unbearable oppression seemed to be crushing him. He hurried to his bed and lay down, hiding his face with his hands.

This crumpled Jui-chueh's last line of defence. Dropping her false smile, she buried her head on the table and wept. Shu-hua and Shu-ying, their own voices tearful, tried to comfort her. Chueh-min regretted he had spoken so hastily. He had been too harsh with Big Brother. He tried to think of something to say to make amends.

Chueh-hui was different. There was too much hatred in his heart for him to find room for sympathy for his Big Brother. He could see a lake before him, and a coffin . . . Ming-feng and Mei. . . . And now . . . this . . . and what it would bring. These thoughts made him burn with rage.

Like his two older brothers, Chueh-hui had enjoyed the loving care of a devoted mother. After she died, he tried to carry out her teachings—love and help others, respect your elders, be good to your inferiors. But what a spectacle his elder generation was making of itself today! How the dark forces in the family that destroyed love were growing! The life of the girl he had adored had been uselessly snuffed out. Another girl had been driven to her grave. And he had not been able to save them. Sympathy, he was bereft of sympathy—even for his brother. In his heart there were only curses.

"One girl has already died because of you," he said to Chueh-hsin coldly. "I should think that would be enough." He strode from the room.

Outside, he met the nursemaid bringing in little Hai-chen. The child hailed him, laughing, and he returned the salutation. He was miserable.

Back in his own room, Chueh-hui was overcome with a loneliness, the like of which he had never felt before. His eyes grew damp. The world was such a tragic place. So many tears. So much suffering. People lived only to destroy themselves, or to destroy others. Destruction was inevitable, no matter how they struggled. Chueh-hui could see plainly the fate that lay ahead for his Big Brother, but he was helpless to save him. And this fate was not only Big Brother's, but the destiny of many, many others.

"Why is there so much misery in the world?" he asked himself. His mind was filled with pictures of innumerable unhappy events.

No matter what happens, I must go my own road, even if it means trampling over their dead bodies. Chueh-hui seemed to be hemmed in by bitterness, with no way out, and he encouraged himself with these words.

Then he left the compound. He went to the magazine office, to join his new friends.

XXXV

Temporarily suppressing his unhappiness, Chueh-hsin accompanied Jui-chueh to her new abode. Madam Chou, Shu-hua and Shu-ying went with them. There were also the man servant, Yuan Cheng and Sister Chang, the stout maid, who would stay with Jui-chueh. Chueh-min and Chin came out a bit later in the day.

Jui-chueh didn't like the place. It was the first time she and Chueh-hsin would be separated since their marriage. She would have to live without him in this damp gloomy house for over a month. She tried to think of something to console herself, but she could not. Everyone was busy arranging furniture, and she wept behind their backs. But when anyone spoke to her she managed to look cheerful. This made the people concerned about her feel somewhat reassured.

It was soon time for the others to return to the city.

"Must you all go? Can't Chin and Shu-hua stay a little longer?" Jui-chueh pleaded.

"It's getting late. They'll be closing the city gates. I'll come and see you again tomorrow," said Chin with a smile.

"City gates." Jui-chueh repeated the phrase as if she had not understood it. Actually she knew very well that tonight she would be separated from Chueh-hsin not only by distance but by a series of ponderous gates. Between dusk tonight and dawn tomorrow even if she died out here, he wouldn't know, he wouldn't be able to reach her. She was like a criminal, exiled in a distant land. This time she couldn't control her tears; they welled from her eyes.

"It's so lonely here. I'm afraid. . . ."

"Don't worry, Sister-in-law," said Shu-hua. "I'll move out tomorrow."

"I will too. I'll speak to Ma about it," added Shu-ying emotionally.

"Be patient, Jui. You'll get used to it in a day or so," said Chueh-hsin. "The two servants staying with you are very reliable. There's nothing to be afraid of. Tomorrow the girls will move out to keep you company. I'll try and find time too. Be patient. The month will pass quickly." Though he tried hard to appear confident, Chueh-hsin felt more like embracing Jui-chueh and weeping with her.

Madam Chou gave some final instructions, the others added a few words, then they all departed. Jui-chueh saw them to the compound gate and watched them get into their sedan-chairs.

Chueh-hsin had already entered his conveyance. Suddenly he got out again to ask whether she wanted him to bring her anything from home. Jui-chueh said she had everything she needed.

"Bring Hai-chen out tomorrow. I miss him terribly," she said. "Take good care of him," she directed, and she added, "Whatever you do, don't let my mother hear about this. She'll worry."

"I wrote to her two days ago. I didn't tell you. I knew you wouldn't let me write her," replied Chueh-hsin.

"Why did you do it? If my mother knew I was—" Jui-chueh stopped herself abruptly. She was afraid of hurting him.

"I had to let her know. If she can come to Chengtu, she'll be able to help look after you." Chueh-hsin swallowed his pain. He didn't dare think of Jui-chueh's unfinished sentence.

The two looked at each other as if they had nothing to say. But their hearts were filled with unspoken words.

"I'm going now. You get some rest." Again Chueh-hsin walked to his sedan-chair. He turned his head to gaze at her several times.

"Come early tomorrow," Jui-chueh called from the gate. She waved her hand until his sedan-chair disappeared around a bend in the road. Then, supporting her heavy abdomen, she went into the house.

She wanted to take some things out of her luggage, but her limbs were powerless. Her nerves were tense too. Wearily making an effort, she walked over and sat down on the edge of the bed. Suddenly, she thought she felt the child move in her womb; she seemed to hear it cry. In hysterical anger, she beat her abdomen with her hand weakly. "You've ruined me!" she exclaimed. She wept softly until Sister Chang, the maid, hearing her, came hurrying in to soothe her.

The following morning, Chueh-hsin indeed came early, and he brought Hai-chen with him. Shu-hua moved out, as promised. Shu-ying came too, but she had not been able to obtain her mother's consent to live outside the city. Later, Chin also arrived. For a while, the little compound was very gay, with chatter and happy laughter.

The hours passed quickly. Again it was time to part. Hai-chen burst into tears; he wanted to remain with his mother. Of course, this was not possible. After much persuasion, Jui-chueh managed to cajole a smile from him again. He agreed to go home with his father.

Once more Jui-chueh saw Chueh-hsin to the gate. "Come again early tomorrow," she said. Tears glistened in her eyes.

"I'm afraid I can't come tomorrow. Masons are coming to build a simulated tomb for *Yeh-yeh*. The family wants me to supervise," Chueh-hsin said morosely. Noticing her tears, he said quickly, "But I'll definitely find time to come out. You mustn't get upset so easily, Jui. Take care of your health. If you should get sick. . . ." Chueh-hsin swallowed the rest. He was afraid of weeping himself.

"I don't know what's wrong with me," said Jui-chueh slowly with a mournful smile, her eyes fixed upon his face. She patted Hai-chen's cheek. "Each time you leave, I'm afraid I'm never going to see you again. I'm scared. I don't know why." She rubbed her eyes.

"You shouldn't be. We live so near each other, and I come to see you every day. And now Shu-hua is staying with you." Chueh-hsin forced a smile. He didn't dare let himself think.

"Isn't that the temple?" Jui-chueh suddenly pointed at a tile-roofed building far off to the right. "I hear that's where Cousin Mei's coffin is. I must go and see her one of these days."

Chueh-hsin turned pale. He hastily looked away. A terrifying thought possessed him. He took her warm soft hand and pressed it, as if afraid that someone would snatch her from him. "You mustn't go, Jui!" he exhorted. Jui-chueh was impressed with the gravity of his tone, though she couldn't understand why he should be so set against her going.

But he said no more. Dropping her hand abruptly, after Hai-chen again said goodbye to "Mama," Chueh-hsin strode to his sedan-chair. As the two carriers raised the conveyance to their shoulders, Hai-chen leaned out of the window and called, "Mama! Mama!"

On returning home, Chueh-hsin went to the family hall, where the old man's body was lying in its coffin. He met Mistress Chen, who was coming out.

"How is Jui-chueh? Well, I hope," she greeted him, smiling.

"Not bad, thank you." Chueh-hsin forced an answering smile.

"Will she be giving birth soon?"

"It will still be a couple of days, I'm afraid."

"Don't forget, Young Master. You mustn't enter the delivery room!" Mistress Chen's voice suddenly became hard. She walked away.

Chueh-hsin had been given this warning several times before. But today, hearing a person like Mistress Chen issue it in such a tone made him speechless with rage. He stared after her retreating figure. When little Hai-chen, whom he was holding by the hand, raised his head and called *Tieh-tieh,* Chueh-hsin didn't hear him.

XXXVI

Four days later, Chueh-hsin paid his usual visit to Jui-chueh. Because he had been delayed by some business at home, he didn't arrive until past three in the afternoon.

Calling Jui-chueh by name as he entered the courtyard, he hurried to her room. But before he could set foot across the threshold, he was stopped by the stout maid, Sister Chang.

"You can't go in, First Young Master," she said severely.

He understood, and meekly withdrew to the little garden outside Jui-chueh's window. The door closed. Inside, he heard footsteps and the voice of a woman he didn't know.

Chueh-hsin gazed distractedly at the grass and flowers in the small garden. He couldn't tell whether he was happy or sad, angry or satisfied. It seemed to him he felt all these emotions at the same time. It seemed to him that he had been in a similar state of mind several years before, though only to a very slight extent. Actually it had been quite different.

How he had suffered through her struggles then, how happy and grateful he had been when she presented him with the precious gift of their first child. He had been by her side when she won through to victory; his tension had relaxed, his worry had turned to joy. When the midwife handed him the infant, he had kissed its adorable little red face. He had vowed in his heart that he would love the child and make every sacrifice for him; his whole life was deposited in the body of that infant. He had gone to the bedside of his wife and looked at her pale weary face with a love and gratitude beyond words. She had gazed back at him, triumphant, loving; then she had looked at the baby.

"I feel fine now," she had said to Chueh-hsin, happily. "Isn't he a darling? You must decide on a name for him, quickly!" Her face shone with the radiance of a mother's bliss.

Today, she was again lying in bed. She had begun to moan.

There were hurrying footsteps in the room and low serious voices. All that was the same. But now she was in this rustic place. They were separated by a door. He couldn't see her, encourage her, comfort her, share her pain. Today, again he waited. But there was no joy or satisfaction—only fear, shame and regret. In his mind there was just one thought—I have injured her.

"Young Mistress, how are you feeling?" he heard Sister Chang ask.

There was a long silence. Then an agonized cry pierced his ears. He trembled, gritted his teeth, clenched his fists. Can that be her? he wondered. She had never uttered a sound like that before. But who else could it be? It must be her: It must be my Jui.

Again those terrible screams. Cries hardly human. Footsteps, voices. The rattle of crockery and cries blended together. Chueh-hsin covered his ears with his hands. It can't be her. It can't be my Jui. She could never scream like that. Nearly frantic with worry, he tried to look through the window, but the blinds were closed. He could only hear things; he couldn't see. Disappointed, he turned away.

"Be patient, Young Mistress. You'll be all right in a little while," said the unknown woman.

"It won't be long now," urged Shu-hua. "Just be patient."

Gradually, the cries subsided into low moans.

The door suddenly opened and Sister Chang hurried out. She went into another room, then hastened back to Jui's room. Chueh-hsin stared in through the half-opened door. He hesitated, wondering whether to go in. By the time he made up his mind, the door was closed in his face. He pushed it a few times, but inside there was no response. As he dejectedly turned to leave, from the room came a terrible cry. He pushed the door hard and pounded it with his fists.

"Who's there?" shouted Sister Chang.

"Let me in!" There was fear in voice, and pain and anger.

No one answered. The door remained shut. His wife continued to scream.

"Let me in, I say!" He furiously pounded the door.

"You can't come in, First Young Master. Madam Chou,

Elder Master Ke-ming, Mistress Chen—they all left strict instructions. . . ." Sister Chang shouted through the door.

Chueh-hsin's courage ebbed away. He remembered what they had told him. Silently, he stood before the door. He had nothing more to say.

"Is that you, Chueh-hsin?" It was Jui-chueh's agonized voice. "Why don't you come in? Sister Chang, let the First Young Master in! Oh, the pain . . . the pain. . . ."

A chill ran up Chueh-hsin's spine. "I'm coming, Jui, I'm coming! Open this door immediately! She needs me! Let me in!" he yelled, beating a wild tattoo on the door with his fists.

"Hsin, it hurts! . . . Where are you? Why don't you let him in? Oh!"

"I'll protect you, Jui! I'll never leave you! Let me in! Can't you see how she's suffering? Have you no pity!" He heard a violent thrashing about.

Then the cries in the room stopped. A dead silence followed. That awful stillness was suddenly pierced by the bright clear wail of a new-born babe.

A stone seemed to drop from Chueh-hsin's heart. "Thank Heaven, thank Earth!" he breathed. Her pain was probably over now. Fear and suffering left him. Again he felt an indescribable joy; his eyes filled with tears. "I'll love and cherish her more than ever," he said to himself. "And I'll love our second child." He smiled with tears running down his cheeks.

"Sister-in-law!" Shu-hua's terrified exclamation smashed him like a blow. "Her hands are cold!"

"Young Mistress!" cried Sister Chang.

Their cries were a mournful dirge. Besides the midwife, they were the only other persons in the room.

Chueh-hsin knew that disaster had struck. He didn't dare to think. He went on beating against the door and yelling. No one paid any attention. The door stood implacable. It wouldn't let him rescue her, or even see her for the last time. It cut off all hope. In the room, women wept.

"Jui, I'm calling you. Can you hear me?" An insane shout, embodying all his love, was wrenched from the depths of his heart. A cry to bring her back from another world, to restore life not only to her but himself. For he knew what sort of an existence he would lead without her.

But death had come.

Footsteps approached the door. He thought it was going to be opened. But no, the midwife stood with the baby in her arms and spoke to him through a crack. "Congratulations, First Young Master. It's a boy."

He heard her start to walk away, and then the dreadful words, "Unfortunately, the baby has no mother."

The announcement went through Chueh-hsin's heart like a knife. He had none of the father's love for his infant. The child was his enemy, an enemy who had stolen Jui-chueh's life.

Gripped by hatred and grief, he pounded savagely on the door. He had wanted to kneel at his wife's bedside and beg forgiveness for his wrongs. But it was too late. The stubborn door barred their final love, their last farewell. It would not even let him weep before her.

Suddenly it dawned upon him. The door had no power. What had taken his wife away was something else. It was the entire social system, with its moral code, its superstitions. He had borne them for years while they stole his youth, his happiness, his future, the two women he had loved most in the world. They were too heavy a burden; he wanted to shake them off; he struggled. Then, all at once, he knew it was impossible. He was powerless, a weakling. Slumping to his knees before the door, he burst into bitter tears. He wept for her; he wept for himself. His weeping mingled with the sobs inside the room. But how different the two sounds were!

Two sedan-chairs halted outside the compound gate and Chueh-hsin's stepmother Madam Chou and another woman entered. Madam Chou heard the weeping as she came in the gate. Her expression changed. She said to the other woman agitatedly, "We're too late!" They hurried into the house.

"What are you doing?" Madam Chou, surprised, asked Chueh-hsin when she saw him still kneeling outside the door.

Chueh-hsin quickly rose. Spreading wide his hands, he sobbed, "Jui, Jui!" He recognized the other woman and greeted her shamefacedly, then again began to cry aloud. At the same time, wails came from the infant inside.

Not speaking, the woman dabbed her eyes with her handkerchief.

The door finally opened. Madam Chou said, "Please go in, Mrs. Li. Our family is not allowed in the confinement chamber."

Mrs. Li entered, and her penetrating voice was added to the other sounds of grief.

"Jui, why couldn't you wait? Ma came from so far to see you. If you have anything to tell me, speak! Come back, Jui. Couldn't you have waited one more day? You died a cruel death, my poor little girl! Deserted in this lonely place. They drove you out and left you all alone. If I had only come back earlier, you'd still be alive. My poor child. Why did I let you marry into that family? Your Ma destroyed you."

Madam Chou and Chueh-hsin heard it all clearly. Every word was like a needle, piercing deep into their hearts.

XXXVII

"Big Brother, I can't live in this family any longer! I'm leaving!"

Chueh-hsin had been sitting alone in his room at dusk, when Chueh-hui burst in on him. He had been gazing at the photograph he and Jui-chueh had taken when they got married. Although he couldn't see very plainly in the dim light, her every feature was etched upon his heart. Her full pretty face, her lovely big eyes, her shy smile, the faint dimples in her cheeks—they all seemed to come alive in the photograph. He had been staring at it tearfully when Chueh-hui's exclamation brought him back to reality. He turned to see his Third Brother looking at him with flashing eyes.

"You're leaving?" Chueh-hsin asked, startled. "Where are you going?"

"Shanghai, Peking—any place, as long as it's away from here!"

Chueh-hsin made no reply. His heart ached. He massaged his chest.

"I'm leaving. I don't care what they say, I'm leaving!" Chueh-hui jammed his hands into his pockets and heatedly paced the floor. He didn't know that each step fell like a heavy tread on Chueh-hsin's heart.

"Second Brother?" Chueh-hsin wrenched out the question.

"Sometimes he says he's going, sometimes he says he's not. I don't think he'd give up Sister Chin and go off by himself," Chueh-hui replied irritably. Then he added with determination, "Anyhow, I intend to leave."

"Yes, you can leave if you want to. You can go to Shanghai, to Peking, any place you like!" Chueh-hsin said almost sobbing.

Chueh-hui remained silent. He understood what his Big Brother meant.

"But what about me? Where can I go?" Chueh-hsin suddenly buried his head and wept.

Chueh-hui continued to pace the floor, from time to time shooting unhappy glances at his brother.

"You mustn't go," Chueh-hsin pleaded. He stopped crying and removed his hands from his face. "No matter what happens, you mustn't go."

Chueh-hui halted and stood looking at his Big Brother with a distressed expression.

"They won't allow you to leave. They'll never let you go!" Chueh-hsin said in a loud argumentative tone.

"I know they don't want me to go." Chueh-hui laughed contemptuously. "But I'm going to leave just to show them!"

"How can you? They have many arguments you won't be able to deny. *Yeh-yeh*'s body is still in the house; there hasn't been any memorial service yet; he still hasn't been buried. . . ." Chueh-hsin seemed to be speaking for "them" at this point.

"What's all that got to do with me? How can they stop me? They won't dare to kill me—like they killed Sister-in-law!"

311

Chueh-hui furiously uttered this cruel remark, regardless of how it might injure his brother.

"Don't talk about her. Please don't talk about her," Chueh-hsin begged. "Nothing will bring her back to life."

"Why get so upset? After the mourning period for *Yeh-yeh* is over, you can marry again," said Chueh-hui, smiling coldly. "At most you'll only have to wait three years!"

"I'll never take another wife, never. It's for that reason I've given the new baby to Jui's mother," Chueh-hsin explained weakly. His voice sounded like an old man's.

"Then why did you let her take Hai-chen too?"

"It's only for two or three months. What sort of atmosphere is this for a motherless child? He cries for his 'Mama' all day, but there's no one here to look after him. I'll bring him back after *Yeh-yeh* is buried. I'm going to concentrate on educating him. He's my sole hope; I can't let him go. I can't turn him over to another woman."

"That's what you say now. After a while you'll change your mind. You're all the same. I've seen it happen time and again. Our own father is a good example. You say you don't want to remarry. They'll tell you you're still young, that Hai-chen needs a mother. You'll agree. Even if you don't want to, they'll make you." Chueh-hui still wore his chill smile.

"Other things they can force me to do, but this is one thing they can't," retorted Chueh-hsin miserably. "Not even for Hai-chen's sake."

"I feel the same way about leaving. They can't force me to stay!" Chueh-hui couldn't repress a chuckle.

Chueh-hsin didn't speak for several moments. Then he said in annoyance, "I'm not going to help you. We'll see whether you can leave!"

"Whether you help or not is up to you. But I'm telling you this—the next time you look around, I'll be gone!"

"You have no money."

"That's no problem. If the family won't give me any, I can borrow some elsewhere. Anyhow, I'm leaving. I have lots of friends who can help me!"

"Won't you wait a bit?"

"How long?"

"Two years? By then you'll have graduated from the Foreign Languages School. . . ." Chueh-hsin lowered his tone. He thought Chueh-hui was wavering. "Then you can find work outside, or you can continue studying. You'll be in a much better position than you are now."

"Two years?" Chueh-hui cried excitedly. "I don't even want to wait fifteen minutes! I'd like nothing better than to clear out of this city immediately!"

"Two years isn't very long. You're too impetuous. You ought to give things more thought. Don't be so impatient. What's the harm in waiting two years? You've lived here eighteen years already. Surely you can stay only two years more?"

"My eyes weren't fully opened before; I had no courage. And there used to be a few people I loved in this family. Now I have nothing but enemies!"

For a long time Chueh-hsin did not speak. Then he asked in a sorrowful voice, "Do you consider me your enemy too?"

Chueh-hui's heart softened. He pitied his Big Brother. "Naturally, I love you," he said quietly. "We nearly came close to understanding each other once in the past, but today we're miles apart. You loved Sister-in-law and Cousin Mei much more than I did, of course. Yet you let people move them about just as they liked; you even helped. If you had been a bit more courageous, you could have saved Sister-in-law. Now it's too late. How can you talk to me of obedience? Do you really want me to be like you—destroying others and destroying myself? Big Brother, although I love you, that's something I simply cannot comprehend. Please don't give me that kind of advice any more. Otherwise you'll make me hate you."

Chueh-hui turned to leave, but Chueh-hsin stopped him with a tearful cry.

"Wait! We'll understand each other yet. I have my problems—but I don't want to talk about them now. I won't stand in your way. I'll help you. I'll speak to them. If they don't agree, you and I will find some other way. I definitely want to help you."

Just then the electric lights came on, and they saw the tears in each other's eyes. The young men exchanged a forgiving glance. They were still fond brothers, after all. But although they thought they understood each other, that was not the case. Chueh-hui was happy as he left his brother's room, because he would soon be able to get away from the family. Chueh-hsin, after Chueh-hui departed, wept bitterly. He knew that before long he would be losing another person he loved. Although he would be surrounded by many people, he would be isolated and lonely.

Chueh-hsin kept his word. Two days later he had another private talk with Chueh-hui in the younger boy's room.

"I couldn't convince them. I failed," he said in a low voice. They sat facing each other across a square table. "I spoke to our stepmother. While she doesn't approve of your going, she isn't altogether against it. She's always wished us well. She's very unhappy and regretful over your Sister-in-law's death. She and Jui's mother have been looking after all the funeral arrangements; I haven't had to do a thing. I was better to Mei than I was to your Sister-in-law. At least I saw Mei before she was placed in the coffin; at least I arranged for her funeral." Chueh-hsin began to sob. "Poor Jui. She's been dead for three weeks already and not one member of the older generation has gone to see her. Fifth Aunt won't even let Shu-chen go to the temple where Jui's body is resting. They're avoiding her as if she were some sort of evil spirit. I never thought a girl like Jui would come to this. Every time I meet Jui's mother, it's like a knife through my heart. Mrs. Li doesn't say anything openly, but her words are weighted with reproach, and they're all directed at me. You don't know how badly I feel!"

Gnawing his lips and clenching his fists, Chueh-hui listened. He forgot about his own affairs. He could see the full, pretty face of his sister-in-law, Jui, and a coffin. Gradually the coffin became two, then three. The faces of three girls appeared —one full and pretty; one mournful and sad; the third innocent and lively. The faces multiplied. Four, five—he knew them all—more and more and more. . . . Suddenly they all disappeared, and he was confronted with only the tear-stained visage of his Big Brother.

"I won't cry any more," said Chueh-hsin, pressing his fists

314

down on the table-top. Indeed, he halted the flow of his tears.

There was an uncomfortable silence. The brothers could hear the monks chanting prayers and beating gongs and cymbals in the large hall.

Finally Chueh-hsin sighed and wiped his eyes with his handkerchief. "I started to talk about your problem. I'm afraid I've wandered from the subject." He tried to laugh but did not succeed. "Stepmother said she couldn't decide. She told me to talk with Uncle Ke-ming. I did, and he gave me a strong reprimand for not understanding ceremonial custom. He said you would have to wait at least until Yeh-yeh is buried before you could go. The others there with him all agreed. Mistress Chen made some sneering remarks. She even insinuated that your interference with the devil-chasing had something to do with Yeh-yeh's death. Of course she didn't dare to come right out with it, and no one agrees with her—"

"They probably will, in time. It would make a nice new scandal in the family. They all dislike me anyhow. Well, I'm waiting for their next attack!" Chueh-hui said angrily.

"Oh, I don't think they'll do anything against you. They're preventing you from leaving as a means of striking another blow at me." Chueh-hsin bitterly rumpled his hair. "They say Shanghai is a big wicked city, that you'll go bad if you go to school there. They say that Yeh-yeh was opposed to us attending regular schools anyway. They say Shanghai schools produce only trouble-makers, not gentlemen. We talked and talked. This uncle said this, that aunt said that. . . .

"The substance of it is they don't want you to go. Not only do they want you to wait till after Yeh-yeh is buried—they hope you'll never go."

Chueh-hui rose abruptly to his feet and banged his fist on the table. "Well, I *am* going! I'll show them what I am—a rebel!" He paced the floor muttering "rebel" as if he didn't fully understand the term. Suddenly he faced Big Brother and demanded, "What's your idea?"

Chueh-hsin raised his head. His eyes lit up. With a determination that was rare in him, he said, "I promised to help you, and I will. We must act secretly. Didn't you say you had

315

friends who could lend you money? Well, I can give you some too. It's better to take some extra money along. As to what happens afterwards, we'll face that when it comes. Once you leave I don't think there'll be any trouble."

"Are you really going to help me?" Chueh-hui cried joyfully, grasping his brother's arm.

"Not so loud. We don't want them to hear. Whatever you do, don't tell anyone. I can pretend I don't know anything about it. Or you can leave a note, berating me. Then they won't be able to suspect me. We can work out the details later. We'd better meet in the garden. It's not very convenient to talk here." Chueh-hsin's manner was almost gay, but there were tears in his eyes.

"You're right," said a clear voice. "This isn't the place for conversation!" Chueh-min entered, smiling, together with Chin. "Your plan isn't bad," he laughed.

"Why were you standing outside, listening?" scolded Chueh-hsin. "Why didn't you come in?"

"We knew you were discussing something private, so we stood sentry at your door. That was Chin's idea. Isn't she clever?" Chueh-min grinned at Chin and she smiled back at him faintly.

"We hope you'll help us too, Big Brother," Chueh-min continued. "Chin's mother has already agreed to our marriage, and I don't expect any opposition from Stepmother. We're just waiting for the mourning period for *Yeh-yeh* to end and then we'll set a date. But we want to have a modern, new-style ceremony."

Chueh-hsin frowned. Another problem, he thought. "It's still early yet. We'll talk about it when the time comes. We can probably manage." Chueh-hsin said this last to comfort Chueh-min. Actually, he was not in the least confident.

"You must come down to Shanghai," cried Chueh-hui exuberantly. "I'll be there to welcome you."

"It's not very likely. If Chin's mother doesn't want to go, we can't just leave her here. In any event, we have to wait two or three years before both of us can go together."

"What about Chin's school?" asked Chueh-hui.

"She'll be graduating next year. Maybe the Foreign Languages School will admit girls by that time. If not, she can study at home for a year or two. Then, when we go down river, she'll be able to apply directly for entrance to a university." Chueh-min turned to Chin. "How does that strike you?"

Chin smiled but she did not speak. She trusted Chueh-min. She knew he was trying to work things out for her.

Chueh-hui silently regarded the young couple. He envied Chueh-min his happiness, yet he was glad he had no strings to prevent him from leaving this family he so despised. A new life was waiting for him in Shanghai. Shanghai, with its masses of people and its new cultural movement. In Shanghai were also the two or three young friends with whom he had been corresponding but whom he had never seen.

"We'd better continue this talk in the garden. Second Brother, you and Chin go ahead first." A servant outside began calling, "First Young Master!" Chueh-hsin seemed to remember something he had to do. He hastily said to Chueh-hui, "You go along too, Third Brother. Wait for me at the Fragrance at Eventide building. I'll join you soon." And he hurried from the room.

A few minutes later, Chueh-min and Chin followed. Chueh-hui left shortly after. As he came out of the house, Chueh-hui saw Big Brother examining a pair of eulogistic scrolls which had just been delivered. A servant was holding one end of them. Chueh-hui walked over to beside Chueh-hsin and read:

> The whole family weeps, bidding farewell to the loved one. The husband suffers added bitterness because his new-born babe cannot receive a mother's care and affection and has to be raised by his in-laws.

The scrolls were signed by Jui-chueh's brother, who lived out of town. Chueh-hui mournfully went into the garden to find Chueh-min and Chin.

Chueh-hsin remained, staring at the inscription. Then, abruptly, he rolled up the scrolls and told the servant to take them into the house. He himself walked towards the garden.

317

This family needs a rebel, he thought. I must help Third Brother. Through him I can hit back a bit. We'll show them. Not everyone in this family is as docile as I!

XXXVIII

"Once Chueh-hui is gone, our association will again suffer a loss to our gregariousness and loud voice. . . . It was only a little while ago that Hsu Chien-ju left us, and now you are leaving." At the Newspaper reading room, one of the elder members, Wu Ching-shih, said this emotionally first to the other members present and then to Chueh-hui.

"It is not only a loss of voice, we are going to lose one of the best contributors to our spirit and action," Chang Hui-ju immediately said in support.

Chueh-hui was there reading the newspapers, trying to distract himself from his dejection. When he saw his friends there, he couldn't help thinking of what he had shared with them in the recent past in group activities and life experience, and the sincere and honest consolation, sympathy, encouragement, assistance, hope and joy that they gave him, none of which he could get from his own family. In the past months he had been here every day to see these friends; the place and the people had become an indispensable and inseparable part of his life. He had never thought of leaving them, yet now he was really going to desert them to get away, as he was going to desert his family. He felt apologetic and grateful towards them, and hated to part from them. He thought that hereafter the reading room would open every day as usual, the members would come daily as usual, and the publication would be issued every week as usual, but he would not be able to participate in and share all these. He would be gone, far far away, unable to share anymore the pain and joy of these people, unable to hear anymore the ringing words of Huang Tsun-jen persuading payment of the monthly membership contribution, unable to enjoy anymore such stories as Chang Hui-ju's experience at the pawnshop, and unable to come here anymore with his brother Chueh-min. Now he was beginning to be aware of the many things—indeed, too many—that he would be unable to have anymore. He said with great grief in his heart, "I shouldn't have deserted you, we have so many things to do right now, and all of you are so tied up, not a single person can be spared. But I really haven't done much as I know my abilities are so limited, and I sincerely hope that my absence will not really cause you any inconvenience."

"Chueh-hui, you shouldn't say such things! Your family situation is of such a nature that the earlier you can get away from it the better. When you get to Shanghai you will make great strides in knowledge and experience; and since you already have friends there through correspondence, you are certainly going to make many more, and then you will have plenty of work to do there. There the cultural reform movement is much more ardent and widespread, it's not like here where even a girl with her hair shortened finds it impossible to stay on. Our work here is not too pressing, we will be able to handle it. Just don't worry," Huang Tsun-jen said to encourage Chueh-hui.

"Moreover you can still write articles and mail them to us from Shanghai, you will be able to supply us with richer and fresher materials, and sharper and stronger views," Chang Hui-ju said in support.

"Sure, I will mail you an article for each issue, disregarding quality considerations; I will definitely send you something for each issue," Chueh-hui said with great enthusiasm.

"I hope that we will be able to keep up a steady correspondence," Huang said.

"Definitely, I will be expecting your letters much more eagerly than you will mine. As I leave you, I shall be feeling lonely, I am not sure whether I will be able to have friends like you there . . ." Chueh-hui replied with feelings of sincere regret.

"It is we who will have to take the chance of not being able to find a friend as good as you," Chang said earnestly.

"That I am able to go away right now is all due to your

help, especially Tsun-jen, who has already done me great favors in the past," Chueh-hui said in great earnest, with a grateful look at Huang.

Huang smiled warmly, and replied, "What are you saying? It's nothing, it takes no special effort on my part. If you were in my place, you would have done the same for me." Then he asked, "Have you sent all your luggage to my house? What else do you have?"

"Nothing," replied Chueh-hui, and explained, "It's not that there isn't any more, it's that I can't take along too many things. There are books that I will leave behind, my Big Brother has promised to mail them to me later. There are too many spies in my family, and any slip that would betray my secret to one of them would cause a lot of trouble. Thus my pieces of luggage were all stealthily moved out and transported to your house in the very early hours of the morning."

There was a silence, which was broken by Chueh-hui. "Why don't you say something? Everybody is so quiet, you should know that the time that we have to talk together is indeed very limited now . . . Tsun-jen, is the boat to set sail three days from now?"

"I don't know for sure, but my relative will let me know in time. I hope it will leave a day or two later than that, so that we shall have a few more chances to see each other. Furthermore, we friends of the Li-chun Weekly are going to have a farewell party for you tomorrow," said Huang.

"Farewell party? That really isn't necessary," Chueh-hui said declining with a slightly bitter smile. "If we can talk together more, like we are doing now, it will be nice enough. Why should we attach so much importance to formality?"

"We must, we must have a farewell party for you, let us have some good time together although we are going to part right away. I have money now, I don't need to go to the pawnshop again," said Chang, producing a guffaw from all by his last remark.

"We don't want you to finance it alone, we will share it equally," said Huang laughing.

"Then I will have a share too," Chueh-hui offered. "Of course you will not," retorted Wu Ching-shih, who was about

320

to say something else but was interrupted by someone rushing into the room. Everybody looked at the newcomer.

The youth who had just come in was Chueh-hui's school-mate, Chen Chih, also a member of the Weekly. He was in a hurry to get there and was all out of breath from running. His red face was perspiring, and he cried as he entered, "I am late!"

"That doesn't matter, you are always late, so that your name is Chih,"[37] said Chang jokingly.

Chen offered no retaliation, but said seriously to Huang, "Tsun-jen, I just saw your relative Mr. Wang on the street, he told me to tell you that the boat leaves tomorrow morning."

"Tomorrow morning, really?" Chueh-hui was startled. "They had said in three days!"

"I am not kidding you, I heard him saying unmistakably tomorrow morning."

"You were planning a farewell party for me tomorrow," Chueh-hui uttered in great disappointment.

"Never mind, let's do it today. It's late now, let's go to the restaurant right away, you might have to get home early to take care of things to get ready," said Chang emphatically.

"It won't do, I have to go home right now!" said Chueh-hui in a great hurry, with a bitter smile on his face. He now had his brothers in mind.

"You can't go," the other members exclaimed in unison, "we won't let you go."

Huang was surprised at Chueh-hui's embarrassment, so he asked, "Why do you want to go home? Don't you want to have one more dinner with us? When we part, who knows when we will be able to get together like this."

Before Chueh-hui could say anything, the other members again chimed in to persuade him to stay, and Chang Hui-ju started to nail up the boards of the shop front. He was strong and had no trouble doing it, with some help from Chang Huan-ju and Chen Chih. Huang Tsun-jen cleared up the papers and files.

Chueh-hui watched what was going on and felt that he was

[37] Chih means late.

in no position to resist any longer, so he said in pleasant agony, "Well, I'll stay." Yet while he was saying this he couldn't help thinking of his brothers eating at home, which made him feel depressed. He quietly followed his friends to a restaurant, and the earnestness and enthusiasm of friends soon diverted him from his melancholy. Amidst his friends, he felt the happiness of selflessness, for being happy for their sake gradually produced real joy in himself.

It was quite dark by the time Chueh-hui and his friends left the restaurant. An autumn breeze cooled their flushed faces. They stood beneath the eaves of a building, reluctant to separate, watching the hurrying crowds on the street.

"We'll part here," one of the boys said at last. "I won't see you off tomorrow. Have a good trip."

"Thank you," said Chueh-hui. They shook hands.

Several others also wished him luck, and departed.

"We'll see you home," said Hui-ju, his small eyes shining in his ruddy triangular face.

Chueh-hui nodded. He and his three remaining companions entered upon the crowded street. A couple of blocks further on, another boy bade Chueh-hui farewell.

They entered a quiet lane where dim street lights were paled by the moonlight. The entrance-ways to the compounds lining the thoroughfare were like dark caves. Locust trees rising up within the walls cast sharply etched shadows on the silvery stone flaggings. The outline of every twig and leaf stood out dark and motionless, like a drawing by some master hand.

How can the city be so still? Chueh-hui wondered. He could almost forget how much turbulence and trouble the city contained. He looked up at the full moon riding silently through the limitless night sky.

"A beautiful moon!" Hui-ju sighed admiringly. He asked Chueh-hui, "After you leave here aren't you going to miss this place even a little?"

Chueh-hui didn't answer.

"What's so special about this city?" Tsun-jen demanded. "When he goes down river he'll find much nicer places."

"All of my dearest friends are here. Of course I'll miss Chengtu," Chueh-hui said awkwardly.

He bade goodbye to his companions at his gate and walked through the compound directly to Chueh-hsin's room. He found Big Brother and Chueh-min engaged in conversation. After hesitating a moment, Chueh-hui announced:

"I'm leaving tomorrow morning, Big Brother."

"Tomorrow? But I thought you said three days from now. . . ." Chueh-hsin paled and rose from his chair.

Chueh-min, startled, also stood up. He stared at Chueh-hui.

"The ship has been chartered by a relative of Tsun-jen, and he's decided to sail tomorrow. I only found out this evening, myself," said Chueh-hui morosely.

"So soon!" said Chueh-hsin, disappointed, supporting himself with one hand on his desk. "You only have one more night at home."

"Big Brother," Chueh-hui said sadly. Chueh-hsin turned to look at him with tears in his eyes. "I wanted to come home early and have dinner with you both. But the boys insisted on giving me a send-off. That's why I'm so late. . . ." Chueh-hui swallowed the rest of his words.

"I'll get Chin. She'll want to speak to you. Tomorrow, there'll probably be no time," said Chueh-min.

Chueh-hui held him back. "Don't you know what time it is? You'll have to knock at her gate and get everybody up. It will attract too much attention."

"Then she won't be able to see you before you leave. She'll be very disappointed. She told me several times to let her know when you were going."

"We'll call on her first thing in the morning. I'm sure there'll still be time," said Chueh-hui, observing Chueh-min's distraught countenance. Actually he wasn't at all sure whether he would be able to see Chin or not.

"Is your luggage packed?" Chueh-hsin asked hoarsely.

"I've already sent it down to the pier. There isn't much. Just a roll of bedding, a basket hamper and a small trunk."

"You're not taking enough to eat. I have a few cans of ham someone sent me. I'll get them for you." Without waiting for a reply, Chueh-hsin went into the next room and brought out four cans.

"I don't need that many. I'll be able to buy things along the

323

way," Chueh-hui said when he saw his Big Brother wrapping up the cans.

"It's always better to take a little extra. Anyhow, I don't need them." Chueh-hsin placed the bundle in front of Chueh-hui. "I'm sending you money by the method we agreed upon last time. It will be waiting for you in the Chungking, Hankow and Shanghai post offices. Just take your postal money orders in and cash them. If the money I gave you yesterday isn't enough, you can have some more."

"Plenty. It's not a good idea to carry too many silver dollars. Luckily, the roads are fairly safe now."

"Yes. The roads are fairly safe now," Chueh-hsin echoed mechanically.

Chueh-min and Chueh-hui exchanged a few words.

"You ought to go to bed, Third Brother," Chueh-hsin urged. "You have to get up early tomorrow. You'll be living on a crude, wooden ship for several days. You'd better rest."

Chueh-hui murmured an assent.

"You'll be on your own after this. Dress warmly and eat properly. You're often neglectful about such things. It's not like being at home. If you get sick, there'll be no one to look after you."

Chueh-hui nodded.

"Don't forget to write along the way. I'll send you your books when you reach Shanghai. You needn't stint too much on money. Whatever school you enter, I'll pay your expenses. Don't worry about the family. As long as I'm here, I won't let any of them interfere." Chueh-hsin was almost weeping.

With an effort, Chueh-hui controlled his own emotions.

"You're lucky. You've been able to climb out of this sea of bitterness. But we. . . ." Chueh-hsin could not go on. His legs gave way and he sat down heavily on his chair. Burying his head, he wept quietly.

"Big Brother," Chueh-hui called unhappily. Chueh-hsin did not reply. Chueh-hui walked up to him and again spoke his name. Removing his hands from his face, Chueh-hsin looked at Chueh-hui and shook his head.

"I'm all right. It's nothing. You go to sleep."

The two younger brothers left him.

"I want to see Stepmother," Chueh-hui said, when the boys got outside. He had observed the light burning in Madam Chou's window.

"You're going to tell her you're leaving?" Chueh-min asked, surprised.

"No," Chueh-hui smiled. "I just want to see her. It may be for the last time."

"All right, go ahead," said Chueh-min in a low voice. "But be careful. Don't give yourself away." He returned to his own room, while Chueh-hui went to their stepmother's apartment.

Madam Chou was seated on a reclining chair, talking with Shu-hua. She smiled reproachfully when she saw Chueh-hui enter. "You didn't come home for dinner tonight."

Chueh-hui only smiled and said, "That's right." He stood quite a distance from Madam Chou.

"You're always running around outside. What do you do, anyhow? You should be careful of your health," she said solicitously.

"My health is fine. And running around outside is much better than sitting at home being sniped at!" Chueh-hui laughed.

"How you love to argue!" Madam Chou criticized him with a smile. "No wonder your aunts and uncles were complaining about you today. To be honest, you *are* too aggressive. You fear no one. Even I can't control you. Strange, you and your Big Brother were born of the same mother, but your characters are completely different. Neither of you is like her. Big Brother is too docile, and you're too stubborn!" Madam Chou laughed. Shu-hua, beside her, looked at Chueh-hui and smiled.

Chueh-hui wanted to defend himself, but then he thought better of it. Suddenly he longed to give his stepmother some hint of farewell. Later on, she would know what he meant. He came a step closer.

Madam Chou could see that there was something on his mind. "What is it, Chueh-hui?" she asked kindly. "Do you want to talk to me about going to Shanghai to study?"

This remark reminded Chueh-hui of Chueh-min's warning. He decided to be careful. "There's nothing special," he replied with a forced laugh. "I'm going to bed." He looked at

Madam Chou's round face, gazed at Shu-hua, then turned and walked out. As he was leaving the room, he thought he heard Shu-hua make some comment about his queerness.

We may not see each other again, he thought miserably. Once I leave I'll be like a bird released from a cage. I'll fly away and never come back.

XXXIX

Chueh-hui slept only a few hours that night. Although he awakened before dawn, he remained in bed, thinking, until at last it was daylight.

It was time to start. He still had to go with Chueh-min to see Chin. He had to leave home immediately. Chueh-hsin saw him and Chueh-min to the compound gate.

The streets were cool and quiet in the early morning. Abroad were only cooks carrying their shopping baskets to the market, a peasant in from the countryside to collect night-soil, one or two pedlars of breakfast snacks. The sky was very clear; warm sunlight shone on the walls of the compound opposite the Kao family residence. Sparrows twittered noisily in the locust trees, welcoming the new-born day.

"I'm going, Big Brother." Chueh-hui's voice rang brightly in the fresh morning air. He tightly grasped Chueh-hsin's hand.

"I'm sorry I can't accompany you any farther," sighed Chueh-hsin unhappily. "Take good care of yourself. Be sure to write often."

"I'm going," Chueh-hui repeated. Again he pressed his brother's hand. "Don't feel too badly. We'll certainly see each other again." He dropped Chueh-hsin's hand, almost casting it from him, then turned and walked quickly away, carrying the cans of ham Big Brother had wrapped for him.

Several times, he looked back. Chueh-hsin was waving to

him from the gate. Even after Chueh-hui was out of sight, Big Brother still stood dazedly, waving goodbye.

When the boys reached Chin's house, Chueh-min rapped lightly on her window. They heard her cough, and the patter of her feet. Then the curtain was pulled aside, and Chin's sleepy face appeared behind the windowpane, her hair tousled and uncombed.

Chin smiled at them. Suddenly she noticed the expression on Chueh-hui's face. Startled, she asked in a low voice, "Today?"

Chueh-min nodded. "Right now."

Chin turned colour. "So soon?"

Chueh-hui stepped closer to the window. "Sister Chin," he hailed her softly, in an affectionate tone. He could see only her face, and he was separated from that by a pane of glass.

Her gentle eyes scanned his face. "You won't forget me, will you?" she asked with a sad smile.

Chueh-hui shook his head slightly. "Never. You know I'll always remember you."

"Wait a minute. Don't go yet." She disappeared from the window.

She soon returned. "Here's something I once promised to give you," she smiled. Opening the window a crack, she slipped him a recent photograph of herself.

Delighted and grateful, Chueh-hui raised his eyes to look at her, but she had already drawn the curtain. "Sister Chin," he called softly. He didn't hear any answer, and his brother was urging him to make haste. Reluctantly, he followed Chueh-min out of the compound.

The brothers hurried along the street, talking as they walked. When they reached the pier, Tsun-jen and Hui-ju were there waiting for them.

Hui-ju cheerfully pumped Chueh-hui's hand. "We've been here for ages. Why are you so late? The boat's liable to go off without you."

"Not at all. Of course we'd wait for Mr. Kao," a middle-aged merchant who had been standing off to one side interjected, smiling. He was Tsun-jen's relative, Mr. Wang.

Chueh-hui had already met him. He now introduced him to Chueh-min.

"Chueh-hui, come and see your luggage," said Tsun-jen. He led Chueh-hui aboard the boat and showed him his cabin. Chueh-min followed.

"I've opened your bedroll and laid it out for you. . . . This package is some pastries and cookies to eat on the way. It's from Hui-ju and me," said Tsun-jen.

Chueh-hui could only nod.

"Mr. Wang will take care of everything; you don't have to bother about a thing. He'll deliver you to Chungking. From there on, it will be easy. Don't forget to look up my cousin when you get there. He can help you," Tsun-jen chattered.

The boat at the next pier had been chartered by some wealthy official. There were armed guards on the boat; on the pier were many people seeing the official off. Now from the pier came the popping of firecrackers. The boat was about to sail.

"Don't forget to write, Chueh-hui; write lots of letters!" Hui-ju had just entered the cabin. He slapped Chueh-hui on the shoulder.

"You fellows are the ones who have to write," Chueh-hui laughed.

"We're ready to sail," Mr. Wang came in and announced. "Would you three visitors please go ashore?" The friends seeing Mr. Wang off had already left.

Chueh-hui walked with his brother and his two classmates to the gangplank. They all shook hands.

"Take good care of yourself," Chueh-min urged. He walked down the gangplank with the other two boys.

They stood on the shore. Chueh-hui stood in the prow. They waved and he waved.

Slowly the boat slipped away. It began to turn. The figures on the shore grew smaller and smaller; soon they were gone. Standing in the prow, Chueh-hui gazed in their direction. He thought he could still see them, waving. He raised his hand to brush something out of his eye. When he lowered his hand again, even his mental image of them had disappeared.

The past seemed like a dream. All that met his eye now was an expanse of deep green water, reflecting trees and hills. On the boat a few sailors plied long sculling oars, singing as they worked.

A new emotion gradually possessed Chueh-hui. He didn't know whether it was joy or sorrow, but one thing was clear—he was leaving his family. Before him was an endless stretch of water sweeping steadily forward, bearing him to an unfamiliar city. There, all that was new was developing—new activities, new people, new friends.

This river, this blessed river, was taking him away from the home he had lived in for eighteen years to a city and people he had never seen. The prospect dazzled him; he had no time to regret the life he had cast behind. For the last time, he looked back. "Goodbye," Chueh-hui said softly. He turned to watch the on-rushing river, the green water that never for an instant halted its rapidly advancing flow.